Praise for *Vulnerable Communion*

"*Vulnerable Communion* is subversive theology in the tradition of the prophets speaking from the margins of society. It calls the church to confront and dismantle the (world's) 'cult of normalcy,' within which the church has uncritically worshipped. It also calls for a theology of disability that not merely insists on caring for people with disabilities but that allows the experience of disability to interrogate its theology of power. The result is a long-awaited and much-needed theological revisioning of the traditional doctrines of God, Christ, creation, redemption, and church so that the true power of the gospel is released from the underside of history once again."

—**Amos Yong**, Regent University School of Divinity; book review editor, *Journal of Religion, Disability and Health*

"Powerful in its questioning of 'the disabling framework of the 'normal,' Reynolds's unflinching account emits an irresistible lucidity. A theology of life as sheer gift unfurls in the space opened by his profound meditation on human vulnerability."

—**Catherine Keller**, Drew University

"Tom Reynolds has written a theologically profound and deeply moving exploration of what happens to core Christian understandings of God, of Christ, of community, and of embodiment when these are understood in light of disability. His work makes an important and bracing contribution to disability studies. It makes an equally important contribution to theology, making available an awareness of how our vulnerability opens us to each other and to the great compassion of the divine. It would be hard to come away from this beautiful book unchanged."

—**Wendy Farley**, Emory University

"For years, I have thought that the key theological and pastoral issue in ministries with people with disabilities is not disability per se, but vulnerability. Tom Reynolds has taken that premise from his own experience as a father and his own training as a theologian and crafted a theology based on a foundation of vulnerability. I have rarely read a manuscript where I made so many 'amen' marks. This book is an amazing integration of Reynolds's experience in the worlds of disability and theology. This is a wonderful contribution to theological studies—a resource that any clergy interested in understanding vulnerability for ministry will go to again and again—and a theological contribution to the exploding field of disability studies."

—**Bill Gaventa**, editor, *Journal of Religion, Disability, and Health*

"Reynolds provides another vital resource and is a new and important voice in issues concerning the place and presence of people whom the world calls 'disabled' in the life of the church. Reynolds carefully unpacks the baggage of labels and stigmas that have been placed upon the lives of many people with disabilities. With strong, articulate theological arguments, he lifts up the power of being what the world would call 'weak' and 'vulnerable,' in which the presence of the Christ is revealed in all of human life. Yet Reynolds is quick to remind us that this discovery is not a solo journey, but discovered in the very practice of hospitality within the body of Christ, in which we are reminded that this resurrected body is inclusive of all God's people."

—**Brett Webb-Mitchell**, School of the Pilgrim

Vulnerable Communion

A Theology of Disability and Hospitality

Thomas E. Reynolds

BrazosPress

a division of Baker Publishing

Grand Rapids, Michiga

Published by Brazos Press
a division of Baker Publishing Group
P.O. Box 6287, Grand Rapids, MI 49516-6287
www.brazospress.com

Printed in the United States of America

Library of Congress Cataloging-in-Publication Data
Reynolds, Thomas E., 1963–
    Vulnerable communion : a theology of disability and hospitality / Thomas E. Reynolds.
      p. cm.
    Includes bibliographical references and index.
    ISBN 978-1-58743-177-7 (pbk.)
    1. People with disabilities—Religious aspects—Christianity. 2. Church work with people with disabilities. I. Title.
    BT732.7.R49 2008
    261.8'324—dc22
                                                     2007037373

Contents

Contents

Contents

Acknowledgments

This book was written in the presence of many people whose encouragement and assistance have made it possible to reflect at length upon the matter of disability and its important implications for Christian thought and practice.

I am grateful to the Louisville Institute for providing the generous support of a grant during the summer of 2005, during which I initially sketched out the parameters of what became this book. Gratitude also goes to the group of Louisville Institute grantees like myself who met the following January at Louisville Presbyterian Seminary for a follow-up seminar. The stimulating conversations that took place made me realize that I had to write this book.

Thanks to *Theology Today* for giving permission for me to use material in chapters 5 and 7 of this book initially published in two articles: "Love beyond Boundaries: Theological Reflections on Parenting a Child with Disabilities," 62/2 (July 2005), 193–209; and "Welcome without Reserve? A Case in Christian Hospitality," 63/2 (July 2006), 191–202. Thanks also to Hasting College for permission to draw material from "Vulnerable Humanity: Disability and Community beyond 'Normalcy,'" published in *Being Human* (Vol. 5, Fall 2007), 13–17.

Most of the manuscript was written while I was employed at St. Norbert College, De Pere, Wisconsin. I am indebted to the many friends, students, and colleagues at SNC with whom I had the fortune of sharing my work and from whom I gained the sense that what I was doing mattered. Gratitude for financial support also goes to the Faculty Development Office of St. Norbert College for a summer grant in 2006.

For the wide hospitality of my new colleagues and friends at Emmanuel College, Victoria University, the Toronto School of Theology, and the University of Toronto at large, I am grateful and look forward to many fruitful years together.

I am profoundly thankful for friends who have read the manuscript at various stages and offered crucial feedback. Writing is never a solitary affair, but an extension of good conversation. For helping to nourish, clarify, and correct my thinking, thanks go to Juliana Claassens, Deborah Creamer, David Duquette, Robert Matlock, Kim Nielson, Sarah Pinnock, Keith Reynolds, Mary Reynolds, Molly VanDeelen, and Amos Yong. Thanks also to Catherine Rose at Emmanuel College for her help editing and compiling the index. I hasten to add, however, that all lingering faults in the text are my own creations.

I am also grateful for the enduring support of Rodney Clapp at Brazos Press, whose guidance throughout the project has helped sustain my passion, and for the prudent editorial skills of Lisa Ann Cockrel at Brazos, whose literary eye helped reshape many of my awkward sentences.

For a book like this, it would be an unacceptable omission to neglect the many friends and caregiving networks that have helped support our family, thus enabling me to continue with this project when family life required full attention. More than once I felt unable to write because the material was so "close to home."

Special thanks go to our friends at First Presbyterian Church of Green Bay, who embodied the kind of hospitality that befits the community called "church"—Rev. Dr. Steve and Doris Shive, Rev. Dr. Robert and Elaine Matlock, and others too numerous to mention. We miss you.

Heartfelt appreciation for the kindness of other friends in the Green Bay area also deserves mentioning. To friends in the musician community—especially John and Karen Gibson, Steve and Jen Johnson, and Woody and Pam Mankowski—and many friends at St. Norbert College—especially John and Laura Neary, John and Gertie Holder, Lauri MacDiarmid and Dave Peterson, and members of the Religious Studies department: thank you for your friendship and for welcoming our family, warts and all, so graciously. Thanks also to Luna Café (Mark and Angel Patel) in De Pere, for your support and good coffee.

Professional psychiatric and behavior management care from Child and Family Consultants of Green Bay (Dr. Bradford Lyles, Ken Horn, and Cheryl Rotherham), counseling resources from Brown County Mental Health (care of Julie Weinberger), and other services from the Department of Family Services of Brown County and Macht Village, have made a huge positive impact on Chris and our family. We will always be indebted. Warm thanks also to the gifted teachers and administrators who have so vigilantly attended to Chris's well-being and education at Aldo Leopold and De Pere West High.

Most importantly, family has made the difference. Thanks to our parents and brothers and sisters for the bottomless wellspring of support through the ups and downs. I am especially grateful to my brother Keith and sister-in-law Jeffi Farquharson-Reynolds for lovingly bringing their L'Arche experience into our lives. This perspective has been life changing for our family, and crucial for my own reflections in this book.

My lifelong companion, partner, and friend beyond comparison, Mary, has been the main resource of this book. Thank you for your love for Chris, Evan, and me, and for the many hours of memorable conversation about matters in this book.

My "most specialest" thanks go to my children, Chris and Evan. This book is for you. Thank you, Chris, for agreeing to my writing this book, for letting me share some of our experiences, and for your support and counsel along the way. And thank you, Evan, for your brotherly compassion and understanding, with all its privileges and struggles. I am so proud of you both. My hope is that if, perchance, either of you read this book, you will see its musings as a testimony of my desire to more deeply enter into the mystery of being a family, loving you more attentively and completely.

Introduction

About nine years ago my family was regularly attending a mainline Protestant church near our home. We had been introduced to the church through the Mothers Day Out program that it sponsored, and gradually grew to appreciate the community there. It was vibrant and socially engaged.

One day a number of concerned mothers met with the minister to express their frustration and anger over the unseemly conduct of a particular boy in Sunday school. They did not want their children exposed to this child and feared what he represented. For it seemed that this boy was modeling "bad behavior"—verbal outbursts that sometimes involved profanity, a lack of sensitivity to other children's personal space (occasionally biting them when irritated or provoked) and an unpredictably violent imagination when playing with toys. No Sunday school is equipped to handle problems of this magnitude. So upon expressing their indignation, the mothers requested that the minister call the child's parents and ask that he not return to Sunday school. Obviously, there were family issues that needed serious and immediate attention.

The "problem child" was ours. My wife received the call early one morning. The minister was deeply apologetic and pastoral in his approach. But the damage had been done. What were we to do? Where could we go? Over the years, we had been through behavioral programs, family counseling, and psychiatric care. At this point, we were just beginning to come to terms with our son's recent diagnosis: Tourette's syndrome. Later, he would also be diagnosed with Asperger's syndrome, bipolar disorder, and obsessive-compulsive disorder. But at this point he was about seven years old, and we knew only of the Tourette's. We stopped attending this church. In fact, we stopped attending church altogether.

The personal connection is important to the aims of this book. Do my wife and I fault the concerned mothers who confronted that Methodist minister? No, for we too have been concerned about our children hanging around the wrong crowd and being harmed or influenced by unruly behavior. Nor do we fault the minister, for he was in a predicament. Could things have been handled differently? Yes. And other parents did handle it differently, talking with us directly in an effort to understand, even to the point of befriending us and asking what they might do to help. So one of the basic questions of this book is: what could have happened at this church? More broadly, what can happen in our churches and in our daily lives when we encounter not only people with disabilities, but also other people who are different in some way or another? How can we build bridges of understanding and mutuality, fostering mechanisms of support and empowerment instead of barriers that exclude?

The circumstances at this church were complicated by the fact that our son, Chris, had disabilities that were hidden, not readily apparent in physical form, and that we were only beginning to understand. For example, many people with symptoms similar to those of our son remain undiagnosed and untreated simply because they appear "normal," even precocious, in many other respects. I cannot count the number of times friends and acquaintances of ours have exclaimed, "but he seems so normal!" In fact, this has been a source of great pain. For Chris cannot live consistently under these kinds of expectations. Consequently, when "abnormalities" such as obsessions, angry outbursts, or tics have surfaced, people that he has come to trust have brushed him aside or discounted him altogether. Judgment has also been pronounced against us, his parents, by well-meaning friends, teachers, and family members. Perhaps Chris is simply precocious or gifted, and we are to blame for not accommodating his unique needs; his symptoms then are indications of frustrations that we have caused by not doing right by him. Or worse, perhaps we have created his condition by doing something wrong, harming him. Chris is indeed a charming, intelligent, artistic, caring, and sensitive young person. And he thrives in some circumstances—but not all.

There are very real physiological factors that interfere with Chris's cognitive and emotional development, complicate his orientation to the world, and frustrate his relationships with other people. Tourette's syndrome is a neurological disorder of the brain that causes involuntary movements (motor tics) or vocalizations (vocal tics), and in many cases also involves related disorders such as OCD (obsessive-compulsive disorder) and ADD (attention-deficit disorder). Bipolar disorder is psychiatry's name for manic depression, which entails extreme mood cycling that, in children, often appears in symptoms like prolonged raging, separation anxiety, precociousness, night terrors, fear of death, oppositional behavior, sensitivity to stimuli, problems with peers, and so on. Asperger's syndrome is probably the most inclusive of Chris's diagnoses. It is a high-functioning disorder on the autism spectrum that is, in many cases, associated with Tourette's syndrome and bipolar disorder.[1] With medical care and the support of schools in the form of IEP's (individualized education programs), Chris is making his way in the world. But the principalities and powers of the world are not set up to make his way easy.

Given this, and without others understanding the biological nature of Chris's condition, it has been all too easy for others to suspect he is the product of bad parenting or a toxic home environment. At intervals my wife and I have internalized these possibilities, forging our way through individual counseling and family therapy. We have often blamed ourselves, and thus become caught up in a cycle of shame and guilt. In an effort to cope, we have isolated ourselves by avoiding social situations. Especially when Chris was younger, it was enough that we frequently had to negotiate our way through anxieties or embarrassing eruptions in public places like church, a restaurant, or the local grocery store, which always elicited condescending gazes and suspicious whispers.

Gradually, however, through the supportive presence of others along the way, we are emerging from our self-imposed seclusion and the narcissistic world it generated. Why do I say "narcissistic"? Because, in a real way, isolation is a protection mechanism against the pain of being excluded, against being exposed as an atypical family, constantly bombarded by infelicitous commentary from people whose otherwise well-intended advice serves to reinforce the negative sense of ourselves as bad parents. More importantly, however, we have sought to protect Chris from the pain of being misunderstood. Yet protective walls can be deceptively insidious. In defending against possible suffering, they ironically create further suffering by cutting off the possibility of healing and companionship in relationships of trust. We feared exposure, shirked from making our vulnerability visible, and as a result, disengaged from the very processes that had the power to bring wholeness. It was like a vortex from which we have been able to escape only piecemeal; and even then, only through the tenacious hospitality of friends, an empowering network of medical caregivers, a loving church community, and, through them, the experience of God's grace.

How easy it is to misunderstand a person whose humanity exhibits itself in unconventional and ostensibly deficient or dysfunctional ways. In turn, how easy it is to misplace the resulting shame and guilt. The effects ripple outward in uncontrollable and potentially devastating ways. Indeed, mechanisms of exclusion, oppression, and hostility are built upon such grounds. There are implications here that stretch far beyond the theme of disability. In this book, however, the central focus is on disability and the human vulnerability it so powerfully manifests. Why? Not simply for personal reasons, but also because disability is an often overlooked and contested "site" that opens up a range of possible resources and interdisciplinary approaches to the vulnerable and relational character of human existence, bringing to the fore issues of difference, normalcy, embodiment, community, and redemption. For this reason, disability has theological power.

In her excellent book *Copious Hosting: A Theology of Access for People with Disabilities*, Jennie Weiss Block suggests that, of all places, the church should be a model of the accessible community, a point of entry into God's love that is reflected both in thinking and in acting. For, as she puts it, "the Body of Christ presumes a place for everyone."[2] But place is difficult for persons with disabilities. Far too often such people encounter a symbolic, if not palpably concrete, sign that reads, "access denied." This is tragic for both persons with disabilities and non-disabled persons. Certain people are excluded from participation, and thus their humanity is diminished. The result also diminishes church communities themselves, as disabling principalities and powers constrict the redemptive work of God. The humanity of non-disabled people is then diminished, as well.

This book seeks to reflect theologically on how Christians might think differently about disability and act differently toward people with disabilities. Nurturing communities of abundant hospitality is the goal. However, this means more than the courtesy of providing access points for those otherwise unable to enter and find their way. Hospitality involves actively welcoming and befriending the stranger—in this case, a person with disabilities—not as a spectacle, but as someone with inherent value, loved into being by God, created in the image of God, and thus having unique gifts to offer as a human being. Yet we are up against complex social forces and theological assumptions that make the task difficult.

Moving beyond Block's analysis, then, I wish to forge a path forward by rethinking human community in light of the primacy of relation and embodiment, such that the fundamental character of human wholeness through vulnerability and interdependence comes to the fore. It is vulnerability, as I shall argue, that we all share as human beings. Why is this important? Because it provides a way into more firmly acknowledging and experiencing our deep connections with one another, connections that indicate a basic web of mutual dependence but that all too often become obscured by what Stanley Hauerwas appropriately calls "the tyranny of normality."[3] Rather than autonomous self-sufficiency (e.g., the individual's ability to construct, produce, or purchase), our human vulnerability is a starting point for discovering what we truly share in our differences. And, accordingly, it is a source bearing the precious and fragile grace of solidarity with one another, that is, a form of belonging inclusive of disability. There is, in the end, no hard-and-fast dualism between ability and disability, but rather a nexus of reciprocity that is based in our vulnerable humanity. All of life comes to us as a gift, an endowment received in countless ways from others throughout our lifetime. When we acknowledge this, the line between giving and receiving, ability and disability, begins to blur. Theologian Jürgen Moltmann goes so far as to state, "There is no differentiation between the healthy and those with disabilities. For every human life has its limitations, vulnerabilities, and weaknesses. We are born needy, and we die helpless. It is only the ideals of health of a society of the strong which condemn a part of humanity to being 'disabled.' "[4] Conversely, as we shall see, having a disability is not equivalent to being ill and needing a cure.

This is not to downplay or trivialize the real challenges faced by persons with disabilities, but rather to observe just how unstable and malleable the category of disability is. Although we often treat disability as a fixed term with well-defined references, it is inscribed with meanings that are context-dependent and socially derived, varying according to what social groups value and how they understand themselves as a community. Furthermore, the difference between ability and disability is linked broadly to how a society views the difference between normality and abnormality, notions that shift according to changes in a society's perceptions of bodily functioning and aesthetic appearance. Human abilities tend to be measured in terms of what is considered normal functioning, wholeness, and order, making disability a correlate of dysfunction, incompleteness, and disorder. Sadly, this is why disability is stigmatized so often as a symbolic threat to the social fabric, something to be remedied or excluded. It is this correlation that must be called into question and transformed according to a different way of thinking about wholeness and ability, measured not by productive power and individual completeness but by vulnerability and interdependence.

Transforming our sense of disability in this way entails what Nancy Eiesland calls a theological method of two-way access.[5] On the one hand, persons with disabilities are empowered to participate more fully in the social and symbolic life of the church and wider society. This focus emancipates, seeking to liberate persons from restrictive barriers to public and religious access that are erected as by-products of taken-for-granted beliefs about "normal" conditions of embodiment. Examples of such barriers range from the concrete (e.g., lack of ramp access to above-ground-level buildings or the absence of communication provisions for deaf people) to the more abstract yet equally palpable ways that religious language is used to sanction common human experience and thus ignore, misrepresent, or demean the bodily presence of persons with disabilities (e.g., through metaphors like "walking by faith, not by sight" or "hearing God's word," and through theological views that denigrate or trivialize the experience of disability as something plaguing the "sinful," those "lacking in faith," or "God's special ones"). The point is to become mindful of, reconsider, and alter exclusionary practices and attitudes so as to promote the full inclusion of persons with disabilities into church communities.

On the other hand, the second part of this two-way method gives non-disabled persons access to the social-symbolic world of persons with disabilities, such that the disabling framework of the "normal" becomes questionable. Accordingly, non-disabled persons may gain the capacity to recognize their own complicity in sanctioning social and spiritual barriers to persons with disabilities. As illustrated in the examples above, it is not the impairment itself but the community that is disabling, insofar as it makes rules that draw attention to certain impairments as threats to normal role performances. Furthermore, by way of a critique of normalcy, non-disabled persons are able to acknowledge their own vulnerability, making possible a broader and richer human solidarity.

This being said, what this book is and is not becomes clearer. For instance, this book shall not explore disability solely in personal narrative form. While I shall draw from personal experience at various points to help contextualize the discussion and make important allusions, my overall intention is not to place Chris or my family at the center of the discussion.[6] The main focus will be analytical and theological in nature. Indeed, it is my hope that the book will be sufficiently inclusive in scope to interest readers not immediately connected to disability. Thus,

I seek to speak neither for nor directly to disabled persons. Rather, I speak as an advocate, a father trying to forge a path through an uncertain and painful terrain, but in which I have glimpsed rays of hope. Paul Ricoeur calls hope "the passion for the possible."[7] And I see possibilities not only for reorienting the way non-disabled persons think about disability and act toward persons with disabilities, but also for altogether reconsidering theological themes in light of human vulnerability. Connecting disability with vulnerability sounds new theological possibilities. It moves the discussion about disability from a minor to a major key. That is, it helps us understand disability not as a human deficiency or tragedy to be pitied, but as a way of living life's possibilities vulnerably with others and in God.

So I seek broad connections, ways to engage readers who have not thought about disability or engaged persons with disabilities. As Moltmann notes, a "person with disabilities gives others the precious insight into the woundedness and weakness of human life. But a person with disabilities also gives insight into the humanity of his own world. Through persons with disabilities, other people can come to know the real, suffering, living God, who also loves them infinitely."[8] Reflecting on his work as founder of a community of people with intellectual disabilities, Jean Vanier suggests something similar, namely, that those with disabilities call us into acknowledging our own human weaknesses and thus open us up more radically to God's grace.[9]

This, however, leads me to make another disclaimer. My purpose in this book is not to marshal examples of how disability can serve a positive function by teaching us what it means to be better human beings or better Christians. While Moltmann and Vanier have their finger on the pulse of something fundamentally important, serious dangers haunt such an approach. I shall enumerate these dangers more fully in chapter 1. Let me simply state from the start that I do not believe persons with disabilities are simply moral lessons or a means of inspiration for non-disabled people. Robert F. Molsberry counters such presumption forcefully: "I resist being seen as inspirational. There's more to living with a disability than that."[10]

Speaking personally, while I can think of numerous instances when my son has taught me how to be a better father, a more compassionate human being, and a deeper Christian, he is more than merely a vehicle for my parental and spiritual education. To treat him this way would have the patronizing effect of reducing his person to an object made useful by his disabilities. Not only would this trivialize his real challenges and difficult moments of suffering, it would also mute the fact that his is a life that shines of its own accord and with its own dignity, regardless of whether or not it instructs others. His gifts and abilities far exceed the alleged limitations entailed by one diagnosis or another. The measure of a person is not a factor of their disabilities. That is why I follow the lead of writers in the field of disability studies who speak of "persons with disabilities" rather than "the disabled." The latter suggests that people with disabilities are all the same and can be wholly defined by their disabilities, unable to speak with integrity for themselves. As Molsberry again states, "I don't want to allow my life to be the object of hasty generalizations by those who are not intimately acquainted with it. . . . Disability is not the defining aspect of any life. Disability is just one condition among many that contributes to the richness of living."[11]

Hence, it is imperative that any book about disability listen to and take account of the diverse voices that make up what has been called the largest minority group, becoming informed by the disability rights movement and by the emerging field of disability studies. The fact that you are reading a book like this is not accidental. It indicates that the hard-won efforts of people with disabilities to bring their experiences of social disempowerment and injustice to the forefront are paying off. While disability has been present through the ages, and is clearly a part of our lives today, until recently it was considered neither something worthy of social activism nor a subject calling for serious intellectual and religious engagement.

The civil rights movement changed that. It opened up new frontiers for rights-based and anti-discrimination legislation. Stimulated by the example of African Americans and women, disability organizations began to claim a political voice and speak out of their own experiences of marginalization, mobilizing as a group to publicly resist societal mechanisms of exclusion.[12] Thus empowered, people with disabilities launched critiques of prevailing social models, formulated new ones, and started creating alternative forms of service provision that were less restrictive and more humanizing. As a result, the field of disability studies developed. Although there is some debate over the character of disability studies, on the whole it is animated by the desire to interpret disability outside of intellectual frameworks that have proven inadequate to the experience of persons with disabilities.[13] Other books have detailed the character and significance of these events, so I will not rehearse their efforts again. Suffice it to say, however, that this book travels a pathway cleared by pioneers who have done the hard work of breaking through barriers of exclusion. As shall become obvious, I write indebted to their labor.

Keeping in line with the general thrust of disability studies, then, this book shall bring literature on disability into conversation with a range of sociological, philosophical, and theological sources in order to challenge non-disabled persons and resist the disabling principalities and powers that afflict our society and our church communities. My particular method, hinted at earlier, is to highlight the theme of vulnerability through a route that privileges disability and brings it to the center of the discussion. Privileging disability in this way amounts to what liberation theologians have called a "preferential option." It does not simply use the category for theological gain, as if eventually to move on to better or more fruitful territory. Instead, it marks a radical conversion to the afflicted and oppressed as loved of God. Taking such a turn, however, is no easy endeavor.

Disability is a "dangerous memory," to employ Johann Baptist Metz's term, that renders our society, our theology, and our church communities accountable.[14] It is not an issue invoked merely when people with disabilities factor into the equation. Rather, it is a ubiquitous element in all social mechanisms that presume "normalcy" as their touchstone and in so doing rule out of play the non-normal by raising access barriers. Thus, disability has been the occasion for both overt and covert gestures of exclusion, intentional and unintentional acts of oppression. According to the Americans with Disabilities Act of 1990, a disability is defined as (1) a "physical or mental impairment that substantially limits one or more of the major life activities of an individual; (2) a record of such impairment; or (3) being regarded as having such an impairment."[15] Because the notions of "life activities" and "being regarded" are themselves defined socially and involve culturally communicated perceptions, they open up a wider horizon of investigation. For example, why are certain impairments taken to be disabling and not others? Visual impairment in today's world is not considered a disabling condition, but needing a wheelchair, an artificial limb, or medication for bipolar disorder is. In these cases, there are real obstructions created by non-disabled persons that prevent social participation and self-definition. The question is why? And, further, how can this be changed? The dangerous memory of disability opens up the possibility of theological and social critique, and the possibility of a theological revitalization that benefits the entire community of faith.

With this in mind, let me sum up the preceding discussion by highlighting the development of the chapters of this book. Chapter 1 enumerates some of the promises and perils of thinking theologically about disability. This will prove instrumental for understanding what it is we are up against, and act as a kind of testing ground for the theological proposals to follow. Subsequently, focusing on vulnerability in light of disability as a dangerous memory, chapters 2 and 3 explore what I shall call the "cult of normalcy." The task at this point is to expose the false social pretenses upon which exclusionary practices toward persons with disabilities are based, and which are dehumanizing for all people. Following the arc of this critique, chapter 4 then strives to paint a more adequate portrait of being human, a vision grounded in themes of embodied relation, vulnerability, and love. Indeed, being human and whole means more than self-creative autonomy and productive efficiency. And in light of this wider focus, being Christian means more than a fix for our brokenness, a way of maximizing our security and fleeing from our embodied condition of interdependency. Accordingly, chapters 5 through 7 deepen the analysis by examining theological currents that flow from the notions of God and creation (chapter 5), humanity and redemption in Jesus Christ (chapter 6), and the reconciling power of God's kingdom anticipated in the community we call church, implying a vision of hospitality that encourages a wider praxis of inclusion (chapter 7). These chapters are fruits of the theological method of two-way access mentioned above.

The basic argument of this book is this: wholeness is not the product of self-sufficiency or independence, but rather of the genuinely inclusive communion that results from sharing our humanity with one another in light of the grace of God. To exist as a finite creature is to be contingent and vulnerable. This means we are beings that face limitations and are capable of suffering from a range of impairments. There is a profound theological implication here. It is precisely such vulnerability that God embraces in Christ, entering fully into the frailty of the human condition, even unto a tragic death. Jesus is Emmanuel, God with us. Sharing the divine self in this way sends a distinct message: God is in solidarity with humanity at its most fundamental level, in weakness and brokenness. This is not to romanticize weakness. Rather, here God reveals the divine nature as compassion not only by undergoing or suffering with human vulnerability, but also by raising it up into God's own being.

Redemption then is a welcoming, an empowering act of divine hospitality. It does not render human beings "weak," in the sense of passivity. Neither does it negate vulnerability by making humans invulnerable and perfectly whole. Nancy Eiesland correctly notes this by calling our attention to the fact that Jesus's body remains scarred after his resurrection.[16] So instead of doing away with impairments and the capacity to suffer, redemption transforms vulnerability into a communion with God, prefiguring the final eschatological horizon to come when all things will become so transformed. An entire "theology of vulnerability" opens up, wherein the marginal and heretofore neglected (i.e., disability) becomes central.

Understanding redemption this way has dramatic implications for living together. It addresses the often hidden struggles of persons whose "deficiencies" relegate them to marginal societal and/or ecclesiological status. But, more broadly, it opens up the christological implications of Paul's paradoxical proclamation in 2 Corinthians 12:9–10; namely, that the saving power of God is made manifest and perfected in weakness or the lack of ability (*astheneiai*). The intent is neither to valorize disability nor to glorify suffering. For Paul's "thorn in the flesh" must be understood christologically, not as a means to romanticize passivity and self-sacrifice. Attending to this, however, requires giving more attention to the theological bearing of notions such as relation, embodiment, wholeness, sin, redemption, hospitality, and the nature of ecclesial existence. It calls also for a rich social scientific and philosophical inquiry into the character of communal life and the ways it can function to marginalize those considered different and deficient in some way or another.

Hence, I come to the fundamental thesis of this book: there is a strange logic to the Christian witness, one that gives testimony to a strength that comes through weakness, a wholeness that manifests itself in brokenness, a power that reveals itself through vulnerability. The logic here is paradoxical and subversive. Rather than idealize vulnerability, it produces what I shall call a "metaphorical reversal" that exposes the false pretenses of the cult of normalcy. For human communities tend to shun what lacks the power to present itself according to common and taken-for-granted values, whether because it is simply foreign and strange or because it manifests some form of alleged corruption or deficiency. Indeed, we grow to fear the abnormal, the different and other. It disrupts the familiar and safe world of commonplace assumptions, and thus makes us vulnerable. Such vulnerability is no panacea; it is anxiety-ridden. A sense of vulnerability can seek shelter in the cult of normalcy and is wont to assuage its insecurity by justifying the order of things as they are (i.e., the conventions of the cult of normalcy) via all kinds of ideological mechanisms.

The redeemed life, however, exemplifies the reorientation—indeed reversal—of such fear-based anxiety. Such a life marks a conversion (*metanoia*) to God that trades on the experience of vulnerability and inability as a harbinger of divine abundance. This does not mean a mere submissiveness and lack of power in relation to God's utter power. To the contrary, it entails an acknowledgment of creaturely limitation and interdependence that cultivates an active openness toward human differences. A space is made for others, strangers, disabled persons—those without autonomy, power, and completeness measured in terms of the cult of normalcy. It is no accident that the biblical narratives portray a kind of salvation that, far from vindicating the conventional and normal, actually subverts it by pointing to the palpable presence of the divine in human vulnerability as a site of relational interdependence. The power of God is unseemly and strange.[17] It discloses itself paradoxically, not in autonomy but through the stranger's lack of ability. The stranger, however, is not merely a moral lesson. He or she is a person full of dignity, full of humanity, whose call is for us to be present, to listen, and to open up and share our lives.

Jesus Christ is the exemplar of such a stranger, an icon of a vulnerable God. At the heart of the Christian witness is an inclusive love of difference that is christological in shape. In the Christ event God sympathetically enters into our midst and communicates a love that spills over with unconditional regard for all persons. Beyond merely confirming the basic human right to respect, this radical love issues in a recognition and acceptance of human creaturely dependence as a bearer of the image of God. And it does so in a gesture of hospitality.

Reflecting the ancient policy of inviting the stranger into one's home, hospitality is a fruitful metaphor for divine love. In the biblical traditions, welcoming and attending to one who is alien and thus vulnerable, who somehow stands outside the taken-for-granted social world and is thus incapable of reciprocating in like kind, is a moral imperative. Even more, however, hospitality heralds divine presence. It has redemptive power for both host and guest. It bears a relational vulnerability that exhibits the unseemly power of God in human weakness and inability. Such a view emanates from the New Testament remembrances of Jesus's ministry, death, and resurrection. Hospitality is the Christ-shaped character of God's reconciling love, displayed not in power but in vulnerability. Such love is not distributed according to the order of ability, but according to the order of grace, a hyperbolic logic of abundance that functions to reverse the conventions of the "normal" by bearing weakness. For hospitality is a gift offered without preconditions and expectations, an emblem of openness to the other. Accordingly, it is through the practice of hospitality that we participate in God's inclusive embrace, realizing the kingdom of God announced by Jesus.[18]

In this way, we move beyond the cult of normalcy toward living out the presence of God in the praxis-oriented task of being present to and for others. Disability is more than a handy illustration of God's grace; it is redemptively fundamental. Hence, privileging disability not only makes possible, but also requires, a rethinking of theology from the ground up. Bringing what has been considered marginal to the center of Christian faith has radical consequences. Disability's "dangerous memory" provides a prophetic counter to the cult of normalcy far too often assumed in theological formulations. The focus is shifted from talking about disability as something that affects "them" to representing disability as something that affects "us." Not simply because we are all disabled, though all of us at some point shall experience disabilities as our bodies age, but rather, because we participate in systemic social structures that silence and disconfirm persons with disabilities. And this impoverishes our experience of redemption in Christian communities. Our resistance to human vulnerability calls for transformation if we are to experience the power of the biblical witness and participate more fully in God's inclusive love.

In the end, I come to the conclusion that disability is tragically but redemptively fundamental. Tragic, not in the sense of evoking pity, but because disability entails involuntary impairment and real suffering, much of which is the consequence of social alienation and exile. Redemptive, because disability opens up our vulnerability and dependence upon each other and God. This gets to the heart of Paul's proclamation (2 Cor. 12) that God's power is made complete and perfected in weakness. But I must confess from the outset that it is difficult to estimate the true power of such a paradox, a difficulty made manifestly real not only in the writing of this book, but also more concretely in the everyday realities of parenting a child with disabilities. And the result has transformed my theological perspective and offered fresh new ways of understanding the well-worn landscape of Christian faith.

Notes

1. For more information, consult Tracy Haerle, ed., *Children with Tourette's Syndrome: A Parent's Guide* (Rockville, MD: Woodbine House, 1992); Ruth Dowling Bruun and Dertel Bruun, *A Mind of Its Own: Tourette's Syndrome: A Story and Guide* (Oxford: Oxford University Press, 1994); Mitzi Waltz, *Bipolar Disorders: A Guide to Helping Children and Adolescents* (Sebastopol, CA: O'Reilly, 2000); Demitri Papolos and Janice Papolos, *The Bipolar Child* (New York: Broadway, 1999); George T. Lynn, *Survival Strategies for Parenting Children with Bipolar Disorder* (Philadelphia: Jessica Kingsley, 2000); and Tony Attwood, *Asperger's Syndrome: A Guide for Parents and Professionals* (Philadelphia: Jessica Kingsley, 1998).

2. Jennie Weiss Block, *Copious Hosting: A Theology of Access for People with Disabilities* (New York: Continuum, 2002), 131.

3. Stanley Hauerwas, "Community and Diversity: The Tyranny of Normality," 37–43, in *Critical Reflections on Stanley Hauerwas' Theology of Disability: Disabling Society, Enabling Theology*, ed. John Swinton (Binghamton, NY: Haworth Pastoral Press, 2004). This essay originally appeared in *Suffering Presence: Theological Reflections on Medicine, the Mentally Handicapped, and the Church* (Notre Dame, IN: University of Notre Dame Press, 1986), 211–17.

4. Jürgen Moltmann, "Liberate Yourselves by Accepting One Another," in *Human Disability and the Service of God: Reassessing Religious Practice*, ed. Nancy L. Eiesland and Don E. Saliers (Nashville: Abingdon Press, 1998), 110.

5. Nancy L. Eiesland, *The Disabled God: Toward a Liberatory Theology of Disability* (Nashville: Abingdon Press, 1994), 20–23.

6. For a personal account, see my essay "Love without Boundaries: Theological Reflections on Parenting a Child with Disabilities," *Theology Today*, July 2005 (62:2). Readers interested in firsthand, testimonial accounts of disability might consult Francis Young's *Face to Face: A Narrative Essay in the Theology of Suffering* (Edinburgh: T. & T. Clark, 1990), a moving book by a well-regarded historical theologian who discusses her struggles to parent a child with severe disabilities. In a similar vein, see also Kathleen Deyer Bolduc's *His Name Is Joel: Searching for God in a Son's Disability* (Louisville: Bridge Resources, 1999), and *Life as We Know It: A Father, a Family, and an Exceptional Child*, by Michael Bérubé (New York: Pantheon Books, 1996). Also instructive is Robert F. Molsberry's *Blindsided by Grace: Entering the World of Disabilities* (Minneapolis: Augsburg Fortress, 2004), which chronicles a pastor's struggle to come to terms with his disabling condition after a bicycle accident.

7. See Paul Ricouer, "Hope and the Structure of Philosophical Systems," 203–16, in *Figuring the Sacred: Religion, Narrative, and Imagination*, trans. David Pellauer, ed. Mark I. Wallace (Minneapolis: Fortress Press, 1995).

8. Moltmann, "Liberate Yourselves by Accepting One Another," 121.

9. Jean Vanier, *Becoming Human* (Mahwah, NJ: Paulist Press, 1998), 39–41.

10. Molsberry, *Blindsided by Grace*, 57.

11. Ibid., 84–85.

12. For good treatments of the disability rights movement, see James I. Charlton, *Nothing about Us without Us* (Berkeley: University of California Press, 1998); Joseph P. Shapiro, *No Pity: People with Disabilities Forging a New Civil Rights Movement* (New York: Times Books, 1994); and Doris Zames Fleischer and Frieda Zames, *The Disability Rights Movement: From Charity to Confrontation* (Philadelphia: Temple University Press, 2001).

13. On disability studies, see Colin Barnes and Geof Mercer, *Disability* (Cambridge: Polity Press, 2003); Lennard J. Davis, ed., *The Disabilities Studies Reader* (New York: Routledge, 1996); Mark Nagler, ed., *Perspectives on Disability*, 2nd ed. (Palo Alto, CA: Health Markets Research, 1993); Michael Oliver, *Understanding Disability: From Theory to Practice* (New York: St. Martin's, 1996); Tom Shakespeare, ed., *The Disability Studies Reader: Social Science Perspectives* (New York: Cassell Academic, 1998).

14. Johann Baptist Metz, *Faith in History and Society: Toward a Practical Fundamental Theology*, trans. David Smith (New York: Seabury Press, 1980).

15. American with Disabilities Act (1990), *U.S. Statutes at Large*, vol. 104, 327–78.

16. Eiesland, *The Disabled God*, 98ff.

17. The "strange power" of God is a turn of phrase drawn from Daniel L. Migliore, *Faith Seeking Understanding: An Introduction to Christian Theology* (Grand Rapids: William B. Eerdmans, 1991), 52.

18. See Christine D. Pohl, *Making Room: Recovering Hospitality as a Christian Tradition* (Grand Rapids: William B. Eerdmans, 1999). See also Lucien Richard, OMI, *Living the Hospitality of God* (Mahwah, NJ: Paulist Press, 2000), and Thomas W. Ogletree, *Hospitality toward the Stranger: Dimensions of Moral Understanding* (Philadelphia: Fortress Press, 1985).

1

Theology and Disability

Perils and Promises

As a person with disability I want to turn to every part of human society and God's church and urge them: Let us share your world! Because your world is also my world and every person's world, and because, so far, this is the only world there is.

Arne Fritzson[1]

Some time ago, I was casually describing my interest in theology and disability to a friend who is active in the field of disability studies. I was surprised by his response. He sat back in his chair and smirked awkwardly. After taking a sip of his coffee, he exclaimed with a suspicious tone, "You're venturing into a troublesome area." He proceeded to tell me about the "religious" experience of a female acquaintance who is paralyzed from the waist down and uses a wheelchair. On one occasion, after being subject to considerable pressure, she agreed to accompany a group of Christians to a "healing" ceremony. She was called up to the front of a church during the service. The healing "failed." Not only did she remain paralyzed, she was publicly transformed into an embarrassing spectacle, and made the subject of awkward gazes and whispered questions. This diminished her sense of being welcomed as someone unique and loved by God, the same status as anyone else in that church community. Her impairment had been inscribed with theological meanings that reduced her condition to a lack or blemish, a deviance. The focus of the community's gaze was on her disability, and as a result features of her personhood fully capable of making valuable contributions to the community were neglected. Such misplacement, certainly not intended, nullified her creaturely dignity as a gift of God. Sadly, she holds a deep resentment toward both Christians and God, as do many persons with disabilities.

This story is disturbing. That it depicts an experience commonplace for persons with disabilities is perhaps even more disturbing. It exposes the rather uncomfortable relationship that exists between Christianity and disability, a relationship that trades on regrettable but all too familiar misunderstandings of what it means to be physically, mentally, or emotionally impaired.[2] While these misunderstandings may involve cultural and social processes wider in scope than Christianity, it is nonetheless true that such misunderstandings have been—and still are—adopted, transmitted, and justified by Christian means, which augment their influence. Because of this an unfortunate irony ensues: among church communities that seek with all due diligence to incarnate the love of God, disabilities are treated as faulted and pitiable anomalies, stigmas to be extricated. Labels and categories are employed that single out and reduce a certain group of people to roles designated for the abnormal and blemished. And such generalized role projections demean and ostracize. How so? By setting up restrictive norms about who and when people are able to participate fully in civic space. Based upon narrowly defined models of individual autonomy, efficiency, or productivity, certain bodily differences and impairments are perceived as liabilities that amount to deviance. Hence, the place where God's welcome should be most evident becomes instead a place of inaccessibility and isolation for some. Persons are disconfirmed.

In this chapter, I shall place disability at the forefront in order to explore the ways in which it exposes major liabilities in theological discourse and practice. The aim is to prepare the way for a counter-discourse that undoes inadequate theological representations of disability by naming and resisting the flawed premises upon which they rest. Clearing semantic space in this regard will help us defamiliarize disability and see more clearly why the example of the paralyzed woman discussed above is so disturbing. Disability does not simply mark a personal tragedy that calls for healing. Neither does it indicate a diminishment of the image of God imprinted upon human beings. Neither does it suggest that people with disabilities are "children of a lesser God," an ineffective or non-loving God. Rather, it calls into question the Christian community and its understanding of human wholeness, normalcy, impairment, redemption, and God's love and power.

Subverting faulty assumptions will prove critical to the task of systematically rethinking human vulnerability and disability. As Karl Marx once said, the criticism of religion is the beginning of all criticism.[3] Religion commonly relies upon the status quo, which arises and is maintained by mechanisms of social exchange and economic power, reinforcing it with divine purpose. Thus an analysis and critique of theological concepts can aid us in bringing to light the hidden and often faulted practices and attitudes that buttress how we commonly measure what is normal, valuable, and real. In this way we shall be in the position to open up the prospect of a more adequate theological portrait of God's inclusive love.

I. A Disabling Theology or a Theology of Disability?

More than a few factors make the juxtaposition of Christianity and disability problematic. My intention, however, is not to catalogue every theological framework that is "disabling" or oppressive for persons with disabilities. Nor do I wish to point out flaws by painting an historical portrait of how disability has been theologically interpreted for the past two thousand years. Instead, I seek to usher the reader into the subject matter by highlighting general features in the literature on disability, most especially as they offer critical resources for more adequately framing the correlation between theology and disability, such that their connection leads to a theology "of" rather than "against" or "in spite of" disability. There are two widespread impediments to such a constructive correlation, both of which look for a moral meaning to disability. And this is counterproductive.

Defining Disability beyond the Medical Model

First, Christians commonly adopt the prevailing medical model of disability.[4] This model is based on what non-disabled people think is best for persons with disabilities. For example, it is assumed that disability indicates a deficient or flawed human condition, a bodily deviation due to a "loss" of capacity in one way or another, which holds a person back from participation in society. Hence, disability represents an inability, abnormality, or disadvantage calling for management and correction in order to restore proper functioning. And from a societal perspective this means that disability is a liability, a dysfunction legitimating professional and welfare services. While this way of approaching the matter is not altogether blameworthy—for many people benefit from corrective measures made possible by modern technology and medical practices—it is nonetheless limited in scope.

The medical model tends to reduce disability to a problem requiring diagnosis and treatment, a broken object to be fixed, made better, or overcome. In so doing, however, the person becomes reduced to a function of disabilities rather than vice versa. Indeed, the personal becomes obscured. Fostering an impoverished, one-way relationship of dependence between healer and patient, caregiver and cared-for, the medical model can effectively silence the patient as a subject of her or his own experience. For it is assumed that the healer has the knowledge to define illness and the power to rehabilitate, the advantages of which are passively received by a beneficiary regarded as someone with nothing to offer. Indeed, the term "patient" has etymological roots in Latin, where it means "to undergo"—one who endures affliction and receives treatment. Seen in this way, reciprocity is annulled by professional control, repair, and supervision. A service is administered to a non-participant, one who plays the role of an otherwise helpless and useless burden.

And when this happens, even among caregivers who are family or friends, good will and acts of charity become patronizing vehicles of victimization—the person is written off.[5] That many perceive themselves as victims of a personal tragedy, which reduces them to needy recipients of medical care, demonstrates how the medical model can be internalized and appropriated by disabled persons.

The fact remains, however, that disability is neither a defect nor a social burden, the equivalent of personal tragedy. And it does not necessitate an unwieldy dependence upon others. Persons with disabilities have distinct voices and, despite perceived losses or deficiencies, possess both the capacity for self-determination and the ability to make important contributions to society. Well-known examples come to mind, like Helen Keller and Franklin D. Roosevelt. However, these are not simply anomalies, heroes who have made their way despite disability. They mark a certain potential for all people with disabilities, a potential often stymied by social constraints. Genuine healing is more than a matter of an individual's bodily adjustment to fit society's definition of normalcy. It is instead a matter of society adjusting to the presence of diverse people with a range of impairments.[6] And with this we enter the arena of civil rights and social justice. From its early days onward, the disability movement has rallied to the phrase "nothing about us without us," seeking fervently to empower persons with disabilities to assert agential independence and define their needs beyond discriminatory systems organized and operated by non-disabled persons.[7]

Disability, then, is not merely a medical problem for individuals; it is more a social problem. The medical model and its stress on cure and rehabilitation not only fails to address this broader issue, it inadvertently perpetuates processes of disempowerment, exclusion, and isolation, concealing deeper attitudinal, employment-related, educational, and architectural obstacles to genuine inclusion. For example, a person who uses a wheelchair *becomes* disabled when there are access barriers (i.e., when there is no ramp to enter a building or an elevator to travel to the fourth floor). Thus it is that, as a loss of bodily function, impairment is socially transformed into a disability, a restriction of activity that excludes social participation.[8] Perhaps we might then see disability less as something one *has*, or worse *is*, and more a series of moments defined by interactions between people and the public institutions where they occur.

We must therefore supplement the medical model with a social model, addressing disability as both a socially constructed category and a matter of human rights. I say "supplement" rather than "replace" because it is also important not to lose sight of the fact that bodily impairments yield various kinds of physical experiences and personal responses, some of which can be frustrating and painful. So while people with disabilities cannot be reduced to their impairments alone, they are nonetheless bodily affected by those impairments, making possible the experience of disability. Thus, as advocates of the social model sometimes forget in the call for justice and civil rights, disability is not solely a socially constructed reality.[9] It also involves concrete bodies with involuntary restrictions that can cause discomfort, pain, and frustration of their own accord. For example, developmental disorders on the autistic spectrum are a biological factor of the brain that directly impacts thinking, feeling, and social activities. Autistic persons may experience horrible fears, frustrating obsessions, and self-abuse, and not all of these are products of social causes.

It is also true, however, that persons with autism are subject to barriers rooted in societal attitudes and assumptions about what it means to be whole or healthy, which become springboards for representing autistic experience and investing it with attributes and meanings that extend far beyond its physiological conditions. As a form of lifelong disability, then, autism takes on a social role as normalcy's "other," a feature of deviance that automatically pushes it to the margins. Disability theorist Lennard Davis suggests this is why disability and normalcy should be seen as part of the same system.[10] Even as they reference bodily conditions, criteria for measuring human ability are factors of communal assumptions about what makes for normal or healthy functioning. Disability, then, is a physiologically rooted social performance. With this in mind, a more holistic definition of disability might read as follows: disability is a term naming that interstice where (1) restrictions due to an involuntary bodily impairment, (2) social role expectations, and (3) external physical/social obstructions come together in a way that (4) preempts an intended participation in communal life. The stress is indeed on the social, but not in a way that neglects the body.

In this way, we can see how bodily impairments become saturated with meanings external to, and much wider than, themselves. They are interpreted in light of role expectations about normality and human wholeness, which ironically set up conditions for social participation that cannot be met given the real barriers that exist under the auspices of a community's assumptions about what counts for normal and healthy human functioning. I say "ironic" because the logic is circular. A society's conception of normalcy informs and governs exchanges between persons, producing a system of conventions resistant to or incapable of accommodating the non-normal. By inverse implication the non-normal is perceived in terms of being unable to participate. Thus, in the case of certain impairments considered non-normal, a person's subject-position becomes ideologically overdetermined. The perception of inability by "able-bodied" persons functions to define a person's whole being. Disabled, then, becomes something one is—that is, powerless and useless, incapable of participating adequately in social exchanges. This is the substance of the oppression faced by persons with disabilities. It relies on a notion of disability that is absolute and totalizing rather than the consequence of an impairment that a person happens to have, which impedes getting along in ways set down by non-disabled persons.

Understanding Disability Christianly: Is Disability a Tragedy to Be Undone?

This brings us to a second main factor that makes the coupling of Christianity and disability problematic. Insofar as Christians adopt the medical model, disability accrues theological meanings that are reductive in character, leading to perilous consequences. Among Christians, disability is commonly represented as something to be healed or gotten rid of—a fault, a lesson in lack of faith, a helpless object of pity for the non-disabled faithful to display their charity, a vehicle of redemptive suffering, a cross to bear, or fuel for the inspiration of others. Whatever the case, it is clear that such theological reductionism is alienating and oppressive for persons with disabilities, nurturing a traumatic sense of being out of place. How so? Insofar as Christians take for granted assumptions about normalcy that stem from their sociocultural environment and that reflect certain interpretations of the scriptures, they inadvertently give theological sanction to principalities and powers that are disabling. The issue is not simply one of physical accommodations for disabled persons—for example, insuring that there are points of access to a sanctuary. The problem of access is, more broadly, a social and theological problem. For, as we shall see, if "disabled" is seen as something a person is, an impairment becomes inscribed with transcendent meanings that treat it as a reflection of divine purposes.

Disability strikes a fundamental note of ambiguity in the Christian witness. And the implications reverberate outward to unsettle easy assumptions about what it means to be human, whole, redeemed, and related to God in the context of a community of faith. This is precisely why I argue that it is instructive to rethink fundamental theological themes in light of disability. Too often theology simply presumes the operative sway of the cult of normalcy, and in a way that is oppressive for persons with disabilities—that is, in a way that devalues, restricts from social participation, and inhibits aspiration to self-defined goals.[11]

However, questions abound. How, then, should Christians respond to disability? Is it improper to wish curative wholeness and well-being upon someone who appears lacking in these graces? After all, given the redemptive power of God's love testified to in the scriptures, is not impairment an unacceptable condition of human misfortune and flaw? Does not the creaturely dignity of a person with disabilities naturally cry out for, and indeed deserve, healing and restoration to physical or mental completeness? Moreover, would not such healing bear witness to God's saving power? Intuitively, it does not seem fair or right that a person should be consigned to live in a tragic state of dysfunction and bear its social consequences. Why would God continue to allow people to suffer—physically or socially—from loss of movement, loss of possibility, loss of a normal life? What possible purpose could lie behind an unremittingly disabled body? Where is the mercy, the compassion, the transformative power to usher in health? In a nutshell, where is God?

These concerns are as inescapable as they are poignant. And they are voiced not only by persons with disabilities, but also by the non-disabled persons with whom their lives become entwined. Such concerns, however, manifest underlying theological convictions about the character of human life in the context of God's redemptive love, convictions that merit critical analysis. For example, as illustrated in the story of my colleague's friend, those who tried to heal this woman presumed that it is God's benevolent will that people live fully functional lives, normal lives characterized by physical wholeness and motor flexibility. Indeed, there are biblical precedents for such a presumption. One only has to open up the New Testament Gospels to find numerous accounts of Jesus healing the lame, deaf, blind, and sick. It seems only natural, then, for Christians to suppose that God (1) wishes for human beings to flourish in the fullness of their creaturely capacity and (2) is capable of healing and transforming conditions where such flourishing is impeded or imperiled. After all, is not wholeness part of God's saving plan for humanity?

Despite the apparent truth of this conclusion, it brings us face-to-face with unyielding obstacles. For it is painfully clear that such wholeness eludes many. And with this we are brought to other, more difficult, questions. Why then do so many suffer from a dearth of human potential, from brokenness, deficiency, and impairment? More personally, as I have asked, why is my son Chris fated to live with daily neurological and biochemical impediments to his well-being? That innocent children face disease and harm in this way seems an unmitigated tragedy, calling into question the justice of God's sovereignty and love. The specter of what is commonly called *theodicy* looms large. In fact, I submit, lurking behind the awkward relationship between theology and disability are questions of theodicy. The issue amounts to whether and how we can justify God's abiding love and sovereign purpose given the constancy and ubiquity of human suffering and brokenness.[12]

This is by no means a new concern. It arises in biblical texts—for example in Job, Lamentations, and in the Gospel accounts. And many great theological minds in the Jewish and Christian traditions have wrestled with it, and continue to do so. Is it possible to reconcile the evidential fact of suffering with faith's affirmation of God's power and goodness? The question is unavoidable when we begin to think theologically about disability. And I believe its difficulty is part of why Christians are so often disturbed around people with disabilities. We are not sure how to make sense of disability, for several reasons. First, disability confronts non-disabled persons with their own fragility and contingency.[13] For all humans are only partially and temporarily able-bodied. We are subject to limitations, suffering, and finally death—and at any moment. Furthermore, unsure of ourselves and afraid to step outside the insularity of what is comfortable and assuring about normalcy, we often feel like we must do something to cover up or hide disability when we encounter it, making it go away. So we act out of pity, condescending in a detached way that assuages our discomfort but essentially leaves others unaffected. Finally, disability mirrors back the limitations of our communities and the ways they are constructed to serve some and not others, the conscious acknowledgment of which is unsettling and disorienting. Disability confronts us with different ways of being human and living in the world, rupturing the comfy but precarious assurances that we hold to regarding the purpose of human life. So we seek to neutralize it by remaking others in the image of our assurances, fixing their brokenness to more adequately reflect what we perceive to be true and valuable—that is, what is like us, normal.

In a theological context, such a process is endorsed by linking the conventions of normalcy to God's intention. One of the fundamental convictions of Christians is that the physical world is a created order that mirrors a divine archetype. Creation is good. Rosmarie Garland Thompson pinpoints the logic here in stating that when the visible world is posited "as the index of a coherent and just invisible world," we are encouraged "to read the material body as a sign invested with transcendent meaning."[14] So the world as it is reflects a divine intention. Assumptions about human wholeness and normalcy are thereby given theological credence. But what about those elements of creation experienced as lacking in goodness, perhaps tragic and harmful to human well-being? Usually they are perceived as inverse reflections of God's purpose, a tragic mark of something gone wrong. Disability quickly becomes a sign of imperfection, a flaw in God's good order, something to be undone. And because of this, theodicy questions foster an understanding of disability that leads down an erroneous path.[15]

Fundamentally my proposal is that theodicy questions, inevitable as they may be, can produce unintended but palpable mechanisms of exclusion that obviate the call to hospitality at the center of Christian faith. Under the banner of love, the allegedly benign intention to understand, accept, help, and heal disabilities can ironically stymie the genuine welcome of disabled persons into our communities, signifying a deeper and perhaps more pernicious form of exclusion. Hence, we must proceed with great caution and circumspection in the attempt to discern God's hand in human disability.

There are five reasons why we must proceed with great circumspection in thinking theologically about disability. First, because it can speciously presume that disability always entails tragedy and suffering, absorbing it into a curative medical model that treats the condition as something to be overcome by the individual. Second, because it can misrepresent and overdetermine disability as an absolute category, which obscures the reality of persons with disabilities and in effect disables select impairments as representative of a general faulted or incomplete condition. Third, because it leaves unquestioned the cult of normalcy, simply assuming its influence, and subsequently neglecting the need for social critique and transformation. Fourth, because it traffics in mistaken understandings of human wholeness, redemption, and God's power, all of which preempt the inclusive work of love to which we are called. Finally, because it produces a thin theology that in essence regards suffering as a problem to be solved rather than sympathetically and redemptively encountered. All of these justifications indicate the degree to which we must rethink the paradigm by which disability is perceived as an anomaly. And they shall loom large in the remainder of this book.

II. Beyond Theodicy?[16]

I remember the moment as if it were an eternal image etched in my psyche. Holding the hand of my wife, Mary, I watched Chris emerge from the womb and take his first breath. It was an incomparable privilege. A great mystery unfurled before me. As Chris was carefully handed to me and I held him gently, his fragile beauty stunned me into tears. My heart melted and refashioned itself into one, gigantic upsurge of wondrous gratitude. The only words I could muster were, "You're amazing, Mary. Thank you, God." Joy rushed over me. Here was our son, wrapped snugly in a blanket and experiencing his first sense of the world outside the womb. I was humbled and proud, all at the same time.

Sixteen years later, the joy has not abated. That I am privileged to witness the unfolding of a life mysteriously connected to me and yet uniquely its own is still overwhelming and too much to take in. But, if I am honest, I must admit my sense of parenthood has been chastened by struggles that I could not have imagined on that first day. While no parent is ever really prepared for the task of parenting, the life of my son is marked by struggles that stretch Mary and me beyond the usual contours of parenthood. Born with a genetic predisposition that emerged only as he aged, perhaps triggered by familial and/or environmental circumstances, Chris has now been diagnosed with Asperger's syndrome, Tourette's syndrome, obsessive compulsive, bipolar, oppositional defiant, and attention-deficit disorders. This makes his and our family's life a different and often difficult one.

In the throes of daily life, we have been brought to ask, "Where are you, God?" Now this question is no detached, academic matter of speculation. It is deeply personal, a matter of adequately responding to Chris and finding resources for tending to each other. How should one respond, especially as a parent, to an innocent child who suffers? As Robert Massie asks, "if a healthy child is a perfect miracle of God, who created the imperfect child? Why would God create imperfection? Especially in a child? Especially in our child?"[17] Ours is an effort to "be there" for Chris when he cries out after a painful day of social exclusion, emotional outbursts, educational failures, or uncontrollable tics and obsessions. This is not a matter of justifying God in the face of suffering; it is a matter of being an empowering and healing presence for Chris.

What are we to say when Chris looks at us and asks, "Why did God make me this way?" Faced with such a question—literally "faced" by the heartfelt query of my son, who directly confronts me and calls me to respond—I am humbled and silenced, both as a parent and as a theologian. All the prolix answers that could be mustered from the pages of great theological texts seem trivial and heartless before the depth of the circumstances. As in the case of Ivan in *The Brothers Karamozov*, there is a great refusal that wells up inside of me. Not merely suffering in general, but the suffering of this particular one, my son, whom I love more intensely than I ever thought possible, is something I cannot accept as a justified handout from the God whose hand I believe lovingly fashioned him into being. And, I must admit from the outset, there seems to be neither an apparent reason for nor a discernible point to his struggles. The moral meaning of Chris's disabilities is not a cognitive problem for which I have an answer. Nor, as I have come to believe, is it a problem for which I should have an answer.

This predicament is why I contend that the urge to explain suffering vis-à-vis God is a faulty strategy. Whatever the intellectual merits of the theodicy question, it leads down a path with troubling consequences for thinking about human disability. Indeed, it trades upon a medical model and fosters a theological reductionism that equates disability with personal tragedy. If we affirm a God who wishes to eradicate suffering and whose power is able to undo suffering, it stands to reason that there must be divinely ordained grounds for why some experience tragedy to a degree that others do not, perishing or remaining broken in ways that others are not. Could it then be, as Job's accusers queried, a reflection of God's curse or punishment? Could it be related to a person's lack of faith? Could it be that God has a broader, higher purpose to serve by exposing some to unremitting loss and pain or fashioning some with bodily defects and inabilities? Indeed, perhaps some must endure personal anguish in order to cultivate sympathy and love in others. Or perhaps suffering reflects God's way of nurturing moral advancement, an instrument of eventual blessing for the sufferer, for others, or both. Perhaps affliction is a crucible in which virtue and character are formed, becoming an example or inspiration for others.[18]

These are powerful and, to a real degree, unavoidable responses. For human beings, as thinking beings, naturally seek to understand so as to endure predicaments that detract from well-being. But these responses are theologically erroneous, leading down a path that trivializes suffering, explaining it away as a problem to be solved rather than empathetically engaged and potentially transformed. The real challenge is not intellectual, but practical.[19] Practical, first of all, because another person is not a problem, but a presence whose call for affirmation elicits the moral obligation to listen and pay attention, to show compassion in a way that reflects back to them their distinct creaturely beauty and value. Second, because only by tending to the presence of another do we come to recognize when suffering really occurs and is not merely our own projection onto someone with disabilities. The real task, then, as Stanley Hauerwas puts it, is to be present to others, and this requires moral skills gained in relationships of interdependence, not in cognitive propositions.[20]

What is more, these responses belie the redemptive nearness of God to human vulnerability and brokenness, a nearness of solidarity that does not undo or fix such brokenness but, as I shall argue, paradoxically embraces it. Accordingly, such responses depend on faulty notions of human wholeness which bolster assumptions that end up construing lack of ability as an anomaly, an embodiment of insufficiency and deviance. And this has the effect of marginalizing disability, even to the point of oppression, representing it as a freakish spectacle to be shunned and removed from the ordinary space of public life. The urge to explain human vulnerability to suffering vis-à-vis such formulations poses serious and unwieldy impediments to the compassionate display of the power of God's love, which, as this book unfolds, we shall come to see as the opposite of power and ability conceived in terms of autonomous ability and normalized physical, mental, or emotional functioning. If God is love, then God's power must be understood as something other than utter self-sufficiency, which is removed from the human predicament. Love sympathetically engages the beloved by being present to the beloved in a way that undergoes a transformation because of love and, accordingly, empowers the beloved.

Equally troubling, however, is the way theodicy can overlook the social character of disability and mask the ways that communities themselves are disabling. For a community's perception of disability is the inverse projection of its own framework of normalcy.[21] Disability is a factor of the cult of normalcy. An image is cast onto those whose lives disrupt the status quo, manifesting a lack or deficiency of what is construed as standard, ordinary, and familiar. In most instances, this means that suffering is attributed to disability in ways that may not actually involve discomfort or pain. The upshot is that disadvantage is assigned and measured according to social conventions that frame what it means to be able-bodied and to function productively as a contributing member of society. Accordingly, disability is deemed an agential defect, a tragic dysfunction or illness in need of allaying and curative efforts. And because it is presumed to have no overt purpose, no satisfactory social meaning, disability is alleged to involve frustration and pain.[22] This is precisely why persons with disabilities are seen as victims, patients, or liabilities. The real tragedy, then, is not intrinsic to disability; it is socially imposed. It lies in how disability functions as a socially sanctioned category based upon the experiences and expectations of non-disabled persons, which in effect coerces disabled persons into playing roles inadequate to their own experience and which distort their sense of themselves as persons.

So when my son asks, "Why did God make me this way?" I am compelled to inquire into the social conditions and theological premises that bring this question to his lips. Perhaps in another family, another society, his condition would be seen as a gift, a strength, and not a liability. For indeed he is gifted with abilities much wider than those aspects deemed disabled. Perhaps it is my own limited, parental expectations that are, at least partially, responsible for his turmoil. This in no way suggests that I am to blame, or that parents and families of persons with disabilities are somehow at fault.[23] Nor is it to suggest, as a friend of mine once did, that Chris would probably thrive in some other family environment. Nevertheless, it is important to acknowledge that I am part of a systemic problem. I too participate in the cult of normalcy and require ongoing transformation by God's love in the context of human frailty. Most of us do. This is why I believe that the very notion of disability strikes to the core, forcing our theological reorientation as Christians. Disability is not simply about "them"; it is about us.

In order to open up space for a more fruitful theological picture of human wholeness and disability, however, we must examine and critique problematic notions of disability that emerge from the coupling of theology and disability in terms of theodicy. So now we turn to those attitudes and assumptions, often justified via biblical texts, that impart questionable ways of representing disabled bodies.

III. Toward a Hermeneutic of Disability

There are several consistent patterns of characterizing disability that have been drawn from stories in the Hebrew and Christian scriptures, invested with theological meaning, and passed down through Christian traditions, but which are inadequate representations of disability. They are inadequate because they are superficial, either (1) denigrating disability as a human flaw or deficiency or (2) trivializing it as something serving a beneficial or positive end.

I am not simply referring here to flagrantly hostile attitudes toward disability. It is true that persons with disabilities have been subject to verbal diminishment through terms like "invalid," "cripple," "freak," "retard," "idiot," "imbecile," "spaz," and so on, words that disgrace disability as something nonvalid and subhuman. It is also true that persons with disabilities have been disregarded as agents of their own experience, treated as incapable of acting independently and thus in need of surveillance and control by non-disabled persons. Such acts of oppression and disconfirmation, however, do not happen in a vacuum. They imply a disabling framework of attitudes and assumptions that often goes unexamined, hidden behind conventions presupposed as normative. They are symptoms of a deeper, more entrenched problem that merits investigation, especially as it arises in the Bible, is given theological vestments, and is promulgated by Christian communities.

It would be irresponsible to overlook the fact that there are resources in the biblical witness for the inadequate representations of disability described above. While these may cause a certain measure of embarrassment, we cannot simply sweep them under the carpet and pretend they do not exist. We must be honest and admit, in the words of Roy McCloughry and Wayne Morris, "that disability language is used negatively in many parts of the Bible." Like McCloughry and Morris, however, we should probe further and not admit defeat. For they immediately go on to ask, "Is there a perspective in Scripture that celebrates diversity and the life of all people made in the image of God?"[24]

But this question introduces an interpretive problem. How do we adjudicate between less and more helpful alternatives in the biblical texts? On what basis can we distance ourselves from texts that present harmful portrayals of disability while embracing those which are empowering? Answering these questions and moving forward requires developing a critical hermeneutic of disability. Such a hermeneutic allows us to read the Bible against itself. By no means does it entail simply discarding those texts that do not agree with certain contemporary beliefs presumed as foregone conclusions. That would be as irresponsible as simply ignoring parts of the Bible that are problematic.

A theological hermeneutic of disability involves a careful juxtaposition of texts which are themselves polyphonic and at times contradictory, so as to negotiate theologically between them and discern possible routes of fruitful analysis. Such a process is not new; it is part and parcel of all biblical interpretation.[25] It has inspired allegorical interpretations of the past and been the source of major theological shifts, such as Martin Luther's Pauline notion of justification by grace through faith. Moreover, this process has been made requisite in our time through advances in historical-critical studies, which recognize that biblical writings are themselves representative of various social, cultural, and political frameworks, each germane to a situation in time and place that influences the biblical writers. The Bible itself is a compilation of many interpretations with many theological aims, all of which seek to discern, preserve, and foment God's work of salvation, but none of which are transparently absolute.

A hermeneutic of disability, then, is not merely a matter of hunting through the biblical witness and finding select passages on disability that can subsequently be applied to our theological task in some straightforward manner. We must instead wrestle with the text, like Jacob wrestled with the angel and refused to let go until granted a blessing. And because the Bible is ambiguous on the account of disability, this means becoming cautiously selective as interpreters, choosing certain themes over and/or against less favorable alternatives, explicit in providing warrants for our selections vis-à-vis their consistency with other biblical texts, themes, and norms as well as with our own present experience, sociocultural context, and general knowledge base.[26] This will help us gain a faithful yet critical distance from some representations of disability presented in the Bible. It will also better equip us to counter contemporary interpretations of the Bible that project social and cultural assumptions onto the texts in ways that are unproductive. Drawing from authors in the fields of disability studies and philosophy can aid us in this task, helping us to adjust our apertures as readers in a way that subverts common presumptions and opens up new prospects for discerning what it means to be human, created in the image of God, redeemed, and in community with others. Indeed, there is a larger story of redemption disclosed in the biblical narratives that can provide a foothold for the kind of hermeneutic of disability I am describing. For the positive thrust of this program to take shape, however, negative attitudes and stereotypes toward disability must first be addressed.

IV. Dismantling Alienating Notions of Disability: Developing a Typology

Returning to the two-pronged framework of identifying inadequate viewpoints mentioned in the first paragraph of the previous section, let us break the analysis into two groupings: (1) denigrating views of disability and (2) trivializing views of disability. Whereas the first view represents disability in negative terms, as a blemish, the latter assesses it in positive terms, as something constructive. Both, however, serve to objectify disability in ways that demean persons with disabilities.

Avoiding the Theological Denigration of Disability

Regarding the first grouping, perhaps the most well-known way of representing disability in the Bible is as a blemish or stigma signifying a divine punishment or forsakenness. Here, disabled bodies are portrayed as less than whole, suffering from an incompleteness or lack of some significant, creaturely wholeness that is perceived as sacred and reflective of God's nature and perfection. This view adopts widely held beliefs in ancient Babylon and Egypt that disability was an evil omen or the product of evil spirits. On the premise that there are divinely ordained reasons for such a condition, in more than one case it is quite straightforwardly taken as a product of sin, as God's curse or punishment.[27] The Bible time and again depicts a God who shuns and exiles, sends debilitating plagues and diseases, inflicts pain, and prevents prosperity to the sinful and disobedient (e.g., Exod. 9:14–16; Lev. 26; Jer. 9:13–16; Matt. 3:7–12; Rev. 11:17–18). That affliction is brought about by God is also the operative assumption behind the coupling of moral impurity and physical stigma in the priestly system of the Hebrew Bible (e.g., Deut. 28:15ff. and Lev. 21:17–23).[28]

It is also the premise behind some of the New Testament accounts of Jesus's redemptive work. For example, Jesus is portrayed as the unblemished sacrifice for human sin, as one who suffers and dies in the place of human beings, who rightly deserve punishment for their sin (e.g., Rom. 3:25; 1 Cor. 5:7; Heb. 7:27; 1 John 2:2). There is also a link made between healing and the forgiveness of sins. As Nancy Eiesland notes, Luke 5:18–26 equates Jesus's healing actions with forgiveness; and in John 5:14, recounting the healing of a man who could not walk, Jesus states, "Do not sin any more, so that nothing worse happens to you." Eiesland goes on to suggest that even when Jesus heals the man born blind in John 9:1–3, he both supports and contradicts the sin-disability link—"neither this man nor his parents sinned; he was born blind so that God's works might be revealed in him" (9:3).[29] Clearly, with reference to this man, Jesus disconfirms the traditional connection between sin-punishment-blemish; but he nonetheless leaves the question open whether the connection is appropriate in other instances. Ambiguity thus remains, for the real focus is neither sin nor disability but God's work. As in most of the healing accounts, the story here primarily functions to confirm the christological identity of Jesus.[30]

This brings to mind another related way of representing disability, namely, as an instance of not having enough faith. On more than a few occasions in the gospel narratives, Jesus heals afflicted people and exclaims, "Your faith has made you well" (e.g., Mark 5:34; 10:52; Luke 17:19). The implications here are dangerous if we are not careful. As faithfulness yields healing, so too can failure to be healed be interpreted as a lack of faithfulness or, as Eiesland comments, "a personal flaw in the individual, such as unrepentant sin or a selfish desire to remain disabled."[31] The example of the paralyzed woman at the opening of this chapter is illustrative: if only she had more faith, she would be cured. Hence, in this way of thinking disability marks the moral culpability and spiritual imperfection of people. For it is assumed, conversely, that prayerful obedience to God leads to wholeness and well-being.[32]

In these two versions of the denigrating view of disability, there is a theodicy at work that presumes a medical model of disability. They both collapse the distinction between illness and disability, treating the latter as something to be fixed and cured, gotten rid of as a case of suffering and inadequacy. However, people with disabilities are not sick. Though sometimes an illness can cause disability, we must remember that disability involves social restrictions that follow from an impairment. Focusing solely on the cure of the individual glosses over this point.[33] Moreover, impairments need not entail physical suffering. Clinging to the ideals of self-sufficiency and bodily perfection, non-disabled people tend to project suffering—and hence the need for a cure—upon people with disabilities by assuming conventional standards of normalcy. Suffering is more consistently the product of exclusionary restrictions than bodily impairments. People with disabilities "suffer our society" and "suffer our difference," as Rod Michalko puts it, because impairments are perceived to be all the same—a blemish.[34] And by trading on such perceptions, finally, disability becomes objectified as the focus of curative efforts, reducing persons to anonymous and voiceless subjects whose sole purpose it is to receive the blessing of health. These are oversights connected to the medical model's view of disability as a personal tragedy or a body-gone-wrong.

There are also unsound theological suppositions at work here. The linkage of sin-punishment-blemish with faith-forgiveness/salvation-healing claims too much. By treating disability as a faulted, person-defining condition, it is easy to take the next step and conjecture that the whole person is somehow imperfect, morally flawed or lacking adequate faith. For if it is taken for granted that God's power can and God's love wishes to eliminate creaturely imperfection and suffering, restoring the dignity of health and wholeness, there must therefore be something that is blocking God's healing presence. Set up in such a way, making the victim responsible is a typical path toward resolving the issue. Human beings are prone to ask "why me?" when things go wrong. We look for a reason, a scapegoat, someone or something to blame. And if God is not culpable, and a community refuses to question its social order and/or theological framework, then the individual is presumed at fault, either bringing on divine punishment as a response to sin or preempting the healing process because of lack of faith. Even worse, in cases of what we now know to be epilepsy and mental retardation, it can be conjectured that such anomalies are the product of possession by evil spirits. Believing strongly in the presence of evil forces in the world, Martin

Luther famously typifies this approach when he recommends the drowning of a mentally retarded boy whom he alleged had no soul and therefore could only be an instrument of the demonic.[35]

Not only do these attitudes wrongly assume that persons with disabilities suffer from a diminished humanity, they also claim too much about God's work. After all, as the Psalms and Ecclesiastes suggest, blessings fall equally upon the wicked and the righteous (e.g., Ps. 73:2–5; Eccles. 3:15ff.). The wicked even seem to prosper in instances where the faithful suffer. Things are not always as they appear; nor do they portend in some calculable manner how the course of events will turn out in the end. God's ways cannot be mapped out and measured neatly according to a one-to-one correspondence between sin and punishment or healing and faith, as if wholeness and normalcy are signs of divine approval or successful healing is a sign of the fullness of saving faith. The example of Job is instructive. As Job suffers, his friends call upon him to repent for his hidden sins and alleged arrogance. Yet God ultimately denounces them for speaking wrongly of God—that is, for trying to justify God's ways by presuming to know why Job suffered (Job 42:7–8). Even in the example of John 9:13, where the blind man is healed, Jesus contests the easy assumption that disability is always caused by sin. And while in other passages Jesus does associate faith with healing, he never reverses the logic to equate healing with saving faith. Indeed, we must acknowledge that, in all probability, many who became faithful followers did not also get cured of their disabilities.

In the final analysis, then, theologically denigrating views of disability diminish the creaturely worth of persons with disability, overlooking the broader vision of inclusive love and hospitality to which the biblical texts bear witness (e.g., Lev. 9:14; Isa. 29:18–19; 43:1, 9–10; Matt. 25:36, 40; Luke 14:15–24). This alternative biblical witness requires retrieval; otherwise we assume too much and risk too little.

Avoiding the Theological Trivialization of Disability

The second main grouping of inadequate representations of disability are views that glibly dismiss the concrete reality of impairment and its personal and social consequences by treating disability in romanticized terms—that is, as a means for non-disabled persons to demonstrate their charity, a theological example from which Christians can learn, or a kind of virtuous suffering. There are thus three primary ways that disability can be theologically trivialized.

The first example of the trivializing perspective is a classically patronizing means of reducing persons with disabilities to objects upon which non-disabled persons act as benefactors. Here disabled persons are projected as poor needy beggars, "the least of these," essentially helpless people in need of grace. Presumed to have little to offer, "the disabled" become perfect candidates for Christian charity, for selfless giving. I am deliberately using "the" to qualify the term "disabled" because this point-of-view traffics in generalizations about disability that conjure attitudes of low expectation. It is simply taken for granted that non-disabled persons must lower their expectations for disabled persons, who lack the independent resources to participate in the activities of conventional society. Therefore, inclusion in the life of the community entails condescending acts of care and assistance, making special allowances for persons who are otherwise incapable of functioning normally and contributing to the community. Pity becomes the operative mode of attending to persons with disabilities, a giving of what "we" have in abundance to "them," who are deficient in such graces. Entire service systems, such as "Jerry's Kids," are set up according to this framework of understanding. They are frequently given theological sanction as vehicles for sharing God's love with the less fortunate.

Despite its positive-sounding emphasis, this viewpoint is obviously disabling. That it reduces persons to a perceived helplessness is harmful enough. The person becomes obscured and rendered anonymous, demeaned as one whose role it is to receive. But there is also at work the rather narcissistic notion that disability serves the common good, namely, because it cultivates love and generosity in non-disabled people. Whatever noble intentions may underlie such a presumption, disability advocates find it hideously infantilizing. It cloaks a self-serving agenda trained not upon the empowerment of disabled persons, but rather on the moral advancement of non-disabled persons. The focus is subtly shifted to the non-disabled benefactor, whose gesture of charity perpetuates societal exclusion and overdetermines disabled persons as helpless victims, passive receptors of care. This inadvertently fosters a spiritual self-centeredness that contributes to the problem rather than alleviating it, rendering persons with disabilities anonymous and on the outside. Disability is not a way for non-disabled Christians to grow in charity.

By no means is this to decry any and all gestures of support or institutionalized programs of provision. It simply exposes us to the possibility of misjudgment and misplaced intentions. This is precisely why it is crucial to listen to what persons with disabilities are saying about disability. And many are echoing what Joseph Shapiro suggests, "that there is no pity or tragedy in disability, and that it is society's myths, fears, and stereotypes that most make being disabled difficult."[36] It is not pity that is required; it is the empowerment that comes from solidarity and advocacy, built upon the premise that persons with disabilities are self-defining agents—like non-disabled persons—who are capable of contributing to society and Christian communities in ways not necessarily defined by their disabilities. There is no adequate reason to suppose that disability entails tragic suffering and that persons with disabilities must be cured or rehabilitated before they can participate productively in society. Charity without concern for human dignity and restorative justice preempts genuine social equality and religious inclusion.[37] At stake is a shared humanity that joins human beings in a larger circle, disabled and non-disabled alike.

Hence, if pity is trivializing because it objectifies disability as a means for non-disabled caregivers to demonstrate charity, equally trivializing is a second viewpoint that objectifies disability as special, a source of inspiration for non-disabled people. This is a gross oversimplification of disability. At work here is the narcissistic shift that we saw a moment ago in the case of pity, creating disability as a mirror for non-disabled persons to gaze flatteringly back upon themselves. Only now, persons with disabilities are appraised as those from whom we can learn. By being represented as a moral object lesson, however, disability is idealized, loaded with biases that refract the purposes of those without disabilities. Not only does this perpetuate the notion that disability is a tragedy that affects "those other people," it colonizes disability by infusing it with romanticized moral meanings. Accordingly, persons with disabilities are treated as subjects without individual histories and identities except as they play generalized roles that serve to ennoble non-disabled Christians. Illustrations that come to mind are those that treat disability as an example of Christlike human tenderness, dependence, weakness, or spiritual openness.

The temptation to use disability in these ways is strong in theological circles. Stanley Hauerwas courageously admits as much, confessing to using disability as a vehicle to understand the claims of the Christian narrative and its call to genuine community.[38] Whether this amounts to subjecting persons with disabilities to a theological agenda is a concern that haunts him even as he would like to deny it.[39] I would hasten to add that I struggle with the same tension, and in this book will continually come back to the question as a means of keeping the analyses honest while maintaining the preferential option for persons with disabilities discussed earlier in the Introduction. For, like other inadequate approaches, a theologically trivializing view of disability refuses to recognize disabled persons at the speaking center of their own lives; it neglects the contributions they can make, and glosses over the concrete personal and social suffering entailed by disability. In so doing it overlooks the range of challenges and disabling conditions to which persons with impairments are subject. Indeed, disabilities are not all the same; there is great diversity. Acknowledging this fact makes it problematic to use disability to extract univocal moral lessons.[40] People with disabilities must not be assimilated into romanticized moral meanings foreign to their experience. Unique persons are involved, in each instance possessing an irreducible dignity that shines of its own accord and is fully capable of achieving self-defined goals regardless of whether or not they instruct non-disabled people; or regardless of whether or not impairments can be wrapped in diagnoses of one kind or another and alleviated. Employing disability for mere theological gain is something to be vigilantly guarded against.

Accordingly, we must also resist appraising disability as a condition that is common to everyone. Claiming that "we are all disabled" is only a partial truth; it overlooks the concrete forms of physical and emotional suffering that may accompany certain impairments and also sweeps away the realities of exclusion and oppression faced by persons whose impairments preclude participation in a world designed by and for non-disabled people.[41] I say "partial truth" because, as I noted in the Introduction, it is factually correct to say that no one is physically complete and wholly self-sufficient, able to function without dependence upon others for survival and well-being. There is a kind of continuum on which all human abilities can be located, where shadings of grey eliminate dualistic distinctions between ability and disability.[42] Human beings are limited and vulnerable, subject to the unpredictable contingencies of embodied existence, to becoming impaired, and ultimately to bodily deterioration and death. Indeed, as I shall argue, it is this vulnerability that, when recognized in a certain way, has the power to transform our relationships and open us up to God. But this is not to suggest that persons with disabilities are somehow special because they are more attuned to our generic human vulnerability and, hence, are more open to God. Neither is it a way of suggesting naively that we are all disabled and simply need to recognize our own disabilities. If everyone is disabled, then the category becomes moot and utterly relative. The experiences of those who face involuntary physical impairment and societal disconfirmation through attitudes and institutions are trivialized.

This is an extremely important but sticky point, for disability is indeed entirely consistent with the human predicament. Jennie Weiss Block suggests as much in her observation that "our support for those who are people with disabilities and the acceptance of the explicit reality of our own limitations are not mutually exclusive activities but are, in fact, deeply related and connected."[43] Acknowledging our shared human vulnerability can be an important route into building solidarity among disabled and non-disabled people, exposing the hollow norms of attractiveness, individuality, and productivity upon which our consumer-oriented culture is built. But it should not do so by romanticizing disability, concentrating solely on how non-disabled persons can learn theological and moral lessons from disabled persons.

A third way of trivializing disability can be found in approaches that treat disabled persons as virtuous sufferers, those whom God favors with special burdens aimed at enhancing their spiritual capacities.[44] This understanding most explicitly depends upon theodicy formulations that represent disability as a vehicle for blessing and a sign of God's grace. It presumes that submission to affliction yields praiseworthy spiritual attributes, such as humility and dependence upon God. Nancy Eiesland cites the apostle Paul's thorn in the flesh (2 Cor. 12:7–10) as an illustrative example.[45] Implied here is an ascetic ethos of self-sacrifice, one that interprets suffering as a redemptive, testing device that God's children must undergo to mature in faith by relying on God's strength alone, and not their own abilities. The message transmitted through the tradition has often come to mean that human beings must acquiesce to hardship and pain as a divinely designed route to sanctification. In all wisdom, love, and power, God allows us to face adversity because God cares for us and wishes for us to enter into a deeper relation of dependence with God that is not possible without experiencing genuine obstacles to our well-being. We are ordained to struggle, created frail and incomplete in a world meant for soul-making, not human satisfaction. By passing through the crucible of pain, character virtues can be formed and souls can grow in stature.[46] Hence, the moral meaning of disability is that it is a cross to bear that perfects human nature, purifying it of its conceitedness, illusion to power, and self-sufficiency. Suffering has redemptive value.[47]

While there may be a measure of truth to this perspective, it is inadequate in that it too quickly rationalizes suffering as intended, perhaps even directly caused, by God. As a means to theologize about disability, this model is dangerous. The notion of virtuous or redemptive suffering fallaciously links disability with suffering. But more seriously and dangerously, it promotes passivity and resignation to situations of personal hardship or social exclusion and oppression that otherwise should be resisted and transformed. Not only does this sanitize impairment by explaining it away in terms of the potential good it produces, it also baptizes the status quo, sanctioning the cult of normalcy. Eiesland states the point forcefully: "Similar to the practice of emphasizing self-sacrifice to women, the theology of virtuous suffering has encouraged persons with disabilities to acquiesce to social barriers as a sign of obedience to God and to internalize second-class status inside and outside the church."[48] The result trivializes disability as God-ordained rather than something that is socially inscribed with disconfirming and unjust ideological projections that themselves require repudiation on the basis of the broader vision of inclusiveness and hospitality found in the biblical witness.

It is true, however, that human beings are fragile and contingent, and that the natural world in which we live is unstable and unpredictable. We are subject to various kinds of involuntary impairments, the intensity of which becomes manifest with age. Often we do become stronger in character because of our weaknesses, bearing fruits from our struggles. But these empirical facts cannot be generalized and turned into normative moral lessons without losing ground. Weakness and suffering do not always yield character virtues. Nor do they necessarily produce moral insight for others. Disability is neither the direct cause of suffering nor a concrete sign of weakness. How then are Christians to understand and reflect God's presence in light of disability? Here is where we can begin to move beyond theodicy formulations.

Conclusion: Toward a Wider Horizon for Theological Thinking about Disability

In this chapter, we have focused primarily on the difficulties of thinking theologically about disability. And there are real perils at stake in our efforts. But there are also signs of promise interspersed throughout the dangers, signs that have emerged here and there like grass through asphalt and that offer hope for an empowering, transformative solidarity between non-disabled and disabled persons. In theological terms, disability need not be denied, decried, or overcome as an incomplete humanity, a defect indicating failure or sin. Full personhood is neither diminished by disability nor confirmed by ability. Instead, it is a factor of the interdependent relationships we share with one another as creatures loved into being by God and in the image of God. There is a wider horizon in which all persons in their uniqueness and vulnerability coexist within the enfolding presence of a gracious God. This horizon is our shared humanity, a fragile and contingent humanity that God is present to, suffers with, and transforms by embracing in Jesus Christ.

In order to draw out the full meaning of this vision, however, we must first investigate the embodied and relational character of human life in communities. This will allow us to understand and critique the cult of normalcy, naming and reevaluating those restrictive values and norms that have been universalized on the basis of individual health, productive ability, or self-sufficiency. Such an endeavor will grant us the leverage to rethink wholeness in a way that fruitfully engages disability and promulgates a justice-making momentum of social inclusion.

Notes

1. Arne Fritzson, "Disability and Meaning," in Arne Fritzon and Samuel Kabue, *Interpreting Disability: A Church of All for All* (Geneva: World Council of Churches Publications, 2004), 22–23.

2. Like many authors in disability studies, I use the word "impaired" to indicate a bodily limitation or impediment. I avoid "physically challenged" because of the glib and paternalistic connotations, and "handicapped" because of the suggestion of disadvantage in fulfilling certain role expectations, which (as we shall see) are socially ascribed more than bodily derived.

3. Karl Marx, "Contribution to the Critique of Hegel's Philosophy of Right," *The Marx-Engels Reader*, 2nd ed., ed. Robert C. Tucker (New York: W. W. Norton and Company, 1978), 53.

4. See Roy McCloughry and Wayne Morris, *Making a World of Difference: Christian Reflections on Disability* (London: Society for Promoting Christian Knowledge, 2002), 8–13.

5. See Robert F. Molsberry, *Blindsided by Grace: Entering the World of Disability* (Minneapolis: Augsburg Fortress, 2004), 69.

6. McClourghry and Morris, *Making a World of Difference*, 15.

7. See James Charlton, *Nothing about Us without Us: Disability, Oppression, and Empowerment* (Berkeley: University of California Press, 1998).

8. McCloughry and Morris, *Making a World of Difference*, 15. See also Lennard J. Davis, *Bending over Backwards: Disability, Dismodernism and Other Difficult Positions* (New York: New University Press, 2002), 12; and Colin Barnes and Geof Mercer, *Disability* (Cambridge: Polity Press, 2003), chaps. 2–3. The distinction between "impairment" and "disability" is key to a more "social" model.

9. For this criticism of the social model, see Barnes and Mercer, *Disability*, 68; and McCloughry and Morris, *Making a World of Difference*, 17–19.

10. Lennard J. Davis, *Enforcing Normalcy: Disability, Deafness, and the Body* (London: Verso, 1995), 2. See also 48–49.

11. On the theme of oppression, see Jennie Weiss Block, *Copious Hosting: A Theology of Access for People with Disabilities* (New York: Continuum, 2002), 42–46; and Barnes and Mercer, *Disability*, 20–21.

12. The term "theodicy" originates with Gottfried Wilhelm Leibniz's *Theodicy: Essays on the Goodness of God, the Freedom of Man and the Origin of Evil* (London: Routledge and Kegan Paul, 1951), originally published in 1710. For an excellent collection of essays dealing with this issue, see *God and the Problem of Evil*, ed. William L. Rowe (Oxford: Blackwell Publishers, 2001).

13. Rod Michalko, *The Difference That Disability Makes* (Philadelphia: Temple University Press, 2002), 95–96. Robert Molsberry quips that disability "may be the best lesson available on contingency" (*Blindsided by Grace*, 88).

14. Rosmarie Garland Thompson, *Extraordinary Bodies: Figuring Physical Disability in American Culture and Literature* (New York: Columbia University Press, 1997), 11.

15. For this critique of theodicy, I am indebted to Brett Webb-Mitchell, *Unexpected Guests at God's Banquet: Welcoming People with Disabilities into the Church* (New York: Crossroad, 1994), 72–73. In the discussion that follows, however, I shall move beyond Webb-Mitchell's analysis to offer additional reasons why theodicy is problematic for thinking about disability.

16. The title of this section is drawn from Sarah K. Pinnock's *Beyond Theodicy: Jewish and Christian Continental Thinkers Respond to the Holocaust* (Albany: State University of New York Press, 2002).

17. Quoted in Helen Featherstone, *A Difference in the Family: Living with a Disabled Child* (New York: Penguin Books, 1980), 33.

18. Some of these responses are discussed eloquently in Kathy Black's *A Healing Homiletic: Preaching and Disability* (Nashville: Abingdon Press, 1996), chap. 1.

19. See Webb-Mitchell, *Unexpected Guests at God's Banquet*, 71–75.

20. Stanley Hauerwas, *Suffering Presence: Theological Reflections on Medicine, the Mentally Handicapped, and the Church* (Notre Dame, IN: University of Notre Dame Press, 1986), chap. 3; and *Critical Reflections on Stanley Hauerwas' Theology of Disability: Disabling Society, Enabling Theology*, ed. John Swinton (Binghamton, NY: Haworth Pastoral Press, 2004), chap. 1.

21. Davis, *Enforcing Normalcy*, 23–24.

22. On this point, see Hauerwas, *Critical Reflections on Stanley Hauerwas' Theology of Disability*, chap. 5. See also Michalko, *The Difference That Disability Makes*, 50–60; and Webb-Mitchell, *Unexpected Guests*, 74.

23. See Harold S. Koplewicz, *It's Nobody's Fault: New Hope and Help for Difficult Children* (New York: Times, 1996).

24. McCloughry and Morris, *Making a World of Difference*, 36.

25. See Black, *A Healing Homiletic*, chap. 2.

26. For an excellent example of what such an approach can look like, though not dealing with disability as such, see L. Juliana M. Claassens, *The God Who Provides: Biblical Images of Divine Nourishment* (Nashville: Abingdon Press, 2004).

27. On ancient Near Eastern traditions, see Robert Scheerenberger, *A History of Mental Retardation* (Baltimore: Paul H. Brooks Publishing Company, 1983), 7–8.

28. See Black, *A Healing Homiletic*, 20–25; and Sarah J. Melcher, "Visualizing the Perfect Cult: The Priestly Rationale for Exclusion," 55–71, in *Human Disability and the Service of God: Reassessing Religious Practice*, ed. Nancy L. Eiesland and Don E. Saliers (Nashville: Abingdon Press, 1998).

29. Nancy L. Eiesland, *The Disabled God: Toward a Liberatory Theology of Disability* (Nashville: Abingdon Press, 1994), 71–72.

30. Colleen C. Grant, "Reinterpreting the Healing Narratives," in *Human Disability and the Service of God*, 73–74. For other explorations of the sin-disability connection, see McCloughry and Morris, *Making a World of Difference*, 98–99; and Block, *Copious Hosting*, 109–13.

31. Eiesland, *The Disabled God*, 117. See also McCloughry and Morris, *Making a World of Difference*, 98.

32. Black, *A Healing Homiletic*, 25–26.

33. Block, *Copious Hosting*, 103–4.

34. Michalko, *The Difference That Disability Makes*, 61–71.

35. David M. Colón, "Martin Luther, the Devil and the Teufelchen: Attitudes toward Mentally Retarded Children in Sixteenth-Century Germany," *Proceedings of the PMR Conference* 14 (1998): 75–84. The passage in question is from *Luther's Works*, ed. Helmut T. Lehmann and Jaroslav Pelikan (vols. 1–30, St. Louis: Concordia Publishing House, 1955–; vols. 31–55, Philadelphia: Fortress Press, 1957–), vol. 54, *Table Talk*, ed. and trans. Theodore G. Tappert, 396–97. See also Webb-Mitchell, *Unexpected Guests at God's Banquet*, 65.

36. Joseph P. Shapiro, *No Pity: People with Disabilities Forging a New Civil Rights Movement* (New York: Times Books, 1981), 5.

37. See Eiesland, *The Disabled God*, 73–74.

38. Hauerwas, "Timeful Friends: Living with the Handicapped," in *Critical Reflections on Stanley Hauerwas' Theology of Disability*, 20; see also 192–95.

39. Ibid., 17.

40. McCloughry and Morris, *Making a World of Difference*, 30–31; and Block, *Copious Hosting*, 29.

41. Block, *Copious Hosting*, 34–36.

42. Molsberry, *Blindsided by Grace,* xii. See also Fritzson, "Disability and Meaning," 7–10, 16–19.

43. Block, *Copious Hosting*, 36.

44. Black, *A Healing Homiletic*, 27–28.

45. Eiesland, *The Disabled God*, 72.

46. This representation can be found in systematic form in John Hick's theodicy. For example, see "An Irenaean Theodicy," 39–52, in *Encountering Evil: Live Options in Theodicy*, ed. Stephen Davis (Atlanta: Westminster John Knox Press, 1981); and *Evil and the God of Love*, 2nd ed. (New York: Harper and Row, 1978).

47. Black, *A Healing Homiletic*, 30–32.

48. Eiesland, *The Disabled God*, 73.

2

Communal Boundaries

Dwelling Together and the Cult of Normalcy

The most stringent power we have over another is not physical coercion but the ability to have the other accept our definition of them.[1]

It is clear that a vigorous inclusion of differences remains one of the more important tasks of Christian communities today. The reality of cultural and religious diversity and the need for justice among people who are marginalized and poor makes the gospel message of love and neighborliness especially relevant. But we must tread with great caution. Inclusion is risky business. Too often it is servant to the status quo, championing the interests of convention rather than attending to the particular uniqueness of persons.

Examples are seen in the dynamics of tolerance and assimilation. Though often touted as benevolent, tolerance can be subtly heavy-handed. It may assume a position of power that grants differences a share of the public space only so long as they do not disrupt or cause inconveniences to a dominant group's way of life. Inclusion then becomes more a matter of insuring that things remain the same than of providing resources to welcome differences as contributions to the group. And because the focus is on preserving group identity, tolerance can easily slip into assimilation. In an effort to maintain social control, assimilation is a community's way of imposing conformity on differences, remaking them in its own image. An overt or tacit pressure is applied to shape appearances, behaviors, attitudes, and beliefs according to what a dominant group takes for granted and assumes about the world. Assimilation repudiates differences. It feigns an inclusion of differences that is at best a paternalistic gesture of charity, helping "those others" get along "like us"; at worst it is an act of coerced subjugation.

A striking illustration of this is found in the medical model we discussed in the previous chapter. If the primary task of medicine is to cure illness, alleviate suffering, and rehabilitate broken bodies, focused attention on those conditions considered anomalies, impoverishments of health and wholeness is required. And for this an understanding of pathology or deviance must be presumed. Illness is measured against representations of a prototypical or ideal body. The goal then is to correct and normalize deviance—that is, get people back to normal functioning so they can be reintegrated into society and, if this fails, manage them with caregiving procedures until they die. Certainly there are positive achievements here that deserve to be lauded. But there is also real danger.

The danger is that such a procedure is founded upon criteria that operate in clandestine ways to sanction the status quo. A vision of health and wholeness is taken for granted that relies upon standards produced by social negotiations, the ideals and norms of which favor some people over others. Hence the limitations of the medical model: it trades on processes of tolerance and assimilation that ritualize normalcy. Pushed to a further degree, these can lead to exclusion by marginalizing, depersonalizing, infantilizing, institutionalizing, rendering invisible, and so on, those differences deemed incapable of integrating into "normal" life and serving its taken-for-granted conventions. The upshot is that medical forms of inclusion often render differences irrelevant or restrict them altogether. It is crucial to note that we are now talking about differences, not simply physiological problems related to bodily impairments. Disability is about difference. But who decides what difference is? What is normalcy? And why is it that certain norms and ideals for embodiment and wholeness go unquestioned?

If we are to formulate a theology that genuinely includes the experiences of persons with disabilities, it is clear that we must find ways to move beyond tolerance and assimilation. This means thinking about disability in a wider field, as something that affects us and not merely "them." There is more at stake here, however, than acknowledging the fact that non-disabled persons are only temporarily non-disabled, subject upon old age, if not before, to conditions of bodily impairment, limitation, and weakness of one kind or another. A deeper reality looms large, one that often remains hidden, perhaps deliberately so.

Human beings are vulnerable and dependent creatures. The ideal of self-sufficiency is an illusion. Non-disabled and disabled persons alike are caught up in networks of dependencies, relationships without which participation in life activities considered normal would be impossible. Once again we come to see that the line between ability and lack of ability is a blurred one. Accordingly, we must eschew the temptation to presume frameworks of normalcy that animate common, yet debilitating, attitudes and practices toward those whose bodily impairments render them allegedly different and non-normal.

This requires going deeper, naming and analyzing the social processes by which the normal and abnormal are constructed and ritually sanctioned. Normalcy operates as a cultural system of social control. On one account, it is simply a way of ordering and bringing meaning to the everyday world shared by a group. It is unavoidable and itself good. There is, however, an insidious undertow that accompanies it, working to draw all into a certain caste or type. Normalcy is a force that flows according to strategic mechanisms of power that serve the conventions of the status quo, which in turn serves primarily those persons whose bodily appearance and abilities fall within a recognizably standard range. The normal then becomes representative of a community's identity or sense of itself and, accordingly, functions by marking out and idealizing those attributes and capacities competent to contribute to its good. To state it plainly, the "normal" is relative to a group's values and aspirations, and, conversely so, what is attributed "abnormal" (disease, disability, etc.).

Unpacking the nuanced character of this requires moving beyond portrayals of human existence that focus mainly on the individual. For the person is not an isolated "something" that is healthy and whole or not, to which life together in community is an extra flavor added to the pudding. We are persons only along with others, in community. So, moving beyond the individualist model, the task of this chapter is to show how it is the relational character of human life that is fundamental, the problem of normalcy being an outgrowth of the need for recognition and orientation in a world shared with others. The focus here is diagnostic, a portrayal of a predicament. I hope to demonstrate with some theoretical depth how health, ability, and the normal are, to a large degree, constructed outgrowths of communal life.

I. The Human Need for Welcome

As I begin to walk away, he exclaims, "I love you; you're a good person; you 'rock'; you're the best dad; you're a good person—I love you." His voice fades but the phrases linger on until he is satisfied I am still present and have heard him. I respond from the doorway, "I love you, too; and you're also a good person." This endearing exchange occurs countless times in a day. Of course, I am flattered to receive such high praise from my son. It is a tender witness to the kind of person he is (of course, I am in no way biased). His heart is genuine and generous, and it humbles me. But there is also more going on here than the display of affection.

Chris is gauging his world, checking for the persistent boundaries and dependable recognition that he needs to feel at ease with himself. All children do this, sounding themselves against the presence of parents or significant others. As developmental psychologists affirm, from early in life we need a reassuring and trustworthy environment in which to explore our limits and eventually gain a sense of self.[2] Personal identity and responsible agency blossom only if there is a reliable social world to negotiate. With Chris, however, this negotiation opens into an anxious set of obsessions. Indeed, children with Asperger's syndrome often have unwieldy fears of death, and they can become preoccupied with intrusive thoughts, many of which involve the loss of loved ones and significant others. I can recall Chris having such fears when he was just three years old: he cried many nights at bedtime because he could not stop having "bad thoughts" about his mother or me getting killed in an accident. His acute awareness of vulnerability to loss made him apprehensive and insecure. And as a result, his sense of our parental presence and authority needed consistent maintenance.

Even now, at age seventeen, Chris is plagued by fears, unsure of his place amidst a fragile and unstable world. He sees the violence, war, and suffering around him and reacts with frightened dismay. In new settings he is compelled to inspect each and every feature of his surroundings, looking into boxes, closets, behind doors, and so on. Transitions of all kinds, such as moving between rooms at school, can cause him alarm, triggering obsessions of one sort or another. Lacking confidence in the stability of his world, he asks for repeated reassurance from authority figures closest to him. Mary and I have adjusted as best we can, given our own limitations, to provide as much structure and consistency as possible. Even so, Chris needs repeated recognition and affirmation from all significant presences in his life—teachers at school, his friends, adult friends of ours, his brother, Evan, and our dog, Natalie. He often looks for tactile reassurance in the form of hugs, but his size and age are making this a problematic "personal space" issue at school with teachers and peers.

Fundamental Trust—A Desire for "Home"

Chris's needs in this regard are not altogether different or abnormal. True, his unique neurological makeup may attune him more dramatically to his vulnerability than most people. But there is a fundamental desire for assurance lodged deep into all human psyches. Such a need seems to be a basic, axiomatic ingredient cutting across all the ordinary circumstances of our daily lives. In order to be selves, human beings require a meaningful and trustworthy world, a world with boundaries that provide security and that offer a dependable sense that all will be well. All will be well? This sounds like an excessive claim, so let me phrase it differently: insofar as we grow and make our way along with others, we are biologically predisposed toward the development of a persistent and comprehensive confidence in the goodness of things, a goodness according to which we come to measure the worth of our lives.

Such an inclination is rooted in the instinct to survive, but extends beyond mere survival. True, there are basic needs for food and shelter that all human beings require. The complexity of our emotional and intellectual capacities, however, makes these needs dependent upon acquiring social skills to navigate the relationships by which we not only survive but also find value and purpose in that survival. This is what makes it so traumatic when basic physical and emotional needs are not met. We are born to flourish, inclined to think and act as if the fabric of reality itself somehow contains a promise that all will be right in the end. Repeatedly waking each morning, facing the tasks of our days, and retiring in the evenings, we live as if our life with others bears value and confirms the inescapable rumblings in our hearts for assurance against principalities and powers that would deny or undo our aspirations and hopes. Why? Because human life seeks more than survival alone. It seeks to flourish and find itself affirmed within a larger framework of value and purpose. Life seeks delight in living. This is what Chris is reaching for with all the tenacity and courage his spirit can muster. And, I dare say, this is what we all are reaching for.

Amidst the intractable uncertainties and perils of our existence in a finite and contingent world, there is at work a life impulse that persistently resists annulment by death-wielding forces and empowers us to go forward. This thesis shall animate much of the discussion in the remainder of this book.[3] I contend that dwelling together in the world cannot help but elicit an affirmation about the capacity of life to sustain the promise of value over against its impoverishment and final invalidation. While it cannot be guaranteed, this affirmation seems inbuilt and inescapable. It acts as an audacious presumption that operates in the background as a fundamental feature of the way we inhabit the world and seek to flourish in communities. It is the stuff of hope and trust.

Indeed, we come to trust in the moral significance of living together, acting as if there is a sense to it all that upholds the integrity of acting rightly toward others and preparing for a meaningful future. When tragedy strikes, we stubbornly resist it, as if it somehow thwarts our anticipation of a more fundamental trustworthiness operative in the world. Such resistance signifies that trust is much more than merely a passive disposition that waits on things, an act of resignation simply accepting its world as it is—closed and determined by necessity. Rather, resisting marks a passionate forward momentum toward the possibility of things being other than tragic. For, as H. Richard Niebuhr insightfully notes, "distrust is only possible where the conditions of trust have first been established."[4] That is to say, distrust feeds off a more original presumption of trust that is somehow let down or betrayed.

To illustrate the point, let me turn again to a personal example. Chris has just come home from school. No sooner than his mother and I greet him, he collapses and cries out, lamenting a hard day of failures at school. My arms snuggle around him and, almost second nature, I say something like, "It will be alright; I am here with you." What is going on here? On the surface, these words seem trivial and perhaps offensive. But I believe they indicate something more than a pretentious claim to parental omnipotence, feigning the ability to make everything better. Neither do I believe they are simply a benevolent but overt lie rubbing fictitious ointment over a wound beyond my capacity to understand, let alone cure. Instead, more profoundly, and as a father, I am convinced they are testimony to a deep-seated confidence that heartbreak and failure should not and cannot be the final words. And what makes these words especially powerful is that they are uttered in the context of a relationship marked by care and love. It is as if to say, "There is hope by which we can carry on together amidst and past the tragic." Physicist, Anglican priest, and theologian John Polkinghorne puts the matter in this way: "Despite all the bitter suffering of the world, there is a deep intuition set in the human heart, that Reality is trustworthy, that the comforting of a disturbed child is not the acting of a loving lie, but the assertion of a true insight."[5] Even if I were to remain silent before Chris, the act of being present to him would still signify the affirmation of something beyond the tragic. And Chris's reception of my presence is his way of affirming this too.

Such an affirmation—of the trustworthiness and purposefulness of things—is no calculative intellectual matter. It is not based in rational queries, the product of a chain of reasoning about the nature of the cosmos. Indeed, we may inquire whether there is finally any meaning and value in existence and come to the eventual conclusion that the world is the expression of a higher order, a first mover, a creator, even a loving God. But such questioning depends upon a more original and heartfelt question: is the world a home for us? The Greek word *oikos* carries the root meaning of "home." It signifies a place of belonging, a house. And because home is where the heart is, this implies more than simply a geographical point or physical residence. Basic to our existence is a desire to dwell in a place that welcomes us, an environment worthy of trust and hope, to which we fundamentally belong. We seek the means to inhabit the world and be "at home," as the Greek verb *oiken* expresses.[6] This plays out as an intractable craving for connection and relatedness, for being part of an organized and meaningful space with others, an economy (with roots in the Greek *oikos*, the management of a house). The essence of being at home is linkage to a place of affirmation, where we are surrounded by the recognizable and familiar, and thus feel recognized and taken in. In such a context, or economy, human beings flourish.

The basic question of human existence, then, is whether there is welcome at the heart of things. Will I be received and embraced? Is there a voice behind all other voices that says, "You are precious, and I will be there for you"? Our heart's deepest impulse hankers after connection with a trustworthy creation—a purposeful macro-context that bathes our lives in meaning and value, thus cultivating a sense of being at home. The world is good. In such a place, tragedy is not the final word—hope is.

Home as Dwelling Together

However, human beings do not find this kind of assurance merely in general and abstract terms. We inhabit the world in particular places of welcome, dwelling in homes that on a local scale mediate a sense of being at home in the larger world. We are like thirsty travelers craving the nourishing replenishment of a home that receives us with cool water. And the wellspring of such welcome is not something we discover alone. Home is a dwelling place marked by the presence of other people. It is a communal place of orientation in which we fit comfortably, grow roots, and reside safely. Its welcome is constituted by relationships formed within a specific social network that nurtures familiarity and preserves trust. We desire to be recognized and accepted, woven together with others.[7] This is why, as Jean Vanier concludes, communities are manifestations of the need to belong.[8] We feel at home in the world by dwelling with others. By belonging to a home, in this sense, we inhabit creation. Home is the way we dwell in the universe as a cosmos, a trustworthy whole.[9]

Conversely, the experience of dislocation and exile, of being a stranger, invisible or excluded and without a home, breeds confusion and anxiety. This makes human disability no sideline issue. For if the notion of "place" is fundamental to our identity as persons, the experience of displacement yields suffering, undermining or blocking our desire for meaning and value. It is understandable, then, that persons with disabilities come to distrust their world, often overwhelmed with a broad sense of being unwelcome. It is also, sadly, understandable how the experience of disability threatens able-bodied people. Their familiar, predictable, and ordered world is thrown into relief, resulting in fear and uncertainty. But what is it that animates this dynamic? What is it that non-disabled persons find so uncomfortable or threatening about bodies with impairments? Why should disability be singled out, marginalized, alienated, and exempted from participation in communal places, from being welcomed? Attempting to answer these questions requires probing further to explore the character of communal formation and its relation to personal identity. From here we shall be better equipped to understand the powerful hold of normalcy on social life.

II. Social Boundaries: Ability and Disability

To proceed, we must recall that disability is a consequence of bodily impairment. It indicates the perception of an inability to perform designated tasks or activities considered necessary within a social environment. That disability is socially constructed will become even more evident as our discussion advances. Remember, however, that this is not to deny the unique biomedical features of various forms of disability, but rather to recognize that human beings understand what an impairment is through distinct sociocultural lenses and the communicative, attitudinal, and architectural barriers that they foster. An impairment becomes a disability when it runs up against a barrier to social participation and is subsequently seen as a lack of ability.

Lack of ability, then, is acknowledged and measured by values that arise within the conventions and role expectations of a shared world; for ability is a factor of performing in ways that are understood by others to be meaningful and consequential. This is precisely why disability is so often taken to be a diminishment, an inability. And it is also why disability is not a thing but a range of physiologically rooted social performances, a series of moments defined by relationships between human beings. In a basic sense, the distinction between ability and disability is built into the fabric of communal life. Our sense of self-worth is not automatic. It is conferred and meted out by a community in terms of its members' capacity to display or contribute goods relevant to that community as a place of belonging, a home.

Community and Identity—Frameworks of the Good

Many anthropologists underscore the point that human beings are born instinct-deprived; we are unfinished animals that require anchoring in networks of relationships. We need others to nurture and sustain us, making it possible to inhabit a safe, predictable, and meaningful world. That humans are not ready-made for getting along in the world is a liability rendering us vulnerable and dependent creatures. We receive our existence from others, and this is at the heart of belonging.[10] Not only do we need basic material goods in order to develop and survive as individuals—such as food, clothing, shelter, and medical care—we also, and more fundamentally, need a sense of connection with others in order to procure these goods and gain a broader sense of place. This is why we possess such a powerful desire for orientation, for a place to call home.

Philosopher Charles Taylor offers some helpful categories that clarify what is at stake here. He describes this desire for orientation as "a craving for being in contact with or being rightly placed in relation to the good."[11] His thesis is that human beings find a point of reference in the world by being rooted in the good, which orders and infuses with significance everyday goods such as food, shelter, relationships, education, and work. But "the good" is not something that floats about in the abstract. It is culturally embedded, tied to the exigencies of a corporate way of life. The good is what we find meaningful about life together. It functions as a kind of background horizon of valuation by which human beings in a specific relational space are able to flourish together. Outlining a general view of who we are as persons, the good creates a context for meaningful interactions between persons and designates what makes a full life.[12] Our life impulse—our passion for being rightly placed in a trustworthy world—is made concrete by reference to the good. And this happens insofar as we belong with others.

Taylor stresses the point by noting how the good is always embedded in and mediated by a particular framework of valuation. Fundamentally communal in character, frameworks are like backdrops for the different stages upon which human beings interact and dwell together. In other words, they create a certain moral space, supplying specific resources for distinguishing between what does and does not contribute to human flourishing within a corporate context.[13] Frameworks are interpretive paradigms that provide discriminating perspective to questions of what is true, worthwhile, and beneficial. Because of this they summon commitments and allegiances that endow the past, present, and future with shared purpose and significance. Visions of health, prosperity, love, education, and so on depend upon the backdrop of a framework to become intelligible. They are given perspective by a wider field of vision.

Insofar as humans crave orientation and being rightly placed in reference to the good, frameworks are inescapable. Staying with this metaphor, we might say that a framework provides the communal home its particular shape and stability, without which it would collapse. Frameworks thus create a shared dwelling place, endowing a group with a sense of identity, a sense of what it means to live and interact together. Indeed, the discovery of what is meaningful is never my own performance, acted out in solitude; it arises by being conversationally initiated into a language, a way of communicating a meaningful world. Taylor muses, "I can only learn what anger, love, anxiety, the aspiration to wholeness, etc., are through my and others' experience of these being objects for *us*, in some common space."[14]

Accordingly, we do more than rely upon frameworks for making judgments; we rely upon them to become productive and responsible agents. Frameworks are constitutive of human identity. They provide the context for understanding ourselves and making choices about what to do. We only become selves insofar as we define how things have significance for us, and this implies the presence of others.[15] Indeed, knowing who I am is related to the issue of where and with whom I stand. We develop the capacity to be authors of our actions not as separate and autonomous beings, but as beings constituted relationally within mutual frameworks and social inheritances.[16] Granted, we act as individuals, as physical bodies with certain biological needs and propensities; yet the meaning of those actions for us, the way we come to interpret their intention and effect, arises in the presence of other people. In such a way, I become a particular person capable of calling this physical body "mine." As Alasdair MacIntyre puts it, self-knowledge is "always a shared achievement."[17] The self is primarily relational, an act of communal belonging. Thus we can say, echoing a famous African proverb, the "I" is insofar as "we" are. Or, as Taylor sums up, "I am a self only in relation to certain interlocutors," engaged in conversation with others vis-à-vis a common reference to the good.[18]

Inhabiting a meaningful and trustworthy world therefore necessitates belonging with others in community. And communities, like organisms, require some measure of integrative focus as they encounter novel circumstances and understand them to be meaningful. This focus, according to Taylor, is created and maintained by stories and narratives, which provide structure, direction, and purpose to a framework by exhibiting its collective sense of the good.[19] Nations, institutions, and groups of all kinds have an identity-forming history that makes them what they are, and which is celebrated, remembered, and passed on through stories and ritual events that commemorate these stories. For an example, think of how, for Christians, the biblical stories of God's saving work in Christ become embedded in weekly worship and commemorated throughout the church year. Or, in the case of the United States of America, how young people early in their education learn about the Revolutionary War and its ideals, annually celebrated on Independence Day. Without this kind of narrative focus communities would dissolve into the Babel of fragmentation and indefiniteness; and, in turn, our sense of meaningful connection with others would dissolve. It is in telling stories together that we come to know a shared past, recollecting it in memory, reaffirming it in fidelity, and anticipating it in hope for a common future. In such a way, assurances become internalized and the world is experienced as trustworthy. Frameworks are encoded in stories.

So the welcome we seek is communally circumscribed. Frameworks create and sustain a provisionally bounded sociocultural community, coordinating practices by shaping shared attitudes and values.[20] I say "provisionally" because, of course, communities are not seamless wholes but always contain elements of internal differentiation, indeterminacy, and instability.[21] Even with these, however, communities do inform personal agency and draw together an "us" out of disparate experiences and interests. They have a kind of force field that is designated by frameworks and mediated through the stories we tell. We thus become oriented to reality. That is, we inhabit the world in certain ways. Hence, communities are more than merely an aggregation of individual selves; they have a comprehensive character vis-à-vis their reference to a mutually relevant center of valuation. And so our sense of what it means to be a person, to be in meaningful relation to others, and to lead a full life, is not a matter of personal choice or preference but is socially generated. It is cultural in nature. We find our way along with others, learning to share common experiences and the stories, symbols, and ideals that represent them. This helps us to see how ideals of wholeness and health are communal constructs, formed under the sway of a particular vision of the good.

It seems only too natural then that we make judgments and behave in ways that protect and preserve the ideals of a community's framework or value horizon. We come to rely upon these ideals for orientation in the world; they grant a sense of place. Negatively, we place under surveillance or exclude those elements and persons perceived as out of place, that do not fit. They cannot be assimilated or integrated and are in effect deemed an impoverishment, perhaps even something dangerous, because they do not present what we consider familiar or acceptable. In fact, we come to fear such elements and people. Their difference puts conventions into question. So the internal differentiation, indeterminacy, and instability mentioned earlier becomes a threat. Strangeness disrupts the predictable world and so disorients, making us conscious of the extent to which we are vulnerable. This is precisely why multiculturalism can be problematic.[22] Strangeness creates a dissonance that threatens to spoil the fabric of a community's mutually reinforcing sense of the good. The social order is jeopardized. The predictable world is thrown into relief. Because of this, communities develop protective strategies through what I call the "cult of normalcy."

III. Recognition, Value, and the Good: Into the Sway of the Cult of Normalcy

Thus far we have explored how human beings seek a place of welcome in the world which is found by becoming oriented socially within shared frameworks. Yet we must not stop here, for the process is not quite so straightforward. Orientation involves more than adopting a framework's worldview. It is bodily instantiated, only possible insofar as we are able to participate in practices that characterize a corporate way of dwelling together and reflect its vision of the good. Moreover, we become conscious of the ability to participate, and thus gain a sense of belonging, from being recognized by others as contributing agents. Our awareness of ourselves depends upon being included in a group, upon how we fit into its story—its taken-for-granted framework of conventions, assumptions, and values.

It is evident, then, that consciousness of worth is not automatic or built into human nature. We desire it and must go outside of ourselves to find it. And it resides not in some abstract form but is embedded within a social network that mediates a particular sense, through everyday relationships, of what is good. From early in our youth we learn what it means to be acknowledged as of worth, as having something to offer, as being somebody—a "body" with value. Our appearance, actions, and attitudes acquire legitimacy insofar as they purchase recognition, living up to the performance expectations and supporting the conventions and values of a social context. Self-definition and social definition are intrinsically related. Consequently, persons can discover themselves and their worth only in the context of relationships that mediate meaning and value, which to a real degree inscribe a community's identity onto their existence. But how does this inscription happen?

Economies of Exchange

Consciousness of worth is something that transpires according to what I call an *economy of exchange*, a system of reciprocity that regulates interactions in a community. I use the word "economy" deliberately. For its etymological roots can be traced back to the Greek word *oikonomos*, which refers to someone who manages a household, coupling *oikos* (home) and *nemein* (to manage). Home is an enframed social space organized around values, commitments, and designated responsibilities. And this implies the existence of some kind of interactive exchange system, which manages resources toward the end of flourishing in that context. The attribution of worth never occurs in isolated form as an individual's thought process, but rather within a complex set of social arrangements and reciprocal relationships that produce, distribute, and appraise values. Thus, an economy of exchange is how a community's sense of the good is parceled out and managed in ordinary affairs that link people up to one another. If frameworks are communicated in story form, they come to life materially in economies of exchange. And this begins with bodies. For we do more than talk and tell stories; we engage one another in concrete practices that involve flesh and blood. Bodily practices form the supportive scaffolding of a framework.

This point is not trivial. Our bodies always negotiate social space by participating in an exchange of goods, whether going to school, playing on a sports team, working in retail, raising children, or meeting for coffee with friends. In every situation, even in the virtual world of cyberspace, we are present to others. That is, we portray or offer something that is recognized and received (or not) as of significance. Each social context—school, sports, employment, family, and friendship—involves its own performance expectations and criteria of value measurement. Yet, in general, all of them have features that represent paradigmatic values which are held by the mainstream of a community, reflecting its broader vision of what is good and desirable.

For example, what it means to be a good parent often varies considerably between and even within societies, depending on a particular group's conception of human agency, meaningful relations with others, and overall well-being. In some cultures, a narrow vision of the nuclear family is prominent, such that being a good parent might not be considered possible if one is single or involved in a same-sex relationship. In other cultures, the status of the family unit is conceived more flexibly, for the broader community may be primarily accountable for raising children. In some cultures strict discipline is administered to insure proper conduct and the cultivation of moral responsibility, whereas in others children have more flexibility to explore boundaries and learn from their own mistakes. While in the former case an overactive and mischievous child may indicate bad parenting, in the latter it may reflect good parenting. For each economy of exchange, it is the ability to (re)present what is commonly valued that becomes the means for being recognized as a good parent, for offering something that is esteemed by the group as contributing to its well-being.

So if human beings desire more than mere survival, desiring instead to be worthy of that survival in the eyes of others, accepted and welcomed, this desire is played out within an economy of exchange. By it a framework is brought down to earth, so to speak, regulating and reinforcing the perceptions of what qualities are worthy and unworthy, acceptable and unacceptable. Because it attributes merit, enabling us to purchase recognition by others, an economy of exchange has the power to govern what becomes appropriate and desirable. And by this it creates the fabric of what is considered commonplace, typical, and generally expected by a group. At work is a system of language, attitudes, and actions that manufactures group consensus on select values. Hence, an economy of exchange designates conventions and qualities that comprise what it takes to belong. We might say it mediates and supports a framework by establishing identification markers that grant the capacity to recognize people by form and function as part of the group.

Body Capital—Measuring Exchange Value

It is no accident that the human body becomes a primary locus of such identification markers, its appearance (form) and ability (function) measured according to common expectations and standardized ideals.[23] Aesthetic qualities and role performances are the most immediate features of our everyday interactions with others. Physical appearance is probably the most obvious marker. It can be hereditary in origin or result from deliberate alterations or accidental injuries and illnesses. But appearance or form is not unrelated to performance or function. Clothes and physique, for example, testify to this in contemporary consumer culture, the outfitted and muscular body often connoting the virile and successful body. Identification markers, in this regard, are also related to gender, race, class, and ethnicity. While inscribed on the body, they get passed on symbolically through various functional mechanisms, such as language, education, rites of passage, diet, leisure and work expectations, political ideologies, and religion. In addition, they become embedded in the wider infrastructures of society, in architecture, transportation networks, mass media, and economic and class arrangements. In each of these instances, identification markers represent communal values in function and form. A social identity is written on the body. How one looks is related to how one plays roles and performs in an economy of exchange.

Economies of exchange, therefore, revolve around identification markers that display what I call *body capital*. The value of a body and its abilities is a matter of how it reflects common assumptions about a community's sense of the good, how it gains legitimacy, purchases recognition, or acquires worth in the context of others. And this exchange value amounts to power—the power to belong. Such power, however, is not wielded as a built-in property of the individual. For, as critical theorist Michel Foucault notes, it is a power inscribed onto the body by others. It is a factor of who and/or what "manages" the household. Body capital is a power value engineered by dominant social institutions and governed by disciplinary technologies such as education, medicine, penal systems, and even architecture. Think of how the young girl or boy becomes accepted by classmates. All kinds of cultural productions are involved, such as beauty, athleticism, and intelligence. And each of these is inscribed with different values according to specific social role expectations.

Foucault is instructive here because he helps us see how economies of exchange traffic in power relations that have an immediate hold on the body—"they invest it, mark it, train it, torture it, force it to carry out tasks, to perform ceremonies, to emit signs." The economic use of bodies is key. For reciprocal relations are largely a "force of production," by which power becomes possible as bodies are subject to forces external to them, "prepared, calculated, and used." Capital is manufactured and managed. So, according to Foucault, "the body becomes a useful force only if it is both a productive body and a subjected body."[24] The body is an icon representing the effects of power, an image ideally cast in the form of the dominant culture's sense of the good.

The notion of body capital, then, highlights Karl Marx's insight that human thought and culture is conditioned by socioeconomic structures of power.[25] He puts it bluntly: "The ruling ideas of each age have ever been the ideas of its ruling class."[26] The practices by which persons become oriented toward the good are embedded in ideological structures of power. That is, select ideas are translated into values and distributed by power. Foucault pushes Marx's insight further to locate the axis of power and knowledge in the body. Modes of exercised power shape our relation to bodies by determining "the forms and possible domains of knowledge."[27] Bodies are formatted, imprinted by various kinds of knowledge. Pharmaceutical corporations, for example, have capitalized on our culture's vision of sexual virility, beauty, and bodily health. Medical advances in knowledge therefore become shaped by and coupled with strategic marketing and the power to shape human perceptions and desires. We can see, then, how frameworks of the good are not discovered or otherwise corroborated by a benign logic of consensus; they emerge and play out within power relations, put to work in the service of specific techniques of production and repression. On repression, one has only to recall how the categories of race, gender, and ethnicity have been employed strategically, where historically white, male, and European bodies signified privilege and accordingly evoked body capital as fully human, the other of which—black, female, and non-European—carried a derivative value.

The Cult of Normalcy

The notion of body capital, therefore, also gives critical leverage to account for bodily differences that are recognized as unrepresentative of a community's good. Such bodies distinguish themselves by being out of place, marked by incompleteness or incompetence in form and/or function. That is, they lack capital, by appearance and/or ability perceived to be incapable of participating in the conventions put down by a prevailing economy of exchange. Anomalies are presented; disorder is introduced; borders are trespassed. Something does not belong. The result is a social disruption that throws into question the capital of taken-for-granted identification markers and, accordingly, mobilizes a need for boundary maintenance, for preserving and reaffirming a community's orientation to its sense of the good.

The human need for orientation and belonging wields a mighty yet corruptible power. When endangered, it can manifest itself collectively in protective strategies that aim to secure and fortify communal stability. For the different and "other" disorients the familiar, threatening to undo the trust we have placed in its conventions. So, in an effort to resist disorder and turmoil, energy is marshaled to repudiate the alien or foreign and reaffirm the ordinary and trustworthy. Borders are ossified and made accessible only to those whose body capital amounts to an exchangeable value. Driven by insecurity, says Vanier, "we build walls around our group and cultivate our certitudes."[28] The doors and windows of the home are policed. And power is consolidated to bolster security and control the ways body

59

capital is administered and exchanged. Ironically, however, the whole dynamic is fueled by a perception of value scarcity. Psychologically, human beings fear the loss of worth, the loss of body capital acquired to purchase recognition and belonging. This has sociological repercussions, however, as we take refuge in the ordered conventions of an economy of exchange and the security they seem to offer. Power and security in this sense are siblings, offspring of the fear of insecurity. A key point in the discussion thus comes to the fore.

It is this fear that is projected onto "the other," the dissimilar and strange. Persons with body markers different than the mainstreamed body, in form and/or function, come to be seen as exhibiting an incompleteness or messiness that signifies an aberration. They mark an anomalous territory of experience that does not readily conform to the values affirmed by the majority, fostering insecurity and instability. And because, as Lennard Davis remarks, the human "body is never a single thing so much as a series of attitudes toward it,"[29] it is easy to see how the differently marked body becomes represented as defective, an inverse and negative reflection of bodily features attributed with significance, such as beauty, efficiency, productivity, and so on. An irregularity is transformed into a deviance, a degeneration of the good. It is not to be desired. It lacks worth and has no exchange value.

Consequently, the different body is treated with indifference, suspicion, or revulsion. Devices of assimilation and exclusion are produced to standardize relations and eliminate infractions. These congeal into what can be called the cult of normalcy, that is, a set of rituals trained upon demarcating and policing the borders of a "normal" way of being. Bodies are regulated so as to remediate and thus neutralize their deviances. This is the product of an economy of exchange that fears the disruption of its management system. At base, then, the cult of normalcy is an evasion strategy trained upon nurturing conformity and manufacturing consent. It is the symptom of an inwardly turned community, one that fears what is outside. Relying on techniques of standardization, bodies are disciplined and made compliant and docile, to use Foucault's terms. The cult of normalcy deals with bodily variations by rendering them pathological and deficient vis-à-vis reference points of power and privilege. Select identification markers are held up as definitive, as prototypical body capital in form (appearance) and function (performative capacities). Taken symbolically to represent group identity, the prototype is accepted as normal. That is, it becomes recognized as common and similar among community members, a paradigm case of what is shared, only here there are also prescriptive connotations.

Hence, in the cult of normalcy there is slippage between the ideal and normal. The normal functions as normative, a way of controlling bodies and judging differences deviant. Normalcy is made desirable and enforced in public venues as the standard. We see this illustrated on network television and in advertisements, novels, and popular magazines. The ideal is held up as normal: the perfectly sculpted and athletic body presented as commonplace, even though it actually represents only a slim margin of thin people. Indeed, the large body is seldom depicted (except perhaps with humor), while statistically most North Americans are overweight. And the impaired body or the above-sixty-year-old body is almost never represented, except in select character roles. Given this lack of representation, television viewers and magazine readers are led to judge their own bodies as deviant. And the result is a proliferation of health clubs, cosmetic surgeries, steroid use, and anti-aging formulas. The North American body thus is inscribed with a formulaic and standardized sense of normalcy. Body capital equals youth, beauty, and muscular slenderness, even to the point of anorexic emaciation.

Lennard Davis has suggested that the idea of the normal is a recent invention of early nineteenth-century Europe, a product of the development of statistics and the concept of the bell curve. Before this, ways of measuring human bodies revolved around the "ideal," an exemplary type that no human could conceivably match. A model of perfection steeped in a Platonic and hierarchical understanding of the universe, the ideal meant that all else was in varying degrees imperfect, inadequate copies of the original. With the advent of statistics, however, the ideal was redefined in reference to the general population, located on a curve of distribution and taken to be what defines the normal and average, the typical. And with this comes the concept of deviations or extremes. Homogeneity became the ideal and heterogeneity was shunned. Such a transformation fits well with the growth of eugenics during the period, which sought to perfect humanity by eliminating anomalous "imperfections." It also connects with the concept of equality that enlivened democratic reforms and with the need for interchangeable factory workers as the Industrial Revolution came into full swing. Davis thus concludes that the normal "is a configuration that arises in a particular historical moment. It is part of a notion of progress, of industrialization, and of ideological consolidation of the power of the bourgeoisie."[30]

However, Davis's historical sensitivity seems strained. For it is also the case that societies across the globe and throughout history have enforced a normalcy representing certain ideals. While the word "normal" might be a recent invention, the cult of normalcy is not. Underneath a society's conventions and taken-for-granted norms lies a standardizing power. And this holds true for all communities. Ironically, Davis's analysis proves the point of showing how modern economies of exchange are caught up in ideological power mechanisms that normalize body capital for expedient means. We shall explore this further in the next chapter. For now, it is important simply to stress that all cultures trade on ideals and representations of the good that become standardized in common identification markers and then accepted as an ostensibly shared body capital. The bell curve is not needed for this. Indeed, the bell curve is one way of embodying the cult of normalcy. We might equally illuminate its presence in medieval society, the concept of the ideal reinforcing feudal or ecclesiastical hierarchies and their capacity to distribute body capital. Through the ideal, bodies became normalized and stamped with the seal of approval or repressed, put away, and isolated as savage, heathen, invalid, and the like. Whether assimilated or excluded, the body in the cult of normalcy is seen as an objective marker of the good, reduced to its function in the system, a tool used to purchase recognition.

What makes the cult of normalcy particularly deceptive is the manner by which it assigns aberrancy to what is perceived as alien. That is, it conceals unexamined assumptions that privilege normalcy as an original embodiment of the good. The normal is what we are supposed to be; the different is a corruption or privation of good, marked with derisive ideological meanings. For example, upon arriving in the "New World," Columbus noticed that the Taino people were "naked" and had "no culture" and thus needed to be civilized, made fully human.[31] The same dynamic, albeit in a different form, occurs with the medical model and its desire to cure the "deficiencies" of the disabled body. Normalcy is legitimated in terms of its contrast, the abnormal, which is invested with all kinds of negative connotations, perhaps even to the point of being evil. Those considered unable to conform to conventional norms of bodily wholeness and completeness are denigrated. Davis puts it bluntly: "Normality has to protect itself by looking into the maw of disability and then recovering from that glance."[32] And throughout the process, normalcy simply goes unquestioned, presumed as fact.

With such deception, differences cannot be recognized and affirmed as such; they are rendered unworthy, pathological, and outside the good. Why? Because they represent a failure on the part of a person to control the body.[33] This is how freaks, monsters, savages, and invalids are created. They function as "the other" in a process of social purification and purgation that ultimately aims to buttress normalcy by denigrating its inverse image, the abnormal.[34] The cult of normalcy thus filters standardized values by selecting and shaping information that upholds them. Attitudes and prejudices coalesce and are passed on in this manner, managed in a way that preserves normalcy—in language, media, and art as well as in labor, educational, and family institutions. Again, this corroborates Foucault's insight that power and knowledge are inscribed onto the body. Seen as a counter-testimony to the normal body's form and/or function, the abnormal is considered deformed and/or dysfunctional.

This prevents people with disabilities from becoming subjects of their own experiences; disability carries a negative symbolic value. The cult of normalcy tells people with disabilities who they are, forcing them by various societal rituals to bear a name that is depersonalizing. When adopted and internalized, this turns into self-loathing, guilt, and resentment ("I am abnormal"; "it is my fault"; "somehow I invite this treatment"). The consequence of the cult of normalcy is alienation, both socially and personally.

What I have offered in this section is a way of supplementing the insights of Taylor, highlighting the social processes by which frameworks and traditions hold sway in human interactions. Economies of exchange govern reciprocity, and they do so by instantiating the good in specific ways. Without body capital, recognition cannot be purchased. To the detriment of some, the cult of normalcy functions precisely to maintain social control by mainstreaming body capital and remedying or excluding what presents itself as lacking body capital. Such a conceptual scheme will prove helpful as we begin in the next chapter to assess modern and North American ideals of normalcy. Before this, however, a further step in the discussion is necessary, one with troubling implications for religious affirmations. Of course, there is an alternative—a way out—that we shall develop in later chapters. But traveling the path of diagnosis and critique is essential for grasping the significance of what is yet to come.

IV. Outside the Good

If it is true that human agency and self-identity are informed by the recognition received from others, it is also the case, as Taylor suggests, that "nonrecognition or misrecognition can inflict harm, can be a form of oppression, imprisoning someone in a false, distorted, and reduced mode of being."[35] Lack of recognition is connected to lack of social worth, and lack of social worth is connected to lack of body capital. Seen as an aberration, such a lack disconfirms and causes suffering for some—the abnormal—in the name of the many—the normal. This process is faulted to the core.

Stigma—The Spoiled Body

In a now classic book, sociologist Erving Goffman offers a way of accounting for lack of body capital, through his theory of stigma.[36] A stigma is a discredited attribute that fails to live up to what is expected and demanded of a person. Thus, its ascription depends upon social interaction. Someone possesses a stigma if he or she is marked by "an undesired differentness from what we had anticipated."[37] Goffman qualifies "we" by the term "normal," noting its connection to a collective identity. The normal is the assumed frame of reference by which a stigma is attributed to someone as a "disidentifier," something that disconnects them from the prevailing social order.[38] And the power animating such perceived disconnection lies in the stigma's undesirability. To be sure, human beings naturally make categorical distinctions between all kinds of things, and this includes bodily and behavioral differences. In this process, however, some distinctions become highlighted as blemished features unworthy of social inclusion. While Goffman does not account for why this is so, as we have done in the preceding discussion, he does stress the socially constructed nature of stigmatization and identifies three general types, which often overlap: physical deformities; moral and behavioral blemishes; and differences of race, nation, and religion (to which we might add gender and ethnicity).[39]

Goffman's analysis of stigma has important implications for our discussion. He offers us leverage to more fully grasp how the cult of normalcy repudiates persons lacking in body capital. In reality, a stigma is not the property of an individual body, but rather the result of complex social projections that represent bodies, lumping them into general stereotypes insofar as they display undesired qualities. This kind of devaluing does not merely focus on the stigmatized, it uses stigma to prop up the rule of normalcy. "One can therefore suspect that the role of normal and the role of stigmatized are parts of the same complex, cuts from the same standard cloth."[40] Stigma is a vehicle for projecting onto others an inverse image of normalcy, imputing deviancy to solidify its power to provide value and meaning, even prestige, to the dominant majority. Rosemarie Garland-Thomson summarizes the point nicely: "Stigmatization not only reflects the tastes and opinions of the dominant group, it reinforces that group's idealized self-description as neutral, normal, legitimate, and identifiable by denigrating the characteristics of less powerful groups or those considered alien."[41] Stigma buttresses the status quo by obligating certain persons to play roles that "manage" interactions with normals so as to avoid social disruption and discomfort.[42] Thus, Goffman helps us see how a dominant group has the means to control which differences are deviant and which are not. This means to control is what I have described as the cult of normalcy.

Goffman also enables us to see the ludicrous narrowing effect that stigma has. First, a stigmatized person is reduced to his or her stigma. The stigma becomes the defining feature of that person's being, thus enabling society to manage and marginalize the undesirable difference it represents. In Goffman's words, we thus "construct a stigma-theory, an ideology to explain his inferiority and account for the danger he represents," imputing "a wide range of imperfections on the basis of the original one . . ."[43] That is, we sum up a person and judge them unworthy on the basis of their particular stigma. Terms like "bastard" and "cripple" have their origins here. A person's lack of body capital becomes fetishized, defining him or her as undesirable and outside the good.

Second, the attribution of stigma assumes a concept of normalcy that goes unquestioned and which, upon further examination, is incredibly thin, disqualifying almost everyone at some stage of life. For example, and with great sarcasm, Goffman defines the prototypical male figure in North American culture: "a young, married, white, urban, northern, heterosexual Protestant father of college education, fully employed, of good complexion, weight, and height, and a recent record in sports."[44] From this common perspective, men gauge themselves and look out into the world, at some point being forced to view their state as inadequate and inferior. Women and minorities are altogether ignored. Here, the normal is an illusory image grounded in a phantom majority, pretending to represent a common condition that neither exists nor ever will.[45]

Both of these narrowing dynamics produce a great irony. Stigmatization is a procedure by which the cult of normalcy ends up biting its own tail, actually undermining the status quo by cultivating a sense of alienation among the majority at the same time that it attributes imperfection to the minority. Reducing persons with stigmatized attributes to their alleged blemishes ends up reducing the scope of what qualifies as normal. The cult of normalcy thus undoes itself, excluding virtually everyone. People are then forced into pretense, living lies by playing roles in order to fit in.

We must ask, then, on what basis a community withstands such an irony. Would not the whole process be self-undermining, eventually waning in influence and power? Goffman points to the problem, but for all of its subtlety, his analysis does not attempt to expose and critique its underpinnings. He is content simply to name the social inequity that results from disqualifying certain people from social acceptance, which forces some to adjust and manage their identities according to the images projected upon them. But from where do such images arise and come to hold social power? Why is someone's particular bodily difference seen as a threat disrupting the fabric of an economy of exchange? The answer, I suggest, lies in a community's sense of the good, which has been normalized in common conventions and attitudes, and which, accordingly, is highly resistant to dislocation and falsification by differences.

Taboo—Prohibiting the Abnormal

Noted anthropologist Mary Douglas offers a helpful way of supplementing Goffman's approach, equipping us with some categories that allow us to see the inverse connection of stigma to the good. Her analysis pivots around the morally charged notion of taboo.[46] Taboos mark those things that are to be avoided because they challenge the conventions of a framework of valuation. Like stigmas, they designate anomalies that threaten to spoil a community's way of bringing order to experience. Some things prove too much for a group to bear, for they deviate from the taken-for-granted order of things. They are considered "contrary to nature." Moral injunctions thus arise to isolate and shield a group against the peril represented by them. In an effort to protect the need for orientation and preserve the good, a community will deem certain classes of things impure, blemished, unclean or dirty, perhaps evil, in contrast to the pure, unblemished, and sacrosanct character of its sense of the good.

How this division is made, of course, depends upon the context of valuation. For example, Douglas cites the priestly dietary restrictions of ancient Israel, which create the condition of "holiness" for entering the temple and being in right relation to God. Four-legged animals, fish, and fowl are classified according to a threefold classification in Genesis of nature itself: the earth, the waters, and the firmament. Such creatures are acceptable for consumption only if their mechanisms of locomotion are appropriate to their place in nature. Douglas states:

> In the firmament two-legged fowls fly with wings. In the water scaly fish swim with fins. On the earth four-legged animals hop, jump or walk. Any class of creatures which is not equipped for the right kind of locomotion in its element is contrary to holiness. Contact with it disqualifies a person from approaching the Temple. Thus anything in the water which has not fins and scales is unclean (Lev. 11:10–12).[47]

By implication, we can see how the distinction between holiness and abomination might extend to gender roles (as in women being unclean during menstruation), class lines (as in the Hindu caste system), race (as in apartheid-like systems), ethnicity (as in colonialist chauvinism), and health (as in illness). We also can see how hybrid combinations between categories of various kinds are often considered contaminations, as in interracial marriages, mulattos, homosexuals, and so on. Such mixing of categories blurs the boundaries between things, creating disorder. This is why distinctions and prohibitions like these, while not the same for every culture, (1) play out in all cultures in some form or another, (2) function according to how the world is socially constructed, and (3) provide a boundary-making locus for evaluative judgments.

Douglas's analysis proves even more instructive by outlining how "holiness" functions as an attribute of where a community finds its power. The root meaning of the word "holy" denotes something set apart, as qualitatively different from the ordinary. Unlike the taboo, however, the difference of holiness is fundamentally positive, signifying that which bestows blessing and is the source of good. This illustrates the interrelationship between power, frameworks, and value. Again, examples can be marshaled by turning to the Hebrew scriptures. According to Douglas, "God's work through the blessing is essentially to create order, through which men's affairs prosper."[48] Value comes from the framework established by God's power. Thus, it is to the holiness of God that the Israelites must conform if they are to flourish. Policed by the priestly specialists, this means being set apart from the unclean, avoiding contact with elements that defile the purity of the good. But it means even more.

It means maintaining wholeness and completeness according to the created order of things. Douglas documents this by observing how much of Leviticus is "taken up with stating the physical perfection that is required of things presented in the temple and of persons approaching it." Quoting Leviticus 21:17–21, she points out how the priest must be exempt from blemish, pure and whole, if he is to preside over the most sacred rites.[49] Holiness entails conformity to the class of things to which something belongs and keeping the different categories of creation distinct. And it is exemplified by completeness, integrity, and wholeness.[50] To be whole, then, requires being vested in the power and authority that governs the social system and its way of articulating and framing the world.[51]

In the Hebrew worldview, holiness is epitomized in God. For God is the power of creation and the covenantal laws, undefiled and whole—in a word, pure. Put in terms we have been using, God is the source of the good that animates and upholds the framework by which the covenanted people find orientation and welcome in the world. Breaking from this source entails disintegration and suffering, the removal of blessing, for it marks a breach of keeping covenant with God. For the law promises blessing and prosperity when obeyed, but evokes curse when violated, manifest in afflictions like impairments and plagues (Deut. 28). This is the basis for the theodicy questions we criticized in the last chapter. And as we saw then, it is the font of many denigrating views of disability. For disability is construed as lacking body capital, representing impurity in the scheme of creation. It manifests what stands outside the field of force supporting normalcy. It marks disorder. Religion, in this instance, is co-opted by the cult of normalcy.

Metaphors of wholeness, therefore, have spatial and bodily connotations that serve to legitimate particular kinds of responses to persons marked by an alleged incompleteness, a deformity or dysfunctionality. Crippled, maimed, diseased, bastard, impotent, idiot, imbecile, retarded, and so on, are terms used to isolate and separate such persons from what is considered whole and "normal"—that is, what fits in with the way things should be. They are corruptions of an ideal embedded in social conventions. A negative value is imputed to deviation, stigmatizing it as outside the proper scheme of things, outside of order. It represents what Douglas calls a danger to the stable world. Access to the community is limited unless the blemished is assimilated through purity rites of one sort or another that ritual-ize normalcy by rendering whole or healing that which is faulted. Restricting or removing defilement is the key to maintaining the blessings of the created order, an order symbolized in the Leviticus holiness tradition by the temple. In our own culture, healthcare and penal systems symbolize this fundamental dynamic.

An important implication of Douglas's analysis comes to the fore, namely, that human "ability" is understood and measured socially vis-à-vis an ideal moral condition. Well-being is connected to the capacity to be self-initiating, able to move one's body through space and direct one's mental energies in a focused and productive way. And being able to focus in these ways entails possessing the power of agency, able to align oneself with the good purposefully and stay within its boundaries, avoiding transgression and deviation, refraining from overstepping one's place and missing the mark. In other words, ability means having the power to move with conventions, to conform, to be normal and whole, even to be holy. It means to control one's body in a certain way. How a community understands power and the good, therefore, has everything to do with how that community understands and responds to disability. For disability is seen as disorderly and out of control. The issue is systemic and social in nature. "Lack" of self power is a liability to the group, rendering a person "needy" and "dependent" upon others to be made whole, or, if deemed permanently "lacking," segregated from public spaces that require wholeness for access.

Consequentially, lack of ability is considered indicative of a faulted moral condition. According to the cult of normalcy, disability is a breach of the order of things. It is a liability to the group, calling for defensive maneuvering. And it is a short step from here to the notion that impairments are the result of sin, curse, or lack of faith, and the person with disabilities bearing the burden of respon-sibility. The good of the community, then, requires that disability be ritualized into normalcy or rendered invisible if the community's sense of orientation and meaning has been threatened with fragmentation and chaos. Disorder is impure. Human beings fear lack of order, which symbolizes falling apart and disorientation.

Monsters are creatures of disorder. They are *unheimlich*, uncanny and disruptive. They are immoral, unreflective of the good, and so throw social cohesion into relief. *Heimlich*, as Davis notes, is a word associated with the comfortable predictability of the home, with familiarity and clean boundaries. And if what we seek is home, a place of welcome, the anomalous and disabled body throws this into relief. It is "unhomey" or *unheimlich*, a creature of disorder.[52] The different is the "un-housed," that which does not belong. Its presence "un-houses" us and should be controlled because it is not in control of its own body.

It is distressingly understandable, then, how the subject positions of persons with disabilities become overdetermined by the cult of normalcy. Disability is a counter-testimony of conventions assumed to mirror a community's sense of the good. Indeed, it is a social product, the consequence of a fear of disorder and disorientation caused by the perception of deficiency in body capital. Disability, in the end, is the systemic result of a fear-based projection, which ironically implicates those caught up within the sway of normalcy. In addition, as a function of social cohesion religious practices and attitudes are disabling insofar as societal norms and ideals are seen as reflections of the umblemished and pure nature of God.

Should we take Chris to church? Such a question has plagued Mary and me, for he often talked about learning from Sunday schools and youth groups of the past how he should "overcome" his disability by praying harder. But he says God does not listen to his prayers, because "nothing happens." How can God matter anyway, he asks, because God is perfect and he is so "imperfect"? Clearly such interpretations are products of theology taken captive by the cult of normalcy. We shall discuss this more later. For now, it is important to take small steps, the first of which is to question the ideal of normalization for people with disabilities.

Conclusion: Against "Normalization"?

This chapter has highlighted the social nature of belonging and explored how it can lead to the marginalization of people with disabilities. One important consequence of our efforts is the gaining of critical perspective. For instance, it now becomes possible to question medical and caring methods trained upon "normalization." This term has a positive connotation in that persons are directed toward rehabilitation and social reintegration, the goal being to grant some measure of independent participation and inclusion in the daily conventions and activities of a community. Independent living is thus often touted as a worthy achievement for persons with disabilities. It entails a freedom to choose living in ways that bring about fulfillments taken for granted in mainstream culture. But, as Eva Feder Kittay writes, "this ideal can also be a source of great disempowerment if applied with too broad a brush." She goes on suggest that even the worthy intention of communal inclusion can get "congealed in concepts and behaviors that have less desirable consequences."[53]

Indeed, there is an unfortunate irony here. The process of normalization depends upon an understanding of the "normal" that goes unquestioned, giving unchecked license to the cult of normalcy. An idealization of what counts for independent living, free choice, and inclusion is simply presumed. The person is (re)made to fit the system. So, for all its noble prospects, too much is yielded to the social mechanisms that set up disability as something incomplete and faulted, something to be fixed and made whole, fully functional. It is not merely the impairment or undesirable inherited trait that needs readjustment; it is the community's conception of normal form and/or functioning that needs readjustment. Independent living and communal inclusion should be measured as subsidiaries of broader and more holistic goals, such as living as richly and fully as one's bodily capacities permit, and doing so in a way that enhances one's capacity for joy.[54] Obviously, terms like "rich," "full," and "joy" are laden with implications that demand investigation. And we shall investigate them later. At this point, it is enough to say that the system should be flexible and open enough to fit the person, in all her or his uniqueness. Also critical of normalization, Hauerwas suggests that "the demand to be normal can be tyrannical unless we understand that the normal condition of our being together is that we are all different."[55] In the following chapters, we shall turn our attention to precisely these kinds of goals.

For now, however, we are brought to ask some fundamental questions. First, is human worth merely a function of utility, a social accomplishment acted out in normalizing systems of value exchange? That is, is a person's significance and dignity measured simply by his or her capacity to contribute in ways that productively reflect a community's sense of the good? Second, is the "lack" of body capital always something that requires rehabilitation or ritualized cleansing if it is not to be excluded and rendered irrelevant to a community? Is deviation really defilement? Is difference a perversion, a danger threatening to spoil the social fabric of community? Third, is it proper to equate wholeness and integrity with an idealized and complete human nature, a being able-bodied, able-thinking, and able-feeling? Is disability an incomplete or fractured human nature, a failure to control the body? As may be obvious, these questions are all interrelated. Indeed, perhaps they crystallize in a final question: is the "normal" the "good"? To all the above questions, I answer resolutely, "no."

Addressing these questions in a way that provides hope and social access for persons with disabilities, however, requires undoing the tyranny of the normal and its confusion with a conventional good. It necessitates finding ways to make space for the different as something that augments a community rather than diminishes it. And this demands a thorough rethinking of human embodiment, the nature of human relation, and the character of human value. As Nancy Eiesland argues, we must engage in a process of "re-symbolizing" what it means to be human, such that new images of wholeness are created and new ways of dwelling together in community are envisioned.[56] Fresh criteria must be introduced to measure the moral character of a society and its way of mediating "welcome." But wherein lies the power to break the hold of the cult of normalcy and its conventions? I suggest that resources for such an endeavor are found in the redemptive pulse of the biblical witness.

However, we must first frame a context for rediscovering the biblical witness through the lens of disability. And this, in turn, requires rethinking human dependency and vulnerability in the context of the cult of normalcy that dominates North America. Such will be the task of the next chapter, which shall help us see more clearly how liberal political ideals in conjunction with free market capitalism produce a "framework" making it difficult for people with disabilities to be empowered as contributors to society, let alone Christian churches. Values like freedom, equality, independence, rationality, productivity, efficiency, and prosperity inscribe themselves onto our bodies. Despite the positive spin these are often given, such values also have harmful consequences. Let us then explore how such a claim is warranted.

Notes

1. Stanley Hauerwas, "Community and Diversity: The Tyranny of Normality," in *Critical Reflection on Stanley Hauerwas' Theology of Disability: Disabling Society, Enabling Theology*, ed. John Swinton (Binghamton, NY: Haworth Press, 2004), 40.

2. A well-known example of this is found in the work of Erik Erikson, who suggests that the earliest stage of an infant's emotional development deals with the issue of "trust versus mistrust," that is, whether or not her or his world is dependable. See his *Childhood and Society*, 2nd ed. (New York: Norton, 1963).

3. For a more philosophical articulation of this, see my book *The Broken Whole: Philosophical Steps toward a Theology of Global Solidarity* (Albany: State University of New York Press, 2005), esp. chap. 4.

4. H. Richard Niebuhr, *Faith on Earth: An Inquiry into the Structure of Human Faith*, ed. Richard R. Niebuhr (New Haven: Yale University Press, 1989), 78.

5. John Polkinghorne, *Quarks, Chaos and Christianity* (New York: Crossroad, 1996), 15; see also 95. I am indebted to Michael Reinardy for calling my attention to this passage. Peter L. Berger suggests something similar in his *A Rumor of Angels: Modern Society and the Rediscovery of the Supernatural* (New York: Anchor Books, 1990), 60–65.

6. See Lucien Richard, OMI, *Living the Hospitality of God* (New York: Paulist Press, 2000), 7–11.

7. Wendy Farley eloquently articulates this sense of "home" in *The Wounding and Healing of Desire: Weaving Heaven and Earth* (Louisville: Westminster John Knox Press, 2005), 3–7.

8. Jean Vanier, *Becoming Human* (New York: Paulist Press, 1998), 36.

9. This point is drawn from Gaston Bachelard's insightful book *The Poetics of Space*, trans. Maria Jolas (Boston: Beacon Press, 1969), chap. 2, see esp. 46–47, 51.

10. Vanier, *Becoming Human*, 44.

11. Charles Taylor, *Sources of the Self: The Making of Modern Identity* (Cambridge: Harvard University Press, 1989), 45.

12. Ibid., chap. 1.

13. Ibid., see 26f.

14. Ibid., 35 (emphasis in original).

15. Ibid., 34f.

16. See Charles Taylor, "The Politics of Recognition," in *Multiculturalism*, ed. Amy Gutmann (Princeton: Princeton University Press, 1994), 25–73, esp. 32ff.

17. Alasdair MacIntyre, *Dependent Rational Animals: Why Human Beings Need the Virtues* (Chicago: Open Court, 1999), 95.

18. Taylor, *Sources of the Self*, 36. This idea of the social origination and character of the self has been made by George Herbert Mead, *Mind, Self, and Society* (Chicago: University of Chicago Press, 1962).

19. See Taylor, *Sources of the Self*, 47ff. See also Alasdair MacIntyre's notion of "tradition" in *After Virtue: A Study in Moral Theory*, 2nd ed. (Notre Dame, IN: University of Notre Dame Press, 1984); and Paul Ricoeur's discussion of narrative frameworks in *Oneself as Another*, trans. Kathleen Blamey (Chicago: University of Chicago Press, 1992), chaps. 5 and 6, and in the three-volume study *Time and Narrative*, vols. I and II, trans. K. McLaughlin and D. Pellauer, and vol. III, trans. K. Blamey and D. Pellauer (Chicago: University of Chicago Press, 1984, 1985, 1988).

20. Taylor's way of describing "frameworks" has a certain affinity to what Clifford Geertz describes as "culture." Like a framework, culture is a semantic web that presides over a group of persons and informs a way of life. See Geertz, *The Interpretation of Cultures* (New York: Basic Books, 1973), 46f. and 89. See also Kathryn Tanner, *Theories of Culture* (Minneapolis: Fortress Press, 1997), chap. 2. The sociology of knowledge perspective, as presented by Peter L. Berger and Thomas Luckmann in *The Social Construction of Reality* (New York: Anchor Press, 1967) gets at a similar point.

21. On this point, underscored by postcolonialist authors, see Kathryn Tanner, *Theories of Culture: A New Agenda for Theology* (Minneapolis: Fortress Press, 1997), chap. 3. See also my *The Broken Whole*, chap. 3.

22. See Taylor, "The Politics of Recognition."

23. I am adapting this distinction loosely from Lennard J. Davis, *Enforcing Normalcy: Disability, Deafness, and the Body* (New York: Verso, 1995), 11–12.

24. Michel Foucault, *Discipline and Punish: The Birth of the Prison*, trans. Alan Sheridan (New York: Vintage/Random House, 1979), 25–26.

25. "Morality, religion, metaphysics, all the rest of ideology and their corresponding forms of consciousness, thus no longer retain the semblance of independence. They have no history, no development; but men, developing their material production and their material intercourse, alter, along with this their real existence, their thinking and the products of their thinking. Life is not determined by consciousness, but consciousness by life." Marx, "The German Ideology," in *The Marx-Engels Reader*, 2nd ed., ed. Robert C. Tucker (New York: W. W. Norton and Company, 1978), 154–55.

26. Marx, "Manifesto of the Communist Party," 489.

27. Foucault, *Discipline and Punish*, 28.

28. Vanier, *Becoming Human*, 39.

29. Lennard J. Davis, *Bending over Backwards: Disability, Dismodernism and Other Difficult Positions* (New York: New University Press, 2002), 22.

30. Davis, *Enforcing Normalcy*, 49. See also *Bending over Backwards*, 105.

31. For an engaging account of Columbus's perceptions, see Tzvetan Todorov, *The Conquest of America*, trans. Richard Howard (New York: Harper Perennial, 1992).

32. Davis, *Enforcing Normalcy*, 48.

33. Susan Wendell, *The Rejected Body: Feminist Reflections on Disability* (New York: Routledge, 1996), 60–61.

34. For an excellent discussion of this theme in North American culture, see Rosemarie Garland-Thomson, *Extraordinary Bodies: Figuring Physical Disability in American Culture and Literature* (New York: Columbia University Press, 1997), chap. 3. See also Richard Kearney, *Strangers, God and Monsters* (New York: Routledge, 2003).

35. Taylor, "The Politics of Recognition," 25.

36. Erving Goffman, *Stigma: Notes on the Management of Spoiled Identity* (New York: Simon and Schuster, 1963).

37. Ibid., 5.

38. Ibid., 44.

39. Ibid., 4.

40. Ibid., 130.

41. Garland-Thomson, *Extraordinary Bodies*, 31. See also Susan Wendell's discussion of Goffman in *The Rejected Body*, 57–60.

42. Goffman, *Stigma*, 41–42, 122.

43. Ibid, 5.

44. Ibid., 128.

45. Garland-Thomson, *Extraordinary Bodies*, 32.

46. Mary Douglas, *Purity and Danger: An Analysis of Concepts of Pollution and Taboo* (New York: Frederick A. Praeger, Inc., 1966).

47. Ibid., 55.

48. Ibid., 50.

49. Ibid., 51. See also Sarah J. Melcher, "Visualizing the Perfect Cult: The Priestly Rationale for Exclusion," in *Human Disability and the Service of God*, ed. Nancy L. Eiesland and Don E. Saliers (Nashville: Abingdon, 1998), 55–71.

50. Ibid., 53–54.

51. Ibid, see chap. 6, esp. 99.

52. Davis, *Enforcing Normalcy*, 141–43.

53. Eva Feder Kittay, *Love's Labor: Essays on Women, Equality, and Dependency* (New York: Routledge, 1999), 171.

54. Ibid., 172–73.

55. Hauerwas, "Community and Diversity: The Tyranny of Normality," 40.

56. Nancy L. Eiesland, *The Disabled God: Toward a Liberatory Theology of Disability* (Nashville: Abingdon Press, 1994), 22f. and 90ff.

3

Able Bodies? The Illusion of Control and Denial of Vulnerability

A society that honours only the powerful, the clever, and the winners necessarily belittles the weak. It is as if to say: to be human is to be powerful.

Jean Vanier[1]

A human being is more than the power or capacity to think and perform.

Jean Vanier[2]

The previous chapter highlighted how, because of the human need to belong and find orientation in the world, communities—including the persons who compose them and the institutions that uphold them—are led to project the fear of disorder and worthlessness onto others who exhibit bodily qualities that are different and unfamiliar. This is the stuff of the cult of normalcy. And its effects are pernicious, setting up social mechanisms that either assimilate by enforcing conformity or exclude by preventing participation in a community's economy of exchange. I have deliberately focused on the construction of normalcy instead of disability for reasons that Lennard Davis articulates nicely—that is, "because the 'problem' is not the person with disabilities; the problem is the way that normalcy is constructed to create the 'problem' of the disabled person."[3] Normalcy creates disability as an obstacle to human flourishing, an incomplete and out-of-control body.

As a parent of a child with disabilities, I am acutely aware of the cult of normalcy. Not only does it shape other people's responses to my son Chris, it informs my own attitudes about parenting and being a family, shaping the expectations I have of him. I am a parent caught up in social currents larger than myself, which come to mold the character of my responses to Chris's specific ways of being. On the one hand, this is only natural, given that we are all finite human beings who understand who we are in terms of our place in a community's economy of exchange, and appraise ourselves and others accordingly. On the other hand, I am disturbed by how much my way of approaching Chris reveals the very communicative and attitudinal barriers I am critical of as his advocate. Despite my efforts to be a loving parent, I often discover how deeply I am caught up in the cult of normalcy of North America. And this plays out in ways that prevent him from discovering and developing his own unique way of being in the world. I wind up projecting role expectations onto Chris that are socially derived and, in fact, help construct his disability. I project *my* way, anticipating for him the contours of what normal development and a meaningful life should look like according to how I understand it. That is, I ritualize normalcy by trying to socialize him into its conventions, reinforcing the debilitating power of the status quo. And the tragic irony here is that I do so under the auspices of seeking his own good.

The issue, then, is whether in seeking the good of people with disabilities nondisabled persons are inadvertently seeking their own good—that is, the good as they perceive it, being products of the cult of normalcy. We must question whether conforming to the markers of a society's economies of exchange is genuinely good, whether it actually makes possible human flourishing. Should Chris control his motor and verbal tics in public? Should he avoid hugging others spontaneously in order to preserve the etiquette of keeping space between people who are not family or friends? Should he be required to chew silently with his mouth closed while eating with others? These questions boil down to a single question: to what degree must Chris shape his "out-of-control body" to function normally in our society, acquire positive recognition from others, and thereby become conscious of his worth? These are hard questions for a parent because, it is true, Chris's own special way of being deserves affirmation apart from whether or not he fits conventional values and social norms. Yet it is also evident that Chris's own capacity to flourish can be augmented by being encouraged to move beyond the orbit of his family and caregivers to participate in and contribute to society as an independent person. Why? Because he can grow in the consciousness of his worth by interacting with others on a wider playing field, not simply remaining ensconced in the private and protected sphere of his significant others. But this raises difficult problems.

There is a two-sided charge that obligates parents of children with disabilities and, by general implication, most caregivers and medical institutions. First, there is a responsibility to affirm, nurture, and empower the unique person, helping to foster his or her own peculiar way of being. Second, there is a responsibility to encourage independence and the capacity to live productively with others in society. However, these two charges often run against one another. Efforts to "normalize" a child in our culture often lead to sacrificing or suppressing genuine uniqueness, creating a docile body. Yet, conversely, efforts to affirm and give license to the uniqueness of children with disabilities often lead to institutionalization and social exclusion, for established social conventions are not set up to accommodate out-of-control bodies. Indeed, convention requires controlling and minimizing the unconventional.

The situation gets more complicated in cases where disabilities are less severe or hidden. For example, Chris's highly functioning autism makes establishing balance between the two charges extremely difficult. Mary and I, not to mention the network of teachers, psychologists, and caregivers that aid Chris, find it almost impossible to identify the boundary where legitimate capabilities end and real impairments begin. Precisely which behaviors are factors of developmental disability and which are factors of developmental immaturity? What behaviors can be "managed" by encouragement, discipline, and behavior-modification skills, and what behaviors cannot? Tragically, this ambiguity ends up confusing Chris and injuring his sense of self-worth. Many normal regimens are expected of him at school and at home, but he often struggles to "measure up" and so becomes frustrated and angry. Yet despite this he also shows very strong signs of being able to communicate clearly, interact sensitively with others, work independently, contribute to the good of others, and create with incredible imagination. So what should be done?

Part of the answer, I have grown to believe, involves unmasking and critiquing the manner by which the cult of normalcy gains sway in our society, determining the ebb and flow of economies of exchange by outlining what it means to be a person and have worth. That the cult of normalcy operates in unexamined, clandestine ways to administer value and ascribe dysfunction and abnormality to out-of-control bodies makes it particularly dangerous. Its subtle way of defining what it means to be a person not only socially constructs disability, but also prevents persons with disabilities from becoming agents of their own unique way of flourishing. Disability is forced to carry a negative symbolic value. Societal and communal structures—on a macro and a micro level—end up projecting and managing an image of normalcy, which becomes manifest in conventional expectations that create abnormality when they run aground. Some bodies become rendered deviant, different, and "other."[4] Boundaries are set up between "normals" and "those others." These condition and thereby limit the capacity to be open to differences.

The previous chapter discussed generally how and why this occurs. However, it is now important to explore the particular manner in which it occurs in our own sociocultural framework, that is, in North America (and to a large degree, Western society as a whole). This shall allow us to fill out with more specificity the schematic provided in the last chapter. The purpose for doing so is to more fully expose how non-disabled and disabled persons alike become complicit in the cult of normalcy, conforming to its standards. For example, as discussed a moment ago, I have become painfully aware how restrictive the assumptions I have about what it means to be a healthy and functional human being can be for Chris. Yet there is hope. Becoming conscious of and understanding these assumptions, many of which I unknowingly project onto Chris, has helped clear a path toward attending more fully to his own unique and gifted way of being. Ultimately, his life is precious in its own right, determined not by the cult of normalcy but rather by its being created in the image of God, loved into being by God. This opens up a new way of being together and confronts me with my own vulnerable humanity as a creature also loved by God. Be this as it may, it is also regrettably the case that much of Christianity in North America has become part of the cult of normalcy, inadvertently baptizing assumptions that are indeed foreign to the redemptive pulse of biblical narratives.

With this in mind, the discussion in this chapter shall address two primary foci of the cult of normalcy in North America, especially the United States. First, we live in a liberal democracy saturated with certain ideals, the most prominent of which are freedom, equality, and rational autonomy. These ideals are deeply embedded in our consciousness, and outline a view of the person that elicits common civic expectations and responsibilities. Second, and connected to this, our cultural framework is controlled by consumer values that are driven by market capitalism and its production-oriented, materialistic ethos. Here the person is defined by the ability to produce and purchase. Now I do not wish to suggest that these features of American life are inherently faulty or by necessity lead to harmful consequences. Indeed, there is much here that is laudable, such as the defense of human rights, the preservation of civil society based upon self-governance, and unprecedented opportunity and prosperity for many Americans.

However, there are also dynamics at play that mitigate these gains with a complex irony. How so? By cultivating an understanding of the healthy and functional human being that marginalizes people with disabilities—among others—under the banners of freedom, equality, reason, productivity, and purchase power. The normal body is the "able" and controlled body, assumed to be autonomous, rational, and efficient. When these ideals are uncritically adopted into a Christian viewpoint, they become sanctioned as part of God's intention for all human beings. In turn, they support the denigrating and trivializing attitudes toward people with disabilities that were discussed in chapter 1. So we must be circumspect. What are the factors that contribute to the cult of normalcy in North America? Answering this question is crucial to exposing the unseemly character of its hold on the way Christians think about disability.

Of course, it is one thing to critique and another to offer up an alternative vision of potentially greater value. Thus, after naming and assessing the problems of the North American framework, it will be the task of the next chapter to propose a substitute model for human flourishing. The aim is not so much to develop new social policy as it is to present a counter-anthropology (which may lead to the creation of new social policies). This kind of anthropology, I shall argue, is made possible by privileging disability, bringing it from the margins to the center. If we understand disability outside the cult of normalcy—which construes impairment as a lack of body capital, a deviance or anomaly—we gain a perspective that allows us to see that it is not rational autonomy, aesthetic appeal, self-sufficiency, or productive power that defines human wholeness and health. Rather, it is a way of belonging with others and cultivating the joy of being "at home" together. Ultimately, it hinges not upon proving our worth through amassing body capital, but rather upon the capacity to welcome and be welcomed, experiencing ourselves as creatures loved into being by God. This amounts to a metaphoric reversal that dislodges the sway of normalcy. Controlling the body does not give human beings dignity. Dignity is an extension of something more fundamental—being with others within the enfolding grace of God. And discovering this dignity is what yields wholeness.

Unpacking this, however, requires first examining how we become caught up in the cult of normalcy in our own particular cultural situation.

I. Theoretical Roots of the Modern Notion of Personhood

There is a fundamental paradox at the heart of modern democratic social existence. On the one hand, it is assumed that persons have an inbuilt dignity and worth, and therefore are free to define their own lives and do so on a par with others. On the other hand, as the previous chapter illustrated, persons can discover themselves and their worth only in the context of others, in relationships that mediate meaning and value and, to a real degree, ascribe a sense of identity upon persons. Through such duality, self-definition and social definition are internally related, symbiotic. Precisely this is what makes governance by and for the people such an advance over more centralized or authoritarian forms of rule. For if preserving group identity and cohesion is politically prioritized, the freedom of self-definition for individuals is constricted. However, the reverse is also true. If individual freedoms are politically prioritized, the collective identity and common good of the group is jeopardized, resulting in fragmentation.[5] More importantly for us in this book, a focus on individual freedom can lead to narrow, even constrictive, visions of what it means to be human. The result ironically fosters the cult of normalcy. So the paradox here produces the need for delicate balance.

The roots of this paradox go back to the origins of liberal political philosophy in the European Enlightenment. Eighteenth-century thinkers like Thomas Hobbes and John Locke painted pictures of an ideal society built upon social contract.[6] They suggested legitimate political rule is a matter of independent individuals coming together for mutual advantage, agreeing collectively to fashion binding regulations and responsibilities for themselves, thereby consenting to be governed.

Central to the notion of contractual agreement is the principle that every person is able to participate, according to Locke, as "free, equal, and independent" agents in the formation of shared public space.[7] Three principles are crucial presuppositions. First is a voluntarism that presupposes the original capacity of individuals to make reasonable choices based on self-interest. Second is an egalitarianism that presupposes a rough parity or symmetrical situation of participation and cooperation among all members of society in the political process. Connected with the first two, the third is an individualism that presumes persons are separate sources of claims and projects aimed at their own happiness. The liberal portrait of a well-ordered and just society, then, regards human beings as free, equal, and independent moral agents.[8] These ideals compose the backbone of the concept of democratic self-governance. And insofar as we are heirs of their historical influence, these ideals contribute substantially to the "framework" of North American society (to employ Charles Taylor's term again). So it is worth exploring what they mean in some further detail.

I shall highlight four premises that underlie the relationship between the three principles listed above. To begin, we must note that there is an inner correlation between egalitarianism and voluntarism. Equal persons are free, and free persons are equal. The question arises: on what basis? And the answer seems to revolve around the premise that what makes us free also makes us equal. For thinkers in the liberal tradition, this connection is independence conceived in the shape of rational autonomy. Out of it arises both the ability to cooperate symmetrically with others, and the capacity to choose what is good for oneself without intrusion or authentication by others.[9] Contrary to Plato and other traditional anthropologies, which set up a hierarchy distinguishing between the abilities of some people and others based upon different natural endowments, the liberal picture of rationality suggests that all people are naturally endowed with certain facilities, such as the capacity for critical inquiry, self-criticism, and accumulating knowledge without reliance upon habit, custom, or authority. This capacity (i.e., reason) distinguishes persons as self-directed individuals, who by independent and self-originating means make assertions and decisions that create and define themselves. So the individual is autonomous, that is, has a rational will competent to author law for itself (*auto-nomos*), able to adjudicate between different courses of action based on preferences and knowledge.[10] And because of this, the individual lays claim to certain rights (i.e., freedom and equality) against coercion from external social forces.

A second premise then emerges, coupled to the first. This is that the self is in principle prior to the social. If rational autonomy produces parity among individuals, who then choose to cooperate as a collective unit, the freedom to determine one's life based upon self-interest is original; it precedes the social contract. Indeed, the ideal society is one that carves out maximal space for individuals to pursue their own perceived interests and ends without external encumbrances. Independent rational reflection not only provides resources for efficiently pursuing such interests, but in the process also indicates the need to join together with others in order to insure the freedom and equality necessary to protect and preserve the right to self-determination. Why? Because of inconveniences that occur without it (Locke), or because the greed, vanity, and selfishness of some can run amuck and infect the social world, consolidating power for their own self-interest and thus denying the freedom of others (Hobbes). So, on behalf of its own interest the individual agrees to curtail some interests vis-à-vis the presence of other individuals with their own interests, consenting to participate in a civic structure aimed at sustaining the most open and effective environment for all to pursue their own ends. In other words, we are free to define and shape our own lives to the degree that this does not infringe upon the rights of others to do the same. All persons have the same basic moral status. And the just society will embody this in reality. Again, we can see how freedom, equality, and independence are connected at the root.

A third premise can be drawn out of the second. That is, the liberal picture of the human person strongly differentiates between the private sphere of the individual and the public sphere of collaborative cooperation. If the self is given precedence over the social, then the private sphere of an individual's good has priority and the public good is derivative. Society is a secondary good required to guarantee private good. In fact, civic responsibility arises from self-interest. The public space essentially exists to provide space for the individual to choose freely the private life she or he prefers. Extreme versions of this, such as libertarianism, go so far as to say that society has no right to interfere with such free choice unless it violates the freedom of others to follow their chosen course of action. But even in less extreme forms, the liberal conception of public moral space is minimalist and primarily negative. It lets liberty reign unchecked until the symmetry of equality is threatened. Only then can societal mechanisms be put into play to curb the actions of some and insure the liberty of others. For example, on the basis of rational autonomy, unequal treatment or discrimination on the basis of gender, race, ethnicity, class, and religion is considered morally culpable. Inequality and injustice occur when the private domain oversteps its boundaries, when the self-interested considerations of some people coerce or displace others. Therefore the moral authority of state government and the public debate that surrounds it is grounded in the value of the private sphere. And this value stems from a respect for the freedom, equality, and independence of all persons. In sum, civic and public space is moral insofar as it carries out the charge to protect the rights of individuals.[11]

All of this culminates in a final premise, that of the inherent dignity of the human being. Since society is deemed an association of free, equal, and independent agents, the authority of the individual is fundamental. By "authority" I mean the power to ascribe meaning, value, and direction. This power renders the person a self-authenticating source of his or her own life-script. And insofar as it is potentially brought into cooperative ventures with others, the person becomes a citizen entitled to certain inviolable rights. Such a capacity marks a shared and essential trait among all human beings, underlying the well-known language of human dignity.

Outlined then in these premises, and culminating in the notion of dignity, are the morally charged contours of what it means to be a person. In a nutshell, the liberal Enlightenment picture of the person portrays an autonomous and self-determining individual capable of entering into social collaboration on the basis of rational self-interest. Reason is that which enables us to govern our own lives in the private sphere, and reach agreement with others in the public sphere. And its benchmark is autonomy. Politically conceived, reason allows the independent agent to discern that the interests of others must be taken into account along with his or her own interests. This kind of respect for others makes us citizens.

Moreover, it makes us moral agents, such that we acknowledge others as persons—that is, as rational agents deserving the private right to self-determination (freedom) and the public right to participate in cooperative strategies that take account of and coordinate their self-interests with others (equality). And from here follows the moral principle suggested by Emmanuel Kant in his famous second categorical imperative, namely, that a person should not be treated as a means to an end, as an instrument defined by the self-interest of other people. Stated positively, this means that the human being should be regarded as an end, a value in itself.[12] It follows, then, insofar as they are woven into the fabric of human personhood, that freedom, equality, and independence are also ends, values inherent to human dignity that must be preserved. A life without these is not worthy of dignity. This underlies Kant's concept of duty and moral obligation, which cannot simply be reduced to self-interest.

II. Problems with Equality, Freedom, Independence, and Reason

However, we must be careful about what we have said above. True, much good has been accomplished under the auspices of liberal conceptions of rational freedom, equality, and independence. For instance, these ideals have emboldened minority groups to mobilize and champion neglected civil rights and liberties, thus opening up new spaces in society for the participation of all people. Regarding disability, this has had beneficial consequences. It highlights the rights of persons with disabilities to a normal life, fostering the worthy goal of integration into daily routines and activities by and large available only to non-disabled people. Advocacy groups have thus come to charge society with the responsibility of removing obstacles that prevent people with disabilities from engaging in public life and freely defining themselves. In turn, this has helped to reduce the restrictions imposed by the medical model, namely its dehumanizing paternalism and institutionalized bureaucratic focus. Government policies directed toward "normalization" have increasingly come to entitle people with disabilities equal access to educational, employment, and family opportunities. Despite cultivating these gains, however, there are deeply problematic assumptions at work in the liberal way of measuring personhood. And these merit scrutiny, especially as they surreptitiously become vehicles of disempowerment for people with disabilities.

Ironic Equality—Like "Us"

First, let us explore the notion of equality. "Equality" is a comparative term that connotes a similarity between things. But this can be dangerous. Stanley Hauerwas puts the problem bluntly: "Often the language of equality only works by reducing us to a common denominator that can be repressive or disrespectful."[13] Why repressive or disrespectful? Because equality implies a sameness and parity between individuals that homogenizes individual differences, washing them away on the tides of normalcy. A paradox is introduced. On the one hand, the ideal of equality promotes the sense that the other is like me in some fundamental sense and therefore deserves to be treated similarly—that is, included as a member of the group. On the other hand, this very awareness can rob the other of his or her uniqueness, projecting an image of sameness onto the other, even to the point of demanding that the other become like me, like us.

The danger here works on two levels. First, real differences can become disqualified, trivialized, and rendered inconsequential to our identity as persons. Yet among the vulnerable in society not everyone is the same. For instance, this particular person with disabilities has specific needs that cannot be addressed adequately if all are treated equally as cases to be handled impartially. Some people wind up being treated more favorably than others, which ironically produces inequity. Eva Feder Kittay puts it nicely:

> We like to think that equality is an inclusive ideal; that its inherent dynamic is to progressively encompass a wider and wider range of individuals. Yet equality always excludes *some* as it includes *others*. When one group defines itself as composed of equals, it so defines itself against those who are not its members. Even the most inclusive conception of equality—the equality of all persons—excludes the nonperson.[14]

Accordingly, we must ask whether and how people who are very young, ill, disabled, or elderly are to be included under the concept of equality. Are they "not yet equal," "soon to be equal," or altogether "not equal"?[15] "Equality" is a term relative to what full humanity is alleged to be, which can be coopted by the cult of normalcy.

The second danger follows: differences can become pressed to conform to standardized conventions and then assimilated. Not only is equality relative, it is a slippery ideal, its application all too often falling short of its intended effect. For in the name of equality a social power can be bandied that pressures minorities to accept the dominant culture's definition of who they are. None of us, quips

Hauerwas, "want to be treated equally if that means we lose our distinctiveness."[16] Given this, it becomes important for us to inquire into whose equality we are talking about. Are we referring to white, middle-class, and able-bodied males? Does this then mean that African Americans need to leave the distinctness of their heritage behind in order to participate in the public forum as equals, an equality defined by white culture? Does it mean that women must become like men? Does it mean that people with disabilities should be made to act (as much as possible) like able-bodied people? As may be obvious, there is an uneasy alliance between how we understand equality and how we ritualize normalcy. Equality can be one way that the cult of normalcy, masquerading as fairness, designates body capital and controls those bodies whose differences are deemed deviant. Ironically, then, equality can be made to serve the status quo, a tool for the dominant group to wield power.[17]

The result is either assimilation through processes of normalization or exclusion through processes of marginalization or confinement. Yes, normalization can be productive for people with disabilities in the private sphere of daily life. But in the public sphere it resonates in ways that can suppress uniqueness and difference. After all, as we saw in the last chapter, persons are recognized according to their place in a collective web of relationships. And if all are presumed to be the same, this can have a flattening effect that actually serves to regulate or restrict those bodies deemed incapable of reflecting normalcy. It is clear that we need some kind of leverage to preserve and celebrate differences as equal, not merely tolerating differences insofar as they can become equal, or like us.

Ironic Self-sufficiency and Freedom—Dis-abling Ability?

With this we are brought to a second troubling feature of the liberal picture of the human person: independent autonomy. On the surface, this ideal proves basic to processes that liberate individuals and groups from involuntary submission to authorities and customs. It means private freedom from public tyranny, from being forcibly measured or governed by others, what Kant called "heteronomy." For persons with disabilities, it means freedom from restricted access to public life and, further, the freedom for self-definition apart from societal projections. But such freedom comes with a heavy price. Underlying notions of self-determination and independence are disconcerting assumptions that threaten to subvert the otherwise positive gains they foster.

First, it is presumed that the individual is self-sufficient and prior to society, having a dignity and self-directed character that precedes the relationships that tie her or him to a social world. This is a false abstraction. It so privileges the individual's independence from others that personhood is reduced to formal capacities, such as the ability to choose without encumbrance from another. However, as many feminist writers have countered, human abilities are never simply givens, ready from the start; the capacity to make choices arises and is cultivated by others within a relational web of interdependence.[18] In fact, these relationships and the way they play out in larger social contexts shape the development of who we are. Recall Charles Taylor's idea of frameworks discussed in the last chapter. Human beings do not simply come forward as self-sufficient and complete individuals from a place outside of a social world. The individual becomes a person only in the presence of others. So it is relational connection and not solely independence that defines our lives and shapes our desires and interests. The idea of an autonomous and self-constituting person is an illusion. It neglects the role community has in identity formation. Relation with others is primary, not secondary.

In developing this point, a further assumption plagues the notion of autonomy. The important function of dependence in human life is overlooked, so much so that the ideal of separate self-sufficiency dominates our conceptions of health and wholeness. This is ironic given that autonomy is an overblown abstraction. From the beginning of life onwards we depend upon others. Even so, in our society we are trained from early on to be self-reliant and independent, capable of meeting our own needs and defining our own values. Dependence upon others is often deemed a moral, developmental, or biological failure, a passivity denigrating human life. We come to regret limitations and weaknesses, and indeed often view them in terms of being victimized by powers not of our own making.[19] The display of neediness becomes a source of shame, something to be hidden from others. That is, in the presence of others whose bodies demonstrate more "autonomy"—more ability to exert control over their bodies—we feel helpless and seek to cover our weakness, instead acting strong, complete, active, and independent. Accordingly, we come to expect this in others. Such autonomy seems required to enter the public sphere of full cooperation among equal and self-directed individuals.[20] As Kittay observes, "the ideology of equality relies on a vision of autonomous individuals who stand outside relations of dependency."[21]

Public life in our society tends to operate according to what Hauerwas calls an "ideology for the strong."[22] It is strength that is deemed normative for free social cooperation, at least cooperation that is mutually advantageous—and strength is defined as being in possession of oneself, of one's bodily faculties. This is precisely why illness and disability are often swept into the corner of individuals' private lives. Active participation in the public sphere is alleged to require the body capital of full-capacity independence.[23] Bodies that exhibit less than autonomous functioning are relegated to dependency-based institutions—homes, hospitals, or other facilities equipped to care for and remediate bodily dysfunction. Their vulnerability marks a deficiency, a stigma to be normalized or removed from public life. It thus becomes possible to see how, committed to the ideal of autonomy, healthcare practices can become dehumanizing for persons with disabilities. Insofar as society follows a paradigm of the human that equates health and wholeness with self-determination, non-disabled people are allowed to determine the needs of those without the body capital of strength and independence. "We" know what is good for "them," for we are fully free and they are not. The dependent cannot assume the burdens of social cooperation.[24] This kind of able-bodied ideology underlies the paternalistic character of the medical model, and it grants full sway to the cult of normalcy.

Kittay offers a masterful assessment of so-called autonomy vis-à-vis what she calls a "dependency critique."[25] She decries the neglect of relationships of dependency in modern social and political theories. This omission is particularly glaring when we take note of how ubiquitous dependency is in human life. Objectively, many people spend a great part of their lives physically dependent upon others. For example, we spend the first two decades of our lives being trained to become independent members of society, and increasingly spend the last decades of our lives tethered to life-supporting medical care of some sort or another. Moreover, despite advances in medical technology, serious disabling conditions prevent some 10 percent of the population from being fully cooperating members of society. Further still, on a subjective level we are all dependent emotionally upon others for well-being. This is not something freely chosen; and it affects our needs and desires—our self-interests—from the root. Human beings need to care for and be cared for by those who are significant and close to them.[26] There is a persistent craving for welcome built into our lives together. And this is incapable of being relegated to the private sphere alone.

Dependency relationships spill over into public life. For example, caregivers— those whom Kittay calls "dependency workers," such as mothers—are charged with responsibilities that naturally shape activities or allegiances that are neither strictly voluntary nor marked by self-interest.[27] Privileging the ideal of autonomy simply glosses over these basic facts, artificially narrowing the conception of what it means to be human. It assumes that caring for others is a calculated and detached achievement, a self-originating and freely chosen effacement of self-interest. Certainly, parenting falls outside the scope of this understanding, as does caring for family members with disabilities. Even more problematic, privileging autonomy assumes dependency is a distortion of freedom, a lack of functionality that merits restriction to the private sphere. Kittay suggests that it assumes that all individuals are equally situated and independent, able to "act from an elevated self-interest" and engage each other with "mutual disinterest." This fails to account for the fact of dependency in human life and the moral commitments of those who care for chronically dependent persons.[28] For people with disabilities, then, the ideal of autonomy is a double-edged sword that threatens to nullify its otherwise laudable intentions.

Ironically Rational—Routing the Irrational (Reason-unable?)

Related to the above, a third problem with the liberal vision of the person comes to the fore which stems from prioritizing the rational. As portrayed by Kant and other authors associated with the European Enlightenment, autonomy is a sail filled by the wind of reason. The ideal of human dignity, in fact, trades on the presumption that all human beings have a rational will that is capable of governing itself. But what does it mean to be rational? Essentially, the term has come to designate the capacity for a range of activities, the most prominent of which are conceptual thought, language, goal-directedness, and self-determination. These criteria can be boiled down to three skills: first, the ability to understand the world and choose a course of action independent of and without determination by others; second, the ability to recognize that the interests of others need also to be taken into account; third, in light of the first criteria and by way of the second, a more subtle possibility emerges, namely, the ability to recognize objective and universal truths in principle shared by all humans.

Kant's categorical imperative stands as a classic example of how the first two skills open up into the third, compelling humans to act in the most impartial and universalizable manner possible in every instance, in every context. In fact, elsewhere Kant describes the universal human man as one who has a "broadened way of thinking if he overrides the private subjective conditions of his judgment, into which so many others are locked, as it were, and reflects on his own judgment from a universal standpoint (which he can determine only by transferring himself to the standpoint of others)."[29] Reason can be self-authenticating and autonomous because it empowers the individual to direct freely the course of his or her life, and do so according to communicable terms amenable to all people. It is thus the source of public agreement and social cooperation. In this way, the rational person arrives at an objective universal standpoint and is thus empowered to participate in civic life, moderating thoughts and actions accordingly.

By these standards, however, we must ask: "Who is fully rational?" If human independence occurs prior to the social, it would seem that, ideally, we all are at base rational creatures. And indeed, this has become one of the most cherished assumptions of liberal society. Unfortunately, however, it runs counter to the empirical data. Not everyone operates with the clear-mindedness Kant seems to advocate. To be fair to Kant, we must note that he is referring to an ideal, speaking of what it means to be rational and not claiming that everyone shares equally in this capacity. Nonetheless, the ideal falls well short of the reality. Young children, and people with low IQ, autism, developmental disabilities, or Alzheimer's disease, provide examples that mitigate rational objectivity. Not only do these persons have difficulty acting according to a universally appropriate sense of duty, in many cases they cannot recognize, communicate with, or take adequate account of the interests of others in order to collaborate in mutually advantageous ways. What should we make of this fact? What is the moral standing of someone "lacking" in the skills of reason? Is the autistic person, for instance, not fully dignified as a human being, unequal in status to non-autistic human beings? Is the developmentally disabled person incapable of cooperating socially as a full citizen with rights and entitlements, relegated instead to the private sector of dependency, reliant on the care of "rationally able" people? These kinds of questions raise the difficulties with privileging rational ability.[30]

The ability to reason is a cherished commodity among modern human beings, so much so that its loss or dysfunction is often perceived as a form of suffering that should be avoided or remedied. However, as Hauerwas argues, this oversimplifies the matter. To be sure, suffering warrants prevention. Some forms of impairment do involve levels of physical pain that ought to be alleviated. But is it the case, asks Hauerwas, that suffering should always be forestalled, and if possible, eliminated? The issue becomes complex when we consider people whose rational capacities are deemed deficient or absent, as with autism or developmental disabilities.[31] Are these examples of a kind of suffering that is so dehumanizing that it should be prevented? And if this suffering cannot be treated, would it be better, "for their own sake," if people with such disabilities did not exist? Serious ethical questions are at stake, and they concern whether certain kinds of children should be born and whether certain kinds of impairments merit the termination of life. Debates over eugenics and euthanasia are fueled by such quandaries. Is human life ever unworthy of itself, so degraded that, for the sake of humane care, it deserves to be eradicated? Obviously there are treacherous implications here, recalling nightmarish genocidal horrors and ill-advised eugenic efforts to perfect the human race. Yet subtle harm is also done if certain kinds of disabilities are measured according to the yardstick of rationality and treated accordingly as a form of suffering.

Again, the cult of normalcy is at work, in this instance judging human differences according to the normalizing criterion of reason. If the capacity for reason is considered an ideal for the fully functioning person, it seems natural then to decry its privation or absence as a form of suffering, making it an urgent category of prevention. For, to invoke Hauerwas, we "try to prevent those kinds of suffering that we do not feel can serve any human good."[32] However, the logic here is deceptively circular. It trades on a framework that presumes rational thought to be the benchmark for serving human good. Consequently, the temptation is to project our assumptions about how we might feel, as "rational" people, in the situation of someone with autism or developmental disabilities. But we are not in their situation. We do not know if or how much they suffer.[33] Yet we make judgments as if we do, attributing to them our own discomfort in their presence, which covers up our own inability to grant their presence and simply be present with them. In the name of reason, we rob persons with disabilities of their own distinctness and difference. Hauerwas thus concludes: "The strong stress on the value of intelligence as the necessary condition for all human activity faithfully mirrors the loyalties of our society." And so we fail to notice that such a criterion really constitutes a goal "through which we manipulate and destroy some for the good of the 'normal.'"[34]

In reaction, many scholars of the so-called postmodern ilk have challenged the modern way of depicting reason and over-esteeming its capacities. For instance, Michel Foucault argues that, despite its claim to impartiality and neutrality, reason is in actuality one more way that dominant social powers have strategically defined the human person in order to rationalize agendas meant to control.[35] According to this view, reason is not autonomous, neither universal nor objective, but instead a cultural-historical construction serving specific interests. It feigns universality to achieve calculated ends, and hence must be exposed for what it is—a technique of power.

Foucault's argument is not new, but builds upon a long twentieth-century tradition that is suspicious of the Enlightenment's way of aggrandizing reason. Characterizing this suspicion as a "rage against reason," Richard Bernstein marks an increasing focus on "images of domination, oppression, repression, patriarchy, sterility, violence, totality, totalitarianism, and even terror" in connection with reasons which not so long ago "elicited associations with autonomy, freedom, justice, equality, happiness, and peace."[36] Any system of communication that claims objectivity and universality is suspect, for it inadvertently works to regulate and so homogenize, distort, suffocate, marginalize, and/or enslave differences. How so? By suppressing the concrete and plural dimensions of human life, reducing everything to a rationalized sameness that empties the world of all but instrumental value. This is not what the Enlightenment intended, but it is one of its more pernicious consequences. Whether as state socialism, fascism, market capitalism, or the empirical sciences, rationalism has the capacity to systematically impose itself on and turn everything into a compliant object.[37] This produces an "instrumental reason." And the end product is domination, which legitimates societal and economic systems built on the calculability, abstract equivalence, and exchangeability of things and persons.[38]

We shall shortly explore this in the case of market capitalism. But for now, it is important to see how reason is implicated in the cult of normalcy. Ironically, it becomes a tool of the coercive and irrational, a technique of productivity and standardization in the service of mass control and manipulation. Contrary to Kant's intention, the person becomes a means to an end. An example is what critical theorists Max Horkheimer and Theodor Adorno called the "culture industry," where individual things and persons are commodified and given value—capital—only insofar as they have a generalized, functional purpose in facilitating, reproducing, and administering the ideology of the status quo. For these authors, rational activity all too easily becomes slave to economic forces, for "the basis on which technology acquires power over society is the power of those whose economic hold over society is greatest."[39] Even technology, then, can be seen as a reifying ideology, repressing differences by turning rational thought into an instrument that "objectifies itself to become an automatic, self-activating process; an impersonation of the machine that produces itself so that ultimately the machine can replace it."[40] Reason winds up becoming dehumanizing, a vehicle of manipulation and mastery in the name of scientific objectivity.[41]

These are trenchant criticisms. And while we might not go as far as Foucault or Horkheimer and Adorno, they help us expose and shake us loose from the negative consequences brought on by privileging the rational and independent self. At the core is a fundamental point: it is social matrices of interdependency that are primary, not the autonomous and self-originating claims and preferences of the solitary person. The attributes of reason are socially composed, arising in the context of relationships. The ideal of rational autonomy is then an illusion that goes against the grain of how we actually come to negotiate and understand our place in the world. For, as Charles Taylor would say, human beings are caught up in an original situation of interdependence.[42] Hauerwas expresses the same point: "Our rational ability is not the prior principle of our moral activity, for we are able to reason because we are fundamentally social beings."[43] Rational thought is not something a separate "I" has; it is a communal event, a "we-based" phenomenon. Human beings are not private, independent selves who happen to be joined with others along the way. Certainly there are other conceptions of rationality that take into account this fact.[44] Nonetheless, anthropologies that prioritize the rational as a capacity for impartiality and objectivity generally alienate persons from the basic relational matrix on which they depend.

A stress on the rational also tends to favor the mind over the body. And the consequence is an instrumental view of human bodies. That is, it treats the body as a tool to be used and harnessed according to rationally calculated ends. Coupled with the consumer-oriented materialism that dominates North American culture, this can be particularly damaging for the way we think about disability.

III. Managing the Body: The Productive Imperative

We now turn our attention to the ways that liberal ideals like freedom, equality, and rational autonomy line up with economic ideas to foster attitudes and practices that domesticate bodies, turning them into instruments subordinate to the ideal of utility. There were glimpses of such connections above, but it is necessary to unpack them here in more depth to notice the extent of their hold on how we measure disability. Indeed, there is a cluster of problematic values that congeal around what can be called the *productive imperative*. By this I mean to indicate a kind of sociocultural obligation that pressures human bodies to exhibit qualities and perform in ways that are useful and thus generate capital. This is mediated specifically by market-driven economies. It steers consumer culture by underwriting the normative status of individual preferences and the capacity to purchase goods. The productive imperative trades upon commitment to a set of ideals that disenfranchises persons with disabilities: namely, wealth accumulation, efficiency, novelty, consumer purchase power, and youthful beauty and potency. Each of these ideals, I shall argue, helps prop up the framework housing the cult of normalcy in North American society.

Wealth Accumulation

Instead of depicting the full range of human capabilities as normal, the productive imperative reduces the spectrum of normality to a thin margin: that is, the ability to produce wealth. Here, to employ language developed in the last chapter, acquiring the body capital to purchase recognition by others in an economy of exchange means achieving material success. And purchase power is gained via the productivity of labor. Lennard Davis puts it succinctly: "Value is tied to the ability to earn money; if one's body is productive, it is not disabled." Davis also points out that, strikingly, disability in this context is not gradual or graded—it is an absolute or totalizing category.[45] It sums up a person, designating whether or not productivity is possible.

This places an unwieldy distance between the non-disabled and people with disabilities, between the fully functional and the somehow dysfunctional. Kittay suggests that such asymmetry is the result of the normative standing of independence or autonomy, which forces the need for welfare as a compromise between capitalism and democracy. It is worth quoting her at length:

> Within a market economy, the satisfaction of needs, the creation of needs, and the negotiation of what constitutes need is tied to one's participation in a relation of reciprocity between the production of wealth and its consumption. To participate in such a reciprocal relation is to be involved in social cooperation which is requisite for citizenship. This participation is marked first and foremost by labor that is compensated in wages and salaries. It defines "independent." To stand outside these reciprocal arrangements reduces one to the status of dependent, and as someone dependent on an individual, a charity, or the state.[46]

Welfare is designed to alleviate the poverty that results from dependency. As poverty is both morally unacceptable and politically destabilizing, various agencies and policies seek to redistribute wealth to mitigate it. However, this can undermine a citizen's sense of participation in the community, and so undermine their sense of self-worth.[47] It also leaves unchallenged the way that the status quo and its economy of exchange marginalizes people. Yet, as Kittay rejoins, the creation of needed jobs can impede the "autonomous functioning of the market," disrupting "the machine that generates wealth." Such disruption, in turn, can end up fostering the view that poverty somehow involves a "characterological flaw." Those who are dependent and rely on public assistance must be morally faulted, abnormally weak, or dysfunctional, for otherwise—so the logic goes—they would be able to get a job.[48]

This is an excellent example of the productive imperative at work. It is simply assumed that normal and functional bodies—that is, complete, whole, or healthy— will be able to participate independently in the public process of generating capital. And if not, according to the norms of productivity, they must be rehabilitated (normalized) and rendered capable of doing so via medical or therapeutic technologies. Or in worst-case scenarios they should be restricted to dependent care outside the mainstream, essentially shamed by their weakness. Never mind that systemic barriers may be preventing social access for certain kinds of bodies, barriers that serve the interests of some and not others (i.e., non-disabled, white, middle-class, male, and so on). Addressing these barriers, in the case of disability, requires examining other values that cluster around the productive imperative, values that strengthen its power to inform how we think about human bodies and their value in productive terms, thus contributing to the marginalization of persons with disabilities. For disabilities might not exist, quips Hauerwas, "in a society that values cooperation more than competition and ambition."[49]

Efficiency—A Competitive Edge on Time

Efficiency is perhaps the most predominant value of the productive imperative. The ideal body is efficient, capable of producing and consuming capital at a tempo that contributes to the ongoing societal mechanism of wealth creation. With the rise of industrial capitalism in the late nineteenth century, the change to mechanized systems of production brought about a dramatic shift in labor expectation. The speed of factory work required the labor capacity to perform in a time-sensitive manner.[50] In our present post-industrial era, with its reliance upon computer technology, performance expectations are linked more directly with effective and timely information exchange. Each context, however, relies upon the ideal of efficiency, the former dependent upon certain physical abilities and the latter upon mental and communicative abilities. Both in their own way contribute to the displacement of persons with disabilities by treating the body as an instrument, a means to an end.

Accordingly, the effective use of time and resources becomes a measure of human labor. Body capital is thus appraised in terms of efficiency, the capacity to do more with less. The efficient is the productive, and vice versa. In a competitive market, time and material resources are goods that are alleged to be scarce, for the corporation has to outdo its rivals to gain a productive edge and generate capital. An economic social Darwinism ensues, where the ability to survive depends upon the capacity to employ resources in the most rapid, streamlined, and cost-effective way possible. The use of technology and human labor as resources in the service of economic survival is based upon functional performance; that is, how well they make possible competitive advantage and, ultimately, profit. Adaptability and mobility become key elements in this process. Indeed, they are the signposts of efficiency, indicating the capacity to respond quickly to market changes.

Like technology, human bodies must be efficient, "managing" time and resources according to rational calculations aimed at achieving advantage. And as the process continues the pace quickens. It is no wonder that North American life consists of constant movement. We are socialized into frenetic activity, perceiving time as a scarce commodity to be itemized by pocket calendars and detailed agendas. Indeed, we expect each other to be experts in controlling how we use time. But to control the use of time, we must control our bodies, fining tuning them for maximum output with minimal expenditure. We train our bodies to produce instantaneous results. Speed is a key ingredient of efficiency. In this way, the ideal of efficiency instrumentalizes bodies as a time-managing resource in the generation of capital. The ironic twist, however, is that by managing time and resources more efficiently, our freedom and individuality themselves become managed. We accede to the external demands of the economic machine, as tools to be used more productively and more effectively. Human beings become instruments, utilities coordinated by corporations to obtain maximal growth in capital with minimal expenditure. The body is a commodity, assigned an exchange value according to its ability to produce and respond quickly and effectively.

As may be obvious, this system operates as a cult of normalcy. It compels persons to remake and streamline their bodies again and again in the image of conventions tied to productive efficiency. A version of the free, independent, and rational person we discussed earlier is created, only now it is fine-tuned to fit market demands. Body capital is measured according to one's usefulness, one's proficiency in entering into cooperative ventures trained upon gaining mutual advantage. A person gets only by having something useful to offer. He must be marketable, forced to package and "sell" himself. She must promote herself in ways that fit the demands of the marketplace, for the person is a commodity to be purchased—an investment. And in order to "pay dividends" for the investor—that is, the employer—he or she must be able to adapt effectively to shifting circumstances requiring immediate responses. An entire feedback loop is engendered under the auspices of efficiency. The competitive market demands efficiency; efficiency feeds the market.

It goes without saying that efficiency is an ideal that cannot help but marginalize people with disabilities. The rapid pace it fosters is, in fact, one way that disability is social constructed. And it leaves many behind (e.g., the aged, the physically and developmentally impaired) who are unable to be re-made in the image of efficiency.[51] The lack of immediate adaptability and expeditious mobility is seen as a liability to keeping the competitive edge. It is understandable, then, that medical care becomes focused on bodily repair and upkeep. The human body is an instrument that must be kept in top shape to remain competitive, acquiring value as a commodity to be purchased and used in the workplace. It is also understandable how developmental disabilities such as dyslexia, along with depression, hypertension, arthritis, and so on, become disabling conditions. When productive efficiency reigns as the paradigm for normalcy, tasks must be performed with maximum cost-effectiveness.

This shapes our thinking about medical care too. While technology has increased the capability to treat patients with more effective care, the concomitant professionalizing and specialization of care is often depersonalizing. The patient becomes tantamount to a technical problem to be managed efficiently. Humanly sensitive care, involving costly resources (such as people) and time (such as patience), is replaced by new cutting-edge approaches to quick problem solving. After all, insurance companies will only pay so much for care, and the health industry has streamlined to accommodate. With this, we come upon another productive ideal.

Novelty—The Tyranny of the New

In a fast-paced and ever-shifting economic environment change is normative. In fact, change becomes esteemed as a positive value, a symptom of growth and the ability to adapt and stay competitive. It is seen as a good that breeds novel opportunities and more effective means of capital accumulation. But in a market setting characterized by efficiency, the new becomes converted into an end in itself, a way of being productive and instep with change. Only now, rather than a response to change, the novel and innovative is deliberately sought after and cultivated. Novelty is better. It anticipates change and thus beats change at its own game, creating market trends instead of reacting to them. So novelty becomes an attribute of commodities with the power to acquire value and generate economic growth. And such growth means staying on the cutting edge, being innovative. The inventive entrepreneur reigns supreme.

Within this mindset persons are caught up in an ongoing process of restyling themselves, remaking and retooling their bodies in light of new and possible future trends. The body becomes an instrument measured by its plasticity and adaptability to the constantly shifting landscape of innovation. Entrepreneurship means new skills must be learned, new ways of presenting oneself tried out, and new ways of thinking assimilated. Interestingly, novelty in this regard represents a key element in the so-called American spirit of pragmatic ingenuity and inventiveness. After all, the United States is the great experiment marking progress toward future perfection.[52] The new is the ideal, marking fresh opportunities. Simply recapitulating past successes is not the way forward into vitalizing growth; rather, embarking into the future is. And the body is an instrument employed to make this possible. We can remake ourselves; we can become better.

While this sounds like optimism on the surface, it actually signifies a deep existential restlessness with the contingencies and limitations of finite human life. Part of this is tied to the modern reaction to what it claimed was servitude to tradition. In the form of the European Enlightenment, modernity represented a liberating break from the tyranny of an authoritative past. New forms of thinking sought to break free from traditional ways of understanding human life which were alleged to hold individuals captive to superstition, ignorance, and intolerance. For a thinker like Kant, true freedom meant daring to think rationally and define one's own life without encumbrance by tradition.[53] Society and culture could no longer simply be a matter of embodying an exemplary past, for this restricted rational autonomy and reduced human thinking and behavior to mere repetition. Hence, dissociated from the normative past, the future became a place of promise, a horizon of expectation. And this future is built by autonomous, rational, and self-creating human beings.[54] We are in control of our destiny. Connected with the burgeoning sciences, this meant a newfound mastery of nature. Connected with the American spirit, from early days onward it meant independence from authority, both collectively and individually. Connected with market capitalism and late nineteenth-century industrialization, it also meant a potentially unlimited future of wealth generation, in which free competition between producers of resources will foster mutual advantage for all participants.

However, problems abound. First, innovation does not always facilitate benefit for all. This is especially true in the market economy. Entrepreneurship does not foster the freedom and mutually advantageous future it promises. In many cases competitive industrial and corporate wealth generation has proven harmful to social and environmental well-being. Not all people flourish under these conditions. Indeed, if we consider contemporary global demographics, very few do.[55] Why?

In part, second, because novelty as self-creative autonomy is an illusion that excludes. It is an illusion in that no one—no "body"—is truly independent of others. Indeed, human beings become who they are, developing as individuals, in networks of dependency which thrive precisely because of cultural heritages and traditions, the very same traditions that innovative freedom and productivity feigns to overcome or recreate. Accordingly, novelty excludes because a great many people cannot constantly remake themselves in the service of production and growth. This not only creates lack of opportunity, it also socially constructs the category of disability. As an ideal emerging from the productive imperative, novelty for the sake of competitive advantage is a form of tyranny that serves the cult of normalcy. It constructs the human person as a rationally self-interested commodity, an instrument in the industry of wealth generation. It may increase economic activity, but the price is high—the management and manipulation of bodies in the service of future opportunities, opportunities that exist only for some. Inventive autonomy and entrepreneurship may suggest freedom, but it in fact obligates all to performance standards that enslave.

Thus, third, market novelty ironically constrains the freedom and rationality it extols, limiting their scope to the pursuit of economic growth, which is treated equivalent to human flourishing. And it does this, in turn, by treating bodies as consumption driven. The focus on wealth accumulation trades upon an understanding of the person as self-interested consumer, one who is directed toward maximizing satisfaction.

The Person as Consumer—Empowered to Purchase

Here the productive imperative shows its commitment to principles dear to social contract theories. Private self-interest is prioritized as the bedrock of public good. Why? Because in market capitalism it is the individual's free choice to benefit him or herself that gives rise to collective competition, out of which rises the need for greater efficiency and innovation in producing further resources which, in turn, create greater opportunity for profit, benefiting individuals. The process is circular, fueled by the desire for private satisfaction and well-being. Commercial success depends upon satisfying private inclinations, yielding more public production and further satisfaction by acquisition. Thus it is that capitalist economic systems traffic in a symbiotic relationship between the production and consumption of resources. The marketplace provides the greatest good for the greatest number.

In such a scheme the person is a consumer, defined by the ability to purchase goods and contribute to ongoing economic growth. But the result is that market principles seep their way into virtually all aspects of human life. Freedom becomes synonymous with unconstrained choice, and choice becomes a factor of rationally calculated preferences that are played out in the consumption of goods. That which has value is purchased as a commodity whose end it is to satisfy individual needs. Writ large, anything has value insofar as it can serve preferences—cars, food, trees, animals, and even people. And this is another example of how the consumer becomes a commodity, an instrument to be used in the further generation of profit. Our worth is ascribed in an economy of exchange which identifies what resources or goods we have to offer. If we cannot accumulate wealth, we cannot purchase. And if we cannot purchase, we do not contribute fuel to the economic engine. We are, in effect, worthless apart from serving the productive sector—specifically, the marketplace.

At this point a further dynamic comes into play. Consumption is based upon preferences, which are based upon needs and desires. But for economic growth to occur there must be more consumption, requiring more needs and desires. Because they are fed by consumer desire (demand), producers of goods must encourage such desire, engendering a sense of need among consumers if they are to remain viable competitors. Tragically, this further objectifies the consumer, who becomes nothing more than an agent with purchase power in the eyes of industrial and corporate manufacturers. It is no accident that the advertising industry, relying upon media technology, is such an important component of capitalist economies. For not only do goods need to be publicized, they also need to be peddled and received as valuable, preferred by consumers. Advertising creates desire, stimulating appeal by calling attention to some good over others. Is it any wonder that the ideal product, the one with appeal, is the efficient and new, the cost-effective and novel? Such commodities grab interest; they "want" to be possessed. And this fosters further consumption, and subsequently further production, all in an ever-extending feedback loop trained upon satisfying individual self-interest. Consumers, then, are socialized by advertisements. Their rational self-interest is trained to prefer—indeed, fetishize—the effective and the innovative, summoned to invest more capital into the production of more and more goods. Of course this necessitates further advertisements to create additional desires for more possessions.

The logic of consumption is one-sided and nefarious when unrestrained. It manufactures desire and fashions docile bodies easily manipulated to serve the industry of wealth creation. Personal worth is an attribute of what possessions one has acquired. Being means having, body capital measured according to acquisitive potential. Thinking like this serves the cult of normalcy. How so? By promoting a sense of dissatisfaction that is two-sided: both as an impression of need—not yet having enough—and as one of scarcity, that there may not be enough to satisfy. The feedback loop between consumption and production leads us to believe that we need more in order to be fulfilled. We experience ourselves as competitors for resources deemed scarce, compulsively driven to acquire them, even if they are not necessary. New, bigger, better, and more efficient—these become catchwords in the manufacturing of needs and desires. The person becomes fashioned in the image of the marketplace. Desires and values are reduced to commodities. The attributes of a fulfilled life—like friendship, love, joy, humor, and play—turn into marketable commodities, objects we can buy among competing alternatives.[56] Human freedom becomes unconstrained purchase power, rationality becomes preference calculation, and equality becomes the homogeneous and docile consumer.

Why homogeneous and docile? Because in reality we are not self-sufficient and independent creatures. Human beings crave worth and fear the lack of worth, so we seek recognition and welcome by those around us. It is thus our insecurity that tempts us. In our anxiety we become willing captives to normalizing conventions and ideals. In North American market capitalism the cult of normalcy functions to ritualize consumerism, making who we are equivalent to what we have. Transformed into the image of our products our lives become domesticated. Self-determined interests are really those that the market has projected onto us. As we saw earlier, this is precisely what Horkheimer and Adorno decried about what they termed the "instrumental reason" of the "culture industry"—that is, persons become managed things whose value exists only in the facilitation, reproduction, and administration of consuming and producing. Human beings are the same; they exist to feed the market.

A tragic irony comes to the fore. We are made to serve a market whose stated purpose is to serve us. Rather than being nourished, our individual freedom is actually diminished. We become docile consumers habituated to self-indulgence. And this makes us pliable, willing subjects of market forces, in the end conceding what is allegedly held in the highest esteem—our freedom. Far from being free choosers, we become managed by an economic system that keeps us from promised well-being and satisfaction by rousing new cravings directed toward innovative, better, and more efficient goods. We are trained to be restless. Our insatiable desire for more devalues what we have and erodes the satisfaction that may come with it, making us ever fearful of not having enough. Rational self-interest degenerates into self-indulgence and a concern for immediate gratification. Yet this only promotes an economy of exchange that, in the final analysis, can never guarantee us the worth we seek. For consumerism entails being perpetually unsatisfied with ourselves, led along into more and more cravings for worth, a worth defined by possessions.[57] As Robert Molsberry laments, it is difficult for "people to accept who they really are in an advertising-driven culture that fuels its economic engines by creating consumer needs."[58]

The self-interest that drives consumerism is self-defeating. What promises future happiness winds up cultivating unhappiness, intensifying our anxiety over insecurity with each turn in the feedback loop. So we traffic in a double frustration, disappointed either because we do not have the capital to procure or produce goods, or because the goods we do procure or produce do not satisfy. We are possessed by the need to possess, deceived into believing that participation in the market is the final judge of our merit. Consumerism disables: persons with impairments become unable to consume normally.

Beautiful, Youthful, and Able Bodies

One prominent way that consumerism is disabling is in its promotion of youthful attractiveness and vitality. Multiple industries are supported by the obsession with youthfulness, connected up with the ideals of efficiency and novelty. The young are physiologically and developmentally fresh, vital, mobile, adaptive, eager, innovative, and adventurous. However, we must note how these terms are invested with meanings that vary from society to society. They are, to a certain extent, relative. In North America, with advancements in media technology and the cultural revolution of the 1960s, a peculiar kind of popular culture developed that was focused on people between the ages of 16 and 30; and it became economically productive. Directed toward young people, pop music, sexuality, athletics, and fashion became consumer goods driven by the entertainment business and rolled together into a spectacular media phenomenon. The trend still continues, shaping consumer culture in now global forms.

Led by advertisement and entertainment media, we crave the ideal bodily form and function—the fashionable outfit, the sculpted body, heightened athletic ability, sexual potency, and the like. Only the ideal becomes depicted as normal, represented as commonplace on the television screen. So the images of a relatively few people, fabricated to manufacture desire, drive our sense of what it means to be normal.[59] For example, it is considered normal to prolong youth and the ideals surrounding it. And we see this modeled for us in the athletes, actors, and pop music stars we purchase and, indeed, fetishize. We then recreate ourselves in the image of our products, becoming products ourselves. Our bodies become commodities, instruments to purchase worth. We buy all kinds of cosmetic devices and clothing to enhance our look. We attend health clubs to work our bodies into shape. We even undergo cosmetic surgery or take steroids to achieve the optimum appearance or performance level. In the case of sex, we manufacture ourselves as sexual objects, voyeurized and potent, able to attract, perform, and purchase.

The human body is reduced to a commodity. Again, however, there is an irony at work, for the youth industry must create more desire to generate further profit. Efficiency and novelty are taken to ever-greater levels, such that even media models become shaped by the industry. New fashions are fabricated. New looks and body ideals are created, along with the diets and workout regimes to foster them. More efficient workout equipment and cosmetic technologies are invented. The feedback loop moves forward with an increasing pace. Who can keep up? Only those with purchase power. In the final analysis, however, even those with purchase power cannot keep up. Nobody is youthful and vital forever. Hence, the entire dynamic is built upon a lie that is ultimately self-defeating. We cannot be worthy in an economy that outpaces itself to create more need for body capital.

The problem is we believe the lie, and so facilitate disabling mechanisms that dehumanize and marginalize persons. We all grow old and eventually become impaired. The illusion of youthful beauty and vitality is seductive, for it makes us seem invulnerable and in control of our bodies. But notice how the cult of normalcy is at work. The physically and mentally able—the potent, acquisitive, efficient, and innovative body—is normalized. Conversely, excluded is that anomalous and dysfunctional body deemed lacking in these preferred and desirable traits. The disabled body is thus created. Able-bodied people fear the lack represented in the disabled body, so it is ostracized or normalized. Consequentially, everyone ends up shunning those dimensions of human existence that are vulnerable and weak, perhaps wounded or imperiled. We hide, ashamed. Instead of facing our vulnerability directly, we participate in the cult of normalcy, projecting shame onto the other, the different—that which is categorized disabled. We then ignore or pity those ugly, deformed, monstrous, senile, retarded, and otherwise unseemly bodies. In doing so, however, we flee from our own bodies, reducing them to instruments, commodities in the service of productive value exchange.[60]

Conclusion: Spiritual Self-Interest?

The purpose of this chapter has been to illustrate how the cult of normalcy holds sway in North America through particular ideals and mechanisms that define what it means to be a functional, healthy, and whole person. Tragically, the upshot is that we are caught up in a narcissistic and materialistic culture that emboldens self-interest and free-market ideals to the detriment of genuine human flourishing.[61] Under the pressure of competition, persons are individualized and set against one another, for there are never enough resources for everyone. Equally tragic is the fact that many Christian churches do not seem to notice. In this they reveal their own acquiescence, inadvertently capitulating to the conception of personhood bandied by modern liberalism and market capitalism.[62] It is no accident that many perceive religious faith as a private affair, a preference determined by rational self-interest, spiritual depth being a commodity freely chosen and acquired among alternatives.

It is also not accidental that spirituality in our time is seen more as a matter of self-fulfillment than service, more entertainment than gratitude. We consume it, perhaps through an inspirational Sunday morning worship or a touching book bought from among hundreds that line the shelves of huge bookselling conglomerates. Spirituality should serve the consumer; it is a product aimed at personal esteem, happiness, and freedom—American style—and perhaps even material prosperity (the prosperity doctrine). And if it does not gratify, we seek other options, buying more books and aspiring to greater spiritual results. This line of thinking mirrors the restlessness of our commodity-driven culture. But it pulls us apart from each other and throws us back on ourselves—free, equal, independent, and rationally self-interested consumers and producers of goods. The healthy and whole person is the self-directed and satisfied person, one with choice capacity to procure more spiritual capital. It is not surprising then that Christians often see disability as a problem of the individual, a deficiency in body capital to be treated, healed, or otherwise used as inspiration for non-disabled people. Accordingly, disability calls either for a purchasing of wholeness for the person in question or for a production of spiritual capital for other non-disabled people. Roy Mc-Cloughry and Wayne Morris conclude: "The notion that value is linked to one's ability to achieve more in less time, to be fit, slim, strong, financially successful and beautiful—notions that the Church has arguably wrongly supported—have been destructive not only to disabled people but also to the whole body of Christ."[63] But where do we go from here?

There is hope. Discovering this hope, however, means adjusting the aperture of our lenses. It means rethinking fundamental values and reinterpreting the person outside the framework of rational autonomy, self-interest, and the productive imperative. It means resisting being coopted into assuming that individual self-interest is the primary way by which mutually beneficial social cooperation and personal satisfaction can be achieved. Certainly self-definition and wealth production are not themselves evil. But treated as ends in themselves they have a narrowing effect that is dehumanizing and disabling, not only disconnecting persons from the nourishing fulcrum of dependent relationships with others, but also reducing persons to their consumptive and productive capacity.

Hence, I propose an alternative that rethinks what it means to be a person in terms of our basic dependence upon others in relationships of mutual vulnerability and love, in terms of communities based upon a vision of the common good that empowers the well-being of all, and in terms of the creative love of God who is revealed in the person and work of Jesus Christ. In the final analysis my hope—as a father of a child with disabilities—is connected to a vision of human flourishing that is relational and redemptive. We are all God's creatures, full of an inbuilt preciousness that radiates of its own accord apart from the cult of normalcy. Because of this our churches can be more than mere reflections of society; they can be inclusive communities acting as harbingers of societal change.

Notes

1. Jean Vanier, *Becoming Human* (New York: Paulist Press, 1998), 46.

2. Ibid., 86.

3. Lennard J. Davis, *Enforcing Normalcy: Disability, Deafness, and the Body* (New York: Verso, 1995), 24.

4. See Susan Wendell, *The Rejected Body: Feminist Reflections on Disability* (New York: Routledge, 1996), 60.

5. For an excellent account of this, see Larry L. Rasmussen, *Moral Fragments and Moral Community: A Proposal for Church in Society* (Minneapolis: Fortress Press, 1993).

6. See Thomas Hobbes, *Leviathan*, ed. Michael Oakeshott (New York: Collier Books, 1962), and John Locke, *Two Treatises of Government*, ed. Peter Laslett (New York: New American Library, 1965).

7. Locke, "Second Treatise," chap. 2 par. 4, chap. 8 par. 98.

8. See Martha C. Nussbaum, *Frontiers of Justice: Disability, Nationality, Species Membership* (Cambridge, MA: Belknap Press, 2006), 28–34.

9. Ibid., 54.

10. Immanuel Kant makes perhaps the paradigm case for the rational individual's autonomy and independence. See *Groundwork of the Metaphysics of Morals*, trans. H. J. Paton (New York: Harper and Row, 1964), 98–99.

11. See Hans S. Reinders, *The Future of the Disabled in Liberal Society: An Ethical Analysis* (Notre Dame, IN: Notre Dame University Press, 2000), 22–24

12. Immanuel Kant, *Groundwork of the Metaphysics of Morals*, 95–96.

13. Stanley Hauerwas, "Community and Diversity: The Tyranny of Normality," in *Critical Reflection on Stanley Hauerwas' Theology of Disability: Disabling Society, Enabling Theology*, ed. John Swinton (Binghamton, NY: Haworth Press, 2004), 39.

14. Eva Feder Kittay, *Love's Labor: Essays on Women, Labor, and Dependency* (New York: Routledge, 1999), 184.

15. Martha Nussbaum raises these concerns with trenchant force in her critique of the contemporary political liberalism of John Rawls. See *Frontiers of Justice*, chaps. 2–3.

16. Hauerwas, "Community and Diversity," 40.

17. See Kittay, *Love's Labor*, 6.

18. For examples, see ibid., 23–29; and Catherine Keller, *From a Broken Web: Separation, Sexism, and Self* (Boston: Beacon Press, 1986).

19. Hauerwas, "Community and Diversity," 40.

20. See Nussbaum's critique of Rawls on this point, *Frontiers of Justice*, 108–27. See also Alasdair MacIntyre, *Dependent Rational Animals: Why Human Beings Need the Virtues* (Chicago: Open Court, 1999).

21. Kittay, *Love's Labor*, 47.

22. Hauerwas, "The Retarded and the Criteria for the Human," in *Critical Reflections on Stanley Hauerwas' Theology of Disability*, 129.

23. Wendell, *The Rejected Body*, 41–42.

24. Nussbaum, *Frontiers of Justice*, 98.

25. Kittay, *Love's Labor*, 13–19.

26. Ibid., 83. See also 29–30.

27. Ibid.; e.g., xiii, 27, 99.

28. Ibid., 63. MacIntyre makes a similar point in *Dependent Rational Animals*, chap. 7.

29. Immanuel Kant, *Critique of Judgment* [1790], trans. Pluhar (Indianapolis: Hackett, 1987), 161, par. 40.

30. See Nussbaum, *Frontiers of Justice*, 66, 127ff.

31. Hauerwas, "Suffering the Retarded: Should We Prevent Retardation?" in *Critical Reflections on Stanley Hauerwas' Theology of Disability*, 92–93.

32. Ibid., 95.

33. Ibid., 99.

34. Hauerwas, "The Retarded and the Criteria for the Human," 132. On this issue, see also Reinders, *The Future of the Disabled in Liberal Society*, chap. 10.

35. In Foucault's words, reason and its so-called truths are nothing but "a system of ordered procedures for the production, regulation, distribution, circulation, and operation of statements . . . linked in a circular relation with systems of power which produce and sustain it, and to effects of power which it induces and which extends it" ("Truth and Power," 74). Truth then functions as a kind of ideological regime or political economy. Again Foucault states, "Truth is a thing of this world: it is produced only by virtue of multiple forms of constraint." Ibid., 73.

36. Richard J. Bernstein, *The New Constellation: The Ethical-Political Horizons of Modernity/Postmodernity* (Cambridge: MIT Press, 1991), 32–33.

37. Examples of this line of critique are Max Weber's *The Protestant Ethic and the Spirit of Capitalism*, trans. Talcott Parsons (New York: Routledge, 1992); Martin Heidegger's "The Question concerning Technology," in *Martin Heidegger: Basic Writings*, ed. and trans. David F. Krell (New York: Harper and Row, 1977), 283–318; Max Horkheimer and Theodor Adorno's *Dialectic of the Enlightenment*, trans. John Cumming (New York: Herder and Herder, 1972); and Horkheimer's *Eclipse of Reason* [1947] (New York: Continuum, 1992).

38. This is a central thesis in Horkheimer and Adorno's *Dialectic of Enlightenment*, and also appears in Horkheimer's *Eclipse of Reason* [1947] (New York: Continuum, 1992), and Adorno's *Negative Dialectics* [1966], trans. E. B. Aston (New York: Seabury Press, 1973). For an excellent secondary source on Adorno, see Martin Jay, *Adorno* (Cambridge: Harvard University Press, 1984). See also Craig Calhoun's superb chapter on the history and import of the Frankfurt School: "Rethinking Critical Theory," in *Critical Social Theory* (Cambridge: Blackwell Publishers, 1995), 1–42.

39. The passage goes on to state: "A technological rationale is the rationale of domination itself." Ibid., 121. See also 145–46.

40. Ibid., p. 25. See Martin Jay, *Adorno*, 68. In a similar vein Martin Heidegger launches a critique of technology as *Gestell* (enframing), representing an ontologizing of the problem of technical reason (see "The Question concerning Technology"). More recently, Jürgen Habermas has spoken of the "colonization of the lifeworld" as the product of societal rationalization. For example, see *The Theory of Communicative Action*, vol. 2, *Lifeworld and System: A Critique of Functionalist Reason* (Boston: Beacon Press, 1988), chap. 8.

41. A further exploration of these issues is provided in my book, *The Broken Whole: Philosophical Steps toward a Theology of Global Solidarity* (Albany: State University of New York Press, 2005), chap. 2.

42. Charles Taylor, *Sources of the Self: The Making of Modern Identity* (Cambridge: Harvard University Press, 1989), 36.

43. Hauerwas, "The Retarded and the Criteria for the Human," 132.

44. For example, see Jürgen Habermas, *The Theory of Communicative Action*, vol. 1: *Reason and the Rationalization of Society*, trans. T. McCarthy (Boston: Beacon Press, 1984). See also chap. 4 in my *The Broken Whole*.

45. Davis, *Enforcing Normalcy: Disability, Deafness, and the Body*, 131.

46. Kittay, *Love's Labor*, 122–23.

47. Ibid., 123.

48. Ibid., 123, 124.

49. Hauerwas, "Suffering the Retarded," 90.

50. Colin Barnes and Geof Mercer, *Disability* (Malden, MA: Blackwell, 2003), 24.

51. See Susan Wendell, *The Rejected Body*, 37–39; and Roy McCloughry and Wayne Morris, *Making a World of Difference: Christian Reflections on Disability* (London: Society for Promoting Christian Knowledge, 2002), 3–4.

52. See Alexis de Tocqueville's appraisal of this in *Democracy in America*, ed. and abr. by Richard D. Heffner (New York: Penguin, 1984), 156–58.

53. See Immanuel Kant, "An Answer to the Question: What Is Enlightenment" (1784), trans. Lewis White Black, in *Foundations of the Metaphysics of Morals and What Is Enlightenment?* (Indianapolis: Bobbs-Merrill, 1959), 85–92. It is worth quoting Kant's celebrated passage at length to make the point: "Enlightenment is man's release from his self-incurred tutelage. Tutelage is man's inability to make use of his understanding without direction from another. It is self-incurred when its cause lies not in lack of understanding but in lack of resolution and courage to use it without direction from another. *Sapere aude!* 'Have the courage to exercise your own understanding!'—that is the motto of enlightenment.... For this enlightenment, however, nothing is required but freedom ... freedom to make public use of one's reason at every point." 90, 92.

54. For a more detailed portrayal of the Enlightenment project, see my *The Broken Whole*, 22–30.

55. For an excellent account of this inequity, see Cynthia D. Moe-Lobeda, *Healing in a Broken World: Globalization and God* (Minneapolis: Fortress Press, 2002).

56. See John Francis Kavanaugh, *Following Christ in Consumer Society: The Spirituality of Cultural Resistance* (Maryknoll, NY: Orbis Books, 1981), chap. 3.

57. See Mary Jo Leddy, *Radical Gratitude* (Maryknoll, NY: Orbis Books, 2002), chap. 2.

58. Robert F. Molsberry, *Blindsided by Grace: Entering the World of Disability* (Minneapolis: Augsburg Books, 2004), 74.

59. Wendell, *The Rejected Body*, 86.

60. See Nancy Eiesland, *The Disabled God: Toward a Liberation Theology of Disability* (Nashville: Abingdon Press, 1994), 110.

61. See Christopher Lasch's famous book *The Culture of Narcissism: American Life in an Age of Diminishing Expectations* (New York: W. W. Norton, 1979).

62. Michael Budde and Robert Brimlow, *Christianity Incorporated: How Big Business Is Buying the Church* (Grand Rapids: Brazos Press, 2002), chap. 6, esp. 149–50.

63. McCloughry and Morris, *Making a World of Difference*, 77.

4

Recovering Disability

The Strange Power of "Weakness"

We are not alone; beyond the differences that separate us, we share one common humanity and thus belong to each other. The mystery of life is that we discover this human togetherness not when we are powerful and strong, but when we are vulnerable and weak.

Henri Nouwen[1]

This is a special toy, this snake. He has disabilities like me. His eyes have fallen off.

Chris Reynolds[2]

As we saw in the last chapter, an undue focus on the individual, rational, and autonomous agent gives license to a reductive view of the person. Two broad consequences now merit our attention in beginning to forge our way into new territory. First, the common good of shared community life and its role in nurturing moral agents not only is underestimated, it is undermined. The common good appears to be the sum total of separate individuals choosing it to be so in the interest of fairness for all. But, as we recently explored, if the person is able to participate fully in the community only by way of voluntary choice, based in rational autonomy, access to public institutions will be curtailed dramatically for many—for example, children, the elderly, and people with disabilities. Dependency relationships are relegated to the private sphere. The common, or public, good thereby becomes narrowed to the consensus of the majority or, more accurately, to the satisfied interests and strategic agendas of those in positions of public influence. The cult of normalcy then functions to legitimate conventions and expectations that exclude persons who cannot be assimilated and normalized; they are deemed unfit for civic participation. Thus, in the cause of benefiting the many a preoccupation with individual autonomy ultimately extends the benefits of citizenship only to the few—the normal.

Second, in this light human beings progressively become subject to societal and economic forces that domesticate and homogenize differences. The community that is formed under the sway of normalcy winds up serving its conventions, not the good of its members. This is the case, as we have seen, with market capitalism. One becomes a community member only by conforming to the market's standards of worth, becoming in effect a commodity reduced to exchange value. However, if civic participation requires competition for wealth production and accumulation, the community itself cannot help but become fragmented. Fully capable agents will compete against each other. This may have an equalizing effect, but only temporarily, for in the process alienation and mistrust are engendered. Because opportunities and resources remain limited, not all succeed in accruing property and wealth. Inevitably, those left behind are shamed, rendered somehow deficient or faulted in body capital. This only increases fragmentation, producing exclusions that foster resentment and grievance.

An alternative conception of community life and the good it serves is required. Providing this, however, is not merely a matter of constructing new social policies or economic models. Something more fundamental is needed, a moral vision of the person that can marshal our collective energies and projects in the service of human flourishing, whatever peculiar political or economic shapes it may take. For this, I shall highlight the relational dimensions of welcome. Indeed, others are not secondary additions to an already constituted and independent self. But neither is the cult of normalcy an inescapable and unstoppable doomsday mechanism circumscribing all human interactions. If it is true that we are not autonomous individuals; it is equally true that we are not determined products of society, simply passive receptors internalizing its norms and values. Human beings are personal beings. That is, we are agents identified by the relationships we have with others. The context of these relationships informs our sense of self, but such that we become responsible agents in our own unique flourishing. In this way our capacity for self-determination and freedom is a factor of our dependence upon and vulnerability to other people. There are dramatic moral implications that follow from this picture of the human, especially as they relate to disability. Responsible agency looks entirely different; it is tied to the flourishing of others.

By "flourishing" I mean to suggest the prospering of an inbuilt human capacity to experience and share with others the multifaceted joy of being alive. Certainly this depends upon many things, such as obtaining basic resources for nourishment, shelter, and social well-being. But more specifically it presupposes being cared for, such that one can develop as the subject of one's own experience. In turn, this means being welcomed into a relational space, a home where one's unique value is revealed and affirmed. Welcome is not a factor of assisting separated individuals in the process of seeking, through self-interest, their own gratification. Neither is it facilitating conformity to the cult of normalcy, remaking persons in the image of youth, beauty, wealth, and so on. Genuinely welcoming others calls for something different, a moral disposition—love. Love is availability to others, a posture wrought within relationships of involvement with others. In love people become sympathetically attuned and vulnerable to one another, considering each other not from a distance but up close, compassionately. Furthermore, love keeps the joy of the other in mind, respecting his or her own way of being, working to nourish the capacity for joy that he or she embodies, and remaining faithful to it over time.

Exploring what this involves will take some doing, for it goes against the grain of the standards and conventions taken for granted in our culture's economies of exchange. However, as we shall see in the coming chapters, it leads straight into the heart of themes like creation and covenant, and culminates in the gospel message. Human beings are creatures made for each other, for community, for creation, and for God. All of these work together as textures within one symphony, complementing by making each other possible. It will be our task in this chapter, however, to begin illustrating how this is so by sketching the contours of an anthropology based upon human dependency and vulnerability. The goal is to show how entering into relationships of mutual vulnerability and gift giving is a way of belonging with others that cultivates the joy of being "at home" together. As we shall come to see in later chapters, this is ultimately possible for Christians in that we are all members of God's household (*oikos*), a true economy of exchange based upon grace instead of ability. Grace manages this household on the basis of an economy of abundance, of giftedness. Such an economy does not traffic in the scarcity of goods and the need for production; it thrives on a plentitude offered by God. But for now, in this chapter, it is important to forge a way toward this understanding by demonstrating how the individual is not whole and healthy apart from the dependent relationships by which welcome is mediated. And this opens up the issue of disability.

I. Vulnerability: Reassessing Wholeness and Disability

The anthropology I shall propose involves a dramatic metaphorical reversal. That is, it inverts the scheme of the cult of normalcy by privileging disability.

Instead of being spurned or made invisible, the so-called deformed and dysfunctional become the normative fulcrum for understanding the human. Not ability but disability is basic. Why? Because, I suggest, how we understand and evaluate bodily form (appearance and/or completeness) and function (productive and/or performative capacity) is secondary, the product of the way we experience our vulnerability in interactions with others.

Disability is not something less than normal, an inferior or broken nature. Disabled and non-disabled people do not count as two exclusive categories of human beings. All people are linked indissolubly, sharing a fundamental condition: vulnerable personhood. Precisely this kind of vision is obscured if we privilege individual autonomy and the productive imperative. For human being is primarily a "being with," a *coesse* (together being).[3] Our existence as persons emerges in the presence of others. We are inherently relational creatures who need each other to become ourselves. That is, we are unfinished and deficient unto ourselves. And this highlights our insecurity and weakness, undoing the illusion of security gained from being inscribed with body capital within the cult of normalcy. Seen in this light, disability is no fringe issue. Through it emerges a more holistic picture of what it means to be a person. When privileged and brought from the margins to the center, disability deconstructs the cult of normalcy and opens up the possibility of a wider human solidarity. Our way of seeing things changes.

Dependence—Rethinking "Normal"

Let us build on a point stressed in the last chapter: autonomous self-creation is an illusion based in a false understanding of agency. Human beings are not ready-made. Indeed, we are incomplete creatures that require the presence of others not merely to survive but to flourish. We desire welcome, craving a place to call home. Precisely this obliges us to become conscious of and open to our dependence upon others. In his provocative book *Dependent Rational Animals*, Alasdair MacIntyre helps us to understand why this is so. He stresses what he calls "the virtues of acknowledged dependence," which extols vulnerability and disability as essential to becoming fully human.[4] For MacIntyre we become agents or "independent practical reasoners" insofar as we acquire habits and appropriate a language that come to us in a matrix of ongoing dependence. We cannot help but rely upon others—most directly upon family and interpersonal relations but also indirectly upon a larger societal framework—to make the transition to self-awareness and become empowered to evaluate our actions reflectively.[5] In other words, we need others in order to stand back from our immediate desires and ask as independent agents, "Why should I behave this way rather than that?"[6] Thus more is involved than reliance upon others to sustain us and teach us about the world. MacIntyre argues, "Our self-knowledge too depends in key part upon what we learn about ourselves from others, and more than this, upon a confirmation of our own judgments about ourselves by others who know us well, a confirmation that only such others can provide."[7] Given this, the recognition of our dependence is key to our independence.[8]

That we are incomplete, vulnerable, and need others to become complete proves an insightful step into acknowledging, as MacIntyre puts it, "that there is a scale of disability on which we all find ourselves." Disability is an unavoidable part of all human agency. Different individuals, "disabled in different ways and degrees, can have their own peculiar talents and possibilities and their own difficulties." While some persons may struggle with a higher degree of disability than others, all human beings are disabled to some degree—often unpredictably and at different periods of our lives—from infancy to old age. And each of us, threatened by various contingencies, need each other to take note of our own particular condition and become empowered as individuals.[9] Disability is an element intrinsic to human flourishing.

The point is not to trivialize disability or discount the very real struggles created by biophysical impairments of various kinds. Rather, it is to open up the prospect of more fruitfully attending to people with disabilities as persons, people who love and care for others and on whom the temporarily non-disabled also depend, people whose lack of ability may be different and unique in its own way but which should not be seen as entirely outside the scope of the various kinds of lack endemic to being human. Moreover, it is clear that there is crossover between disability and non-disability. One situation may highlight disability more than another, calling forth different capacities in a person, such as crossing a street versus solving a math problem. This is why some prefer the term "differently abled," for human beings function differently at different times in their lives and in different contexts. We do things differently.

So neediness, vulnerability, or lack of ability is not a flaw detracting from an otherwise pure and complete human nature. Rather, it is testimony to the fact that our nature involves receiving our existence from each other. As we shall explore more fully in a moment, appreciating this is a source of relational openness to others who are, in the end, similarly constituted in their differences. By privileging disability, the relational dependence that characterizes the human being as personal is brought into focus. Disability is not an anomalous dimension of human experience, something to be shunned. It is not constitutive of an identity, but something a person happens to have, a feature of the way he or she inhabits the world and relates with others in certain moments. Recognizing this is key to undoing the ill-conceived ideological line of demarcation between normal and abnormal. There is no hard-and-fast separation between non-disabled and disabled people, "us" and "them."

With this we come a long way toward reversing the ideals that uphold the standards of normalcy. Rather than being trivialized, disability is underscored and honored, for it reveals a shared human condition from which no one is exempt. Disability is not a deviance to be assimilated into the normal or otherwise excluded. Indeed, the virtue of acknowledged dependence relativizes ability as a factor of disability, placing both in the context of a shared humanity. It places us together in the context of an inclusive solidarity, advancing the prospect of welcome for all. Genuine sharing becomes possible in a community life where disability itself—in various shapes and forms—is considered normal. This is not a moral lesson that people with disabilities teach non-disabled persons; it is rather an opening to the humanity of disabled and non-disabled persons alike.

The upshot is that personal wholeness is found not through ability but through an acknowledgment of vulnerability that is made concrete in relations of dependence upon others. Notice the word "acknowledgment." It is not just the brute fact of our vulnerability and dependence upon others that is important here. Rather, it is the explicit recognition of this fact. The acceptance of our dependence is key to our flourishing, the means by which we become unique persons, free subjects of our own experience. Paradoxically, freedom is not a property of the self-determining subject, but a qualification of the dependent relationships by which the subject becomes who she or he is. I am free only insofar as I am with others. Jean Vanier, founder of L'Arche, a network of communities for intellectually disabled people, sums it up eloquently: "We do not discover who we are, we do not reach true humanness, in a solitary state; we discover it through mutual dependency, in weakness, in learning through belonging."[10] Human personhood is an intersubjective affair, not a quality possessed by the solitary individual. This undoes false oppositions between ability and disability, and thus begins to undercut the means by which persons with disabilities are marginalized and excluded. Vulnerability is the warp and woof of being human, and accepting our vulnerability opens us to others.

The Difficult Strength of Vulnerability—Neediness and the Reality of Suffering

How difficult it is to process what we have been saying under the influence of the cult of normalcy, for it runs counter to assumptions that animate exchange value based upon productivity and rational autonomy. We suppose that our identity, our worth, derives from the power of completeness, the capacity to be independent thinkers and self-initiating bodies. The irony is, in the words of Stanley Hauerwas, that "our neediness is also the source of our greatest strength, for our need requires the cooperation and love of others from which derives our ability not only to live but to flourish."[11] Living out of this reality is a source of genuine good, for it entails caring for others—in their disabilities—as essential not only to our own flourishing but also to the common good of the communities in which we flourish. Thus, as MacIntyre puts it, how the needs of persons with disabilities are "adequately voiced and met is not a matter of special interest, the interest of one particular group rather than of others, but rather the interest of the whole political society, an interest that is integral to their conception of their common good."[12]

Yet neediness is a thorny reality because it requires recognizing that we are not in control, that we are—at the core—exposed to imperilment and suffering, which makes us contingent and incomplete creatures in need of others. Indeed, the expression "vulnerable" derives from the Latin word *vulnerare*, meaning to injure or harm. Human beings are open to being wounded. We suffer. But, as Hauerwas rightly stresses, suffering is a reality more complex than it at first seems. Most often we perceive it negatively, as an unwelcome intrusion that detracts from well-being. Suffering marks a dimension of life in which we are brought to undergo what we do not like. In suffering we become subject to experiences that are unpleasant and physically or emotionally painful but which, at the same time, we find ourselves powerless to avoid. It can be direct and immediate, such as in the loss of a loved one or hurting one's leg on the stairs. But it can also take on a more indirect and subtle meaning, connoting difficulties, such as disappointments or failures, that frustrate our desires and impede obtaining certain goals. In either case, suffering indicates what cannot easily be domesticated or integrated fruitfully into our lives in the service of some greater end.[13] We are made to endure alien interferences to our well-being, things we did not plan for. Suffering, then, connotes a strong element of passivity, of being out of control and, in a real sense, victimized.

However, not all suffering is negative in this way. When suffering is interpreted as contributing to some wider end or purpose it can be seen positively. That is, it can be domesticated, its alien quality made familiar and acceptable. Examples of this might be the difficulties incurred while training for an athletic event, or the suffering involved with job relocation or coping with a difficult person in church. It is possible in these instances to claim suffering as part of our larger identity or life projects, an intrusion, to be sure, but one that is manageable. It becomes part of a choice freely made and is thus in our control, beneficial though not preventable in the course of our actions. In this case we do not see ourselves as passive victims. Yet difficulties arise; the line between the negative and positive senses of suffering is often quite blurry.

It is those experiences of suffering that cannot be claimed positively that we find distressing and intrusive because they cannot be owned or domesticated. Such suffering and pain disturbs, in Hauerwas's terms, by alienating us from ourselves. Our identity is threatened. Something is not right. So we try to find the means to interpret its presence as integral to our identity, accordingly transforming suffering into a benefit.[14] Conversely, we seek to prevent or eliminate those kinds of suffering that we cannot integrate into our personal or social projects, those that seem, in Hauerwas's words, to "intrude uncontrollably into our lives."[15] Obvious categories of prevention include the body that is deemed permanently out of control and thus incapable of serving any human good. Unrelenting and incurable suffering is particularly disorienting because we cannot imagine its productive purpose. Instinctively, we seem to refuse and deny its presence.

There are dangers that surface here, to which Hauerwas is quick to call our attention. The refusal of suffering can foster grave consequences in our relations with others. To be sure, he is not claiming we should simply accept all suffering. This would be morally absurd. Repudiating certain kinds of suffering, or at least interpreting them in light of a broader purpose, is "essential for our moral health."[16] But Hauerwas wants us to ask whether the general policy of escaping from or domesticating suffering is the right move. For example, how are we to decide what suffering is unnecessary and unacceptable? And if such suffering is, in fact, determined to be acceptable, how are we to decide the manner by which it should be integrated into our lives?[17] These ambiguities are troublesome. Not only do they lead to unfruitful theodicy questions, but they also point us toward dehumanizing ways of living with others. We may represent persons with disabilities as passive victims, falsely attributing suffering to them on the basis of societal projections. We may seek to marginalize or exclude those others that cause us to suffer, not just physically, but socially because they represent anomalies that make us uncomfortable or get in the way of our larger projects. More subtly, we may seek to avert or eliminate those whose suffering we deem incapable of serving any larger good. The desire to prevent suffering, then, can lead to preventing certain kinds of people. It is with this problem in mind that Robert Molsberry counters, "There is more to disability than the desire to escape from it."[18] For disability is too often construed as tragic and unnecessary suffering.[19]

Accordingly, Hauerwas is led to argue that we are morally diminished if we do not recognize that suffering is an inescapable and inevitable part of human life. He asserts: "Suffering is built into our condition because it is literally true that we exist only to the extent that we sustain, or 'suffer' the existence of others." And this includes others unlike us, even mountains, trees, animals, and so on.[20] Human beings are not independent and self-secure creatures, but needy and vulnerable, subject to elements that cannot easily be suppressed or domesticated. Perhaps not all of these elements should be suppressed or domesticated; perhaps by doing so we diminish our own humanity. So, Hauerwas concludes, instead of focusing solely on how we should prevent, mitigate, or explain suffering, perhaps we should, more fundamentally, seek to discern who we ought to become as moral agents capable of recognizing suffering as an unavoidable part of our shared human condition.[21]

Why is this important? Because, as Jean Vanier reflects, "weakness is at the heart of the need to belong; weakness that we may fear, because we have been hurt."[22] Human beings are vulnerable to suffering; we are not in control. This is why the craving to belong is so powerful. Human beings desire worth and fear the lack of worth, so we seek recognition and welcome from those around us. Welcome by others mediates a trustworthy world, orienting us in life. Inevitably, however, we suffer the presence of others, undergoing pain because of things done to us and not done for us. We suffer the humiliation of rejection or exclusion, being told "you are not good enough." Fearful of being wounded again, we attempt to cover our vulnerability, protecting it by denying our dependence upon others. We try to prove that we are okay, hiding behind masks of self-sufficiency. The irony, however, is that this is an illusion, for this belies the fact that we need to be recognized by others as of value. Nonetheless, our anxiety over insecurity tempts us to feign security.

So we live in an incongruous state of affairs: we come to use belonging to a group as a means to escape vulnerability and assure ourselves of strength and completeness by conforming to its measurement of body capital. We search for false security, presuming it entails assimilating to the projected strength of others, bolstered by the conventions of society and its power mechanisms in an economy of exchange. It is as though acquiescing to the status quo offers protection by rendering us immune to life's contingencies and perils. Such false pretense is what fuels efforts to build protective walls around the normal and stigmatize certain differences as deviances. We thereby come to judge certain others according to our fears—that is, the fear of other human beings who lack reason, autonomy, productivity, and body capital in general. The cult of normalcy swings into full operation, assimilating or excluding the strange and anomalous, that which is deficient in value because it does not fit into the ordered scheme of things.

Refusing to own up to our vulnerability cultivates an aversion to difference. This, in turn, yields ideologies of exclusion and violence, for prejudice is nourished by fear. It feigns the status of strength by connecting well-being and wholeness with power, ability, and sameness, idealizing an imaginary completeness that suppresses or denies the capacity to be wounded. Fear insists on preserving the status quo and demands that it be protected against disruption and change. In the name of doing good, then, we lay down the different or strange on the altars of rituals and ideals that bind us to conceptions of shared strength and body capital. We seek to sacrifice—refuse, prevent, or eliminate—that which threatens our world and thus elicits a sense of vulnerability, getting rid of it and so purifying or immunizing ourselves against its perceived potential to contaminate. Anxiety over vulnerability, as Vanier notes, seeks an object. In a state of insecurity we hunt for a scapegoat to symbolize our fear, someone or something to turn into the object of fear, and subsequently our contempt.[23]

The different is frightening because it is experienced as out of control, untamed, wild, freakish, and undomesticated. It is *unheimlich*, un-housed, and threatens to un-house us by defamiliarizing and disrupting the familiar, stable world we depend upon. Thus we suffer from the presence of the anomalous and strange— the disabled body—whose abnormality brings to awareness our own weakness and vulnerability.[24] Hauerwas concurs: "We do not like to be reminded of the limits of our power, and we do not like those who remind us."[25] They rupture the conventions of normalcy and force us to acknowledge that which we shun and seek immunity against: contingency, inability, incompleteness, and neediness. Deviation from the norm or existing order is considered a weakness because it concretely reveals to us what we come to despise in ourselves: fragility and weakness.[26] We are ashamed of weakness, the fact that we too can be rejected and are, in the end, finite and mortal. So we strive to cover it, hiding from our capacity to suffer. In this process, driven by an aversion to vulnerability, the need to belong progressively hardens into a constrictive cement cast. Writ large in social terms, it falsely binds a group together over the fears that preoccupy its constituents. As

Jennie Weiss Block laments, we come to "cling to the cultural norms of attractiveness, independence, self-sufficiency, and productivity to avoid coming face to face with two of our great fears: we are not perfect and we are not in control."[27]

This amounts to a moral failure. Not only does it lead to representing vulnerability as a flaw, it also seeks to objectify such flaw as an attribute of others who are different, disabled, or freakish. By projecting our own fear of vulnerability onto others, we become cut off from the wellspring of our own flourishing: mutual dependence. We deny others, and so ourselves. For mutual dependence emerges concretely from within local spaces of interpersonal relations. Face-to-face relations are where we suffer and undergo each other, our vulnerabilities made most palpable. But because to suffer means to be out of control, with our self-sufficiency threatened physically, psychologically, or morally, we fear disability when we encounter it. We are made unsure. Accordingly, we seek to do something to prove our worth, appealing to conventions rather than simply being with another and entering into a space of fellow suffering.[28] And this breaches relationships, objectifying another as lacking in some way or another. We therefore gain power over another in order to gain power over our own exposed sense of vulnerability. We shame others in order to avoid confronting our own shame.

II. Encountering Disability, Suffering the Other

In light of the preceding discussion we can understand why, when viewed from the position of power and strength, it is all too common to consider disability as something to be overcome. It marks a territory of human experience that suffers from lack or deficiency and which, therefore, merits prevention or elimination. Why do we use the word "suffer"? We use it because, when perceived from the posture of strength and security, disability seems a degradation that inherently involves pain and frustration for the person—as if disability means that someone has nothing creative to offer others. Yet here is the rub: this tells us more about ourselves, and how we have been coopted by the cult of normalcy, than it does the reality of disability. In reality it serves to expose the fear-based agendas and ableist assumptions of the economy of exchange in which we find ourselves. Instead of encountering persons with disabilities, we inadvertently impose foreign categories on out-of-control bodies derived from illusions of control and strength. We define disability as separate from us—as "other." In this we project suffering onto the person with disabilities and then seek to recover from our own fear of vulnerability by ridding the other of it. We become caught in a narcissistic feedback loop, seeking more to assuage our fears than to attend to the presence of the person.

That disability is a category linked to presumptions about suffering defined by the illusion of normalcy is obvious, for we claim that another suffers by attributing to them our own assumptions (from strength) about how we might experience things if we were in their position (of weakness). Yet we judge wrongly. Hauerwas reminds us that we do not know the extent to which another—for example, someone with developmental disabilities—is harmed by or feels pain from impairments.[29] What is clearer, however, is that such projections cause suffering for persons with disabilities, suffering that is the consequence of social or personal acts of discrimination. We create disability as an individual's tragedy, but in the process overlook the person, who is reducible neither to his or her disabilities nor to the alleged suffering we might ascribe to the condition. The irony here it is that we too suffer. We suffer because it is only in relationships with other persons that we are most fully alive, whole, and human. We miss out on the possibility of learning to love.

Creative Openings—An Autobiographical Excursus on Love

I have been deliberately using the word "we" here to include myself, because my relationship with my son Chris makes the point personal. Far too often, admittedly, I have found myself placing on him my own reading of how he suffers and needs to be helped. I am in a position of strength, and Chris is dependent, the needy one. Is this not to be expected? After all, I am the parent and should know what is best for him. While this may be partially true, it is deeply problematic when taken for the whole truth. For example, I have discovered that it has the unfortunate effect of closing me in on myself and preventing me from simply being with and attending to Chris's unique way of being. Feigning control, I come to expect certain things of him as well as myself, managing our affairs and judging their successes and failures according to projected yet artificial categories and roles: disability, father, son, family, love, and so on. Encountering Chris's own distinctiveness and the struggles that accompany it make the limitations of these projections painfully obvious. His particular difference sets him at a distance from the way I have set up parameters and calculated conditions that—often falsely—measure what counts for a normal family life, for the way my son should be, for the manner in which I should love him, for what is good for him.

Disconcerting thoughts arise. It might seem that loving one's own child is a much easier task than loving a complete stranger. For there is a basic biological tie that stimulates instinctive family bonding. A child, after all, is an extension of oneself. Indeed, every child is born into a symbolic household upheld by many taken-for-granted assumptions about who he or she will be. Yet there is a negative side to this. One need only attend youth athletic events to see the phenomenon in action—disappointed parents yelling at their kids to cajole them into performing up to expectations. Parents often strive to see themselves in the successes of their children. Or conversely, and with great subtlety, they can suppress in their children those visible signs of inadequacy that they find so uncomfortable in themselves. Compensating for their own insecurity, parents sometimes obsess over their child's performance in school, athletics, the arts, and so on. This is a symptom of control, of over-identification with a child such that the parent's happiness or suffering is tied up with the child's abilities or disabilities. Hence even, and perhaps especially, with one's own child, encountering the uniqueness of another person—whose genuine difference from us calls us to acknowledge, respond to, and affirm his or her distinctiveness and creative potential apart from our own projections or agendas—makes it difficult to love.

Learning to love my son has meant putting aside presumptions about what love is, what counts for value in a person, what being human entails. This has not been easy. When there is struggle and pain in the process, I must confess my first impulse is to feel disappointed, cheated, even betrayed by life. Chris's presence ruptures my controlled, planned, and predictable world. I am inclined to think that somehow things have gone awry, pieces scattered in disarray, hopes deferred. Because of this, it is easy to feel a sense of failure, as if I am flawed in some basic way, have done something horrible to traumatize Chris, or have not done enough to help him accommodate to how a "normal" child should be, essentially fashioning him in my own ideal image. Indeed, I suffer. Encountering Chris exposes me to my own vulnerability. I am not in control, and I feel impoverished and insecure in his presence. In an effort to shun this sense of weakness, I am tempted to seek avenues of control and strength. I may push Chris away and reclaim security behind an air of parental authority or condescension, essentially shunning his weakness for my own benefit. But doing so makes him bear the burden of my projections. I thrust upon Chris my feelings of inadequacy and confusion, naming him their cause. He then becomes the "other," the one who suffers from disabilities.

This depiction follows a logic played out commonly when non-disabled people encounter disability concretely, up close, in allegedly out-of-control bodies. We feel helpless, not sure what to do or say. We struggle to find a point of connection, to relate to what we might experience as frighteningly alien to our otherwise normal way of experience. The disabled body is then perceived through the lens of our vulnerability, interpreted by way of our insecurity, which calls up prejudices and attitudes linked to our own deep wounds and fears. We may deem the disabled body abnormal, even monstrous, but it is only because we feel out of control in its presence. Unsure how to interact and elicit a common purpose or meeting point, we appeal to the strength and security offered by the cult of normalcy. Why? Because the encounter has put into question and made unstable the values garnered from a taken-for-granted economy of exchange. The strange and uncanny world of disability has disrupted the familiar and predictable world.

Thus we become disoriented and displaced, threatened by being exposed to our weakness. Such exposure can cause anger and resentment, perhaps even leading to violence. Most often, however, our reactions fall into two broad camps, both of which are linked inextricably. First, there can arise a more negatively directed desire to eliminate or cure disability as deviance involving suffering, getting rid of it in order to reestablish control. Some of the consequences of this logic have already been discussed, such as the medical model, social exclusion through marginalization and institutionalization, and eugenics. These, however, often arise from a second, more positive, concern for the "other." This reaction is embodied in the condescension of pity, which is sometimes linked up with benevolent acts of charity. Pity and charity avert the vulnerability required by genuine love, a love that does not keep distance but attends to another sympathetically and up close. Control is maintained. To grasp how these two reactions are interconnected, let us discuss pity and charity in more detail.

Against Pity and Charity?

Of course I do not mean here to discount all acts of benevolent concern and giving. Certainly there are a great many benefits for persons with disabilities that have been made possible by the generous giving of others. Instead I mean to suggest that the encounter with disability often triggers a response that wants to do for the other, which assumes a position of power, strength, and security. This in itself is neither morally wrong nor always based on false pretense. But it can indirectly serve the cult of normalcy. Indeed, benevolence often functions to preserve the conventions of an economy of exchange by which we escape from our own vulnerability. Those persons with ability—autonomy, freedom, wealth, intelligence, and power—reach down from a superior position to "feel for" or "help" the inferior, deviant, and helpless.[30]

Pity is a deceptive emotional response to perceived suffering. Why deceptive? Because it feigns a closeness that is really distance. When unsure of ourselves and afraid to step outside the insularity of what is comfortable and reassuring about normalcy, we respond to undomesticated suffering with pity. Pity emerges from the presumption that we must do something to hide affliction when we encounter it, making it go away. This urge to cover up suffering is a symptom of shame, the shame we attribute to another whose out-of-control body elicits our own sense of shame. So we condescend to others as pathetic, feeling sorry for them in order to connect with their suffering as though it would be tragic if it were our own. It is as if to say, "There but for the grace of God go I." This feeling is not to be equated with compassion or sympathy, a feeling-along-with the other. For pity is a feeling for the other that presumes the other is unlike us, subject to a state of affairs that we are relieved to have avoided. Hence, the real focus of pity is directed toward the perceiver and not the perceived, who is left on the outside. In pity we respond to another in a way that assuages our discomfort in their presence. We see suffering not as it is experienced by the other person but more as it is understood by us, according to our own assumptions about what it would be like to be in their situation.

Pity is thus an emotional state of being that sees persons with disabilities as passive objects upon which non-disabled persons act as benefactors. Disabled persons are projected as needy, "the least of these," essentially helpless people in need of assistance. Presumed to have little to offer, people with disabilities become perfect candidates for charity, for self-less giving. Pity takes for granted that another cannot help him or herself, the product of undue suffering. Inclusion in community life thus entails condescending acts of care and assistance, making special allowances for persons who are otherwise incapable of functioning normally and contributing to the community. Pity fuels gestures of giving of what we have in abundance to the less fortunate, those unlike us who are deficient in such graces. Of course, as Joseph Shapiro counters, "there is no pity or tragedy in disability," for "it is society's myths, fears, and stereotypes that most make being disabled difficult."[31] The point is clear. Under the influence of pity, the allegedly benign intention to understand, accept, help, and heal disabilities ironically stymies the genuine welcome of disabled persons into our communities.

This irony only deepens social exclusion. Ultimately, we end up doing for another in order that we receive a benefit in return—feeling better about ourselves, reassured of our strength and control. Precisely this is the deception of pity: it feigns emotional closeness to the other but actually refuses relational connection. It resists exposure to vulnerability by attributing it to the other. So the center of attention is the benefactor, whose gesture of charity perpetuates the projected neediness of persons with disabilities and overdetermines them as helpless victims of suffering, passive receptors of care. In this way charity is also deceptive.

In the name of charity special provisions may be made to accommodate the sufferer, the one whose disabled condition renders him or her out of control. We might establish care facilities and offer aid. On the surface this may be well and good. Motivated by pity, however, acts of charity keep those who do not naturally fit in at a distance. This is why charity, as it is commonly understood, tends to favor the ideal of donation. We give of those values we possess in plenty and condescend to the needy, who by our standards have been judged as wanting.[32] This, however, trades on and nourishes a disingenuous sense of privilege, presuming that those who receive aid are of no use and have nothing to offer in return. The fact that suffering—and so disability—is ascribed with meanings that depersonalize and often lead to institutionalization and isolation from mainstream society exemplifies the point.[33]

The problem with charity is compounded by the fact that it is commonly idealized as genuine love. When seen as charity (*caritas*), love is regarded as a disinterested and unilateral act of self-denial. According to such a view, love is selfless, and so can be only indiscriminate and general. I give to the other not out of an experience of the other's own value, but because of some external criterion of measurement by which value is conferred upon the other and by which I am directed to forget myself and attend to it. Not only does this logic uphold the paternalism described above—generosity flowing out of what I have in abundance to wherever there is a scarcity—but it entails no real relation, no vulnerability, no zone of mutual encounter. Disinterested love is directionless, often inappropriately deemed "blind." It does not take account of the uniqueness of another, nor does it receive from another the distinctive gifts she or he may have to offer. The difference of a person—that which makes someone alluring and special—is disregarded and overlooked. Hence, indiscriminate love renders a person essentially anonymous, of no particular value at all except insofar as he or she can passively receive the benefit. This is ironic, given that such love is prized as an ideal form of relation. Love in this manner cannot help but reflect the condescending gaze of pity even if enforced by an external authority, determined by a sense of duty, or motivated by a desire to see oneself recognized by others as loving. The concrete presence of another person, along with their specific needs, is neither acknowledged nor loved up close. Indeed, it becomes easy to see how, in the name of charity, we may even resort to violence, eliminating suffering by eliminating the other altogether, of course under the auspices of doing so "for their own good."

To sum up, insofar as they are animated by pity, acts of disinterested love remain captive to the mechanisms of an economy of exchange which continues to produce and mete out body capital according to the cult of normalcy. Societal systems of marginalization and exclusion remain unchallenged and intact. Ironically, when it is considered an impoverishment of the normal and whole body, suffering is attributed to persons with disabilities in an effort to uphold the status quo. Control and security are preserved. How so? By a distancing mechanism that feels (pity) and does good for (charity) the other from a position of height and plenty.

Is it possible to break from this paralyzing feedback loop? Is it possible to "suffer the other's presence" in genuine care and love—up close and not from a distance—without recoiling from being exposed to one's own vulnerability? My relationship with Chris has helped me come to believe that it is possible, even if only in a finite sense and gradually.

Getting Closer—Loving Chris

By honestly confronting and accepting my own vulnerability and limitations I have grown in the capacity to let go of my need for control and to risk moving beyond my own fears, affirming Chris for who he is. Chris is not pathetic. His genuine otherness continually breaks through pity and astonishes me as something surprisingly precious in its own right. His is a young life seeking creatively to affirm itself, thwarted by conditions that he did not ask for and for which he is not responsible. This vulnerability rouses me to attend to him in ways that lure me outward beyond self-preoccupation; and the first taste of this conjures something akin to repentance. Confronted by Chris's vulnerability, I am humbled and brought to recognize how my own needs, expectations, and ideals have closed me in on myself and limited my capacity to be open toward him, to be there with and for him in *his* struggles as well as joys. Being with Chris is what love is all about. Rather than forcing him to adapt and conform to preconceived ideals, love adapts to Chris by welcoming his own way of being.

Love is life-giving generosity, a compassionate regard that draws near and attends to the beloved for his or her own sake and with his or her good in mind. Such generous concern requires that we adjust or even give up our hold on reality as we see it and open ourselves to the unfamiliar, strange, perhaps threatening presence of another without imposing conditions that restrict or exclude their own particular capacities and ways of being. Genuine love signifies being summoned into a relational space of giving that happens outside the order of predetermined calculations and expectations, beyond the boundaries of an economy of exchange and the cult of normalcy. This is what makes love so difficult, indeed traumatic: its gesture of giving hinges on letting go of those things by which we domesticate and manage reality so as to feel ourselves secure and in control. It entails attending to another such that we become vulnerable with that particular and concrete other, up close; and love includes receiving from the other.

III. Relational Wholeness: Love's Interdependence

Our efforts to suppress it notwithstanding, interdependence is originary. It is the fulcrum from which we emerge as persons. It is the source of a relational wholeness that, even as we conceal it, rises like an irrepressible force to call us out into the open. How so? Vanier puts it beautifully: "Weakness carries within it a secret power. The cry and the trust that flow from weakness can open up hearts."[34] The vulnerability of another is a window into our own vulnerability, evoking a sympathetic relation that eludes the cult of normalcy, sweeping under the radar of conventional economies of value exchange. There is, oddly enough, a strength in weakness, a usefulness in being of no use. Embracing our own weakness allows us to welcome weakness in another. But it is by encountering weakness in another that we discover it in ourselves. A humanizing feedback loop is created that undoes the pernicious feedback loop we saw above.

The Strange Power of Weakness—Enabling Love

Vanier suggests that those who embody weakness and are considered nobodies in a society, such as people with disabilities, "have profound lessons to teach us."[35] They invite us to move out from behind closed walls of false security and exclusion to acknowledge and accept our vulnerability. Jürgen Moltmann confirms the point in stating, "A person with disabilities gives others the precious insight into the woundedness and weakness of human life."[36] Disability is a profound symbol of human brokenness.[37] We are incomplete and unfinished beings. Of course we can suppress or deny the weakness this signifies, fleeing from it by pushing away those others whose difference overtly exhibits it as something we deem ugly or dirty, flawed or deficient. But by doing this we shun what is perhaps most human about us—the need to belong and be recognized as of value. We all at the core are vulnerable and receive our existence from one another.

We must, however, tread cautiously. There is real danger here, the danger of trivializing disability as an instructive tool. For their part, Vanier and Moltmann seek neither to reduce people with disabilities to a moral lesson for non-disabled people, nor to justify disability as serving some positive purpose, rendering it useful by what it helps non-disabled people do. Instead they seek to privilege disability as the measure of personhood. Vulnerability is a positive feature of every human life, a life that becomes its own through dependency upon others in relationships of belonging. Each of us is disabled to a certain extent in varied contexts, and will inevitably become more so as we age. In different ways some of us are more vulnerable than others, perhaps living with a greater degree of impairments. But we all participate in a shared humanity. So when we engage another human being at various levels of weakness and disability we confront in ourselves something of their weakness and need. This is not a source of shame. Indeed, I suggest it is the beginning of a moral conversion. And this conversion sets us on the track toward attending more fruitfully to persons according to their own unique needs, rather than according to generalized practices influenced by the cult of normalcy.

Learning to embrace ourselves and others as we are, in our specific weaknesses, releases us from narcissistic self-enclosure and empowers us to risk the openness of genuine relationship. Only in relationship is human wholeness possible, a wholeness that comes not despite but through disability and vulnerability. What is being claimed here amounts to a reversal of the logic that tends to animate society's conventional wisdom, which suggests that wholeness means power and independence, ability and completeness. Disability is not a useless weakness in the negative sense, as seen through the cult of normalcy. But neither is it therefore positive, justified as useful, a calculated good of utilitarian value. This would simply continue to construe disability according to the cult of normalcy. Disability is part of the fragile character of human existence in general, wherein we can find genuine good in relationships of mutual vulnerability. Wholeness comes through mutual dependency; and dependency marks vulnerability, which involves disability. Our weaknesses open us to each other.

The point brings us back to what has become something of a mantra in this book: living out of our interdependency is a source of genuine good. It entails caring for others—represented by a range of disabilities—as essential not only to our own flourishing but also to the common good of the communities in which we flourish. Human solidarity is not found inside the cult of normalcy, but rather in sharing space and welcoming each other vis-à-vis a condition of vulnerability from which no one is excluded.[38] Hence, to quote MacIntyre again, how the needs of people with disabilities are "adequately voiced and met is not a matter of special interest, the interest of one particular group rather than of others, but rather the interest of the whole political society, an interest that is integral to their conception of their common good."[39] Privileging disability is essential to the good of society. It calls us to attend more adequately to the interpersonal nexus of vulnerable openness to others. More specifically, it calls us to responsibility as agents capable of loving and welcoming others.

Love—To Welcome the Presence of the Other

As we have seen, human life seeks more than survival alone. It seeks to flourish and find itself affirmed within a larger framework of value and purpose. Life seeks delight in living; it seeks joy. And this is not something found in separateness and self-sufficiency, but rather in belonging with others. The basic question of human existence is whether there is welcome at the heart of things, whether we can find a home with others who recognize us, value us, and empower us to become ourselves. Is there space for me in the world? Is there a safe place where I can flourish? Will I be accepted and embraced? These questions strike the heartstring of vulnerability, resonating in ways that enliven our basic capacity to receive and give love. Love is the relational power that animates belonging together. It gives and receives life, and the process radiates joy. Correspondingly, love has two poles, a receiving and a giving. These poles are not isolated elements but intertwined. They oscillate and mutually support each other, for giving is a receiving, and receiving is also a giving. Let us take time to explore how.

Fundamentally, love involves welcoming another into a space of mutual vulnerability. Yet this is not something I do to or for someone, a skill I possess in myself and offer to another out of a surplus of sufficiency. Rather, love is the nature of a certain correlation between myself and someone else, a certain way we belong together. Love signals the fact that I have become involved and invested, vulnerable to another, drawn into a relation by the proximity of an "other" who stands before me. But there is more at stake than another just being there. I am rendered unable to remain indifferent, a neutral onlooker or dispassionate observer. Someone has evoked in me a desire to respond, to yield way and pay attention. In relation to me, another claims a certain priority, standing before or in front of me. I am summoned and lured outward, caught up in an event that is larger than me and occurs between me and someone else. And this in-between zone is the dynamic, expansive space of reciprocity, of giving and receiving. In the language of philosophers Martin Buber and Gabriel Marcel, it is the stuff of meeting and relation.[40] It is the arc of human intersubjectivity.

What turns me outward to invest myself, however, is neither merely an object or thing nor a *Doppelgänger*, another version of my ego. Employing Marcel's term, it is an experience of another's presence.[41] A Thou with personal force reveals itself up close as precious in its own right, embodying an initiative as a subject that invites me to attend to it for its own sake. There is an immediacy here that links me to another outside the influence of conventional attitudes, ideas, and expectations I may bring to the experience. Marcel states: "Presence is something which reveals itself immediately and unmistakably in a look, a smile, an intonation or a hand shake."[42] Something happens that sweeps under the radar of projected meanings. In this way the presence of another leads me beyond the orbit of myself, marking the mysterious fullness of a reality outside my own project. It is not simply a matter of an inner feeling or experience. I have been touched by a singular value that cannot be measured according to conventional standards of exchange or absorbed into my own agendas or desires. This sets it at a distance from me even as it entices me into relationship with it and makes me answerable to it. According to Marcel, the encounter with presence is described as coming up against a mystery, something incapable of being reduced to a problem managed and solved according to established standards or principles. A mystery is something in which I find myself involved, but which cannot become objectified as an acquisition or property because it transcends every conceivable technique of mastery.[43] Presence is not in our power to control; it makes us unprotected and vulnerable.

Hence, the relation that is established is not one of easy bliss. It can be quite disturbing and painful. I suffer the other, undergoing its presence. For the other is by nature different, set apart from me, not as a separate object isolated from me but as a fullness that resists being grasped and treated like a possession. There is an involvement that puts me into question, disrupting my world—my way of seeing things and mapping out what should or should not be the case. Neither a calculable nor an exchangeable object that I grasp among other objects, the presence of the other grasps and takes hold of me like an interruptive force. In this regard presence grants or gives itself as an invocation. An appeal is made which throws me into question and makes me answerable to it. It invites recognition and bids me pay attention to it. That is, a concrete, non-objectifiable, and noninterchangeable presence calls out to me, "Love me."[44] The other beckons me to welcome and will its good. My world is thereby adjusted. My way of being is transposed, not merely in some general or disinterested sense, but in a specific direction—toward the other. I am invited to recognize, show regard for, and celebrate the other for its own sake, to reveal to it its own value.[45]

What is it about the other's presence before me that elicits such a response? Here we supplement Marcel's account with that of the Jewish philosopher Emmanuel Levinas, who insightfully calls this element "the face" (la visage).[46] Meeting up with another human being's face means to encounter her or his distinct locus of personhood. Levinas is saying something here that seems intuitively correct. For we speak with each other "face to face," looking into the eyes, directing ourselves to the front portion, not the back, of another's head. The face is a bodily point of access to another person; it signifies that which is irreducible to any condition or horizon of expectation. But in what way? As the intrinsic fragility and vulnerable preciousness of an unrepeatable singularity, something most genuinely "other." The experience of the face cannot help but invoke reply, not because of its capacity to supplement and enrich my world but because of its capacity to be ignored and violated.[47] There is nothing the face has or possesses that justifies response, as if it offered something positive. For this would render it subject to my own agendas in an economy of exchange. Put into language that reflects Marcel's analysis, the face signifies not a thing that is at my disposal, but a presence who seeks my becoming disposed to it—in a word, who seeks welcome.

The face is perhaps the most transparently vulnerable part of the human body. It launches a thousand ships, is a window into our souls, expresses emotions, kisses and receives kisses, and trades glances with another. Not accidentally, we hide our faces when shamed by another's face turned disapprovingly toward us. Instinctively, we protect our face from perceived threats. Think also of the tender face of a child sleeping soundly, the weathered face of an elderly person who has worked long years in the sun and seen her family killed in tribal warfare, the fragile smile on the face of a friend with whom you have just been reconciled after a long winter's bitterness. In ancient times a king's face was said to shine with glory, radiating blessing, such that his subjects were to lower their gaze and not meet it directly. A king could also turn his face away, indicating displeasure and the removal of blessing. These examples confirm how powerful a metaphor the face is for human personhood. It can be recognized, admired, and respected, or disregarded, abused, fetishized, and commodified. The former personalizes, the latter depersonalizes.

There is thus pathos in the presence of the other's face, for an intrinsic vulnerability is exposed that calls to be recognized and heeded. It invokes attention as something toward which I cannot remain indifferent. An agential quality emerges that outlines the shape of a person, a subject with its own initiative, one with possibilities of meaning and value that are distinct from mine and that emanate from its own center of being. So, at base, the face transposes me toward the other, not merely in a superficial acknowledgment of something pretty or attractive, but in a state of reverence before something with dignity and power in its own right, something of worth beyond my horizon and its expectations. Now I may subsequently choose to ignore, shun, or abuse the face. But originally, before this can happen the defenseless exposure of the face invokes in me a moral response. Here the presence of the other radiates a preciousness that can be mistreated, defiled, even murdered. There is something immeasurably good before me, a gift. An intrinsic value is disclosed. Accordingly I am led to react. In the most basic positive sense an affirmation arises, "Here I am."[48]

In the space of this kind of a relation love is born. By being subject to the other's vulnerability I am brought to my own vulnerability, not as a sterile form of self-contemplation but in a posture of vulnerability to the other. I am disposed toward and made "response-able" to the other, brought into a relation that changes me. Without appeal to some utilitarian economy of exchange or logic of equivalence I am carried beyond myself toward a personal presence that is of itself, apart from projected meanings, worthy of response. A love-filled exertion of the self wells up, a desire to draw near the other, aspiring to attend to and be with otherness for its own sake, as beloved. This dynamic power of linkage with the other goes beyond mere pity and charity. Vanier puts it this way: "You are not just being generous, you are entering into a relationship, which will change your life. You are no longer in control. You have become vulnerable; you have come to love that person."[49] It is not out of sufficiency but in relationship with the presence of another that love is born. I become invested in someone and am vulnerable. C. S. Lewis affirms the point: "There is no safe investment. To love at all is to be vulnerable. Love anything at all, and your heart will certainly be wrung and possibly be broken."[50]

Neither is love born merely from a gift that I offer, but rather out of receiving the gift of the other's presence. Love introduces vulnerable connection, solidarity, and reciprocal belonging. It is a way of living in the between zone of genuine relation.

In love another person is received as a gift, a presence to which I respond. In turn I share myself with that other person, revealing back to them their own value. Together we then form a bond of reciprocal mutuality by which we each become more than ourselves alone. Love becomes a back-and-forth dynamic of giving and receiving. Indeed, with every turn each "I" is progressively enlarged, becoming a "we" through identifying with and belonging to something larger than both. Love is not additive, a one-plus-one. It is a dynamic connection of two wherein the sum overflows with something greater than the addition of parts. This does not mean that selfhood loses its integrity by being assimilated into a united fusion. Neither does it mean that one party is absorbed into the world of the other. Nor does it mean self-sacrifice.[51] To the contrary, love actually enriches and expands the integrity of the self. In opening myself to receive another I receive something precious, not something obliged or intended as an exchange value but instead as an unintended moral consequence. Love establishes a relation that transgresses self-enclosure and its debilitating paralysis, enticing the self beyond the gravitational pull of its own orbit, thus serving as the fertile ground from which acts of life-giving generosity can blossom. In this way it involves self-transcendence, a liberating release from the deadness of fear-based individual isolation into a life-giving mutuality of vulnerability and empowerment. The result leads us to become larger and more fully alive. I am expanded and transformed, brought into a relationship that makes me more than I was before. Love marks a moral conversion of self to another in relationship.

Precisely this is why love, as we are describing it, happens outside of the economy of exchange that dominates our social order. The process begins neither because love is socially useful or expedient nor because it is a general ethical duty or obligation owed universally to everyone, but because the particular, unique presence of the other bids me to attend to it as an exception, precious in its own right, apart from the standard rule. I do not love simply in order to fulfill a social prescription or become richer as a human being; these are by-products of love that are misplaced if given priority as ends in themselves. I love because of the revelation to me of the other's intrinsic value.[52] Moral transformation originates in the deep fullness and joy contained in this experience, not in puritanical acts of self-effacement and asceticism. Paradoxically, such fullness and joy come without seeking them intentionally. They appear as a surprise, an unsought bonus rather than a fulfilled objective. Why? Because the gift of another's vulnerability and singular worth invites me to let go of conditions that reflect my need for security and control and to risk a relation beyond foreseeable calculations and expectations, so becoming "response-able" to that person's peculiar way of being.

Love is the moral heart of human existence. This is no sentimental assertion; it is a hard truth. And it is why caring for a child with disabilities has been a vehicle of moral conversion for me. Chris is teaching me how to love, to become more open to the revelation of his own particular value and, in turn, to become more able to attend to him in a way that reflects back to him his own particular value. Vanier observes: "To love is not just to do something for [others] but to reveal to them their own uniqueness, to tell them that they are special and worthy of attention. We can express this revelation through our open and gentle presence."[53] Seeing Chris's own life-giving potential, his own distinctive way of loving, come into its own has been and continues to be a source of great joy. Chris is a creative, intelligent, funny, and deeply caring person with much to offer the world. The gift of my son has opened me to the unique differences of the many people and things that surround me, to which I would otherwise have been dead. Such deep satisfaction and joy are the fruits of a love that I could never have planned for or arranged on my own terms. And in the process he too has grown.

IV. The Moral Fabric of Love: Availability

There is a paradox at work in what we have just observed: the apparent weakness of vulnerability has become a humanizing strength. Far from a liability inhibiting or mitigating love, vulnerability actually works to establish the mutuality in connections that love embodies. Our human vulnerability opens us to each other, enabling the possibility of love. It allows us both to receive and to give love, fostering mutual dependency. And the kind of relationship that is characterized by mutual dependency is one based in an openness that suffers the other, that undergoes its difference and vulnerability. True, we have no direct or immediate access to what another feels. Human beings are creatures physiologically distinct and different. Yet it is also true that we share a human condition constituted by vulnerability and weakness. Because of this we are beings capable of becoming transposed to identify with experiences that are not our own. All human beings have vulnerable hearts, hearts that need to be recognized as valuable.[54] We are thereby open to one another, such that when encountering the face of the other I undergo a summons to draw near to its presence, experiencing a non-possessive desire that wills its good. What is the nature of this non-acquisitive desire for the other?

Encountering another's presence I am enticed outward, made available to the other in a gesture attuned to its difference. It is in this way that love participates in the distinct preciousness of the other. This is not some mystical union of alienated parts. Rather, it is a relationship constituted by responsibility. But the term "responsibility" can be construed in ways that connote disinterested duty, charity, and self-sacrifice, and these do not characterize the genuine mutuality, interdependence, and love we are talking about. So, drawing again from Gabriel Marcel, I propose we think of love as availability to the other, a posture of caring attentiveness that is attuned to the other's preciousness and vulnerability by way of sympathy or feeling-along-with. Availability is a sympathetic attunement in which I am brought into relation with the other's own way of being, experiencing the other's invocation as of moral substance by disposing myself to it in three interrelated postures: respect, fidelity, and compassion.

Availability (*disponibilité*) means to be appreciatively disposed toward the other. It is desire in the form of a nonacquisitive aspiration, receiving the other as a gift. And by this it opens to possible others as well. Marcel offers a brief definition: availability is "an aptitude to give oneself to anything which offers, and to bind oneself by the gift."[55] Availability marks a morally charged willingness to participate in and undergo—that is, to suffer—the presence of another. This is no mere passivity that simply tolerates or accepts the other's presence. Rather, it is an availing of oneself which risks vulnerable openness to another's vulnerability. It is disposing oneself to the other for its sake and on its terms. This is the fulcrum of being with the other, binding together a relation of mutuality. Put negatively, as the converse of indifference and callous exclusion, availability resists letting the other's need for welcome go unheeded. And in this it also resists managing and controlling the other according to external systems of value measurement—that is, the cult of normalcy. Availability recognizes the vulnerable humanity and intrinsic worth of other people. It goes without saying, then, that it entails an active openness to difference. Another is willingly welcomed because of what he or she is—or, more pointedly, because he or she is.

Respect—Giving Way for the Other

That availability is not a possessive or domineering posture can be seen by its way of creating space for the other. The other is "let be," recognized for its own unique difference. The opposite of exploitation, availability shows respect, outlining a concern that the other person grow and unfold at his own pace and on his own terms, not for serving me or some systemic end.[56] This means granting another a certain freedom to be who he or she is. Of course, this also means that I am a free agent capable of recognizing my own vulnerability and letting go of my own projections and need for control. Furthermore, it involves an ever-extending effort on my part to understand another's distinctness apart from my projects and ambitions. This makes availability's respect for the other quite different from the classic liberal portrait of human freedom discussed in the last chapter. Moral agency here is contextual and responsive rather than calculative, and is not based on homogeneous equality and individual rights. Respect does not center on feigned impartiality and generalized judgments but, as Eva Feder Kittay puts it, "on judgments partial to participants within a caring relationship."[57] It is contingent upon coming to know another in specific situations of dependency and vulnerability and, accordingly, giving space for others to flourish according to their own capacities.

While she does not employ the terms "availability" and "respect," Kittay is insightful in articulating the point. She speaks intimately of her experiences raising her daughter Sesha, who is developmentally disabled. According to Kittay, learning what is normal for Sesha has been key to the process of accepting and enabling her individuality, which is nascent and struggles to emerge in a culture that refuses it. "Enabling the development of a disabled child involves attuning oneself to the individual's unique tempo."[58] Kittay cites the story of one of Sesha's caregivers recounting a transformative moment of giving herself over to Sesha. The caregiver states: "Thank you for being my teacher, Sesha. I see now. Not my way. Your way. Slowly."[59] This proclamation epitomizes the respect of availability, demonstrating an attuned openness to the difference of the other, without pretext or conditions that limit welcome. Kittay admits that she has been forced to rethink independence, normalization, and development, for these terms take on very different meaning when brought into the context of Sesha's own unique way of being. "Independent living," she quips, "is a subsidiary goal to living as full and rich a life as one's capacities permit." Knowing these capacities and respecting them as part of her daughter's uniqueness is fundamental to loving her and providing an environment that fosters her development. Thus Kittay continues: "Development for Sesha means the enhancement of her capacities to experience joy."[60] My own experiences with Chris corroborate Kittay's remarks; he bears in himself a life that resonates with its own worth, pulses with its own tempo, and radiates with its own unique joy that I am privileged to share along the way.

Fidelity—Faithfulness to the Other

This leads to another mark of availability: fidelity. If respect for another yields to her capacity for joy, which is distinct and different in its own right, fidelity to another binds me to a process of accompaniment which recognizes the enduring quality of another's capacity for joy. Fidelity means being disposed to another as a presence that abides over time. It is availability in the mode of faithfulness and trustworthiness, a posture that says, "I will be there for you," and thus commits itself to accompanying another along the way. This does not simply entail my involvement in a complacent or detached way, as if I can just passively be "there." Rather, there is an implicit promise made. Availability is not a temporary event; it does not stop or withdraw. It prolongs itself in time as a continual process of openness to another, for presence endures. In Marcel's words availability involves fidelity insofar as it entails "the active perpetuation of presence, the renewal of its benefits" which "corresponds to a certain kind of hold" another has on us.[61] Connoted here is a kind of promise to maintain receptivity to the gift of another's presence. I am no mere onlooker, but consecrate myself to another, testifying to this in acts that demonstrate permanency. Availability has duration, extending implicitly into the future. In this light Marcel goes on to claim "fidelity consists in maintaining ourselves in an actively permeable state."[62] Thus I bear witness to belonging with another, binding myself to abide with and for this or that person over time.[63]

Being with and for someone over time, in this sense, is different than "doing for" them. The latter is a momentary event that finishes, whereas the former implies a faithfulness that is "timeful." While he does not employ Marcel, in an essay with the suggestive title "Timeful Friends: Living with the Handicapped," Hauerwas helpfully expands the meaning of fidelity by noting how it includes becoming "friends of time."[64] Fidelity requires giving time to others on their own terms, patiently and persistently, and without treating them as a means to some other end that I may have in mind, like being helpful. Indeed, knowing and respecting someone necessitates being with them such that they experience welcome and can claim you as a friend. For Hauerwas, who appreciates Vanier's wisdom, this is especially the case with people with disabilities, who disrupt the hurried pace of our culture of efficiency and its quick-fix brand of generosity. Caring then involves less "doing for" and more being with people with disabilities timefully, as persons. Hauerwas puts it nicely: "We have to become not only friends of time, but friends of those who make such time possible."[65] Friendship in this sense is not unilateral but mutual. Indeed, it is a gift rising out of the ordinary things we do for one another and the gentle concerns we show each other daily. And over time this "encourages fidelity."[66] Hauerwas approvingly quotes Vanier, whose L'Arche communities embody timeful friendships "made of the small gestures, of service and sacrifices which say 'I love you' and 'I'm happy to be with you.' "[67] This is a far cry from disinterested charity. It is genuine friendship, implying an attunement to another that stems from an extended relation of involvement. And this brings us to the third mark of availability.

Compassion—Sympathy with the Other, for Its Well-being

Compassion literally means to undergo, feel, or suffer with another. "With" is key. Compassion signifies participative connection, what we might call sympathetic attunement. It does not hide or flee from suffering but shares it—respecting and affirming the vulnerable presence of another enough to abide with them faithfully so that they are not alone—as it also desires another's well-being and works to alleviate suffering and expand joy. To this end Richard B. Steele, a parent of a chronically ill daughter, suggests that compassion is an emotion as well as a virtue, a spontaneous affective response to the pain and need of some specific other, as well as an acquired trait of character that grows in its concern for the well-being of others.[68] It implies the moral readiness for another's presence that characterizes availability, affirming the other as distinctly precious and sharing in the other's vulnerability—that is, suffering the other by suffering with. Certainly this is not the distanced condescension of pity. But neither is it a union that literally undergoes what another feels. It is rather an attunement to the other.

Drawing from Adam Smith's *Theory of Moral Sentiments*, Hauerwas describes this process as sympathy. Sympathy is a fellow feeling that suffers in accordance with another's condition as if it were our own, undergoing the sense of its pathos. For example, it derives sorrow from the grief of others. But since we can never actually experience what another feels sympathy depends upon the imagination. It is comprised of an imaginative leap that projects what we ourselves might feel should we undergo the same experience.[69] This is not to say that sympathy is created by self-conscious effort, a hypothetical conjecture or duty-bound endeavor. Nor does it have the distancing effect of pity (though Smith uses this term positively). It arises intuitively as a kind of reflex, indicating a basic participative and emotionally laden involvement with another. In fact, it arises from a disclosure of fullness and intrinsic value in the other, from what we, along Marcel's lines, have called presence. Sympathy suggests that we are already connected in a manner that empowers us to see, hear, and feel like another, not in their place, but with another.[70] Some form of group tie to the other is presupposed, some kind of commonality—that is, friendship, familial kinship, ethnicity, and so on. To undergo another's pathos as our own is to recognize another as our neighbor.[71] The imagination is only able to transpose itself toward another's way of experiencing insofar as it is shaped by and grounded in its author's capacity to recognize him or herself in similar experiences. A shared sense of mutual vulnerability is the axis upon which this recognition takes place, linking persons together "as if" they coincided.

In this way sympathy is a key feature of availability, the stuff of a participative engagement with the vulnerability of another.[72] To sympathize with another is to respond to her presence by way of participative attunement. It involves an affective drawing near to the other's presence, hearkening to its appeal for recognition and welcome. Thus sympathy cannot help but trade on an experience of vulnerability which, when openly embraced, enlivens a sense of humanizing connection with another that blossoms into a relation of mutuality and interdependence. And this exemplifies belonging.

The point where sympathy often runs aground, however, is in the encounter with another whose difference exceeds our imaginative power to share. When another is experienced as foreign and not our neighbor we find ourselves lacking the resources to attribute our pathos to that of another.[73] We cannot conceive of how they feel. And consequently, as Hauerwas muses, "we seek to avoid their presence in order to avoid the limits of our own sympathy."[74] The strange and different makes us unsure of who we are. It intensifies our vulnerability, for we know not how to respond. There is no perceived affinity, no common horizon with which we can identify. Because of this, we are not sure that the other will reciprocate, receiving and mirroring back our sympathy. Unable to feel connected, we may seek to assimilate the other, attributing to them our preconceptions of suffering, straining artificially to elicit fellow feeling. This is the stuff of pity, which condescends to the other as if from a distance. We may even claim that the other is inherently flawed and lacks the means to reciprocate, becoming resentful or disgusted, thereby vindicating tactics of exclusion. But these responses only serve to reinforce our sense of strength, cheating the other of its own unique way of being, its own pathos.[75] Fundamentally they represent a failure of imagination.[76]

What constitutes this failure? It is a lack of the moral openness of availability. It is a refusal to recognize in ourselves the vulnerability represented by the foreign and different. This refusal makes us incapable of receiving the other and letting it be on its own terms, neither respecting it nor binding ourselves to it in fidelity. For our refusal presumes that we are sufficient unto ourselves and thus have no need of making room for another, someone unlike us who is deemed incapable of sharing our space. After all, the different has no apparent affinity with us, lacking the conventional traits that bind us together according to the cult of normalcy. We thus lose the means to hear the vulnerable voice of the other because we have closed our ears to our own weakness.

This is precisely why weakness harnesses a strange power. It breaks through the false pretenses that have numbed our sensibilities. It disturbs the normal and in so doing excites the imagination. How so? By rendering us insufficient to ourselves. And the medium of this is our capacity for sympathy. In a fundamental sense sympathy means that we have been brought into relation with the pathos of another, and not merely that of our own. This suggests that it is not something conjured in the self but rather is a response to an invocation or summons from outside the self. Sympathy thus depends upon the presence of another who exists apart from and prior to the expectations and conventions that mark out what may or may not be shared in common. Through sympathy, we are brought into relation with something more than ourselves, something singular and precious in its own right. Made vulnerable by our incapacity to do anything other than respond out of our own vulnerability, we suffer the other, undergoing its unique claim upon us. In turn, we respond as if to say, "Here I am," simply being present with another. Love in the shape of availability thus emerges as a moral conversion.

The insight here is as profound as it is disorienting—the vulnerable stranger is us all. We are all different, singular beings who are fundamentally similar in our vulnerability and neediness. From this recognition the moral disposition of compassion arises, a modification of the fellow feeling of sympathy. Compassion is a feeling-with the other for its own sake, preconditions aside. It does not simply undergo and suffer with another, it reaches out and desires the other's well-being and joy.[77] In the posture of compassion I am brought to resist dehumanizing powers and defend the refusal or abuse of another's vulnerable face, making his or her cause my own. Thus compassion signifies a mutual relation of vulnerability that exists beyond conditions established by the status quo. Because of this it requires an imaginative leap outside the conventions of a community's sense of itself. Compassion acknowledges that another may lack the means to reciprocate according to an economy of exchange but desires the good of that other despite this. Without self-protective guardrails, compassion sympathetically undergoes the vulnerability of the other and strives for its good. A paradox comes to the fore. We too are fragile and dependent upon others for our well-being and wholeness in ways that we can neither articulate nor reciprocate.

We discover that the stranger is fundamentally like ourselves. This affinity, however, rises from the sympathetic attunement of compassion, not from preceding conventions. It is the relation that is primary. And from such relation comes wholeness. We become more than what we were before. There is a being with the other that transgresses the boundaries of the familiar world and passes through the limits of self-sufficiency to mutuality in vulnerability. Weakness opens us to being available for one another, which opens us to a shared humanity. Vanier claims: "As the human heart opens up and becomes compassionate, we discover our fundamental unity, our common humanity."[78]

Conclusion: Empowering Community

Communities are a manifestation of the need to belong. And what are communities but extended matrices of interdependent relationships by which we belong to each other. While such belonging can become subject to assimilative and exclusionary practices that judge others according to fears and prejudices based in the cult of normalcy, there remains a gentle but persistent moral tug beyond the urge for control and sufficiency. This tug stems from the basic fact that human beings are vulnerable beings who need each other. Vanier puts it in the following way: "We all belong to a common, broken humanity. We all have wounded, vulnerable hearts. Each one of us needs to feel appreciated and understood; we all need help."[79] Without dependence upon one another, we cannot grow and develop the capacity for joy. We close up in fear. Love, however, opens us up.[80] And this opening is established vis-à-vis relationships of mutual vulnerability in which people respect and take time to be with and for each other.

The community that nurtures this is a community whose good is genuinely humanizing. Put differently, the common good of a community is that which cultivates and preserves our capacity for love, our capacity to foster each other's joy, which cannot happen outside of relationships morally charged and shaped by our basic availability to one another. The humanizing community must hold up respect, fidelity, and compassion as common ideals oriented toward the mutual flourishing of all who belong. Certainly we cannot engage everyone in relationships of mutual vulnerability. We only do so at restricted levels, in our families, our circle of friends, and our local communities. This is precisely why the common good of the larger society—that is, the public matrix of interdependent relations in which families, friends, and local communities reside—must be oriented toward vulnerability rather than normalcy in its forms of productivity, autonomy, efficiency, strength, and rational control. Vulnerability and dependence is normal. Accordingly, the moral measure of a society lies in the way it treats its most vulnerable. So disability is in the interest of the whole political society and its common good.[81] All people have gifts to offer, and this should be instantiated publicly in policies directed toward recognizing and facilitating the contributions of people with disabilities. For the networks of giving and receiving by which we flourish together happen most authentically at the level of vulnerability, at the level where love becomes possible. This is the grassroots level from which arises the welcome we all desire.

Hence, neither the solitary individual nor the social community is primary. They are secondary offshoots of a more basic horizon of interpersonal dependence upon one another, a horizon that makes us whole persons and creates moral agency in the form of availability.[82] Indeed, wholeness is not the property of the individual, a quality of self-sufficiency. It is a relational term; we are not complete persons without each other. What is "mine" is really "ours." My own joy, my own good, is connected with that of others. The common good of a community is thus not an external constraint imposed on me, but a horizon that empowers the flourishing of relationships in which I can flourish. It is together with one another that the distinctive value of every person is accorded recognition and welcomed— indeed celebrated—as a good that is part of us all. This is why vulnerability is key to our openness to each other. It nurtures a community of diversity rather than of sameness or uniformity dictated by normalcy. Society becomes an open rather than a closed circle of belonging. It preserves and celebrates differences as equal, not pressuring differences to become equal, normal like "us."

Therefore, vulnerability must be protected, making justice necessary to prevent undue exploitation, dominance, and closure. For, as we have noted, society often seeks to refuse and prevent suffering that it deems unable to contribute to its exchange functioning. So under its illusions of control, society comes to marginalize and exclude others whose bodies represent abnormality—as difference in the form of an undue weakness or vulnerability. This has a tragic interpersonal effect: it fosters unavailability to others. To counter such an effect, we must measure love by the empowering justice that results, a justice that makes way for more love. This is not to say that justice is the condition of love, rather that love's availability to others is a dynamism of respect, fidelity, and compassion that affirms by creating and preserving space for others to be in their own right, on a par with everyone else. Without justice, love can become sentimental and cheap, or worse, a tool for domination and exploitative imperialism that merely pretends to have the good of others in mind.

Justice testifies to the intrinsic value of other persons by according all their due. As Paul Ricoeur notes, it depends upon love to avert slipping into tit-for-tat forms of reciprocity in which one party gives merely in order to receive. Justice qualifies love's availability in the direction of a restorative praxis of egalitarian sharing, a mutual edification that builds upon the value and dignity of all, not merely some. Hence, the criterion of justice names, resists, and seeks to dislodge oppression and dehumanizing violence, not out of hatred but in love. Accordingly, Ricoeur suggests that love and justice must supplement one another.[83] Love empowers genuine community and justice makes this community one in which equal regard among diverse subjects can prevail. As it insures an equality of connection and interdependence—not autonomy—love welcomes and supports all. Yet in the end, tempered by justice, love must hold the right of refusal to those powers and principalities that neglect or abuse the vulnerability of persons. Vulnerabilities are unequal; some bear the burden of vulnerability more than others. This is why it has been important for us to understand the cult of normalcy (chapter 2) and critique its particular influence upon our society (chapter 3). For people with disabilities have been the recipients of deep injustice. And, in the famous words of Martin Luther King, Jr., "injustice anywhere is a threat to justice everywhere." Why? Because we "are caught in an inescapable network of mutuality, tied in a single garment of destiny."[84]

The center of attention in this chapter, however, has not been on justice. Rather than propose social policies and laws to rectify injustice, I have instead focused the discussion on the strange power of weakness to open up loving attentiveness. This is not to deny the importance of a concern for justice. To the contrary, it is to place the concern for justice in the relational framework of love. Justice, as Kittay argues, must reflect a "connection-based equality" which explicitly attends to different ranges of vulnerability—for example, to people with disabilities as well as to their caregivers—in order to support the relational capacities of each for well-being.[85] Otherwise the capacity for welcome and joy in loving relationships can be neither promoted nor sustained. For Kittay, the basic principles for such justice read as follows: "To each according to his or her need for care, from each according to his or her capacity for care, and such support from social institutions as to make available resources and opportunities to those providing care, so that all will be adequately attended in relations that are sustaining."[86] Seen accordingly, social cooperation does not emerge out of narrowly conceived economic or self-interested gain, but out of love for others, which promotes the sense that our lives are intertwined to the point that we share common goods, instead of compete against each other for them. Persons, each with vulnerable capacities for relationship, are the primary subjects of justice. For we are linked to a community as persons through caring relationships, not as autonomous subjects joined abstractly through contractual consensus.[87]

Love grounded in human vulnerability, I suggest, can be a grassroots moral criterion for social responsibility. Through sharing our weakness with each other we become whole persons, our capacities for giving and receiving welcome empowered. And this happens within the morally charged contours of availability—that is, in loving postures of respect for, fidelity to, and compassion with others. Living our vulnerability, then, is a source of genuine public good in three ways; it entails (1) being with others—represented by a range of needs and disabilities—as essential to (2) our own mutual flourishing, and also to (3) the common good of the larger communities in which we flourish. Vulnerability links us to a human community.

In the final analysis, privileging disability makes this kind of vision possible. It gives substance to the metaphoric reversal we have been talking about. For paradoxically, vulnerability is more than a liability. It has a strange humanizing power. It is a fundamental asset necessary for wholeness, freedom, and love. It is a strength that enlivens the human desire for welcome and rouses us to one another's presence, spreading joy in its wake. Rethought in terms of vulnerability, disability does not make someone unlike us, a flawed condition worthy of remediation or exclusion. Disability is testimony to the fact that human beings receive existence from each other. Hence, personhood is neither diminished by disability nor confirmed by ability. Wholeness, freedom, and love are not products of the "controlled body," but of an acknowledgment of weakness and limitation made concrete in relations of mutual openness and dependence. It is from this point that we enter into a religious space of orientation.

Notes

1. Henri J. M. Nouwen, *Our Greatest Gift: A Meditation on Dying and Caring* (San Francisco: HarperSan Francisco, 1994), 27.

2. This was his statement to me one night as I tucked him into bed.

3. "Being with" (Mitsein) comes from the German philosopher Martin Heidegger. It is his way of describing the ontological status of our being with others. See *Being in Time*, trans. John Macquarrie and Edward Robinson (New York: Harper and Row, 1962), div. I.4. However, unlike Heidegger, who tends to stress the individual, I stress here the priority of relation. *Coesse* is Gabriel Marcel's term. See "On the Ontological Mystery," in *The Philosophy of Existentialism*, trans. Manya Harari (New York: Carol Publishing Group, 1956), 39.

4. Alasdair MacIntyre, *Dependent Rational Animals: Why Human Beings Need the Virtues* (Chicago: Open Court, 1999), 1–2, 8.

5. MacIntyre here expresses views that fall in line with those of Charles Taylor, as discussed in chap. 2.

6. See ibid, 69–73; 82–84.

7. Ibid., 94.

8. Ibid., 85.

9. Ibid., 73. See also Brett Webb-Mitchell, *Unexpected Guests at God's Banquet: Welcoming People with Disabilities into the Church* (New York: Crossroad, 1994), 47–48.

10. Jean Vanier, *Becoming Human* (Mahwah, NJ: Paulist Press, 1998), 41.

11. Stanley Hauerwas, "Suffering the Retarded: Should We Prevent Retardation?" in *Critical Reflections on Stanley Hauerwas' Theology of Disability: Disabling Society, Enabling Theology*, ed. John Swinton (Binghamton, NY: Haworth Press, 2004), 97.

12. MacIntyre, *Dependent Rational Animals*, 130.

13. Hauerwas, "Suffering the Retarded," 93.

14. Ibid., 94, 102.

15. Ibid., 95.

16. Ibid.

17. Ibid., 96.

18. Robert F. Molsberry, *Blindsided by Grace: Entering the World of Disability* (Minneapolis: Augsburg Books, 2004), 120.

19. See Rod Michalko, *The Difference Disability Makes* (Philadelphia: Temple University Press, 2002), chap. 3; and Hans S. Reinders, *The Future of the Disabled in Liberal Society* (Notre Dame, IN: University of Notre Dame Press, 2000), chap. 10.

20. Hauerwas, "Suffering the Retarded," 96.

21. Ibid., 97. See also Hauerwas, "Reflections on Suffering, Death, and Medicine," in *The Suffering Presence: Theological Reflections on Medicine, the Mentally Handicapped, and the Church* (Notre Dame, IN: University of Notre Dame Press, 1986), 25–26, 28.

22. Vanier, *Becoming Human*, 46.

23. Ibid., 73. This also reflects the theory of René Girard, which explains why scapegoats are chosen—to bear symbolically and thus alleviate conflict in the community. See his classic *Violence and the Sacred*, trans. Patrick Gregory (Baltimore: Johns Hopkins University Press, 1997).

24. Jean Vanier, *Encountering 'the Other'* (Dublin: Veritas Publications, 2005), 28.

25. Hauerwas, "Suffering the Retarded," 103.

26. See Vanier, *Becoming Human*, 74–81; and Michalko, *The Difference Disability Makes*, 95–96.

27. Jennie Weiss Block, *Copious Hosting: A Theology of Access for People with Disabilities* (New York: Continuum, 2002), 37.

28. Hauerwas, "Suffering the Retarded," 102.

29. Ibid., 99.

30. Vanier, *Encountering 'the Other,'* 12.

31. Joseph P. Shapiro, *No Pity: People with Disabilities Forging a New Civil Rights Movement* (New York: Times Books, 1981), 5.

32. This criticism of charity is made forcefully by Ada Maria Isasi-Diaz in "Solidarity: Love of Neighbor in the 21st Century," in *Lift Every Voice,* ed. Susan Brooks Thistlethwaite and Mary Potter Engel (Maryknoll, NY: Orbis, 1998), 30–39.

33. This point has been well established by Michel Foucault. See *Madness and Civilization: A History of Insanity in the Age of Reason* (New York: Vintage/Random House, 1973) and *Discipline and Punish: The Birth of the Prison* (New York: Vintage/Random House, 1979).

34. Vanier, *Becoming Human,* 40.

35. Ibid., 45.

36. Jürgen Moltmann, "Liberate Yourselves by Accepting One Another," in *Human Disability and the Service of God,* ed. Nancy L. Eiesland and Don E. Saliers (Nashville: Abingdon, 1998), 121.

37. See Stuart Govig, *Strong at the Broken Places: Persons with Disabilities and the Church* (Louisville: Westminster John Knox, 1989).

38. See Block, *Copious Hosting,* 34–36.

39. MacIntyre, *Dependent Rational Animals,* 130.

40. The in-between space of relation is a central theme in the influential works of Gabriel Marcel and Martin Buber. For Marcel, see "On the Ontological Mystery" and "The Ego and Its Relation to Others," in *Homo Viator: Introduction to a Metaphysics of Hope,* trans. Emma Craufurd (Gloucester, MA: Peter Smith, 1978), 13–28. For Buber, see *I and Thou* (New York: Charles Scribner, 1958) and "Elements of the Interhuman," in *The Knowledge of Man: Selected Essays,* ed. Maurice Friedman (Atlantic Highlands, NJ: Humanities, 1988), 62–78.

41. See Marcel, "On the Ontological Mystery," 36–40; *Presence and Immortality,* trans. Michael A. Machado (Pittsburgh: Duquesne University Press, 1967), 236–38; and *The Mystery of Being,* vol. I, trans. G. S. Fraser (London: Harvill Press, 1950), 204ff.

42. Marcel, "On the Ontological Mystery," 40.

43. Ibid., 19–22; *The Mystery of Being,* vol. 1, 211–19; and *Being and Having: An Existential Diary,* trans. Katharine Farrer (New York: Harper and Row, 1965), 110, 117.

44. This is one of Franz Rosenzweig's key points in his famous *The Star of Redemption,* trans. William W. Hallo (Notre Dame, IN: University of Notre Dame Press, 1985); for example, see 177. Paul Ricoeur picks up the theme in "Love and Justice," in *Figuring the Sacred: Religion, Narrative, and Imagination,* ed. Mark I. Wallace, trans. David Pellauer (Minneapolis: Fortress Press, 1995), 315–29.

45. Vanier, *Becoming Human,* 22.

46. On "the face," see Emmanuel Levinas, "Signification and Meaning," in *Philosophical Papers* (Dordrecht: Kluwer, 1987), and *Totality and Infinity: An Essay on Exteriority* (Pittsburgh: Duquesne University Press, 1969). For a good introduction to Levinas, see the collection of interviews in *Ethics and Infinity* (Pittsburgh: Duquesne University Press, 1985).

47. See Levinas, *Totality and Infinity,* 194–201; and *Ethics and Infinity,* 85–92. Edward Farley makes a similar point in his *Good and Evil: Interpreting a Human Condition* (Minneapolis: Augsburg Fortress, 1990), 39–40, 191.

48. See Levinas, *Ethics and Infinity,* 97; and *Otherwise than Being or Beyond Essence,* trans. Alphonso Lingis (Pittsburgh: Duquesne University Press, 1998), 114, 142, 145, 199, no. 11.

49. Vanier, *Encountering 'the Other,'* 12.

50. C. S. Lewis, *The Four Loves* (New York: Harcourt Brace Jovanovich, 1960), 169.

51. Those familiar with Levinas will note that I am softening his language here in a way that places more stress on love as a correlative relation between me and an other. For Levinas, the relation to the other is tied principally to the ethical call of responsibility (see *Ethics and Infinity,* chaps. 7–8). In this regard, Levinas sees relation in ethical terms as a unilateral act of giving myself over to another, a gesture of service and self-sacrifice.

In my view, this tends to overlook the celebrative, joyful, compassionate, and even playful elements in love as a mutually life-enhancing endeavor.

52. See Vanier, *Becoming Human*, 22–23. Here Vanier makes the point that love begins with the revelation of value.

53. Ibid., 22.

54. Ibid., 82.

55. Marcel, "The Ego and Its Relation to Others," 23. See also "On the Ontological Mystery," 39ff.

56. I am drawing here from Eric Fromm's notion of respect in *The Art of Loving* (New York: Harper and Row, 1956), 23–24.

57. Eva Feder Kittay, *Love's Labor: Essays on Women, Labor, and Dependency* (New York and London: Routledge, 1999), 54.

58. Ibid., 169.

59. Ibid., 157.

60. Ibid., 172, 173.

61. Marcel, "On the Ontological Mystery," 36.

62. Ibid., 38.

63. Marcel also develops these ideas elsewhere. See "Creative Fidelity," in *Creative Fidelity*, trans. Robert Rosthal (New York: Noonday Press, 1964), 147–74; "Obedience and Fidelity," in *Homo Viator*, 125–34; "Testimony and Existentialism," in *The Philosophy of Existentialism*, 91–103; and "Fidelity," in *The Existential Background of Human Dignity* (Cambridge: Harvard University Press, 1963), 54–74.

64. Hauerwas, "Timeful Friends: Living with the Handicapped," in *Critical Reflections on Stanley Hauerwas' Theology of Disability*, 11–25. The term "friends of time" is borrowed from Vanier, *Community and Growth: Our Pilgrimage Together* (New York: Paulist Press, 1979), 66.

65. Ibid., 22.

66. Ibid.

67. Ibid. See Vanier, *Community and Growth*, 19.

68. Richard B. Steele, "Unremitting Compassion: The Moral Psychology of Parenting Children with Genetic Disorders," *Theology Today* 57 (2000): 161–74.

69. Hauerwas, "Suffering the Retarded," 100. See Adam Smith, *The Theory of Moral Sentiments* (Amherst, NY: Prometheus Books, 2000), 3–9.

70. Wendy Farley eloquently describes this in *Tragic Vision and Divine Compassion: A Contemporary Theodicy* (Louisville: Westminster John Knox Press, 1990), 70–73.

71. See MacIntyre, *Dependent Rational Animals*, 123–26. MacIntyre makes the point by way of a discussion of *misericordia*, that is, "grief or sorrow over someone else's distress," 125.

72. For extensive treatments of this theme, see Max Scheler's *The Nature of Sympathy*, trans. Peter Heath (London: Routledge and Kegan Paul, 1954); and Edith Stein's *On the Problem of Empathy*, trans. W. Stein (The Hague, Netherlands: Nijhoff, 1964).

73. Hauerwas, "Suffering the Retarded," 101.

74. Ibid.

75. Ibid., 102–3.

76. Ibid., 101.

77. Farley, *Tragic Vision*, 75–81.

78. Vanier, *Becoming Human*, 97.

79. Ibid., 37.

80. Ibid., 68

81. MacIntyre, *Dependent Rational Animals*, 130.

82. I follow Edward Farley's lead here in describing the interpersonal or interhuman sphere as a primary sphere of relation connecting the social and the personal. See his *Good and Evil: Interpreting a Human Situation*, chap. 1.

83. "Love and Justice," in *Figuring the Sacred*, 315–29.

84. Martin Luther King, Jr., "Letter from a Birmingham Jail," in *I Have a Dream: Writings and Speeches That Changed America*, ed. James Melvin Washington (San Francisco: HarperSanFrancisco, 1992), 85.

85. Kittay, *Love's Labor*, 179.

86. Ibid., 113.

87. See Martha C. Nussbaum, *Frontiers of Justice: Disability, Nationality, Species Membership* (Cambridge, MA: Belknap Press, 2006), 216. In chap. 3, Nussbaum critically appropriates some of Kittay's ideas to a similar end, focusing on what she calls a "capabilities approach." She underscores a diversity of individualized human needs and capacities, which together make a good life possible by linking a person to the human community.

5

Love Divine

Vulnerability, Creation, and God

"You are precious in my sight, and honored, and I love you." (Isa. 43:4)

There is a gratuity to love as we have described it that appears to defy common sense. It begins with the revelation of another's intrinsic value, and expands from there. A personal presence discloses itself as precious, having a significance that seems inborn, as it were, built-in from the start and not the product of values parceled out according to normalizing conventions. Love, then, both occurs amidst and exceeds the range of limiting conditions that define our lives. It means being available to another and attuned to that person's singular worth beyond the utility and convenience of standardized systems of economic exchange. Love's respect, fidelity, and compassion traffic in the space of an unconditional regard for another.

On the one hand, this is truly an impossible feat given the limitations of human life. The cultures and societies on which we depend rely upon frameworks of orientation that govern reciprocity and provide for group accord by way of common conventions, norms, and ideals. As we discussed in chapter 2, human relationships are conditioned by tit-for-tat forms of value exchange and are unavoidably shaped by their influence. On the other hand, if we take into account what was asserted in the last chapter, something also happens in human relationships that makes love a reality, an impossible possibility. Most human beings find themselves available to others at some point, beckoned into a space of respect, fidelity, and compassion for others. This can happen in family relationships, romantic affairs, community activism, religious devotion, and even patriotism. In each example, however, relation with the other occurs amidst conventional economies of exchange, but it also transcends them. For example, I may involve myself in volunteer work out of pity, based on a sense of privilege, but upon encountering the faces of real people in their vulnerability, I may subsequently come to recognize myself with them in a deeper mode of relationship, a way that calls me outward to be vulnerably present to others.

Love is unconditioned, charged with a moral pulse that sweeps beyond the limits of the world of ordinary conventions, the world as outlined by the cult of normalcy. If the revelation of the other as precious in his own right is fundamental, as we argued in the last chapter, love is a possibility built into every conditioned relationship. And this opens up the prospect that in every economy of exchange there is already operative an economy of grace, an economy of the gift that underlies and is presumed by all human acts of reciprocity, even when hidden or distorted by acts of exclusion and violence. Love always exists as a possibility within human relations—indeed, within reality itself—as a gratuitous gift. It is the inborn potential of human life.

According to Paul Ricoeur, this economy of the gift implies a "logic of superabundance" that acts as a balancing corrective to the ideals of distribution and equality inherent in the notion of justice. Justice, as we just saw at the end of the last chapter, is grounded in a "logic of equivalency" that gives each its due. While this serves the social order well, legal forms of insuring fairness can neutralize the unique worth of persons, reducing all to exchange equivalency. Rather than preserving society, such equalization homogenizes the concrete, singular value of differences. True, justice is an ideal measured according to the Golden Rule. But "giving unto others as you would have them give unto you" can easily be perverted and drawn into a utilitarian mode of "I give in order that you will give." What protects against this perverse interpretation? Ricoeur suggests it is the commandment to love one's neighbor, to give as it has already been given unto you, even to the point of loving one's enemies. This "hyperethical" injunction runs counter to the utilitarian economy of exchange, not because it entails self-sacrifice, but because it is based in an economy of grace, an awareness of preexisting gratuity built into the nature of human relations from the beginning.[1] Neighborly love stems from the revelation of value in another person that is basic to the way we find ourselves with others in the world. It points toward the always already possible reality of love, of mutual relationships of compassionate regard and life-giving generosity.

Using the language of "unconditioned," "superabundance," "grace," and "gift" brings us into a distinctly religious sphere of orientation. There is something at work that transcends the human condition, its fragility and finite limits. In this chapter, then, I wish to explore how, strangely, vulnerability is a gift radiating with an unconditioned power that can perhaps best be called divine. This shall lead us into the idea of creation. But creation is a term that has complex theological overtones; it is embedded in the meaning of other terms as well, terms that also need unpacking. Too often theologians who have written about disability have glossed over creation. Yet it is crucial to understand creation as the context of human love, this being part of a matrix of other theological themes, such as the nature of God, revelation, covenant, providence, salvation, and so on. While the biblical narratives highlight these themes mainly in relationship to human beings, there is much that can be learned about the theological importance of vulnerability from extending considerations to include creation as a whole, and God's relationship to it.

So the discussion that follows seeks to forge a path into a theology of disability by beginning with the broader issues of (1) how the concern for God generally emerges in human life and, in turn, (2) how this comes concretely to the fore in biblical texts and (3) in an understanding of creation as a whole and God's relation to it, culminating in (4) a vision of creaturely and divine vulnerability. However, as an explicit theme disability shall loom in the background and will not directly be addressed. Instead, building upon the last chapter, vulnerability will be central. The next chapter will more specifically pick up the issue of disability as we explore the creation of human beings, the problem of sin, and redemption in Jesus Christ. But first we must rethink vulnerability in theological terms so that we can open up the prospect of reorienting theological thinking about disability, especially as it relates to creaturely vulnerability and God's unique vulnerability to creation. It is of utmost importance to take this theological step, for our theology informs our practice.

The overarching thesis of this chapter is this: creation opens up to a creator God who loves. To be is to be a creature, loved into being by a transcendent source of abundance that becomes palpable in vulnerability and fulfilled loving relationships. If love trades upon the fact that another's vulnerability is disclosed as of singular worth, inviting us to let go of conditions that reflect the need for security and control and risk a relation beyond foreseeable calculations and expectations, so becoming available to that person's peculiar way of being, then love's power reflects the presence of a transcendent reality. Indeed, loving another is a kind of conversion to God. Thus we begin with how the sense of God arises in human life.

I. Love and Conversion to God

In the loving posture of availability toward another, a fundamental affirmation is at work that exceeds estimation and escapes containment within any finite framework of value orientation.[2] I wish to suggest that this emerges as a declaration of gratitude for the gift of existence, which rises to the surfaces of our lives in a tenacious posture of hope. Thus the particular presence of another person holds out before us a gift—the promise of mutual relation as an empowering grace. Because of this we continually push past the apparent finality of senselessness and failure, destruction and violence, and risk affirming life amidst and in spite of the reality of death. Human beings seek welcome, a place to call home. While such a gesture is mediated in finite relationship, it cannot help but transgress the limits of finitude, invoking a sense of the divine. I wish, then, to maintain that traces of God's presence are woven into human experiences, an elemental part of our existence. Let us examine this assertion in more detail.

Gratitude—Existence as Gift

Recognizing another as vulnerable and precious means embracing a gift, welcoming an empowering value. I am confronted suddenly, unexpectedly, by a presence that is more than I arranged for or expected, one that surprises me by its very appearance in weakness and fragility, in its capacity to be denied and broken. Astonished, I am awakened and lured into another way of being that suspends the laws of production and distribution so characteristic of the typical economy of exchange. Another more primary economy is at work here, one in which the other's presence offers me nothing useful, nothing at all according to standard conventions—nothing, that is, but its own being. Here there are no calculable reasons drawing me into a contractual relation in order that I may gain something in return, for the other's presence shows itself as a value precisely in its weakness. Apart from all external conditions and utilitarian appraisals of worth, a human being stands before me in sheer givenness. And from this surprising, incalculable occurrence rises in me a profound acknowledgment: to exist is good, a grace received.

Presented in vulnerable uniqueness and difference, the other is precious merely because he or she is. Accordingly, another person comes as a gift set before me, with whom I am invited into relation. And this astonishing fact testifies to the sheer gratuity of my own existence too. Such gratuity, opened up by the presence of another, has extraordinary moral power. I am lured into the between-space of relation, and thus become available to another, involved to the point where my own good is caught up with and connected to his or her good. Sympathetically attuned, I participate in the giftedness of the other as someone akin to me. The other is not merely the limit of myself, but part of me, enriching my world. We are joined in a relation that opens up something extraordinary, even spiritual. Together, we become more than we were before. I am not for myself, but with and for the other in a larger circle of "us." In a real sense I do not exist without the gift of the other's presence. My existence itself is gratuitous, contingent and vulnerable, a gift handed over to me, something for which I can take no credit.

Because such gratuity seeks appreciation, human beings desire to be—that is, to discover their value, and in turn see it reflected back to them through the recognition of others.[3] This is fundamental. Human life seeks more than survival alone. It seeks to flourish and find itself acknowledged within a larger framework of value and purpose. Life seeks delight in living, and this delight blossoms most fully in the dance of relational mutuality and love. Thus it is we aspire for love's welcome and the joy it announces. Built into our hearts is an implicit affirmation that "to be" in the fullest sense means to be welcomed, invited into a place of belonging that binds me with others and outlines the personal shape of a home (*oikos*). And being at home links us to a place of loving affirmation, an economy (*oikos* + *nomos*) where we are recognized for our unique worth and taken in. Put succinctly, to be is to be received as good; being signifies gratuitous welcome. In this sense the relation of love opens us up to the joy of being part of something genuinely good, a belonging to reality.

Being part of my son's struggle to affirm life and wrestle with his condition has brought this truth home with particular poignancy. There is a joy at work deeper than the struggle, a joy, in fact, testified to in the struggle. This is the joy of welcome, of love, of being confirmed and fulfilled in the presence of each other. Implied within the dynamic sway of love's giving and receiving is an affirmation of the goodness of being. Thus the experience of love's self-transcendence not only is able to bring me to acknowledge and accept my own contingency and vulnerability; it also can elicit in me the affirmation of existence as an inestimable value.

The point is this: being in relation to another attests to the fact that existence is trustworthy and good. In giving and receiving we come to act together as if the world is capable of confirming and sustaining the welcome we offer one another. It is as if we bear witness to the goodness of things, exclaiming jointly, "It is good to be." Such an affirmation traffics in what Paul Ricoeur calls a "logic of super-abundance," a surplus of value that exceeds quantification and control.[4] The fact of existence is a given, a grace received. I did not do anything to deserve to be, to justify the essential worth of being. That I am simply alive is an incalculable mystery for which I cannot account on my own terms.

The recognition of this prodigality yields nothing less than gratitude, a gesture of thanksgiving by which we concede to the fact that we are radically dependent, and not our own possessions.[5] As individuals we are only part of a complex network of relationships that is itself contingent and gratuitous. After all, the universe might not ever have been; it is a wonder that there is something and not nothing. The fact that we "are" is a gift. It is good in itself, apart from matters of functioning—displaying an extravagant generosity at work in the universe, a superabundance of grace that spills over and endows my life and all things with inestimable individual value. In all its concreteness and multiplicity the universe is a horizon of excessive plenitude, a fathomless mystery given over continually and creatively in each moment of finite existence. In the Augustinian sense, being is good simply because it is (*esse que esse bonum est*).[6] To be is to express value and, accordingly, to speak an inescapable and original "thank you." Welcome is at the heart of reality, and we glimpse this in relation to others not under the sway of an economy of exchange, but in an economy of grace.[7]

Hope—Relation beyond Tragedy

Gratitude, however, is no easy panacea or superficial optimism. It is tenacious and realistic. It affirms the gift of existence amidst those things that would deny or suppress it, or cause despair. We are fragile and vulnerable beings living in a contingent world. This makes our condition tragic in character, inevitably subject to deprivations, limitations, and sufferings. Tragedy is not merely an aspect of human life; it characterizes our vulnerability. Yet it would be wrong to say that tragedy necessarily leads to pessimism and despair, for it is a persistent and elemental ingredient of the affirmation of being. Edward Farley defines "tragic" as referring to "a situation in which the conditions of well-being require and are interdependent with situations of limitation, frustration, challenge, and suffering."[8] Finite and interdependent beings are diverse and vulnerable to harm. Diversity is the precondition for interrelationship, but also can make disharmony, conflict, and alienation inevitable. Gratitude is not indifferent to tragedy. Tragedy is gratitude's situation.

Hence, gratitude is not a static affirmation, but a restless exigency, a resolute dynamism of the human spirit. It acknowledges tragedy forthrightly, yet refuses to let its apparent word on failure, dissolution, and absurdity become final. It engages imperilment by way of an attitude of expectancy which trusts that things will ultimately be all right. This determination fuels the posture of hope—what Ricoeur calls a "passion for the possible"—that asserts meaning and value over bland repetition, chaos, and destruction.[9] Hope refuses and pushes past all closures and finalities, even death. It acts as if the sheer fact of existence holds out a promise now only partially and fragmentarily realized, but opened up toward a future of possibility. Hope anticipates, audaciously awaiting goodness in a posture of confidence or trust. However, it is not a passive, but a willful and active, anticipation.[10] In the words of Farley, "hope is a sign of life, something vibrant, interested, concerned, and engaged."[11] Furthermore, hope is not merely a matter of for what I hope, but with whom I hope. Hope is a creative power that is relational—for us. This distinguishes it from an ego-centered desire or wish. Love and hope are bound indissolubly.[12]

In this regard, caring for Chris is for me a prime example of hope, an anticipatory gesture that holds out for his good, working toward a future of possibility for him even as limiting conditions daily impose themselves. Is this gesture in vain? Perhaps. Perhaps human beings are nothing but momentary flicks of life in an indifferent nexus of cause and effect. Perhaps mistrust is justified and we are condemned to live in an absurd universe, making the best we can of things, our longing for welcome a useless passion. But I cannot love Chris and believe so. Witnessed in respect, fidelity, and compassion, my availability to him reflects an acknowledgment that his existence is value-laden and full of promise despite its imperilment. So despite evidence to the contrary, I hope. Moreover, I seek to validate and cultivate in him the disposition of hope, reflecting back to him the giftedness of existence in his own being. To do otherwise would be disrespectful, unfaithful, and uncompassionate, a breach of the relation. Isolation and hopelessness are siblings.

Hope survives then, as Gabriel Marcel acknowledges, not by denying despair through some naive optimism or utopian vision, but precisely amidst the very real temptations to despair.[13] Hope arises only with a felt lack or deprivation, and in terms of an acknowledgment of vulnerability. Existence is tragic in its gratuity; it radiates a goodness that is fragile, conditioned by situations of interdependency that limit the scope of well-being and invariably cause discontent and suffering.[14] In this fragility, hope overcomes the possibility of despair by stretching forward and pushing through disappointments, imagining concrete fulfillments that actualize the fundamental affirmation of value underlying gratitude. Farley puts it powerfully in claiming that "hope is an existential refusal of the domination of the tragic."[15] It intuits a world that is open, not closed, to possibility, nor subject to a deterministic fatalism or ultimate dissolution. Furthermore, it thrives on the sense that this openness is trustworthy, signaling welcome as the possibility that tragedy is not the final word. But hope is precisely hope because we cannot see such possibility clearly right now. We are not in control. Hope is a surplus that always occurs in a situation of limits and contingencies, even while it refuses to be reduced to them. Thus hope implies an incalculable possibility that can never be brought to complete fruition in this life.[16] There are no guarantees, only finite and fallible approximations. Despair remains ever an option.

At the same time, however, beyond all probability, beyond all conditioned expectations, hope asserts that the heart of existence is not anonymous and indifferent, that the world is not merely a collection of interchangeable quantities reducible simply to their function in the whole. Rising in the context of relation, hope asserts that the mysterious heart of things somehow wills my being, Chris's being—all beings.[17] Existence is open and trustworthy, holding out the eschatological promise: "It will be all right." In this, hope extends ever forward toward a fullness of life—indeed, a salvation—an exigency animated by gratitude.[18]

Hence, in hope a fundamental affirmation of being takes place that accepts vulnerability even while refusing to let its suffering or tragedy have the last word. It is as if it would somehow betray our nature to give in to suffering as the decisive word of existence. We experience affliction and harm as something foreign, a distortion of something essentially good. Because of this, we are compelled instinctively and continually to struggle against the apparent heartlessness of things. With typical fluency Wendy Farley explains why: "Awareness of how deeply we suffer is possible because it arises out of an intuition of something more fundamental to us. Deeper than the distortions of our lives is a beauty and luminosity that makes suffering seem an utter contradiction to our true nature."[19] Hope happens amidst suffering but does not passively yield to it. Implicitly, human existence is declared an unspoiled good, a declaration which rises in gestures that consent to creaturely vulnerability and interdependence. Even in dehumanizing situations, however, gratitude and hope find ways to spring forth in surprisingly powerful ways, affirming life and resisting ultimate dissolution.

The Sense of God—An Extraordinary Possibility in Vulnerable Ordinariness

It is precisely the hope-filled tenacity of gratitude that points toward the religious sense of God. Something is signified here that eludes signification, that is "more" than can be expressed and exceeds our capacity to contain. In this way the conditioned nature of human existence gives testimony to something unconditioned. More specifically, the unconditioned character of love suggests a logic of superabundance at work in human life that trespasses the limits of finite standards and categories. Our existence thereby becomes opened up to the possibility of a transcendent source of being. That we attend to the other as precious in his or her own right breaks the hold of all conventions and boundaries, leaving in its wake a surplus giving itself over in things, bestowing a grace to which we are indebted. We become conscious that we are neither simply "here" by fiat or happenstance nor merely the machine-like result of causal determinations, but somehow willed into being. This sense of giftedness rises from an inbuilt proclivity not merely to give thanks in some vacuous and inchoate sense, but directed toward an unconditioned reference point that houses and gives over superabundant value. Simply put, we can't thank nobody, only somebody. As Mary Jo Leddy puts it, "in the awareness of having received something for free, there is a movement to wanting to acknowledge the giver."[20]

Who is this giver? Ultimately, the gift we receive points to a plenitude that can only be called divine, a transcendent power of generosity from which existence originates and toward which hope is directed. We are indebted. Indeed, hope's unspoken gratitude, in the words of Marcel, "appears as a response of the creature to the infinite Being to whom it is conscious of owing everything that it has and upon whom it cannot impose any condition whatsoever without scandal."[21] Friedrich Schleiermacher suggests something similar in the often-misunderstood phrase, "the feeling of absolute dependence."[22] As I interpret Schleiermacher, this feeling indicates an awareness of being utterly affected, not in the sense of helplessness or passivity, but as one whose very existence is experienced vulnerably as gift. We did not make ourselves, but simply find ourselves here, placed into the world, as it were. Hence, using Schleiermacher's language, "God" is a way of designating the "whence" of that feeling of absolute dependence, the origin of gratitude's impression that our existence is given.[23] Gratitude and hope are testimonies to a basic sense of God that flows through our experiences like a deep current.

Marcel carries the point further by describing the impression we are talking about as an exigency or desire, not a passive emotional state. Reflecting what we saw earlier in terms of gratitude and hope, he suggests that the human desire "to be," as a fundamental affirmation of being, is a desire for God, the ultimate source of being.[24] To recognize that one has received a gift means, in some sense, to give thanks in return, which implies seeking connection with a giver. The gift, however, is not one thing or another, but our very being, the wonder-producing fact that we are here at all. The desire to be thus invokes a desire to thanksgiving that pushes past limited horizons toward the unconditioned. This is why it is not altogether outlandish to say, along with Augustine, that humans are disposed to something akin to praise.[25] By this we are not suggesting a rose-colored and superficial optimism. To the contrary, in the midst of imperilments our hearts are restless and search for a home, a resting place. We hope. And in the space of this hope we long for a higher power or object to worship that is in some sense personal, a life-giving power that wills us into being, welcoming us into the value-laden and purposeful tapestry of reality. We long to be creatures in a creation. The symbol "God" functions to house—to locate and fulfill—this longing in Abrahamic traditions.

The sense of God as we are describing it, however, is not the indirect product of a process of reasoning about the world (a posteriori), but an immediate intuition, a sensibility that is inscribed upon the human heart (a priori). How so? Insofar as I participate in the presence of another, connected by a relation of mutual vulnerability and love, becoming more than I was before, a self-transcending spiritual momentum is inaugurated.[26] Marcel calls it a kind of conversion experience wherein the self is "called to become a witness," testifying to an abundant and unconditioned grace.[27] This perception of such grace is what stimulates the dispositions of gratitude and hope, which are clues to the valuable goodness and ordered purpose of the world. True, we may rationally infer God from value and order—as did Aquinas, for example, in the fourth and fifth arguments for God's existence in his famous Five Ways. But such a process itself is energized by the prior perception that the world is a home, invested with a meaning and moral significance that, in its gratuity, ushers us beyond itself.[28] It happens after we have already been taken hold of by the desire to thank, to praise. And this means that God has already been invoked at the core of life as its presupposed and unconditioned source. The sense of God does not occur at the end of a chain of reasoning.[29]

Experienced through the lens of availability, finite being resonates with a goodness that is insufficient to itself, that sings with a superabundance opening us to something more. In the words of Gerard Manley Hopkins, "the world is charged with the grandeur of God." It testifies to a surplus of reality and power that cannot be reduced to the ordinary, as we know it. There is an extraordinary dimension woven into the tapestry of our lives that exceeds reckoning in everyday conventions and terms. It comes to awareness in a way that surprises us, arresting the calculated, utilitarian, and predictable world of commonplace assumptions, shaking up our sense of the way things seem to be. Beyond the cult of normalcy love is possible. Tragedy is not the final word. The vulnerable giftedness of beings elicits a self-transcending affirmation that anticipates a different order of existence amidst and despite finite imperilments. Welcome is at the heart of the world. This affirmation is an implicit openness to God. It is not always overt, but it nonetheless beckons us into a space of gratitude and hope. Indeed, gratitude and hope trespass on the logic of the ordinary and predictable. The preciousness and abundance of the world is a witness to God (see Rom. 1:20; Acts 14:17). Things spontaneously seem to cry out, as Augustine exclaims, echoing Psalm 19: "We did not make ourselves; he made us who abides forever."[30] Because of this, John Calvin famously concludes: "There is within the human mind, and indeed by natural instinct, an awareness of divinity" (*Divinitatis sensum*).[31] Or, put in terms we have been using, built into human life is an affirmation of being that indicates the presence of God.

Here, however, the divine presence is not focused or concretely understood. It is more implied than explicit. So while the sense of God animates a spiritual impulse in human life, it functions as a corollary of gratitude and hope that does not necessarily connect to one specific religious perspective or another. In this way the sense of God is not yet overtly religious but rather is a kind of departure point, a creaturely readiness for explicit religious meanings and the revelations that mediate them. That is, it disposes us toward being shaped concretely by the religious traditions we inherit, giving them broad, existential connections in our lives. Concrete religious traditions cannot be deduced from the sense of God. We cannot simply unpack it and find some ready-made religious meaning inside, for it is ambiguous and incomplete. More is required. We do not yet know who God is, only that something extraordinary seems to call to us from the giftedness of being. Hence, rather than being a distinct revelation of God, the sense of God tilts us toward the possibility of such a revelation. It provides a backdrop or context of recognition within which divine revelation becomes anticipated as relevant and credible. Through it human beings are inclined toward specific religious meanings. The sense of God is an opening to revelation, a capacity to receive God's reality concretely disclosed in history.[32]

Human beings are restless. Our hearts seem engraved with a God-shaped hole. We hunger for narratives, rituals, symbols, and concepts that consecrate the con-ditioned, finite world we experience as a creation, a grace given. Living amidst ambiguities and imperilments, we look for ways to amplify and make concrete our sense of gratitude and hope amidst tragedies that undo us and cause suffering. We need to know where to look for resources and direction. We require specific nurturing. That is, we need some framework of interpretation to orient us to existence as good, from which we can double back to understand gratitude and hope as a call from God. We long to see our lives as part of an ongoing story, with a beginning and end that makes sense of the present perils we may face. After all, how do we empower availability, living more fruitfully into the vision of relational mutuality despite its suppression by the cult of normalcy? How can we name the goodness that is so often distorted by suffering and wrongdoing? Furthermore, where is God in the afflictions we undergo? These questions require a distinctly theological turn to the vision reflected in the biblical narratives, a place where the human desire for the divine meets a particular God of grace who comes to humanity, welcoming us as the creative, sustaining, and redemptive source of all things.

In the biblical witness we find a distinct language for the gratitude and hope of which we speak, and for the creative God of love to which we aspire. Carried forward in Christian traditions, such language makes manifest and thus enables us self-consciously to enter into the gifted nature of human life, giving particular shape to the fundamental affirmation we have just discussed more genericically. This gives direction to the desire to praise, providing content that orients us to transcendence. The result is faith, that is, a "belief-full trust" taken hold of by God's gracious and welcoming love. Christian faith proclaims a God who creates the world and fashions human beings in the divine image, and who, as sin comes to distort this image, enters lovingly into covenant relation with the people of Israel to bring about salvation. That salvation is fulfilled for all humanity in Jesus Christ and will be made complete in the kingdom to come. This is a story of love, grace, and hope. Because of this, it is also the story of a God whose power is revealed as vulnerable and available to creation. Thus a theology of creation is the crucial beginning point, making sense of our instinct for God by giving it a concrete reference point in God's creative love.

II. Creation's God: A Theological Matrix

While occurring in Genesis 1–2 as the overture to the whole Bible, the theme of creation is celebrated throughout the Bible, in the prophetic and wisdom literature as well as in Paul's writings and the gospels. And it is saturated with theological meanings. The most crucial notion is that the universe is neither eternal nor self-originating, but derives from a divine order of being that cannot be reduced to finite and contingent processes. This makes it impossible to separate the theme of creation from the knowledge of who God is. It also, therefore, makes it impossible to understand without attending to how God is experienced and revealed concretely as redeemer. So we have a kind of theological matrix that includes various loci: God's nature, revelation, redemption, and creation. Creation is a theme that cannot stand by itself. Discussing these loci intelligibly and noting their interrelations is important for forging the way into a theology of vulnerability that privileges disability. For disability is neither a blemish in God's creation nor something God deliberately creates to punish, to illustrate a point, or to work blessings through. To grasp this we must excavate the broader biblical horizon in which creation becomes meaningful.

For purposes of clarity, at this point we shall look mainly at the Hebrew scriptures. This seems at least provisionally right, since the New Testament literature adopts the Jewish conception of God along with accompanying themes of creation and covenant. The next chapter shall directly engage how the experience of redemption in Christ augments this portrayal of God and God's relationship to creation.

God's Transcendence and the Redemptive Encounter

Central to the biblical traditions is belief in a God whose reality transcends the world in both value and being: "For my thoughts are not your thoughts, neither are your ways my ways, says the Lord. For as the heavens are higher than the earth, so are my ways higher than your ways and my thoughts than your thoughts" (Isa. 55:8–9). God's way of existing is qualitatively different from that of the world, standing out from the world as its creative and redemptive source. As the actualizing power behind the forces of nature and history, the divine mode of existence is wholly unlike that of ordinary beings, surpassing the contingent, temporal, and spatial limits of finitude as an unconditioned "other." But what does this mean? What kind of "other" is God? And how are we able to talk about such a mode of existence?

Talk of God's transcendence depends fundamentally on the issue of how God comes forth concretely as God for human beings, experienced as a significant or pertinent reality evoking some kind of "belief-full" conviction, worship, and redemption. That is, how we think of God's transcendence depends upon how we see the reality of God as of consequence for us. This is why transcendence should not be seen as connoting merely an abstract separation or domineering distance from the world, though metaphors of height and power may suggest this. For the term bespeaks a certain kind of experience in the world, a certain way of the world that attests to something more than or different from the commonplace and mundane. Something sacred or divine comes to pass, designating itself set apart from the ordinary. It is mistake, then, to see God's transcendence as something removed from or outside the world. God's presence is near, experienced within the world. It overflows from within the ordinary, recognized as such by being more than routine everyday events. In theological language this means that God holds transcendence in immanence. Transcendence suggests that God is irreducible to the ordinary world, though it need not imply a chasm between God and the world. As we shall see more clearly as the chapter unfolds, God is intimately involved in the world and associated with creation, filling heaven and earth (Jer. 23:24). Abraham J. Heschel exclaims: "God remains transcendent in His immanence, and related in His transcendence."[33] So even while the reality of the divine exceeds that of the world, the two are related.

To fill this out, however, we must assume a revelation, an encounter with God, the effect of which yields transformation, redemption, or liberation. In the Hebrew Bible we find testimony to a God who expresses a unified and purposeful will, a presence made palpable through historical events. The unity of God, as a plurality of powers wrapped up in single divine presence, acts as a guiding force informing the thrust of Hebraic monotheism, giving it the momentum to break from the polytheistic fertility religions of its Semitic neighbors: "Hear O Israel: the Lord our God is one Lord . . . you shall not go after other gods" (Deut. 6:4). Because God is a living and personal will that enters into purposeful relationship with an historical people through saving deeds and ethical exoneration, the principle of divine unity gathers together the drama of ancient Israel.[34]

Yahweh becomes venerated as deity on the basis of Yahweh's ability to create and preserve the Hebrew nation, delivering it from various powers that threatened to squelch the people's collective life, and through the spoken word (*dabhar*) coordinating their historical existence by entering into a covenantal dialogue with them. Behind God's redemptive manifestation, then, lies a faithful volitional subject—a Thou—who makes promises and remains steadfast through historical flux and flow. "And I will walk among you, and will be your God, and you shall be my people" (Lev. 26:12). The framework of the religious imagination here is the moral dimension of personhood and its practical ethical implications concerning the communal-historical identity of a people. God is not an abstract power of nature or principle of being, but a righteous will disclosed in the liberative transformation of an historical community, calling persons into right relationship with divinity and each other. As personal presence is an agency that confronts the world of others in the mode of encounter, so, analogously, the model of divine disclosure or revelation is one of agential encounter: God comes to the people; God redeems.

Naming God's Redemptive Presence

The reality of God comes to human awareness in a shape that depends upon the way God is known and named meaningfully, disclosed concretely in human life—a living presence that offers salvation from life-opposing forces. This disclosure or revelation suggests the establishment of a relationship, which is represented in public form through cultic remembrances and narratives. Covenant is one way that this relationship is formalized, as narrated differently through Noah, Abraham, Moses, and David. In an important essay Paul Ricoeur highlights this relationship as the resource for naming God. He states:

"The theology of traditions names God in accord with a historical drama that recounts itself as a narrative of liberation. God is the God of Abraham, Isaac, and Jacob, the Actant of the great gesture of deliverance. . . . *God is designated by the transcendence of the founding events in relation to the ordinary course of history. . . .* God is named in 'the thing' recounted."[35]

In essence, Ricoeur is claiming that God is named in a communal act of interpretation that recounts past experiences of revelation. God is named as a relationship-establishing, covenant-making, and promise-keeping God. And in this remembrance God is experienced anew in a present situation, transforming lives by offering resources for gratitude and hope.

However, while covenant is the broad category often employed to express this, biblical scholar Terence E. Fretheim contends that the Hebrew Bible "clearly understands that the God-human relationship is much more comprehensive in nature and scope than the word *covenant* allows."[36] Resources for gratitude and hope play out not through a single medium but in many diverse forms, each of which is based in a narrative way of confessing the divine trace in events. Not merely covenant languages, but also prophecies, laws, hymns, prayers, liturgical formulas, and wisdom writings employ the referent "God." And they do so in various ways, manifesting different purposes that at the same time converge as part of an ongoing story. But there is no seamless coherence amidst it all. There is, instead, what Ricoeur calls polyphony, the overlapping of partial and incomplete discourses.[37] It is an established fact that the Bible is written by many people, who write in different contexts and with different concerns in mind. In this way the meaning of God is animated by the cross-fertilization of multiple ways of remembering, each of which gives witness to a distinctly revealing reality: "The God-referent is at once the coordinator of these varied discourses and the index of their incompleteness, the point at which something escapes them."[38] That which escapes and makes all discourse incomplete marks God's transcendent presence.

God is qualitatively different than anything else, having a name exceeding all others. In fact God is unnamable. There is but one deity, comparable to no created thing, and the ways of this deity are past finding out (Isa. 44: 6; 55:9; see also Isa. 40:18, 25; 45:15 and Job 11:7–9; 36:26). God dwells in deep darkness, concealed by an impenetrable cloud (Ps. 18:11), remaining hidden even as disclosed and revealed (Isa. 45:15). Divine self-disclosure itself is a concealment because God can never be immediately guaranteed and made subject to human manipulation. Hence, the referent "God" signifies the inconclusiveness of all language about God, the common goal of each form of biblical discourse but one that exceeds all of them. It surpasses human naming and cannot be reduced to knowledge. As illustrated by the burning bush episode in Exodus (3:13–15), God's name is such that no human can claim power over divinity. "I am who I am" indicates a kind of existence that, as Ricoeur puts it, "protects the secret of the 'in-itself' of God," which is something beyond nominative ascription and cannot be held at the mercy of human language. Such a secret, in turn, "sends us back to the narrative naming through the names of Abraham, Isaac, and Jacob, and by degrees to the other namings." That is, we are made to look for God's reality not in abstract, otherworldly heights but concrete in worldly occurrences, such as redemption and, as we shall see, creation itself. God's transcendence happens immanently. The appellation "Yahweh" is therefore not a name so much defining God as a sign marking acts of deliverance and giving substance to future hopes.[39]

This has several important consequences, leading into the theme of creation. First, by pushing discourse to excess the referent "God" allows the extraordinary, creative, and new to break forth into the ordinary, monotonous, and predictable. For Ricoeur this illustrates how parables, prophecies, proverbs, and eschatological sayings function. They transgress usual literary forms by hyperbole and paradox, becoming "limit-expressions," ways of signifying what trespasses and lies beyond the capacity to be signified.[40] They seek to remember so as to retrieve the redemptive past in the present, construing anew its power through varied literary and liturgical strategies. In this way the named God—Yahweh, Elohim—has transformative potential to empower praise and hope precisely when they seem impossible.[41] Because God cannot be measured, domesticated, or circumscribed by human efforts, divine transcendence remains unbound by the manipulative tactics associated with human ways of appraising value. God breaks the hold of idols, unsettling constrictive mechanisms of injustice and opening up space for new possibilities.

Second, the importance of God's incomparable transcendence plays out in the unconditioned trustworthiness it evokes. In times of peril and dissolution God's faithfulness is assured (Ps. 105). God is steadfast in all acts and decrees, trustworthy even in judgment and condemnation. There is only one God acting in the legion of worldly forces. This singular uniqueness of God distinguishes God as wholly dependable, unlike the seemingly capricious powers governing the multiform and contingent world. Thus in the context of oppression (such as in the Babylonian exile) it becomes possible for the community to recount its founding story in a way that names God as a resource for gratitude and hope. Here the people recall God's binding covenant with Abraham, wherein God's promise is unilateral, unconditional, and everlasting (Gen. 17:7). They also recall the equally unconditional kingly covenant God makes with David (2 Sam. 23:5), through whom shall come an anointed one to restore the kingdom of Israel (Ps. 89, Isa. 9 and 11).[42] New things are possible: a new covenant (Jer. 31:31–34) and even a new heaven and earth (Isa. 65:17; 66:22).

Thus even in the midst of desolation, final justice and well-being are assured, for God's steadfast love (*hesed*) rings true and shall prevail. Nothing—whether gods, natural forces, or other nations—can separate us from God's love. Even while for a time, and as the result of sin, God's judgment and wrath seems to prevail, it is not lasting like God's love (Isa. 54:7–8). God's promissory word stands forever; it is transcendent and does not change (Isa. 40:8; 55:8–11). The incomparable God forgives and offers grace, making things new (Isa. 43:18–19, 25). God has chosen Israel and there is no need to fear, for God is God (Isa. 41:8–10). This God is not only redeemer, but also creator of all things (Isa. 40:12–31), and thus can be trusted. Here especially, covenant faith merges with creation faith. The stability and hope of Zion is assured by the stability of the cosmos, the order of which is maintained via God's unshakable faithfulness.[43]

Hence a final consequence of the singular transcendence of God is the idea of creation itself. The story of creation is not simply a metaphysical conjecture or prescientific way of explaining the universe, serving then as a foundation point for all theological thinking. It is doxological, the result of a peculiar revelation of God in history from which humans are brought to experience and know God's loving will.[44] This revelation—which is recounted in many ways—becomes the key to interpreting traces of God outlined in nature as well as the human heart, a way of naming and deepening the affirmation of being. It sharpens distorted visions and transforms hardened hearts, opening up availability, nurturing love. So, as we shall soon explore more fully, the revelation of God allows us more clearly to recognize the world as creation, a divine gift inscribed with promise.[45]

The point comes to this: insofar as faith has been grasped by God's loving manifestation in relationship with Israel—and for Christians, as we shall see, in Christ—we can speak specifically of creation as the expression of that same love. So in a real sense we have begun not with a theology of creation but revelation. In revelation and the concomitant experience of redemption we come to recognize God's role as creator, tying past origins, present predicaments, and future hopes into an overall tapestry. This does not, however, make creation faith derivative, dependent upon redemption faith. Rather, it opens us to the double primacy of God's creative and redemptive work. Experientially, redemption clears our vision. But in actuality God's work as creator precedes and makes possible God's redemptive work. For creation is the theater of redemption, and redemption frees human beings, in Fretheim's words, "to be what they were *created* to be, the effect of which is named salvation." Creation language gives "cosmic depth to God's historical activity."[46] Redemption effects a new creation, offering new possibilities for creatures in the midst of imperilment by empowering gratitude and hope.

III. God's Creative Power: Toward a Theology of Creation

With the preceding discussion in mind, we can draw out several implications about God and God's relationship to creation, highlighting themes as they have been developed in Christian traditions to anticipate the discussion of chapter 6. Drawing biblical themes together into a sweeping synthesis, Augustine states: "There is no life which is not of God, for God is supreme life and the fount of life."[47] His words glow with a familiar hue, calling to mind the classic account of creation in Genesis 1, which sets forth a religious-cosmic vision by declaring the world a creation. All things are fashioned by a God who is not reducible to the world and who purposefully creates and declares that all is good. Gratitude and hope are anchored in the ordered goodness of creation.

The details of this vision come markedly to the fore in what scholars know to be the later Priestly account of creation (sixth and fifth centuries). Found in Genesis 1:1–2:4a, this account expresses concerns that were formulated during exile in Babylon, highlighting themes just raised above. The earlier account (tenth and ninth centuries), beginning at Genesis 2:4b and concluding at 3:24, can be distinguished from the Priestly account by its use of Yahweh as a name for God. The Priestly writer however, who edits and puts Genesis together, most likely intends for the entire account of creation to read as a whole. But because the earlier Yahwist account focuses more on humanity's origin, nature, and fall, we shall postpone exploring it until the next chapter, when we explore sin and redemption in Christ. So we shall focus the discussion mainly on Genesis 1 as it addresses creation as a whole, developing six primary themes insofar as they help us forge a theology of creation.

Throughout the process it will be important to remember that the Hebrew account of creation is narrative in structure. It is confessional and liturgical, concerned more with ceremonial praise than with systematic or thematic explication. As Ricoeur would remind us, it is part of a richly polyphonic way of naming God. Creation is a way to signify what is also signified—though differently and in other genres of literature—by redemption, covenant, wisdom, and so on. All these discourses are partial discourses supplementing one another. So our work here is not so much an exegetical undertaking as it is a theological interpretation, one that draws out certain implications insofar as they help better outline how creation fits into the matrix of themes we have been exploring thus far—that is, divine revelation, transcendence, redemption, and covenant.

In the Beginning, God

The first and most basic theme recapitulates what we saw above, namely, that God is the transcendent source of all that is.[48] God has no beginning, but *is* the beginning. "In the beginning when God created the heavens and the earth" (Gen. 1:1). Because the beginning has no preconditions, God does not depend upon creation in the same way that creation depends upon God. God is not merely a part of the world system, but distinct from it, the precondition of all happenings in space and time.[49] The beginning marks an absolute source. This suggests that the beginning does not happen in time, but rather that time comes from the beginning, an aspect of creation.[50] So, as Bernhard Anderson notes, the text here shows itself to be concerned with origins, with the source of both history and the natural world.[51] And as time has its beginning in God, so shall its end be in God: "I am the first and the last; beside me there is no god" (Isa. 44:6).

This also suggests that God should not be understood as a person, being, or entity among others, even a supreme one. The being of God is its own unique category transcending time and creation. Theologians often make efforts to indicate this by employing analogical language. That is, they try to find continuity of some sort between God and the world by speaking in categories of being drawn from creation and working by inference toward the Creator. If the world is created, it stands to reason that it should reflect finite and imperfect marks of God's infinite perfection. By analogy, terms like "absolute being," "being itself," "the power of being," and so on, come to signify in highly qualified ways the transcendent nature of God's reality. But even with these qualifications, language like this often does not go far enough to preserve the ontological difference between God and creation, preferring instead to envision God in categories of being (*ontos*) drawn from creation. The danger is a lurking idolatry that reduces divine transcendence to features of worldly life. This is why Langdon Gilkey calls the doctrine of creation "a great bulwark against idolatry."[52] It helps prevent the creature from being confused with and worshipped as the creator.

Furthermore, "in the beginning" names a God who neither comes from nor struggles against anything else to produce order and form. First, God is unconditioned, uncreated or ingenerate, because God is the source of all creation. Second, God's creative effort is not subjected to preexisting powers contrary to God's purposeful intention, because this would render creation a violent engagement thwarted by inimical forces. So, unlike the Babylonian creation myth, the *Enuma Elish*, where the god Marduk overcomes, sacrifices, and creates the world out of the body of the sea monster Tiamat (grandmother of Marduk), the God of Genesis does not wage war upon a personified chaos to impose order. Cosmic dualism is ruled out. This is not to say that preexisting material in no sense exists for the Hebrew writers, as would be common in the Mesopotamian context, only that it appears amorphous and depersonalized before God's formative will.[53] There is no cosmic conflict between God and alien powers of chaos. While many passages in the Hebrew Bible do recall the conflict structure found in the *Enuma Elish* and other Near Eastern creation stories—where God's sovereignty is established via struggle for mastery and the world is precarious, with the potential to return to the abysmal depths of disorder (Jer. 4:23–26)—it is also the case that they more often soften the conflict to affirm God's trustworthy agency and everlasting faithfulness (Ps. 104:24–26).[54]

The point of Genesis 1 seems to be, as Walter Brueggemann suggests, to enact by liturgical narrative an alternative world, "a well-ordered, fully reliable, generative world for Israelites who are exiles in Babylon."[55] An "in the beginning" God is a resource for future hope. The whole earth is the Lord's domain, a productive and habitable place of flourishing for creatures. Even the waters—an ancient symbol for chaos, destruction, and disorder—are subject to and harnessed by God: "The sea is his, for he made it; for his hands formed the dry land" (Ps. 95:5). The metaphor of royal power looms large (Ps. 93:1–4), not that God controls everything with utterly domineering might but that all is part of God's realm from the beginning of creation. In many places in the Hebrew Bible God's power is repeatedly seen to rebuke and hold the waters of chaos at bay (Pss. 18:13–15; 74:12–17; 77:16–18; 104:5–13; Hab. 3:15; Isa. 17:12–13). The analogy with the exodus from Egypt is striking: just as God divided the sea to forge a liberating path for the Israelites, so too does God arrange an ordered, secure, and trustworthy world, separating earth from the dangerous waters with a heavenly dome (Gen. 1:6–8). Even the powers of chaos serve God's work of creation, contained as they are within fixed boundaries that are part of God's ordering purposes. And this purpose is achieved through neither violence nor imposition.

Creation Called into Being

However, the discussion above by no means implies that creation emerges from God automatically, made invincible because it is created out of God's being according to necessity. In Genesis 1 we encounter the words, "And God said . . ." (Gen. 1:3, 6, 9, 14, 20, 26). This crystallizes a second theme: creation, in Hebraic thinking, is called into being by purposeful speech. Saying makes it so: "By the word of the Lord the heavens were made, and all their host by the breath of his mouth. . . . For he spoke, and it came to be; he commanded, and it stood firm" (Ps. 33:6, 9). The divine word is primary, not naturalistic forces or categories. Creation does not naturally flow out of God's being, emerging from God as of the same substance. So, unlike pantheistic systems assert, the world is not God, nor is it necessary. Things do not follow an impersonal logic of fate. Rather, the world is a meaningful communication of God, spoken deliberately and with intention. Speech implies agential action, a directive to produce order and fashion meaning. "Let there be"—this language marks a God who chooses to create out of a resolve that commands, gives form, separates, and names. A personal nature is required for this, a "who" that also redeems and calls Israel into covenant. It is God's purposeful word that both saves and creates. Indeed, God's word is deed, a making power. Making language thus accompanies speaking language.[56]

Furthermore, as Fretheim observes, "the divine creating often entails a speaking *with* that which is *already* created."[57] For example, God says, "let the earth put forth vegetation" (Gen. 1:11), "let the waters bring forth swarms of living creatures" (1:20), "let the earth bring forth living creatures" (1:24). Earth and water contribute to creation. God's creativity is not one-sided and controlling, but is mediated through creatures. Creation, then, takes place not merely from the outside, through God's word, but also from the inside, from within the abundance and potency of the created realm. Creation itself participates in God's work; the sea animals, birds, and human beings are blessed, called to be fruitful and multiply (Gen. 1:22, 28). It has a creative charge of its own that is self-generating. As we shall discuss later, this means that God does not directly or immediately assume responsibility for all creaturely generation and activity. The world has a natural integrity and creative momentum. God's power is not imposing power.

Creation from Nothing

Yet where then does creation come from, if neither out of conflict with alien powers nor out of God? In an effort to resist Hellenistic theories that asserted pantheism or some sort of dualism, early Christian theologians like Tertullian, Irenaeus, and Augustine tried to remain faithful to the Genesis 1 account by claiming God creates out of nothing (*creatio ex nihilo*).[58] To be sure, the creation story in Genesis does not use this phrase at all. But later biblical texts have been read as implying it, and the phrase, "In the beginning when God created the heavens and the earth," hints of it.[59] Questions occur, however, over whether the formless earth, its dark depths and waters, come first from God or are simply there as preexisting elements subsequently given form when God speaks. Indeed, the text does describe some things being fashioned from nothing by God's word, such as light and the heavenly firmament—but not the formless earth, darkness, and waters. Thus, the opening verses of Genesis probably function more like a literary preamble setting the stage than an actual moment of creation.

Even so, the important message conveyed by affirming that creation is out of nothing can still be retained. Not only does the Creator transcend the world, being irreducible to it, the Creator's purposeful will is the origin of all that exists. Consequentially, the theme of *creatio ex nihilo* supports the assurance that God's redemptive purposes cannot ultimately be thwarted. This does seem to square with the biblical texts. Literally, no thing stands outside God's process of willing beings into existence. Everything is radically dependent upon God, called into being from the formless void and darkness of nothing, the breath of God sweeping over the waters (Gen. 1:2). Nothing has a substance of its own; literally, it has no being.

Given this, perhaps we should say that creation is not out of a negative absolute nothing, but rather out of a positive relative nothing, a matrix of chaotic non-being full of potentiality for God's ordering work. The problem with creation out of an absolute nothing is that it comes dangerously close to affirming creation out of God—that is, nothing else exists but God. While classic theologians like Augustine stressed this option to maintain God's utter sovereignty, it so subjects creation to God's unqualified omnipotence that the finite world becomes tantamount to a playground of divine predetermination and necessity.[60] Contemporary theologian Jürgen Moltmann seeks to avoid this problem by claiming that God withdraws into the divine self to open space for creation, but this hollowed-out space quickly turns into a negative, God-forsaken space of *nihil* equivalent to hell.[61] I suggest that a biblically sound alternative is possible, one that also remains consistent with the basic thrust of the tradition's subscription to *ex nihilo* creation.

"Nothing" could be some kind of primordial material or energy out of which the divine separates elements and shapes the created order, just as the artisan employs clay to fashion the pot (Isa. 29:16).[62] Therefore, the chaos of nothing would not be seen as the negation of existence, but rather, as James Barr suggests, "a source from which certain elements in the created world were drawn."[63] This source would then be a contributing, vital part of God's creative work. Perhaps God's creative activity calls into being, separating and ordering things in a way that employs amorphous chaos as an integral part of the divine scheme, making it less prominent but not altogether eliminated. Perhaps its nothing is validated, not negated, as the "stuff" out of which beings are called, the brooding darkness and waters that the text seems to presuppose.[64]

God, then, creates out of the formlessness of nothing, but in so doing does not eradicate it. In fact, God's creativity acknowledges and activates latent possibilities in the disordered elements neither by conflict nor sovereign control but by, as William Brown puts it, "coordination and enlistment."[65] After all, formlessness is required for creativity, undergoing transformation in the process of becoming formed. In such a way, as many theologians and biblical scholars are now asserting, order is not opposed to chaos but emerges from it, called out of its nothing, which is a potency open to actualization.[66] An intriguing possibility surfaces: perhaps nothing/chaos still remains a part of what we are and the world we live in. We shall explore this in further detail later in this chapter and in the next—it has important implications for a theology of vulnerability and disability.

As we are using the term here, however, the focus of *ex nihilo* is to stress that whatever is created has God's initiative behind it. Brown confirms this by stating: "Nothing lies outside God's creative direction and approbation, not even 'chaos.'"[67] As the Psalmist expresses, "It is God that has made us and not we ourselves" (Ps. 100:3). The creature is not self-sufficient, but relies upon God. If God brings about beings from the formlessness of nothing, the creature belongs to the creator. This is so not only for salvation, but also for existence as a whole, which provides a framework for salvation. Hope is given substance in creation. For, as Ricoeur concludes, "the God of beginnings is the God of hope."[68] Because nothing created existed before the beginning, there is no time outside of creation. God is the creative origin of all coming to being and passing away in time. So the one in whom we place trust for our salvation is reliable, because God is the source of all that is. Past, present, and future are in God's hands.

Continuing Creation and Providence

Creatio ex nihilo helps clarify the character of what we mean by divine providence. This term signifies God's immanent presence in creation, God's persistent care for and guidance of the universe. Creation is not simply dependent upon God at the beginning of time, then subsequently possessing its own autonomy. God does not simply leave the world after producing it, flinging it away to follow its own preprogrammed course without divine sustenance, as Enlightenment Deists suggested. Why? Because if it is true that God creates out of nothing, creation is nothing—that is, it remains formless—without God's constant sustaining presence. To be and persevere in being, existence continues to depend upon God at every moment (Ps. 104:27–30).

Often the idea that creation participates in God has been employed to communicate the point. This not only makes the creative process ongoing (*creatio continua*), but more profoundly suggests that God—by means of God's communicative word—remains actively involved in the world, preserving it from dissolution and ordering it according to divine wisdom (Ps. 104:24; Prov. 8:27–31). Dietrich Bonhoeffer gets to this point by saying "God's Word is itself work." Divine transcendence means that God is not bound to the work by necessity, but "binds the work to himself" through a resolve that is expressed in word.[69] Hence, even as God remains different from the world, unable to be reduced to the world, God is immanent and at hand as creation's ongoing source. The point is, there is not one thing that does not live, move, and have being in God's presence. Or, as Bonhoeffer puts it, "God is beyond in the midst of our life."[70]

Thus the idea of providence stems from that of creation. It flowers in three general principles: first, that God preserves the world, upholding it continually. Second, that God governs the world, ordering it meaningfully by working the divine purpose in the act of preserving the world. Creation is not left to chance, but remains within the envelope of God's will. And third, that God's transcendence is paradoxically not far off but near, immanent in the world and engaged dynamically with all things. Not one incident happens outside of God's enfolding and communicative presence. God is not confined to one place or another, but is everywhere and omnipresent, not in some vague and homogeneous sense, but concretely, with each and every existent creature. God is with us, to the point of being acquainted with each of the hairs on our head; even the sparrow cannot fall without God's knowledge (Matt. 10:29–30). The Psalmist exclaims poetically, "You hem me in, behind and before, and lay your hand upon me. . . . Where can I go from your spirit? Or where can I flee from your presence?" (Ps. 139:5, 7). All beings and events are expressions of God's governing plan, which creates and sustains out of nothing according to divine will.

Creation a Free Act of God

The fact that God wills creation into being means that God is free, having, as Peter C. Hodgson puts it, "the power of being absolutely."[71] This is neither to say that God is absolute being—as if to place God at the top of the ladder of being— nor that God is the power of being—as if God and the world are not distinct—but rather that God's reality is being's power in unconditioned and limitless shape. That God is infinite (not finite or conditioned) means, to stress again, that God is not literally a thing or a person. For if God's reality was imperiled by anything other than God's own purposeful intention, this would circumscribe God and undo God's freedom. God is not compelled to create out of a divine deficiency. Rather, God freely chooses to create. Consequently, only from the purposeful power of God do creatures have being. As we shall soon see, this upholds the notion of grace.

It may then be instructive to understand God's creative energy as a primal form-giving potency that empowers beings to be, which gives being over to beings in creating them. Put somewhat abstractly, God is the pure possibility of being.[72] Having possibility means having freedom, which God has absolutely. This possibility, however, is not an impersonal or desert-like openness that lacks determination, like the formlessness of nothing. The way the biblical writers speak about divine freedom connotes a living, dynamic, and personal nature with the power to intend and decide in and from itself, without impediment.[73] God is self-initiating, unlike the potentiality of nothing's formlessness. Freedom is thus an aspect of God's transcendence, preserving the ontological difference we spoke of earlier. It is a correlate of the notion of creation out of nothing. The chaos of nothing is a potentiality dynamically attuned to God's fullness of possibility. But it cannot name such possibility in advance, without God's input, so to speak.

Consequently, we are led to insist that God's inner resolve to create the world is a mystery. There is no way to access it concretely from the standpoint of finite creation. The ultimate intention behind creation is hidden within God's infinite and inscrutable will.[74] This makes clear the religious notion of creation. For at least as presented in the biblical texts, God does not function as an explanatory principle or solution to the question, "Why is there something rather than nothing?" The idea of creation suggests something different, namely, that existence is an incalculable gift freely handed over, sustained, and governed by a transcendent creator. Again, we are radically dependent, preceded by a God who remains unaccounted for by human means. Acknowledging divine freedom places God beyond metaphysics, beyond the speculative urge toward rationalizing the universe. Genesis 1 confronts the reader neither with a principle of intelligibility that makes sense of the cosmos, nor with a scientific account of how the world came to be, but with a God who is personal and freely calls creation into being. The vocation of the finite creature lies in its creaturely status, its finite limits and dependent status before God's mystery. In this way, God's unfathomable resolve to create complements and gives further substance to God's potential to save. God is free, able to bring transformative possibilities to even the most impossible of situations.

Creation as Gift, Loved into Being

However, we must quickly add a qualification, which leads us into a sixth theme of creation. While God's reason for creating remains hidden, this by no means indicates that the divine will is arbitrary, as though God by fiat decides to create just anything, making the creative process a game of chance and probable outcomes. There indeed is stated purpose and intention behind creation. Yet this comes not from human inquiry about what must or must not be the case according to natural processes but rather from divine proclamation. God resolves to create and declares the fashioned world to be good.[75] Repeatedly, "God saw that it was good" (Gen. 1:10, 18, 21, 25, 31). It is no accident that the phrase rhythmically reoccurs: every moment of God's creation is good.

Understood in the light of Israel's experience of redemption, the creation account confirms what the people knew historically by faith: God is good and seeks to bring forth what is good. Through the spectacles of faith, formed also by other discourses that name God, creation is envisaged as the product of the same trustworthy divine will that enters into covenant and brings about salvation.[76] Creation is thus a theater of redemption, the worldly milieu in which God becomes revealed—both generally, through the sense of God, and specifically, through calling people into right relation according to God's good purpose. As such, creation itself is a communication of God's loving intention to give. The purpose of creation, then, lies in God's desire to create good. And the consequence is a good, a grace received.

God creates out of nothing from freedom and in love. Jürgen Moltmann perceptively notes the importance of coupling freedom and love:

> God's freedom is not the almighty power for which everything is possible. It is love, which means the self-communication of the good. If God creates the world out of freedom, then he creates it out of love. Creation is not a demonstration of his boundless power; it the communication of his love ... *creatio ex amore Dei.* ...

In his love God can choose; but he chooses only that which corresponds to his essential goodness . . .[77]

Divine freedom is not whimsical, but loving. In a way, then, God's creativity is not altogether unconditioned, for divine power has the character of love, giving generously to bestow blessing and benefit. It is not capricious but desires to share goodness. Insofar as divine love is freely given, it is unmitigated and irrepressible. But in so giving, God's freedom is qualified: it is for the world. This kind of overarching vision led Karl Barth to conclude that God is "the one who loves in freedom."[78] I would only rephrase Barth's formula in the following way to summarize what we have said thus far: God is the power of being absolutely in love. For God, who is transcendent, all things good are possible. And this possibility is communicated immanently in the act of creating what is good, intrinsically precious, whole, and blessed.

The discussion here swells to a crescendo: creation is an ongoing act of love, the sharing of God's goodness. The earth is full of God's steadfast love (Ps. 33:5; 36:5). Being is a gift, good simply because it is. And this goodness exuberantly witnesses to God (cf. Ps. 19:1–6): "Praise him, sun and moon; praise him all you shining stars! Praise him, you highest heavens, and you waters above the heavens! Let them praise the name of the Lord, for he commanded and they were created" (Ps. 148:3–5). An economy of grace is evident not only in the historical life of covenantal relation, but also in creation itself. "The Lord is good to all, and his compassion is over all that he has made" (Ps. 145:9). Love is at the heart of existence, neither limited exclusively to some beings nor simply spread out in some homogeneous way, but rather taking on a particular, incalculable form with each created thing.[79] Every being is loved abundantly into being. And insofar as this love is freely given, no conditioned reason can justify or account for the fact that beings exist. There is nothing we did or do to make and confer goodness upon ourselves. The gift is total.[80] We are simply welcomed, and welcomed continually by God's preservation. All finite things are infinitely affirmed as good; nothing is taken for granted and all are included. As God is not reducible to anything conditioned, God's favor is universal and unconditional; it is for the world's benefit and not because of something that the world does for God. Hence, created beings are good in a deeper way than human economies of exchange can attribute. A transcendent, superabundant love flows immanently through creation's abundance. This is God's self-communication—an effulgent welcome that overflows.[81]

IV. Relation and Vulnerability in God and Creation

The foregoing analysis puts together six themes, each of which supplements the others and culminates in the affirmation of creation's goodness. It is now important to unpack three supplementary themes that flow from the theology of creation as we have outlined it. These are crucial, helping to clarify certain misgivings not only about God's transcendence but also about creation's integrity. Furthermore, they open up into full bloom a theology of vulnerability, paving the way for a deeper sense of God's solidarity with creation and of the tragic character of creation's contingency. Ultimately, as we shall see, tragedy is taken up by God and held close to the divine being, such that it can be transformed within the arc of God's love.

Creation's Difference, God's Giving

Implied in our theology of creation is a theme often overlooked by theologians. That is, God's creative power is not a domineering and all-controlling power, but loving power. God's transcendence is available, opening itself to relation. In creating the universe, God makes room for something other than God, actively disposing the divine self to relationship with difference. While God has the power of being absolutely, God's love freely gives being over to others. Such giving involves a willful releasing or letting go of absolute power. God voluntarily limits absolute freedom by absolute love, becoming open to the creature in its being. Given this, creation might best be seen as an act of free love wherein God extends outwardly, going out of God's own being to let beings be, granting them an integrity other than God.[82] How can there be anything other than God? Because God's love freely "hovers over the face of the deep," embracing by entering formatively into the space of the void or formless nothing in order to create. God extends, not withdraws, the divine self. God builds a cosmic home, a dwelling place of "filled formfulness" symbolized by the tabernacle but extended through all things, a resting place of well-being. Sabbath rest temporally implies precisely this spatial completeness. Creation is God's sanctuary.[83]

In this way, God is difference making, empowering the household of a world teeming with diversity. That creation is affirmed good requires that it be distinct, different than God. This means that it is finite, other, uniquely differentiated and diverse. Accordingly, finitude involves fundamental limitations that not only set beings apart from God but also from one another. Creation is not a homogeneous whole. In a strictly empirical sense this seems obvious: every existent thing is conditioned by elements of a bodily nature that is environmentally situated. Beings are not uniformly the same but different. Where the biblical notion of creation pushes further is in its declaration that this difference is good. Each step of the Genesis 1 account concludes with God's affirmation. All the elements of existence—from the star-ridden firmament of the heavens, the dry earth, and the watery seas, to the thriving life of plants, animals, and human beings—are different and good. The universe is blessed as a milieu of astounding abundance and staggering complexity and diversity (Ps. 104:24–25).

In this way it might be said that God shares divine abundance, giving over to the creature its own distinctness and power to flourish. And in living things such distinctness is empowered to create and multiply of its own accord. God shares power, which leads to further developments of creation through other created things. Thus God is not an ordering force that imposes meaningful structure on what is otherwise meaningless. God is an animating and vitalizing power, setting the rhythm of day and night into motion and activating a creative pulse within creation itself. Energized by God's directive lead, creation is creative in its difference from God and in its diversity. This is why creation's diversity should not be seen in atomistic terms, that is, detailed simply by counting things numerically as separated fragments. For creation is an interdependent nexus within which all beings coexist. God enlists the elements to cooperate with divine creativity. Brown summarizes the point: "Although originally lacking form and substance, creation comes to contribute, under divine directive, to it own formation."[84] Created things are fashioned not as sufficient and complete unto themselves, but as finite parts of a larger, interconnected whole, the fabric of which is relational through and through.

Because it is gratuitous this whole—as God's creation—is rooted in something much more significant than a distributive economy of exchange; it is rooted in an economy of grace.[85] All things have being insofar as they participate in a dance with other beings; and such interrelation connotes interdependence. Everything subsists with and is affected by others. No thing is autonomous, having its own being: it is from God, out of nothing, and with others. This suggests, as Sallie McFague attests, an organic view of creation, one that stresses a common story woven throughout its tapestry, a shared way of being together.[86] It is then not so outlandish to say that the world is home, an economy of relatedness wherein each creature contributes to the other and belongs to the whole.[87] As it lives, moves, and has its being in God, this home welcomes each created thing as a gift. Grace is built into the world; love resonates through all things. And because of this, rather than coercive mastery we should conceive of God's ongoing creative work as an act of solicitude.

Creation and the Tragic

Yet this vision of creation's difference is no superficial optimism; that would be foreign to the biblical witness. So we must note that the graced goodness we are talking about cannot be seen apart from its fragility and vulnerability. If each being cannot help but participate in creation along with others, what happens to one being will affect and shape others. Coexistence entails mutability, a vulnerability to undergoing and being affected by other beings. Creation's complexity and interdependence is therefore marked from the start by an accompanying instability. For God lets beings be in their difference, giving over to them a particularity with integrity and preciousness that resonates in counterpoint relation with other beings. Insofar as this is the case, divine decree does not determine all events and relationships like cogs in a great machine. This would nullify the varied goodness of creation. The universe is not a perfect, static, and thus closed system. Instead, it is interactive and continuous. It is composed of differences in relation, which connotes a fluid, dynamic, and thus open-ended system.[88] While creation has a beginning, it is ever incomplete and ongoing. Why? Because, in Brown's words, "God's world-shaping word activates what is already latent among the elements. What was genuinely lacking (in the beginning) was the divinely set occasion to be called forth, the opportunity for the elements to contribute their potential products to the ongoing process of creation."[89] Perpetually called into being out of nothing's formlessness, and in a matrix of interrelationships, creation is a novelty-generating process. Contemporary scientists employ language of chaos and indeterminacy to describe such creativity, as real novelty entails elements of unpredictability.[90] And new things are brought into being as creation continues. But there is also great risk.

This risk opens up the possibility of tragedy. How so? Diversity and variety, while inherently good, also yield conflicts as creatures pursue varied and sometimes opposing ends.[91] Differences entail attributes that distinguish them from one another, such as physical characteristics and, in the case of living organisms, biological needs. These cannot help but display limitations that are contextual, defined by environmental conditions and relations that are not always beneficial or productive for a particular thing, whether living or non-living. Tectonic plate movements create volcanos and earthquakes; weather patterns create hurricanes and floods. Movement by one thing engenders an alternate effect, and sometimes with dramatic and far-reaching consequences. Beings are contingent and fragile in their interdependence. Their dance with one another contains the potential for compatibility and cooperation along with incompatibility, alienation, and conflict. The very goodness of creation includes deprivations that are components of the differences and variety that make such goodness possible.

Hence, change happens naturally in a world conditioned by the complex contrapuntal play of differences. And in this great nexus some beings come into existence while others pass away, often coextensively. Indeed, life-forms flourish not only by stimulating, empowering, and enriching one another, but also by challenging, resisting, and preying upon one another. Lions eat gazelles, especially maladapted ones weakened by disease, mutation, or age. Influenza, and HIV are living organisms vying for life amidst other living organisms.[92] The simultaneous well-being of all organisms is not possible, especially given that the material resources that enable organisms to flourish are themselves exhaustible. And when scarcity occurs, competition and conflict occur. Finite creatures are conditioned by and live in a relational environment full of limits, the good of which is also accompanied by perils, frustrations, suffering, even death. Furthermore, in an open universe new and more complex forms of matter and life emerge only by incorporating—utilizing, modifying, or feeding upon—the old, which dissolve and leave space for the new.[93] So even while creation remains a gracious gift, in Wendy Farley's words, "tragedy is the price paid for existence."[94]

Acknowledging this is an important vehicle for eschewing the theodicy temptation, which would somehow rationalize God's controlling purpose in creating and providentially guiding a world with a tragic structure. It suggests neither that tragedy makes possible the goodness of creation nor that tragedy is actually a beneficial or constructive part of God's sovereign plan, the sense of which lies hidden in God's inscrutable will. Tragedy is best seen as the shadow feature that accompanies creation's interdependent and relational structure. To be different requires being relational, which in turn implies not being self-complete and perfect. Creatures are a mix of being and non-being because they, unlike God, do not have the power of being absolutely. To be creaturely means to be contingent, called into and upheld in being out of nothing. We do not have our "own being"; it comes ultimately from God and occurs in relation to other existents. And this is the same as being susceptible to suffering, to being imperiled by influences not of our own making. Existence is a blessing with a tragic structure.

Notice we are avoiding the term "chaos." Tragedy is not chaos as such. It is an undertow made possible by the wondrous good of relation and difference. Unlike the chaos of nothing's potentiality for being, tragedy accompanies but does not necessarily serve or make possible this good. For this would essentially make meaningful what in many—perhaps most—instances cannot be made meaningful, controlled, and integrated into our life projects constructively. While in some cases creatures do in fact benefit—adapt and grow—through suffering, there is no immediate sense to it. Its hold on us may be explained as part of what it means to be limited and transient, even justified as part of the good we experience, such as back pain is endemic to the bipedal and erect features of human mobility. But this does not ascribe inherent purpose to it as a blessing. In this qualified sense perhaps we can speak of chaos negatively.[95] Affliction is not directly experienced as a gift, but as a surd, an ultimately inexplicable yet inevitable part of the created condition. This makes its out-of-control character part of what we are, vulnerable beings subject to what we cannot control. The universe is open, containing ambiguous, indeterminate, and unpredictable elements. Hence, because it is part of the relational fabric of creatureliness, suffering is not something that can (or should) be rationalized, avoided, or eliminated in all cases. The swift, strong, intelligent, and skillful—"time and chance happen to them all"; "no one can anticipate the time of disaster" (Eccles. 9:11–12).

However, unlike the tragic, chaos has its positive side. Its nothing is potentiality for being. Creation is called out of the void-like chaos of nothing through divine incorporation. So not only does the indeterminacy of chaos remain a substantive part of everything, but out of its formlessness—that is, the brooding darkness and waters of Genesis 1—arise the blessings of order and transformative novelty. Such formlessness need not be tragic. Darkness not only obscures, it offers respite from the burning sun, cultivating rest and healing. The waters not only wash away, they nourish vegetation in the springtime and quench the thirsty. Chaos, then, is larger than tragedy. It is not simply one feature of interrelationship but is endemic to the entire creative process of bringing interrelated creatures into being. Indeed, within its space possibilities beyond the tragic can occur, much as mistakes in jazz improvisation can be transformed into creative opportunities. Through its potentiality God can make all things new. Accordingly, it is more instructive to see the chaotic formlessness of nothing in anonymous and neutral terms; it has the potential for blessing as well as tragedy.[96] The tragedy that it makes possible is derivative. So chaos is not evil.

This leads to another point. That finitude includes the prospect of harm, frustration, and death does not make it an evil that resists God. It is necessary to be vigilant against conceiving creation itself as evil, the product of some primordial fall, as in Gnostic cosmologies. For finitude itself neither opposes God nor distorts the goodness of creation. It is loved into being by God and consequently is naturally good. Thus, in many forms, though certainly not all, suffering is not an evil as such. This is why we should be circumspect in using the term "natural evil" to describe the harm done by floods, earthquakes, and the like. These events are tragic, to be sure, but the pain they cause occurs as a concomitant aspect of creatureliness, the product of a world structured interrelationally and open for novelty (though they are evil when human sin is implicated, which we shall discuss more in the next chapter). Furthermore, they should not always simply be accepted but resisted, as in diseases. Living things are biologically disposed to avoid pain in order to persevere and flourish. Life seeks life. Here, however, the point is that created beings are not perfect—that is, immutable and everlasting—but vulnerable, and good because of it.[97] They are mutable and transient, part of a world that exists before and will exist after their existence. They are conditioned and have a beginning and an end, like the grass grows and then withers (Pss. 90:5–6; 103:15–16). Living things are created from dust and shall return to dust.[98]

Divine Vulnerability and Tragedy

We must admit, then, that God is in a way responsible for creating a world in which tragedy occurs. God gives the world a distinct worth, the intrinsic precariousness of which allows for the possibility of conflict and suffering. Yet this is not to say that God purposely engenders conflict or wills harm. There is no greater harmony that God intends by producing suffering, such that a better or more complete world will be created. Recall that God's creative and providential power is not controlling power. It releases and lets beings be, and so does not determine all events, triggering natural disasters and creating impairments. Neither is God helpless, powerless before tragedy. Instead, out of nothing God creates beings with unique differences, the events resulting from their interaction taking a course determined by the nature of those differences. This is what we mean by natural laws, and this means that God is not the sole actor in cosmic process. Events are not preordained according to a calculus of divine necessity. The universe is an open system. It is unstable, containing elements of indeterminacy and chaos within its ordered structure. Because of this God can be understood as creating the conditions of possibility for tragedy, but not immediately causing it. While there are indeed passages in the Hebrew Bible that name God as the source of both well-being and tragedy (Deut. 32:39; Ps. 104:27–30; Isa. 45:5–7), it must be stressed that God's love for creation is the more consistent message, a love that does not fatalistically determine all events but opens them up toward possibility. Fretheim sums it up nicely: the "divine way of creating, in choosing not to act alone (but enlisting creatures), is also revealing of a divine vulnerability, for in so involving those who are not God, room is given for the activity of finite creatures, with all of the attendant risks in allowing creatures to be themselves."[99]

God's creative and providential presence is vulnerable. Vulnerability, the capacity to undergo and suffer the other, is an inescapable part of giving. As God becomes relationally open to God's gift of creation and lovingly embraces creatures as distinct and valuable beings, God shows vulnerability. God is voluntarily limited and qualified by creation, suffering its presence and being affected by it.[100] This is displayed in the creation account by God's affirmative delight in difference as something good. For something to be good, it must stand out on its own as precious. Such goodness, as a whole creation, is celebrated with Sabbath rest (Gen. 2:2–3). It is also displayed in God's pathos for relationship with creation, especially for covenant with human beings.[101] God cares for creation, desires its well-being, and accordingly reveals the divine self as an historical field of force that restlessly seeks to bring about wholeness, mutuality, and salvation, a process that in the Hebrew scriptures highlights the unique place of human beings in God's sacred order. "I have observed the misery of my people who are in Egypt; I have heard their cry on account of their taskmasters. Indeed, I know their sufferings, and have come down to deliver them"(Exod. 3:7–8). This is a God who is affected by events in the world. Indeed, according to Ellen F. Davis, vulnerability is "the condition of covenant," its enabling factor.[102] As Israel stumbles and the covenant is ignored or distorted, God is pained and angered, reproaching wrongdoing and the broken relationship it fosters. When suffering occurs and injustice gains sway, God empathizes and mourns. God has compassion and gives of the divine self. This God shows special concern for the plight of the outcasts and poor, those who suffer. Hence, according to Fretheim, God suffers because, with, and for, or on behalf of, the people.[103] For Christians, as we shall discuss in more depth in the next chapters, such vulnerability is embodied humanly in God's self-revelation through Jesus Christ, poignantly culminating in the weakness and suffering of death on the cross.[104]

God's vulnerable love is, as Daniel C. Migliore asserts, a "strange power."[105] Strange, because one would think the creator and providential governor of all things has ultimate control, a sovereign power determining everything according to an infinitely harmonious master plan. This is why God's transcendence is often expressed in terms of omnipotence, impassibility, and immutability. It is commonly alleged that God must be wholly self-sufficient, passionless, or unaffected by what is other than God, to be unconditioned.[106] For conditioned things have limits and boundaries, which God goes not. God is complete and cannot suffer the other or change if genuine divine freedom is to be preserved. But like Aristotle's unmoved mover, such a God would be imprisoned in solitariness, alone in infinite perfection and unaffected by anything else. That God, then, could only appear to love, to be in relation; its being enclosed in self-absorbed contemplation, an absolute egocentricity. Neither personal nor free, that God is, in final analysis, unloving. As Moltmann insists, a God who cannot be involved cannot be affected and suffer, and "one who cannot suffer cannot love either."[107] The difference of creation goes unnoticed and unwelcome.

According to the scriptures, however, God's transcendent power does not keep to itself. It is freely open to others and is expended in creation, redemption, and covenant. It is not coercive but sharing, not domineering but relational, a love that gives and receives in communicating itself. True, monarchical or kingly metaphors for God proliferate in the Hebrew Bible, but they strongly qualify royal sovereignty with tender trustworthiness and affectionate reciprocity.[108] It is understandable, then, that the scriptures also use metaphors for God that draw upon relationships of affection and solicitude. For example, "As a mother comforts her child, so will I comfort you" (Isa. 66:13; see also 46:3; 49:15–16). Like a shepherd who cares for sheep (Ps. 23; 95:7; 100:3; Isa. 40:11), God's love values the difference of what is other, remains faithful to it, and shows compassionate regard for its well-being. Recalling the discussion in the last chapter, God's power is the primordial possibility of availability, with its aspects of respect, fidelity, and sympathetic attunement with and for the other. Hence, God's love is an intrinsically relational power, one that risks suffering by becoming vulnerable. William Placher summarizes the point in claiming that God's vulnerability "is a perfection of loving freedom."[109] God's is a freedom that gives. It models availability, and indeed makes possible creation's availability to God. Creation is the gift of divine free love which opens up reciprocity between God and world. God is open to the world, and the world opens up to God.

So even as tragedy occurs God is not distant. God hovers over the face of the deep and creates, upholding our being even in tragedy. In this way tragedy happens in God who, in Arthur Peacock's words, "suffers in, with, and under the creative processes of the world."[110] There is a "tragic structure" to God's love, the love that communicates value by creating difference.[111] God is vulnerable to creation's interdependence, feeling pain and loss with creatures. God's love is a sympathetic attunement that draws near and is present to creatures. God is with and for creation. And because God is good, God desires the goodness of creation to flourish, actively seeking the well-being of creatures, such that God's providential presence offers transformative resources to uphold and redeem them.[112] God comes and delivers, offering hope. God's creative, redeeming power then is not domineering, but inviting. The offer is a summons or invocation that bursts forth unexpectedly, in the midst of impossible situations. One would not think anything could emerge from nothing, but God's invitation into form and order noncoercively engenders beings, drawing creatures into their own from the depths and in cooperation with others.[113] Accordingly, divine grace can work amidst tragedy through the power of love, bringing opportunities for healing, wholeness, and mutuality.[114] God does not cause pain in order that wholeness can occur. Nor does God guarantee a beneficial outcome, overcoming by vanquishing tragedy. This would have the ironic effect of nullifying creation's vulnerable goodness, closing the universe by prohibiting genuine relation among differences. Yet transformation can happen in the midst of tragedy. Why? Because love, not tragedy, is the final word of existence. God is in the midst of creation, affirming its infinite value. Thus the divine presence offers resources of creative resistance to the tragic.

That creation is an open system, however, also indicates something more. According to Moltmann, creation "has neither its foundation, nor its goal, nor its equilibrium, within itself . . . but is from the very outset ec-centrically designed, and aligned in the direction of the future."[115] The beginning establishes the conditions that make possible both tragedy and deliverance. But the beginning is not the final moment of creation; it points toward a yet-to-be consummation point in which all things shall be fulfilled. Such a fulfillment does not mean a return to beginnings as the primordial ideal, but rather the "fulfillment of the real promise implanted in creation itself" from the beginning.[116] The openness of life systems to innovation and relational complexity is a drive toward the fullness of divine life, which is only now glimpsed dimly in creation and remains to be fully realized in the future. And this drive is a response to God's invitational love. Israel's messianic hope, figured prominently in the prophetic literature, embodies this kind of eschatological vision, an aspiration for the carrying through of God's communication of love (Isa. 35). The New Testament writings speak of "a new heaven and new earth" (Rev. 21:1). Creation "waits with eager longing," "groaning in labor pains" (Rom. 8:19, 22) for the day when its gifted potential breaks through brokenness, death, and destruction and is transformed in God's inclusive presence—that is, in the kingdom of God.

The very notion of providence testifies to the fact the creation has a promise embedded in it. Creation's goodness establishes an inherent purpose—the glory of God. God's work of preservation is then properly conceived as a preparation anticipating the saving consummation of creation, an activity constantly offering new possibilities of being to creatures, precisely amidst tragedy. Creation offers grounds for hope. The ongoing creativity of God continually gives birth to new life, engendering novelty and innovation in and through the relationships between creatures. It is a gracious movement oriented toward "bringing the cosmos into a new condition," a final perfection that is presently only hinted at.[117] Creation is unfinished. It is a work in progress, summoned into more complex and fulfilling relationships. The tragedies of annihilation and suffering are openings to the possibility of a future glory in the divine.

However, presently we wait, perhaps with anguish and lament, even angry protest. For we live in the midst of dissonance, a gap between beginning and end, a time when God seems to hide the divine face. We cry with the psalmist, "How long, O Lord, will you look on? . . . Wake up!" (Ps. 35:17, 23). The promise of creation appears dim, seemingly countering the giftedness of things and obscuring God's inviting presence. Yet out of contrast and strife, out of broken relationships, new possibilities can emerge (Isa. 43:19). Hope is born not in facile optimism, but in the midst of genuine grief. And here, in our grief, divine grace suffers with creatures to offer renewal and facilitate new creation. God is present in creation's travail. Moltmann concludes: "Through his inexhaustible capacity for suffering and readiness for suffering, God then also creates quite specific chances for liberation from isolation, and quite specific chances for the evolution of the various open life systems."[118] God's transcendence is a "making possible" of possibilities beyond tragedy precisely because God suffers in sympathy with creation, a fact that the New Testament underscores with great poignancy in the death of Christ on the cross. Unpacking this, however, must wait until the next chapter.

Conclusion: Theology of Creation in a Key of Gratitude and Hope

Thus far, in light of the theology of creation we have outlined it, should be evident how the biblical idea of creation—as witness to God's generous act of self-giving—not only confirms but calls forth and cultivates gestures of gratitude and hope. God's creative power is vulnerable love, a power that is not controlling but, by comparison, weak. Paradoxically, weakness is the way God is a resource for a creation that utterly depends upon God. So the welcome we seek is made available in divine vulnerability; not through omnipotence and immutability but through weakness is God's power manifest. By giving over the gift of being in a self-limiting act of love, God shows openness and reciprocity, the capacity to suffer. This is not to say that God is a wimp, a pushover who feels deeply but nevertheless cannot make a difference. Rather, God's power—the power of being absolutely—is love, the power to generate difference and hold it close to God's own being. God is available, continually creating space for others, welcoming them into being. Hence, creation is a home, an abundance that is fragile in its goodness. Tragedy is not fundamental. There is down deep in things a preciousness that remains fresh and unspoiled, such that we are empowered to resist destruction and despair in gratitude and hope.[119] Hope traffics in gratitude and trust despite uncertainty and peril and the possibility of despair. It refuses the triumph of tragedy on the basis of a fundamental affirmation of being's goodness.

Indeed, the biblical God reveals the power of such goodness—love in the shape of creative-redemptive power. As Moltmann repeatedly stresses, redemption marks a divine strength that is made possible by weakness and suffering. That is, the strange power of God is made efficacious in its vulnerability. Bonhoeffer agrees: "The Bible directs man to God's powerlessness and suffering; only the suffering God can help."[120] This has crucial implications for understanding God's power revealed in Christ. For now, however, it is enough to conclude stressing its importance for how we envision God's presence in creation.

God is the transcendently immanent, life-giving, and relational power of the whole of reality. This is basic to the biblical witness. "The whole earth is full of his glory" (Isa. 6:3). Or, as Paul affirms, "from him and through him and to him are all things" (Rom. 11:36). Even in Revelation we find the exaltation of God's creative power: "You are worthy, our lord and God, to receive glory and honor and power, for you created all things, and by your will they existed and were created" (4:11).

What has all this to do with disability? By now I hope the answer is clear: everything! Understanding creation as God's free gift adjusts the aperture of the lens by which we perceive disability and act toward persons with disabilities. Disability is made neither by God nor by chaotic forces contrary to God's purposes. It is part of a vulnerable world which God loves. But neither is disability necessarily tragic. Indeed, impairments may involve physical suffering and concrete imperilments to well-being. However, we must be careful to avoid reducing all accompanying features of someone's life with impairments to tragedy, as if something is wrong with the person. The cult of normalcy turns disability into tragedy, with the tragedy social in nature, and "sinful."

With this, we see how the full weight of a theology of creation must also include a discussion of human beings and sin. For we are created in the image of God, created for relation with one another, the world, and God. Yet somehow this purpose gets distorted. I have deliberately postponed examining such a scheme until the next chapter in order to bring it into clearer connection with redemption in Christ. Nevertheless, enough has been said to conclude with several autobiographical remarks.

In terms of my relationship with my son, the truth of what I've said has become apparent in two basic ways. First, my own religious sense of gratitude has been amplified by daily encounters with Chris's precious uniqueness. This is not to say, of course, that I am thankful for the privilege of not having to struggle in the way that he does. Rather, I have learned through his distinctive presence that each and every person, created and loved by God, has something beautiful to give the world. Consequently, because my life is itself a gift I am more aware that it is not its own possession, but something to be given back and invested in others, offered in life-giving generosity.[121] The experience of sheer gratuity opens my world up to the fact that creation is not simply there for me, something to be taken for granted or exploited for my own interests. Creation exists by, with, and for love. Specifically, Chris is not there to meet my expectations; rather, my wife and I have been given one who helps us see that our lives are meant to be available and open to what lies outside the boundaries of all our expectations, something more humanizing: love. Loving is a way of thankful celebration. And this has opened up the reality of God to me in radically new ways.[122] It has also deepened Chris's own sense of giftedness, sparking a concern for God.

Second, the nature of Chris's disabilities has made the tenacity of hope real. Hope keeps alive the possibility of his unique fulfillment as a person—despite there being no immediate "remedy" or "cure" available. And such hope has made the difficulties we have faced seem like stepping stones to his greater good, a good undetermined yet real. I cannot guarantee the future for Chris, but I do trust the grammar of the universe in a way that faith in God upholds and deepens. When he cries out to me in frustration, I can say to him without false pretense, "It will be all right." But God is no easy answer, an opiate for covering up Chris's pain and ignoring the pain of human suffering in general. If we are to be realistic, we must admit that, even as it is a gift, existence is also vulnerable and tragic. God is not another term for false optimism and a sense of controlled security, but rather a way of naming the element of trustworthiness in the fragility of things, a way of persistently living out the affirmation that "it is good."[123] My hope is that such hope blossoms in Chris, and that he will grow in the sense of his own giftedness as a child of God, loved into being by God. Chris's germinating hope is reflected in the following words, which are part of a poem he wrote:

> One could say, a person who is bound for dismay
> May not just be in dismay,
> But might, perhaps, be able to pray.
>
> For in one's mind a snapped twig
> Might just lead to piecing together
> A Mona Lisa.
>
> Thus in my mind,
> A spider spins a web so complex that, if God
> Could possibly give birth to new life,
> Maybe I could spin my disabilities, in time,
> Into the prayer of a lifetime. . . .
>
> My disabilities are only a step toward new life.

"A step toward new life." These are beautiful and powerful words. They open up further queries, calling for more theological nuance as it relates directly to disability. How might we mean new life in the context of the Christian story of redemption?

Notes

1. See Paul Ricoeur, "Ethical and Theological Considerations on the Golden Rule," 293–302, and "Love and Justice," 315–29, in *Figuring the Sacred: Religion, Narrative, and Imagination,* trans. David Pellauer, ed. Mark I. Wallace (Minneapolis: Fortress Press, 1995).

2. With some modifications, I am drawing the idea of a "fundamental affirmation" from Paul Ricoeur. See his employment of an "original affirmation" in *The Conflict of Interpretations,* ed. Don Ihde (Evanston, IL: Northwestern University Press, 1974), 341, 452. See also *Oneself as Another,* trans. Kathleen Blamey (Chicago:

University of Chicago Press, 1992), 315–16; and *History and Truth*, trans. Charles A. Kelbley (Evanston: Northwestern University Press, 1965), chap. 6.

3. See Ricoeur, *The Conflict of Interpretations*, 329, 452.

4. Ricoeur, *Figuring the Sacred*, 206–7, 279, 300.

5. On this sense of gratitude, see Mary Jo Leddy's insightful book *Radical Gratitude* (Maryknoll, NY: Orbis, 2002).

6. In a rich and evocative way, Erazim Kohák testifies to this affirmation in his book *The Embers and the Stars: A Philosophical Inquiry into the Moral Sense of Nature* (Chicago: University of Chicago Press, 1984), see esp. 93–97.

7. Leddy, *Radical Gratitude*, 55–59.

8. Edward Farley, *Good and Evil: Interpreting a Human Condition* (Minneapolis: Fortress, 1990), 29.

9. Ricoeur, *Figuring the Sacred*, 207.

10. Gabriel Marcel, "On the Ontological Mystery," in *The Philosophy of Existentialism*, trans. Manya Harari (New York: Carol Publishing Group, 1956), 33.

11. Edward Farley, *Deep Symbols: Their Postmodern Effacement and Reclamation* (Valley Forge, PA: Trinity Press International, 1996), 100.

12. Marcel, *Homo Viator: Introduction to a Metaphysics of Hope*, trans. Emma Craufurd (Gloucester, MA: Peter Smith, 1978), 48–51, 66.

13. Ibid., 36, 47–50. See also "On the Ontological Mystery," 27–28.

14. Farley, *Good and Evil*, 121–24.

15. Farley, *Deep Symbols*, 102.

16. Ricoeur, *Figuring the Sacred*, 211.

17. Marcel, "On the Ontological Mystery," 28.

18. Marcel uses the language of salvation; see ibid.

19. Wendy Farley, *The Wounding and Healing of Desire: Weaving Heaven and Earth* (Louisville: Westminster John Knox Press, 2005), 20.

20. Leddy, 51.

21. Marcel, *Homo Viator*, 47.

22. Friedrich Schleiermacher, *The Christian Faith*. 2nd. ed., trans. and ed. by H.R. Mackintosh and J.S. Stewart (Edinburgh: T. & T. Clark, 1928), 4, 12.

23. Ibid., 4, 16.

24. Marcel, *The Mystery of Being*, vol. 2, trans. René Hague (Chicago: Henry Regnery Co., 1951), 3.

25. Augustine, *The Confessions*, trans. Maria Boulding, OSB (New York: Vintage Books, 1998), I.1.3.

26. Martin Buber notes this spiritual dimension of relation in *I and Thou*, trans. Ronald Gregor Smith (New York: Charles Scribner's Sons, 1958), 39.

27. Marcel, *The Mystery of Being*, vol. 2, 133.

28. In a different vein, Karl Rahner makes this point in *Foundations of Christian Faith: An Introduction to the Idea of Christianity*, trans. William V. Dych (New York: Crossroad, 1987), 68–71.

29. A similar line of reasoning can be found in Paul Tillich's "Two Types of Philosophy of Religion," in *Theology of Culture*, ed. Robert C. Kimball (London: Oxford University Press, 1959), chap. 2.

30. Augustine, *The Confessions*, IX.25.189. See also X.9.202–3.

31. John Calvin, *Institutes of the Christian*, ed. John T. NcNeill, trans. Ford Lewis Battles (Philadelphia: Westminster Press, 1960), III.1 43.

32. Karl Rahner develops this perspective at length in *Hearers of the Word*, trans. Michael Richards (New York: Herder and Herder, 1969).

33. Abraham J. Heschel, *The Prophets* (New York: Harper and Row, 1982), 486.

34. See H. Richard Niebuhr, *The Meaning of Revelation* (New York: Macmillan, 1941).

35. Ricoeur, *Figuring the Sacred*, 225 (emphasis added).

36. Terence E. Fretheim, *God and World in the Old Testament: A Relational Theology of Creation* (Nashville: Abingdon Press, 2005), 15 (emphasis in original).

37. Ricoeur, *Figuring the Sacred*, 224–25.

38. Ibid., 45–46.

39. Ibid., 228.

40. Ibid., 230.

41. For excellent examples of this, see Walter Brueggemann, *Israel's Praise: Doxology against Idolatry and Ideology* (Philadelphia: Fortress Press, 1988).

42. Bernhard W. Anderson, *Understanding the Old Testament*, 4th ed. (Englewood Cliffs, NJ: Prentice-Hall, 1986), 98–101, 232, 357. See also George E. Mendenhall, *Law and Covenant in the Ancient Near East* (Pittsburgh: Biblical Colloquium, 1955).

43. Bernhard W. Anderson, *Creation versus Chaos* (Philadelphia: Fortress Press, 1987), 62–65.

44. Anderson, *Creation versus Chaos*, chaps. 1–2.

45. On this point, see Jürgen Moltmann's Gifford Lectures, *God in Creation: A New Theology of Creation and the Spirit of God*, trans. Magaret Kohl (San Francisco: Harper and Row, 1985), 63–64.

46. Fretheim, *God and World in the Old Testament*, 10–11 (emphasis in original).

47. Augustine, "Of True Religion," *Augustine: Earlier Writings*, trans. John H. S. Burleigh (Philadelphia: Westminster Press, 1953), xi.21.235.

48. Langdon Gilkey, *Maker of Heaven and Earth: The Christian Doctrine of Creation in the Light of Modern Knowledge* (Garden City, NY: Anchor Books, 1965), 44.

49. Moltmann, *God in Creation*, 73–74.

50. See Augustine, *The Confessions*, xi.30.271–72.

51. Thus Anderson argues that "in the beginning" is a better translation of *bereshith* than "when God began to create," which is found in some translations. See *Creation versus Chaos*, 183–87. James Barr suggests something similar in, "Was Everything That God Created Really Good? A Question in the First Verse of the Bible," 55–65, in *God in the Fray: A Tribute to Walter Brueggemann*, ed. Todd Linafelt and Timothy K. Beal (Minneapolis: Fortress, 1998).

52. Gilkey, *Maker of Heaven and Earth*, 57.

53. William P. Brown, *The Ethos of the Cosmos: The Genesis of Moral Imagination in the Bible* (Grand Rapids: William B. Eerdmans Publishing, 1999), 46.

54. On this point, see Anderson, *Creation versus Chaos*, chap. 5, and Fretheim, *God and World in the Old Testament*, 43–46. For an intriguing alternative that argues for a version of the conflict myth of creation in the Hebrew scriptures, see Jon D. Levenson, *Creation and the Persistence of Evil: The Jewish Drama of Divine Omnipotence* (Princeton, NJ: Princeton University Press, 1988). Other similar alternatives argued on more scientific grounds are David A. S. Fergusson, *The Cosmos and the Creator: An Introduction to the Theology of Creation* (London: SPCK, 1998); and Sjoerd L. Bonting, *Chaos Theology: A Revised Christian Theology* (Minneapolis: Fortress Press, 2002).

55. Walter Brueggemann, *Theology of the Old Testament: Testimony, Dispute, Advocacy* (Minneapolis: Fortress, 1997), 153.

56. Fretheim, *God and World in the Old Testament*, 37–38.

57. Ibid., 38 (emphasis in orginal).

58. See Gilkey, *Maker of Heaven and Earth*, 44–58; and Moltmann, *God in Creation*, 74–76, 86–93. For other good discussions of this theme in the patristic period, see Gerhard May, *Creatio ex Nihilo: The Doctrine of 'Creation out of Nothing' in Early Christian Thought*, trans. A. S. Worall (Edinburgh: T. & T. Clark, 1994); and Anne M. Clifford's essay "Creation," in *Systematic Theology: Roman Catholic Perspectives*, ed. Francis Schüssler Fiorenza and John P. Galvin (Minneapolis: Fortress Press, 1991), 210–16.

59. For example, 2 Macc. 7:28; Rom. 4:17; and Heb. 11:3.

60. See Augustine, *The Confessions*, xii.22.285.

61. See Moltmann, *God in Creation*, 87. For a critique of Moltmann, see Catherine Keller, *Face of the Deep: A Theology of Becoming* (London: Routledge, 2003), 17–18.

62. Curiously, Augustine seems to suggest that creation comes out of formless matter, an abysmal, invisible, and unorganized substance, "a nothing-something" (*Confessions*, xii.3–7. 274–76). Only he maintains this was first created by God, even though Genesis 1:2 does not support this view. So Augustine holds to a kind of double creation—first the primordial stuff, then ordered creation.

63. Barr, "Was Everything That God Created Really Good?" 60.

64. Ibid., 63.

65. Brown, *The Ethos of the Cosmos*, 50, cf. 47.

66. For examples, see Fretheim, *God and World in the Old Testament*; Brown, *The Ethos of the Cosmos*; and Catherine Keller, *Face of the Deep*.

67. Brown, *The Ethos of the Cosmos*, 46.

68. Ricoeur, *Figuring the Sacred*, 299.

69. Dietrich Bonhoeffer, *Creation and Fall, Temptation: Two Biblical Studies*, trans. John C. Fletcher and Kathleen Downham (New York: Macmillan, 1959), 23.

70. Bonhoeffer, *Letters and Papers from Prison*, ed. Eberhard Bethge, trans. Reginald Fuller et. al. (New York: Macmillan, 1971), 282.

71. Peter C. Hodgson, *Winds of the Spirit: A Constructive Christian Theology* (Louisville: Westminster John Knox Press, 1994), 145–50.

72. Ibid., 147. For a philosophical interpretation of this point, see Richard Kearney, *The God Who May Be: A Hermeneutics of Religion* (Bloomington: Indiana University Press, 2001); and my *The Broken Whole: Philosophical Steps toward a Theology of Global Solidarity* (Albany: State University of New York Press, 2005), chap. 5.

73. Gilkey, *Maker of Heaven and Earth*, 111–12; Bonhoeffer, *Creation and Fall*, 15–16.

74. Bonhoeffer, *Creation and Fall*, 17.

75. Ibid., 66–79.

76. Ibid., 78. See also Ricoeur, *Figuring the Sacred*, 299.

77. Moltmann, *God in Creation*, 75–76.

78. Karl Barth, *Church Dogmatics*, 2/1, trans. T. H. L. Parker et al. (Edinburgh: T. & T. Clark, 1957), 28, 257.

79. Leddy, *Radical Gratitude.*, 57. This is also one of the key points in Jonathan Sacks's book *The Dignity of Difference: How to Avoid the Clash of Civilizations* (New York: Continuum, 2002).

80. Katheryn Tanner, *Economy of Grace* (Minneapolis: Fortress Press, 2005), 63.

81. Ibid., 67. Daniel L. Migliore speaks of God's creative welcome in *Faith Seeking Understanding* (Grand Rapids: Eerdmans, 1991), 85.

82. "Letting be" is a fundamental ingredient in John Macquarrie's theology of creation. See *Principles of Christian Theology*, 2nd ed. (New York: Charles Scribner's Sons, 1977), chap. 10.

83. Brown, *The Ethos of the Cosmos*, 26. See also Fretheim, *God and World in the Old Testament*, 26.

84. Ibid., 47–48.

85. See Ricoeur, *Figuring the Sacred,* 324–29; and Tanner, *Economy of Grace*, 72.

86. Sallie McFague, *The Body of God: An Ecological Theology* (Minneapolis: Fortress Press, 1993), 38–47.

87. See ibid., 111.

88. Fretheim, *God and World in the Old Testament*, 19.

89. Brown, *The Ethos of the Cosmos*, 47.

90. For examples, see Ian G. Barbour, *Religion and Science: Historical and Contemporary Issues*, rev. ed. (San Francisco: HarperSanFrancisco, 1997), 172–73, 182–84, 206–7. On the notion of improvisation and creation, see Ann Pederson, *God, Creation, and All That Jazz* (St. Louis: Chalice Press, 2001).

91. Wendy Farley, *Tragic Vision and Divine Compassion* (Louisville: Westminster John Knox Press, 1990), 60.

92. Kathy Black, *A Healing Homiletic: Preaching and Disability* (Nashville: Abingdon Press, 1996), 34. See also the illuminating book by Mel Greaves, *Cancer: The Evolutionary Legacy* (Oxford: Oxford University Press, 2000).

93. Arthur Peacocke, *Paths from Science towards God: The End of All Our Exploring* (Oxford: One World Publications, 2001), 84.

94. Wendy Farley, *Tragic Vision and Divine Compassion*, 61.

95. See David A. S. Fergusson, *The Cosmos and the Creator: An Introduction to the Theology of Creation* (London: SPCK, 1998); and Sjoerd L. Bonting, *Chaos Theology: A Revised Christian Theology* (Minneapolis: Fortress Press, 2002).

96. This is a key point in Keller's *Face of the Deep*.

97. Fretheim, *God and World in the Old Testament*, 41.

98. See Migliore, *Faith Seeking Understanding*, 101.

99. Fretheim, *God and World in the Old Testament*, 38.

100. This point is elegantly argued by Keith Ward in *God, Chance, and Necessity* (Oxford: One World Publications, 1996).

101. On the theme of divine pathos, see Abraham J. Heschel, *The Prophets*, esp. chaps. 12–14.

102. Ellen F. Davis, "Vulnerability, the Condition of Covenant," in *The Art of Reading Scripture*, ed. Ellen F. Davis and Richard B. Hays (Grand Rapids: Eerdmans), 277–93.

103. Terence E. Fretheim, *The Suffering of God: An Old Testament Perspective* (Philadelphia: Fortress, 1984), 108.

104. See David H. Jensen, *Graced Vulnerability: A Theology of Childhood* (Cleveland: Pilgrim Press, 2005), chap. 2.

105. Migliore, *Faith Seeking Understanding*, 52. See also William C. Placher, who quotes Migliore, in *Narratives of a Vulnerable God: Christ, Theology, and Scripture* (Louisville: Westminster John Knox Press, 1994), 17.

106. For a classic statement, see Anselm's "Monologium," chap. 25, in *St. Anselm: Basic Writings*, trans. S. N. Deane (La Salle, IL: Open Court Publishing, 1962), 130–31.

107. Jürgen Moltmann, *The Crucified God: The Cross of Christ as the Foundation and Criticism of Christian Theology*, trans. R. A. Wilson and John Bowden (Philadelphia: Fortress Press, 1974), 253.

108. Fretheim, *God and World in the Old Testament*, 13–22.

109. Placher, *Narratives of a Vulnerable God*, 19.

110. Peacocke, *Paths from Science towards God*, 86.

111. Wendy Farley, *Tragic Vision and Divine Compassion*, 98, 106–10.

112. See Black, *A Healing Homiletic*, 36–37.

113. Here I am drawing language from Brown, *The Ethos of the Cosmos*, 46–49.

114. Peacocke, *Paths from Science towards God*, 86–90.

115. Moltmann, *God in Creation*, 207.

116. Ibid.

117. Ibid., 210.

118. Ibid., 211.

119. Farley, *Tragic Vision and Divine Compassion*, 99, 126–29.

120. Bonhoeffer, *Letters and Papers from Prison*, 361.

121. See Ricoeur, *Figuring the Sacred*, 324–26.

122. Before his death Henri Nouwen wrote a beautiful book depicting his experience of caring for a disabled person at Daybreak, a L'Arche community in Toronto. He writes that his sense of God's radical love was deeply enhanced, in fact pulling him out of a prolonged period of depression. See *Adam: God's Beloved* (Maryknoll, NY: Orbis, 1997).

123. See Schubert M. Ogden, *The Reality of God and Other Essays* (Dallas: Southern Methodist University Press, 1977), 37.

6

Worthy of Love? Humanity, Disability, and Redemption in Christ

I have made, and I will bear; I will carry and will save. (Isa. 46:4)

In chapter 5 we explored how the basic openness of gratitude and hope are windows into the goodness of creation, a goodness that is confirmed explicitly by the testimony of biblical narratives to a God who in free love not only reveals and redeems but also creates. Indeed, revelation and redemption are corollaries of God's universal and life-giving creative power. All conditioned things are unconditionally affirmed as good; nothing is taken for granted. No conditioned reason exists that could justify or account for the fact that we are loved into being and sustained by God; God's love is freely given.[1] At the very heart of this, in the words of H. Richard Niebuhr, "is the assurance that because I am, I am valued, and because you are, you are beloved, and because what ever is has being, therefore it is worthy of love."[2]

This has dramatic consequences for how we think about disability, for an economy of superabundant grace surges through the created world that undercuts the economies of exchange animating the cult of normalcy. Vulnerability and weakness carry a secret power because they radiate with divine plenitude, a surplus of love that ruptures conventional categories of instrumental value. Each being is loved into being, precious in its own right and because of its unique difference, even amidst the perils that accompany its finitude. In additiion, each being is fundamentally relational, open to others in a vast web of interdependency with roots in God's gratuitous love. Indeed, openness to God and openness to relationships with others are intimately connected. Availability is a readiness for God.

Here we gain access to the moral sense of creation. That is, finite human gestures of compassionate regard for others are themselves sacred invocations that participate in the infinite, life-giving generosity of the divine. The transcendent God is not far off, but near, immanent in creation. Hence, God's love sweeps horizontally, not simply vertically. It spills outward toward creatures, attending to the particular value of concrete others, up close and personal. Giving thanks to God then entails giving recognition to the inherent worth of others—accepting the generosity that God has already given—and letting it run over into the between-space of human relations. Because existence has been given to me, I give to others.[3] In this way loving creatures is a way of loving God. When I affirm the goodness of the other and attend to it for its own sake, recognizing the unique value that inheres in its being, I am also affirming God, riding the wave of an excessive power rolling through all creation. Existence is a gift overflowing with generosity. My own life is a gift meant to be life-giving for others, to be available for and with them. The New Testament writer expresses this by stating: "Beloved, let us love one another; for love is of God, and the one who loves is born of God and knows God" (1 John 4:7). Love is not only possible; it is a window into the divine. Its "yes" reflects the divine "yes" that is embodied in the gift of existence itself.

This chapter, then, shall unpack and extend such a vision by attending to the question of what it means to be human and saved by God through Christ. With this we echo themes that have already resounded in this book. Only now the focus shall be on the Christian witness, particularly as it broadens and transforms attitudes and practices that are disabling for persons with impairments. We shall build from precedents established in the Hebrew Bible to explore how the New Testament testifies to a power that reveals itself through vulnerability, a strength that comes through weakness, a wholeness that manifests itself not in self-sufficiency but in relationship. The vision is paradoxical and subversive. More than simply idealizing vulnerability, it produces what I have called a "metaphorical reversal" that exposes the false pretenses of the cult of normalcy and opens up the possibility of living in light of God's love. And such love is represented redemptively in the person and work of Jesus Christ. Christians affirm that through Christ human beings are transformed into new creatures, opened to others and God in a way that frees people to be what they were initially created to be but for the effects of sin.

This holds theological weight for thinking about disability in essentially three ways. First it bears directly on the nature of human creatures as created in the image of God (*imago Dei*). I shall argue that the image of God is an elusive category loosely signifying that we are fashioned bodily to be creative, relational, and available agents in God's world. Of course, second, human sinfulness distorts this capacity, obscuring but not destroying our creaturely value. The result disrupts our relationship to each other, God, and the whole of creation, giving grounds for the cult of normalcy in economies of exchange. However, third, the redeeming work of Christ exemplifies the reorientation—indeed reversal—of the character of sin. It makes possible a conversion (*metanoia*) to God that trades on the experience of vulnerability and lack as a harbinger of divine abundance. Theologically interpreted, it is precisely such vulnerability that God embraces in Christ, entering fully into the frailty of the human condition, even unto a tragic death. God is in solidarity with humanity at its most fundamental level, in weakness and brokenness. This is not to romanticize weakness. Here in Christ, God reveals the divine nature as available to creation not only by undergoing or suffering with human vulnerability, but also by raising it up into God's own being.

Jesus Christ is the icon of a loving God, and as such he recreates humanity, the new Adam. Drawing from Nancy Eiesland we might speak of a "disabled Christ," one who understands by embodying disability even in his transformed, resurrected body. This helps us understand the christological implications of Paul's paradoxical proclamation in 2 Corinthians 12:9–10, namely, that the saving power of God is made manifest and perfected in weakness or lack of ability (*astheneiai*). This is neither to valorize disability nor to glorify suffering. Rather, it must be understood christologically, as God's loving nearness to the creature, not as a means to romanticize passivity and self-sacrifice.

Reflecting these points, this chapter grows into a theological vision that highlights the presence of God's transformative power in the midst of human vulnerability, such that disability becomes transformed, not cured but welcomed in the minds and hearts of Christians as loved by God. Wholeness is a way of living with others before God. The concluding chapter will draw out the radical implications this has for Christian practice.

I. Reconsidering the *Imago Dei*

This theme is a perilous topic for people with disabilities, because Christians have often interpreted disability as a distortion of God's purposes, a marring of the image of God. Thus we must tread with great care. Rather than provide a definition of humanity or outline criteria constituting the human person, I shall propose an intentionally loose way of understanding the *imago Dei*. This shall help avoid reductive views that are disabling, and instead foster the inclusion of a wide range of human possibilities. I suggest that to be created in the image of God means to be created for contributing to the world, open toward the call to love others. Three dimensions are implied: creativity with others, relation to others, and availability for others. The point to be stressed is that all people can be contributors, representing a range of both gifts and limitations. Disability is not an incomplete humanity in this regard. God neither spurns nor purposefully makes disability. As Roy McCloughry and Wayne Morris confirm, "God has called each one of us into being."[4] While the Bible contains passages that denigrate disability (see chapter 1 for examples), we must remember that its larger message celebrates lovingkindness toward marginalized persons; furthermore, it witnesses to God's purposes being fulfilled by persons who otherwise might be considered abnormal—for example, consider Moses's stuttering, Jacob's limp, and Paul's thorn in the flesh.

Imago Dei *as* Imitatio Dei

Bearing the image and likeness of God (Gen. 1:26–27) marks a special kind of relationship between human beings and God, each other, and the earth. Human existence is what it is by somehow reflecting God's being. Yet the simplicity of the formulation is misleading, for questions remain as to precisely what it is about human being that reflects and what it is that is reflected. At issue is the very character of the human vocation, what it means to be human in the world vis-à-vis God. Certainly, being a creature means that humans are not God but finite, limited, and vulnerable, like the rest of God's creation. Indeed, we are a part of creation, embodied beings susceptible to tragedy. But there is more. Initially formed from the dust of the earth, Adam is given life by God's breath (Gen. 2:7). So while we are of the earth, we are also quickened by an element of the divine life itself. Human beings are citizens of the earth but also belong to God—indeed, belong to God in the context of creation. This makes humans somehow special. But in what ways?

It is crucial to observe that the Genesis account never precisely defines what the image of God is. The language is elusive, perhaps deliberately so. We are not told that humans literally replicate God in bodily form or appearance. We are not told that human beings are rational souls or autonomous pockets of consciousness standing over against the rest of creation. We are not told that human beings are defined by productivity and the ability to achieve. We are not even told that human beings are free individuals, set loose to define the world as they choose. There is no trait determinable as the image of God and set against others. In fact, the *imago Dei* appears more as a cluster of loosely defined features than discernable traits like reason or freedom.

Subsequent to its claim that God creates humankind in the divine image and likeness, the texts tells us that God intends for humans to have dominion over all other living things (Gen. 1:26). It goes on to say that God created both male and female in the divine image (1:27). Then, verse 28 states: "God blessed them, and God said to them, 'Be fruitful and multiply, and fill the earth and subdue it; and have dominion over the fish of the sea and over the birds of the air and over every living thing that moves upon the earth.'" Finally, as part of the sixth day of creation, the text witnesses to God's giving of every plant and tree to humans and animals for sustenance (1:29–30). However, a key to unlocking what is going on here appears missing. Not only do these verses avoid telling us forthrightly what the image of God in human beings is, they seem to tell us even less about the God whom the image reflects. Because of this, it is perhaps most instructive to widen our lenses to interpret these passages in light of the creation account as a whole, focusing on the character of God's creative doings in order to access what it means to be human in this image.

Such a hermeneutical step is crucial because the image we have of God has dramatic consequences for how we interpret the image of God in human beings. In Terence Fretheim's words, "if the God who is portrayed in Genesis 1 is understood only or fundamentally in terms of overwhelming power, absolute control, and independent, unilateral activity, then those who are created in God's image could properly understand their creaturely role in comparable terms."[5] If God is perfect, self-sufficient, and sovereign, the vocation of human beings in the created order can be conceived in like terms. This can lead readers to perceive dominion and subduing as dominating power over creation, a kind of utterly controlling mastery that easily justifies the exploitation and manipulation of the natural world.[6] As if this is not damaging enough, it can also lead readers to consider the fully human nature in terms of control, dominance, and self-sufficient power such that if these qualities are alleged to be lacking, the person can be deemed deficient, lacking humanity. Furthermore, this viewpoint can be subtley reinforced if chaos and formlessness are seen as inimical elements conquered by God to create order. By implication, humans can easily construe their creaturely task—in the image of God—to be one of imposing order on chaos, a chaos equated with the "out-of-control" body, the abnormal and strange, the monster. The logic is obviously damaging for persons with disabilities. Tragically, these are indeed common renderings and the results have been catastrophic.

The image of God both marks and fosters a human imitation of God: the *imago Dei* is an *imitatio Dei*.[7] That is, what human beings are is connected to how their role in creation is conceived and played out. So we must be careful in our musings. An alternative rendering of the above passages is needed, one that would sit more comfortably with the vision of God we have been articulating from scripture. There is no need to rehearse what was discussed in detail in the last chapter. Suffice it to say that in Genesis 1–2 we find a creative God who freely and lovingly fashions cosmos out of chaos. The creator God is a personal and dynamic God who wills creatures into being, forming an abundant world comprised of variety and interrelationship. But we must remember that God's creativity is not unilateral and controlling, for God works with the elements by enlisting their cooperation, subsequently calling forth creativity from creation itself. God's power does not keep to itself but gives over; it is not coercive but sharing, not domineering but relational. It is a love that gives and receives in communicating itself, embracing, showing compassion for, and suffering with creatures. God is a vulnerable God, open to creation. In all, God is creative, relational, and available. Perhaps, then, the *imago Dei* can best be seen as a form of creativity, relationality, and availability.

Imago Dei *as Creativity—Human Being as a Cocreative Agent of God*

Creativity is a broad term that is filled out by relationality and availability. It means a creaturely participation in God's creativity, which entails connection with, openness to, and responsibility for creation. But isolating the term momentarily can help us gain some clarity in unpacking what it means to be created in God's image. For starters, human creativity involves a divine bestowal of power. Again, in Fretheim's words, "if the God of the creation accounts is imaged more as one who, in creating, chooses to share power in relationship, then the way in which the human as image of God exercises dominion is to be shaped by that model."[8] To illustrate this, Fretheim calls our attention to the very first words that God speaks to newly created humankind—be fruitful, multiply, fill the earth, have dominion, and subdue the earth (Gen. 1:28). This commission to human beings reflects a blessing, an empowerment that results from divine sharing of power. Accordingly, it is a call to imitate divine creativity, to generate new life and perpetuate it in word and deed. Not only does this involve procreation; it also entails naming, caring for, guiding, nurturing, harnessing, and thus managing the economy of living things.[9]

In this sense, the words "dominion" and "subdue" connote a process of ordering from disorder, aiding the divine activity of fashioning the formless and undetermined into formed and determinate being. Furthermore, they connote a responsibility to contribute to God's work of bringing fullness, vitality, and well-being to creation. Human beings are given a cocreative, world-shaping role in making creation an inhabitable and stable place for creatures to reside. "They intercede for God before the community of creation," according to Jürgen Moltmann, as "God's representatives on earth."[10] We are like tenants, entrusted with a house to occupy and care for—the graced economy of creation. And we are a part of this house, made of its elements and commissioned to manage the forces that contribute to its economy in order to ensure their flourishing.[11] So the image of God in humankind is not a stable substance or identifiable trait embedded in everyone so much as a dynamic correspondence to God that plays out variously in relationship to other creatures. Indeed, it is an extension of God's creative relationship with the world. God invites participation in God's own creative activity, giving over to human beings the task of tending to the becoming world. We are called to create from chaos, to nurture order and provide blessing.

Imago Dei *as Relationality—Human Being as Embodied along with Others*

Implied above is the fact that humankind is fundamentally relational. We are caught up in a web of interdependence with the created world, inescapably dependent upon creation for sustenance and well-being. As the creative power of God extends itself in relationship with others, so does the *imago Dei*. Creative power essentially is a relational power.

Fundamental to human relationality is a material, bodily existence.[12] We do not have bodies; we are our bodies. Human beings are living souls, not souls trapped in a material body, but organically unified, embodied creatures.[13] And our bodies define our limits. To deny this is to deny our relationship to other creatures, for relationships depend upon the differentiation created by bodily limits. Furthermore, denying the body denies the God who lovingly sculpted it from the earth. God is invested in our bodies, near to us bodily in that God forms humans directly as part of a creation within which God is immanent.[14] It is God who knits us together in our mothers' wombs, fearfully and wonderfully making us, intricately weaving us from the depths of the earth (Ps. 139:13–15). Our bodies are woven into the fabric of creation, connecting us to the elements in a way that makes us a part of the dynamic interdependence of all things.

So, unlike what has often been suggested in the history of Christianity, there is no absolute line between human beings and the rest of creation.[15] Rather, there are wide threads of continuity; we are part of the common creation story.[16] Moltmann affirms the point by stating that the human being is "a creature in the history of creation," linked inseparably with animals and all other creatures in the continuing creation.[17] Humanity, referenced in prototype singularly as Adam (the Hebrew 'adam is not a proper name but a word for humankind), is made from the dust of the ground ('adama, a play on words) and located within an abundant matrix of created things, referenced as Eden, a place of well-being (Gen. 2:7–8).

That God empowers the human to name creatures, an act that parallels the divine naming in Genesis 1:5–10, is testimony to the creative and relational character of the image of God.[18] Naming presupposes a relationship to the named and, further, creatively empowers the relationship. How so? By establishing a kind of ordered symmetry between parties, an acknowledgment of meaningful connection. Contrary to views that would place undue weight on the conscious use of language as definitive for human nature, we must note that such naming is only possible because human beings are embodied, related intrinsically to the world. True, language is a signifying medium through which humankind orients itself in the world. But it is our bodily relationship to the world, our incarnate existence, which is fundamental to the acquisition of language skills. Language is biologically situated. Even more, it is socially dependent.

Thus, a further aspect of human relationality comes to the fore in the social nature of humanity. The embodied good of the human being (Adam) relies upon having a partner, a companion: "It is not good that the 'adam should be alone" (Gen. 2:18). It is no accident that the image of God is male and female, together and equal (Gen. 1:27). In our sexual differentiation we thrive creatively through procreation and, writ larger, through relationships with other people within the context of creation and in relation to God. The relationship between man and woman, then, seems to be more a metaphor for companionship, for partnership and complementarity in general than a narrowly focused lesson in gender roles. Our human differences are the means by which we thrive in partnership with each other, and in an open relation with God and creation. Without variety relationship is impossible. As we have stressed all along in this book (especially in chapters 2 and 4), human beings are social creatures dependent upon others for well-being and welcome. Differences are good and blessed, the stuff of relationships. Alone we are incomplete; we need each other to be whole. Human beings desire welcome, and this embodied desire is the pretext of love. So if love opens up to an economy of graced abundance, it does so through our differences and the desire for relationship between those differences that animates our partnerships. Human being is a being-with others.[19]

Indeed, it is through recognizing differences that we reflect God, catching a glimpse of God in each other. It is no accident that the scriptures suggest time and again that we find divine blessing in the face of the stranger, the different, the other (e.g., Deut. 14:28–29; Matt. 25:45; Heb. 13:2). As rabbi Jonathan Sacks writes in *The Dignity of Difference*, this "is the Hebrew Bible's single greatest and most counterintuitive contribution to ethics. God creates difference; therefore it is in one-who-is-different that we meet God."[20] We shall have the chance to develop the ethical overtones of this idea in the next chapter. For now it is simply important to stress that while God creates every person in the same relational image, this image is woven differently into each unique individual. Our shared humanity is expressed in variation.

Imago Dei *as Availability—Human Being as Freedom for Love*

Human beings, however, are not solely the product of their connections with creation, determined by antecedent causes and thereby predictable in all behaviors. There is something irreducible about human experience. Philosophers and theologians alike have used terms like "reason," "self-transcendence," "freedom," and "openness" to describe this irreducibility. It is what is often called the spiritual dimension to humanity, that which makes us stand out from creation. However, we must stress, along with John Macquarrie, that this quality is not itself a fixed trait or endowment but rather a "potentiality for being."[21] Defined in the context of our discussion, "being" signifies the fullness of possibility for creativity and relationship. It is what God is absolutely and what human beings reflect finitely as embodied creatures created in God's image. Such potential marks a dynamic openness to relation, a capacity to respond creatively to others and ultimately to God. Humans are thus capable of responsibility, which entails the freedom to self-consciously acknowledge and enter into relationships. Indeed, having dominion entails the capacity to engage other creatures in freedom. Like God we are able to arrange and order things—for example, naming creatures and cultivating the soil to bear fruit. We are response-able: responsive, opened up to engage God and other creatures freely.

This openness by no means indicates an individualistic notion of freedom, whereby we are autonomous and self-making creatures of rational choice. Human freedom is earth-bound and embodied, arising out of finite contexts and the interdependent relationships that comprise them. Yet it is also the case that our capacity to respond to these contexts and relationships grows to become our own in a way that cannot be reduced to strict causal determination. There is something that escapes simple cause-and-effect explanations of human behavior. For example, we are our bodies, but in a way that renders us capable of being self-conscious, aware of our bodies, able to call this particular body mine vis-à-vis other bodies. Put in the broadest terms, this indicates a consciousness of self and others. It is as if the material universe coalesces in the peculiar form of human life to become self-aware and conscious.[22] Formed from the earth, we come to act toward ourselves, others, and the world in ways not narrowly prescribed by past events. Human beings stand out as creative beings capable of desiring and achieving the new. Our bodies transcend themselves in being open to novelty, to the possibility of things being different. We are not held captive by tragedy or suffering. We stretch out to the possibility of something more. But how does this happen?

Human openness is a desire for welcome. It is a desire for a meaningful and vitality-giving place with others in creation.[23] This desire, however, is more than the desire to survive. It cannot be described solely in biological terms, a striving for self-perpetuation vis-à-vis assimilating or consuming things. A more balanced—and more Augustinian—perspective shows how such desire can be conceived broadly in volitional terms, as a power of the will that seeks value or good. Eugene TeSelle, an Augustine scholar, calls our attention to three factors of willing: first there is *suggestion*, which occurs through the senses or associations of ideas; then there is *inclination*, which is an arousal or movement of the affections toward a perceived good, though not yet a deliberate act; and finally, there is *consent*, which freely gives in and yields to or ratifies an inclination, acting upon it. True, as TeSelle notes, human beings can resist consenting to one inclination and instead choose to follow another, and there can remain an internal conflict between varied inclinations.[24] But the point is that consent deliberately yields to a certain inclination over others. Why? Because the will is oriented toward happiness. It follows inclinations that are presumed to offer a greater promise of happiness and joy. This following constitutes human freedom. And such freedom is fulfilled when our inclinations, motivated by a desire for value, produce not the consumption of value but an affirmative connection with something through consent. For Augustine this is what it means to love. Love is an intentional energy of the will, roused by the affections, that both desires and delights in its object, affirming it for its own sake.[25] Through the will we pursue such-and-such an end and direct our course of action accordingly in love with goodness. Loving goodness can properly be said to be our creaturely place in a world among others with God. It is the means by which we find welcome, and is a factor of loving others in God. We are what we love.

God creates room, so to speak, in creation for us to unfold dynamically as intentional, loving beings. We are created for love. In this sense, the *imago Dei* is a desire to give and receive love. And loving requires open space to give itself freely for others. It cannot be love if it is predetermined according to causal necessity. A freedom is necessary which empowers us to become selves. Marked by a unique openness or self-transcendence in relation to others, we can shape our lives as agents of our own flourishing, accordingly engaging others with resolve and purpose. Human beings are persons, and in this capacity reflect divine personhood. As the image of God on earth, human beings can recognize what is different and deliberately enter into creative relationship with it. We encounter the world and respond to others through the will in love, which is a factor of the embodied desire for relation, a part of our longing for welcome. This means that companionship is not automatic but a matter of acknowledgment and mutual giving and receiving between agents. We are free to give ourselves to and receive each other, creation, and God. And there are always more possibilities. So freedom in this sense means that we are unfinished beings. The *imago Dei* is an ever active and extending potentiality. The self is not merely a solitary rational being but an embodied relational task, a perpetual project to be achieved lovingly with others, within creation, and in the presence of God.

We come to a pivotal point. Our volitional self-transcendence is a capacity to love constituted fully in relationship to God. In fact, our self-transcendence *is* God's call to us, a hunger for the divine built into our hearts. We are created for loving God as our supreme good (*summum bonum*), the ultimate terminus of our desire for value and happiness. As Augustine famously states, "You arouse us so that praising you may bring us joy, because you have made us and drawn us to yourself, and our heart is unquiet until it rests in you."[26] As a capacity for love, the *imago Dei* is a capacity for God (*capax Dei*). Indeed, human openness suggests the infinite; its possibilities transgress finitude. Daniel Migliore corroborates this in noting that whereas non-human creatures "have drives or instincts that are triggered by definite needs or particular objects, in the case of human beings there is a restlessness that is virtually boundless." Human beings "search not only for physical and emotional satisfaction but for a meaning in life. . . . They create worlds of meaning that they continually transform, yet without ever finding full satisfaction."[27] Our creativity desires a fullness that lies beyond every possible finite achievement. Why? Because God fashions us such that our openness to possibility is an openness to God. God's call to us is woven into our makeup. We are hardwired for a welcome that radiates lovingly throughout creation and ultimately joins up with the creator. This is what animates the sense of God we spoke of in the last chapter.

However, the desire for God does not merely float vertically in reference to God. It is an openness circulating horizontally through creation and in relation to others. Our freedom is God's call to us for relationship. But the call is not unqualified. Even as it opens to God, it lingers within finite limits defined by the nature of our bodies and the relationships that connect our bodies with other human beings and creation. Our creaturely status places limits upon our freedom and openness, and we are vulnerable because of it, subject to frustrations and imperilments not of our own choosing. But as we have discussed in previous chapters, these limits are not evil. Even as they make tragedy possible, such limits are good, created by God such that relationships are possible. Further, they function creatively to empower our loving recognition of vulnerability in others. That is, while embodied limitations mark vulnerability to tragedy and suffering, they also make possible our response to another's preciousness, another's call for love and welcome. Vulnerability and weakness open up the wholeness made possible through relationships. This is why the effort to eliminate suffering carte blanche is wrongheaded. It denies creatureliness and its limits, thereby cutting us off from the potential for love. Migliore sums it up nicely: "To wish the world were immune from *every* form of struggle and *every* form of suffering would be to wish not to have been created at all."[28]

So as a basic desire for God, human freedom is a vulnerable capacity to receive the other in love, delighting in and caring for his or her good. And as the other's presence is precious and loved by God, it is more than an instrument serving some exploitative end or another. In the natural world, the non-human other is a creature of God worthy of respect and responsible acts of stewardship, care, and cultivation. In the human world, the other is a person bearing the image of God, a person therefore worthy of respect, fidelity, and compassion. Such insights do not emerge because humans are autonomous, have the ability to use reason, or communicate through language. They arise instead in the vulnerable crucible of interdependent relationships. They happen in a loving encounter with the other's difference that transpires in the context of a basic desire for God. Welcoming another is being in relation to God, and being in relation to God means welcoming another.

With this we come to the heart of the creative and relational fabric of the *imago Dei*: human beings reflect God's free love as an availability displayed by solicitude toward what is other. Created in God's image, we are beings with the capacity to respect, be faithful to, and show compassionate regard for others. Our "response-ability" to relationships renders us capable of giving and receiving love. So availability is not simply a freedom from being causally determined and constrained by our relationships; it is a freedom for these relationships. Bonhoeffer makes this point powerfully:

> In the language of the Bible, freedom is not something man has for himself but something he has for others. No man is free 'as such'. . . . Why? Because freedom is not a quality which can be revealed—it is not a possession, a presence, an object, nor is it a form for existence—but a relationship and nothing else. . . . Being free means 'being free for the other', because the other has bound me to him. Only in relationship with the other am I free.[29]

In the final analysis, freedom is a relationship of availability for the other whereby we bind ourselves to her by offering the gift of ourselves. This is what God does for humanity. And being created in the image of God commissions humanity to the ongoing task of doing the same for others. Or, as Macquarrie summarizes, "just as God opens himself into the creation and pours out being, and therefore has 'letting-be' as his essence, so man is most truly himself and realizes his essence in the openness of an existence in which he too can let be, in responsibility, in creativity, and in love."[30]

Human beings, then, are free persons neither because of a fixed trait embedded in their nature nor because of something they produce, but because of something they are: loved into being by God, created in the image of God as vulnerable beings open to the possibility of love. All human beings are therefore precious and marked by dignity in relationships with others. McCloughry and Morris express the implications nicely: "Each person is worthy of respect and dignity because each person has been made by God to convey something unique about God to the world . . . regardless of race, religion, orientation or ability." These authors go on to note a further implication: being created in the image of God "invites us to discover that image in each other."[31] Thus, contrary to messages conveyed by the cult of normalcy, the limitations entailed by variety and differences are humanizing. They are expressions of a shared and vulnerable humanity. In fact, they are invitations by God to dispose ourselves to one another and find our humanity in relation to each other. To be human is to be subject to the call of others and the call of God. Wholeness is not the product of self-sufficiency or independence, but rather of the genuinely inclusive companionship that results from sharing our humanity with one another in love. This is what it means to be God's representatives on earth, a counterpart to the divine.

In conclusion, then, we can affirm that being human is an incarnate desire for relation, not simply a desire to be but a desire to be with others and, ultimately, with God. This takes place in an empowering matrix of bodily connection, in a home that welcomes. The creatively relational and available character of human being is what it means to be whole, which is the *imago Dei*.

The Imago Dei *and Disability*

Do persons with disabilities signify a lack of wholeness, a deficiency that blights the image of God? Emphatically, no! Every human being has the image of God in common, even as it is expressed in variety and difference. Differentiation is part of God's intention for humanity, so it does not indicate an inequality between some, but the equality of all. Here disability does not mark an incomplete humanity—a failure, defect, or sinful nature. It models one way of being human as vulnerable yet creative, relational, and available. Notice the absence of terms like "reason," "productivity," and "independence." Full personhood is neither diminished by a paucity of these nor confirmed by their abundance. Instead, personhood lies in being affirmed by God as a dependent creature loved into being with others. Chris, my son, put it best in something he wrote for me: "I am special just like everyone else, except in a different way. Even though I am 'different,' I just like being who I am."

186

Disabilities, then, need not be suppressed and normalized, decried with pity or overcome with curative aid. Living with impairments is a way, like other ways, of being human that it is fully capable in most instances of giving and receiving love, and thus capable of living life's creative possibilities under the image of a God who loves, draws near, and suffers with. People with disabilities are not "children of a lesser God," but persons who, like everyone, are created vulnerably in the image of the one true God. The fact of each human life "contributes something unique in terms of 'being' even if it cannot in terms of 'doing'."[32] In other words, simply being is more fundamental than the acquisition of body capital measured in terms of an economy of exchange. A divine economy of grace is at work that undercuts the management systems of the cult of normalcy.

The question arises, however, whether God creates people with disabilities. On the one hand—yes— insofar as people with impairments of one kind or another are persons created in the image of God. But on the other hand, as something negatively tragic—no. There is nothing inherently wrong with disability or with the people who have disabilities. Disability is a factor of being finite and contingent in an open universe subject to elements of unpredictability, instability, and conflict. Humankind lives in a relationally composed and ongoing creation. And this means that we are to a large degree vulnerable, out of control of our bodies, each of us subject to tragedy according to the limitations implied by relationships. Persons are not perfect and autonomous beings but depend upon their environment to live, and depend upon the welcome provided by other people to flourish. When these dependencies are put at risk by maladaptive or conflictive biophysical relationships, impairments occur. Limitations like this are part of the tragic structure of creation.

Insofar as bodily impairments cause suffering and foster disabling conditions for persons, God is not a direct causal agent. God does not purposely create tragedy. Recall that tragedy is a shadow feature, a kind of undertow which accompanies creation's interdependent and relational goodness. God is continually at work hovering over the face of the deep, calling chaos into fruitful possibilities, but not in a controlling and coercive way. The blessings of creaturely uniqueness and novelty require flexibility, unpredictability, and elements of formlessness. In this way, God works with chaos to form creatures out of indeterminate nothingness as a potentiality for determinate being. But determinate beings are always changing in relationships to other beings such that potentiality remains part of what they are. Creation is not complete; it is ongoing and therefore includes a mixture of indeterminancy in its very composition. Thus, as created beings connected with all creation and open to possibility, human beings contain components of the indeterminacy of chaos in their very being. Because of the relational structure of creation, there is the possibility that our bodies can be influenced in a way that causes harm.

Disability, however, should not be construed as a "description of life as a tragedy."[33] The image of God in human beings remains untarnished by the tragic.

That is, tragedy does not define a person. There are always humanizing possibilities, even in the most tragic of circumstances. Yet the fact remains that a large portion of the tragedies experienced by human beings are themselves caused by human beings, directly and indirectly, through willful violations and passive negligence or complacency. Indeed, the social systems in which we participate are often disabling, marking out body capital according to a cult of normalcy that distinguishes ability from disability, normality from abnormality, strength from weakness, fullness from lack.

II. Sin's Tragedy and the Possibility of Redemption

In the face of the tragic character of existence, human beings have an aching sense that things are not what they are meant to be. Something is not right. More specifically, our human potential for creative relationality in love is not readily apparent. We long for welcome but look around and find ourselves in a world marked by disasters, fear, abuse, hatred, and violence. The *imago Dei* does not shine out from our relationships. This is noticeably accentuated for people with disabilities, as social powers and systems brand disability a stigma or taboo, a human deficiency, and foster barriers to access. Despite being loved into being by God, people with disabilities are excluded or trivialized as social nonentities in ways that mar their sense of being created in the image of God. As we saw in chapter 2, the process stems from the insidious sway of the cult of normalcy. Now, however, we can note how it represses creativity, relationality, and availability. In different ways, the cult of normalcy prevents both people with disabilities and non-disabled people from discovering their unique value and preciousness in relationships of genuine love and care. The result is tragic, but now in a morally qualified way—as moral evil. Welcome is denied.

But how did we get here? What factors contribute to such an unwelcoming human situation? Let us explore these questions a bit further, highlighting the potential for redemptive transformation even amidst such tragedy.

Sin—Creative Freedom for Love Gone Awry

Without question, the fundamental problem of existence from the Christian perspective is sin. But what does sin mean? Essentially it is "missing the mark" (Greek *hamartia*), signifying a turning away from an original relationship with the divine Creator upon which all other relationships are founded. Accordingly, sin distorts the primal life connections human beings have with each other and the created world. And it does so, I suggest, as a disruption of the fundamental powers of the *imago Dei*—that is, creativity, relationality, and availability—thereby introducing into the landscape of creation mechanisms of power that falsify and/or deny the possibilities of welcome. Sin breaks down relationships, causing a general alienation from God, creation, and other human beings, which in turn leads to exploitation, domination, and violence in human life. In this way the social harm produced by the cult of normalcy itself is a symptom of sin. It is a moral evil.

Sin is simultaneously personal and social, a truth that can be articulated in three ways. First, sin involves concrete acts of consent for which human beings are personally responsible. Yet, second, as humans are relational beings sin inherently involves a breach of relationship with others. Thus it has immediate social consequences. These consequences foster systems of alienation and domination that, in turn, further exacerbate broken relationships between human beings. Sin is somehow "out there," structurally embedded in the corporate powers and principalities that comprise social arrangements and cultural conventions. It therefore appears impossible to avoid sin, as its destructive implications are passed down from generation to generation. Sin, then, precedes us. Third, this brings us to what theologians have called original sin, the fact that human beings are fallen and innately disposed toward sin, corrupted in some fundamental sense, such that sinfulness is a universally shared human condition. The danger with this notion, however, is that it can make sin seem necessary, biologically inscribed and predetermined. Clearly this cannot be the case if human beings are held personally accountable for their actions. We come up against a paradox, but one that can be understood instructively if sin is conceived in relational terms, as both personal and social. Human beings become who they are in and through relationships which have been somehow ruptured, with this rupture grafted onto the social matrices upon which they depend. By no means should such an admission leave society responsible for corrupting an otherwise sin-free person, for this would exempt the person from moral responsibility. Yet neither does it make the person fated to sin. Individual persons participate in sinful configurations that precede them but for which they are also liable. Let us explore how.

That human beings can turn away from their original relation to God, creation, and each other indicates a freedom for relationship that can be violated and abused. We are responsible creatures, and not solely determined by past experiences and relationships. However, this power of freedom entails a marked instability. That is, there is within the openness to possibility a volitional indeterminacy. Many options present themselves. God creates space in creation for human freedom to enter creatively into relations without which love would not be possible. But this space entails risk, for freedom implies the possibility of its misuse, of not loving, of turning away from relationship. The presence of such risk is there from the start.

Our human possibilities are formless and without determinate shape until deliberate decisions are made. Such decisions form us as moral creatures in relation to others. Recall the earlier discussion of Augustine's notion of the will, where we saw that while the affections incline us toward certain things, it is consent that ratifies an inclination by acting upon it. Human beings become who they are not merely by their inclinations but also by consenting to certain inclinations, becoming responsible agents directed toward certain goods. We come to love certain things and persons, and in so doing come to serve them. What or whom we love, then, defines our character and shapes our lives. If human beings are created in the image of God, we are fashioned to enter freely and lovingly into relationship with God, imitating God by consenting to God's purpose for us. Yet we are not mechanically predetermined to do so. There is openness to possibility. In the throes of such openness God invites us into relation through the desire or inclination for welcome and the happiness that it yields. The longing for purpose, meaning, and vitality is a longing for God built into the human heart. But consent to this inclination is ours to make. And we can refuse to consent to our creaturely vocation. We can deny the image of God in us. Hence, paradoxically, the seeds for this refusal are inscribed into the image of God. The constitutional openness to possibility renders human beings unstable, making both consent to and turning away from God possible. But this all sounds too abstract. How does the refusal we are talking about take place?

As we discussed in chapter 2, humans gain a sense of self by being placed in a framework of orientation, a situation of welcome whereby the world is made purposeful and vitalizing. Precisely this is what God does for humankind in the Yahwist account of Genesis 2 by placing Adam and Eve in the Garden of Eden. Human beings as individuals are incomplete, needing others to be whole. Persons depend upon being received by others to recognize their own preciousness. And in the creation story it is God who proclaims the value of human beings, placing them in the created order with each other and the animals. God welcomes and tells us who we are—loved beings. Indeed, we are hardwired for such welcome, finding our creaturely fulfillment in the presence of God. Even as we are not coerced into the divine presence, our affections tilt us toward it, and given the absence of alternatives we consent.

However, according to the portrayal of the fall into sin in Genesis 3 there is an alternative, which is illustrated poignantly in the presence of the cunning serpent, one of God's creatures (3:1). While the story here cannot be taken literally as historical fact, there is nevertheless great moral and religious insight packed into the account as an interpretation of the origin of sin. A serpent comes upon the scene to suggest that God is holding something back from the humans. Putting this into context, we must bear in mind that God had forbidden touching and eating from the tree in the middle of the garden. The presence of this tree implies that the creativity of humankind is not free from all limitations. Indeed, God had said death would result from transgressing this creaturely limit. What the snake proposes, however, is that God is not being straightforward and truthful: "You will not die; for God knows that when you eat of it your eyes will be opened, and you will be like God, knowing good and evil" (3:4–5). There is more possibility at hand, hints the serpent, than consenting to God's arrangement. Here, a "good" other than God suggests itself, excites the affections, and influences the will toward consent. "So when the woman saw that the tree was good for food, and that it was a delight to the eyes, and that the tree was to be desired to make one wise, she took of its fruit and ate; and she also gave some to her husband, who was with her, and he ate" (3:6). Mysteriously, then, the possibility of refusing relation to the divine exists in the finite, created world.

At issue is fundamental trust in God's welcome. The serpent presents possibilities to the humans that conjure a suspicion of God's good intention for them. It is true, as Terence Fretheim notes, that God had not told the full truth. God kept something from humans, something that the serpent's cunning now makes appear beneficial. What the serpent does, however, is stir the humans into anxious questioning: Why had God done this? Could they trust God that not all knowledge, especially such appealing knowledge, is for their own good?[34] Given the anxiety created by being exposed to an alternative good, the humans decided to act for themselves and eat. This is the primal sin—disobedience. But willful disobedience or defiance is not the only ingredient at work. There is more. The anxiety created by new options causes unbelief, a basic mistrust. Accordingly, Fretheim suggests that the originating sin may "best be defined as mistrust of God and God's word, which then manifests itself in disobedience and other negative behaviors (e.g., blaming)."[35] Disobedience follows from a mistrust conjured in the throes of anxiety.

In this picture the serpent functions as an ambivalent metaphor for temptation in the form of mistrust, which can sneak up silently and expose one to peril, striking when least expected. The overall point seems to be this: built into creation (remember that the serpent is one of God's creatures) are possibilities for human beings, some of which, when consented to, lead away from a trusting relationship with God.[36] The serpent also represents the roots of mistrust in deception. It lies about God's good intentions and misleads humans regarding their situation, telling them it will be all right to go ahead and reach beyond their limitations. By suggesting an alternative that conjures anxiety about the human situation, mistrust or unbelief is introduced at the level of the affections, which results in a decisive act of consent that refuses relation to God. This outlines a threefold structure: (1) anxiety over alternative possibilities, which invokes (2) a mistrust in God's welcome, yielding (3) a consenting refusal of relationship to God.

In the end there is a heavy price to pay for this transgression. Out of anxiety and in mistrust the humans wished for control, to take matters into their own hands and become like God, reaching far beyond the capacity for which they were created. Freely acting upon this structurally infects human creativity, relationality, and availability. For example, immediately after eating the fruit the humans recognized their nakedness and fashioned clothes to cover themselves (Gen. 3:7). They knew they were exposed, vulnerable to each other, literally and metaphorically. There is a breach of relation, a distance between human beings is created. Mistrust in God has swept out horizontally to rupture the relational landscape of human life. We are exposed to our being exposed, and so cover our nakedness, our sexuality, our bodies, to shield ourselves and hide our dignity. In the sweep of being exposed, our creative openness to possibility becomes oriented to self-protection. We recognize our incomplete and finite natures, but mistrust others and the potential harm they represent. Others negatively expose our human vulnerability, even unto death. And such exposure cultivates further anxiety and fear instead of the creative openness of availability. The opposite of love, such fearful mistrust hinders our creative, relational, and available capacities as creatures fashioned in the image of God.

The primal sin is lasting in character, distorting the image of God such that the effects of sin escalate and spin out of control. Rather than acknowledge its vulnerable limits and extending outward in the creative risk of love, the desire for welcome turns inward on itself and becomes relationally stifling and security seeking. This is borne out in Genesis 3:8–10, when God comes walking in the garden, calling out, "Where are you?" The breach of relation is obvious. Humankind and God are no longer in sync. In fact, God's presence is no longer perceived as welcoming, but as a threat. The humans hide themselves in fear, for they knew they were naked. Hiding is a quintessentially self-protective maneuver that occurs when we are anxious and mistrustful. God interrogates: "Who told you that you were naked? Have you eaten from the tree of which I commanded you not to eat?" (3:11). But rather than accepting responsibility for their actions, they justify themselves by blaming something else—Adam blames Eve, Eve blames the serpent (3:12–13). Again we see a self-protecting dynamic at work. The accord between humans, God, and creation has been severed. Humans deny their limited relational character, seeking instead to become like God, to secure welcome by creating their own security, hiding when threatened and shifting the blame when guilty of wrong.

Because human beings are not built to guarantee their own meaning and purpose, the historical aftermath of sin is devastating. Death and suffering are introduced. This is not to say these were not already a part of the garden, otherwise the Tree of Life—that other forbidden tree—would have been irrelevant. Rather, as Fretheim suggests, the limits of mortality are now realized on a new experiential level.[37] We might even go further to suggest that death is a metaphor for broken relationships. It signifies life apart from the presence of God's welcome. For example, exiled from the garden by God and left to themselves in an arid land, fear and alienation run rampant. Intimacy and community collapse, as evidenced by Cain's competition with Abel for God's approval. The worth generated by God's welcome is no longer apparent as God initially intended. And murderous violence ensues when Cain cannot gain God's favor like Abel (4:1–8). The meaning of this story lies not so much in the reason why God rejects Cain's offering—for in the text the reason is not apparent, known only to God—as in how Cain responds to his frustration and God's subsequent rapprochement.[38] Cain does not seek to change but becomes enraged, and in a calculative manner kills his brother to rid himself of competition. Cain's desire for welcome in this instance is strikingly self-absorbed, to the point of violence when denied. Fundamental mistrust has led down a pernicious path to death. Literally, the wages of sin is death.

Here we see the general picture of a human pathology that runs deep. The Yahwist account of the fall into sin shows both how sin precedes us as a universal human reality and how we each are contributing agents in its perpetuation. Craving control and self-sufficiency in a situation of anxiety and mistrust, human beings appraise value (what we called body capital in chapter 2) according to economies of exchange based in human ability and productivity. We are exposed to our insecurity in a way that compels us to draw incessantly from the drama of competition, our worth measured against others. Creation's economy of grace is obscured. Accordingly, the thirst for welcome and the secure home it provides becomes insatiable. Wrenched away from the arc of God's gratuitous welcome, we are brought to pine for welcome by imitating the attainments of others, insofar as these attainments are esteemed as having the potential to purchase worth and value for us. Yet we find such worth only in fragments, a fact that leaves us perpetually frustrated. We calculate human value by what successfully achieves recognition, leading us to compete with others for worth. But as we are created for God, our achievements never seem to measure up. We are perpetually shamed, forced to cover up our human weaknesses. In order to secure needed recognition we seek more and more control of our environment and our relationships with others. In the process, human beings increasingly hide from vulnerability and grow to fear and mistrust others whose difference threatens the controlled world—the world created by cultural conventions to provide security. Contempt for others becomes rampant. Communities reflect this dynamic socially insofar as they are informed by the cult of normalcy and assuage human insecurity by justifying the values of an artificially imposed order. Assimilation and exclusion become the operative modes of behavior toward perceived threats. The other—the strange and different—is not welcome. A logic of the strong prevails, holding us captive.

If the desire for welcome is an embodied striving for well-being that connects us with others, an affective power situating us in the world enfolded by the presence of God, its distortion fundamentally affects how we relate to everything. Sin, then, might be seen as human desire gone astray, a corruption of the basic potency for relation. Carrying to an extreme the natural human dynamism toward welcome, sin is a refusal to face the vulnerability of interdependent relationships. It is desire in the form of a will to control that aspires to secure itself by mastering all around it. Ridden with anxiety about it own lack of control, especially given the reality of death, desire reaches beyond its limits. Accordingly, it reduces what is other than the self, placing a stranglehold on all that is "not I" in order to guarantee and, hence, absolutize its own happiness. By effectively closing itself off from others, genuine availability is negated in a posture of existential solipsism or self-centeredness.[39] Differences are denied and reduced to the ego. There is a proportionate relation between the inability to accept vulnerability and live out of its limits and the inability to embrace differences. Insofar as human beings are driven by the will to control, sin manifests itself as the creative freedom for love gone awry. It infects both personal and social life by stifling creative openness to relation. Creativity decays into control and domination. Relationality erodes into fear-based competition. Availability flattens into an isolating contempt for others.

Sin, Idolatry, and the Possibility of Redemption

This way of understanding desire can be deepened by turning to Augustine, who fashioned arguably one of the most influential depictions of sin in the history of Christian thought. Augustine locates the central problem of human existence in a misdirected act of willing, one that centers itself in some created reality, as if it were the Creator, providing life-giving welcome. The finite and immediate—a humanly appraised value, convention, or idea that fosters security of welcome—is thus absolutized over and against its infinite source, treated as if it provided ultimate happiness. This perverts our relationship with God, and by implication our basic mode of relatedness to each other and the world. Such is the nature of idolatry, whereby relative goods at hand are forced into playing a role that only God, as the *summum bonum*, can rightfully play.[40] And what fuels such idolatry? Nothing less than human willing turned in on securing itself as opposed to acknowledging its radical creaturely dependence upon God.

Augustine calls this self-oriented attachment to finite reality *cupiditas*, a need-based form of love or desire which inordinately seeks its own security and satisfaction above all else, therein refusing its genuine relation to creation and the Creator. Recall that for Augustine love is the energy of the will, searching after and delighting in its object. By insisting that perishable and finite goods fill its own need for the enduring welcome of the infinite, however, *cupiditas* clings to these as if they were ultimate good, forcing them to fit into a mold ill-suited for anything finite. The result warps our entire sense of the world, disordering the will. The fault of *cupiditas*, then, is that it looks for its fulfillment in the wrong place. An unfulfilled and never satisfied craving, this kind of desire extends its reach outward, but only in a self-enclosed modality. It seeks to absorb into its own orbit the whole of reality—though in actuality, for Augustine, what it desires is none other than God. It is desire turned inward on itself (*encurvatus en se ipsum*). Hence, the distorted, negative form of love Augustine also describes as *concupiscentia*, which connotes desire spinning out of control, absolutizing its own sweep. It is unfortunate that Augustine too closely associated human desire with lust and sex, for clearly it is not desire itself that is culpable, but rather its directedness to finite goods in place of the infinite, such that by serving only itself it makes itself into a god.

Now this does not merely connote pride or ego inflation as a defiant hubris or arrogance. Though Augustine sees pride as the key element in sin, we must note there are also other forms of *cupiditas*. As feminist and postcolonial theologians remind us, sin can be reflected in servility or passivity, an ego deflation or diffusion. This latter possibility marks an abnegation of creative responsibility in which a person or group acquiesces to the will of another in order to find security. Displaying a lack of empowerment, one surrenders one's own identity to take refuge in and thereby gain legitimacy from the identity of another. There is here an anxious refusal to assert one's own creative possibilities as a person in order to acquire a sense of belonging. This helps us explain why some ways of desiring welcome can, ironically, accede to domination, subsumed and assimilated by the normalizing sway of another's way of being. In order to secure itself, the genuinely creative openness of availability becomes preempted by "losing" itself in the other.[41] A person thus becomes swallowed up by his or her dependency. This is not the positive sense of dependency we have articulated in previous chapters. Often, however, it is a symptom of a learned dependence based in derision, repudiation, marginalization or exclusion. A discourse of domination, such as the cult of normalcy, can so affect the dominated's self-perception that the latter forgets himself and sees himself as the reverse underdetermined image of what feigns powers of determination. This asymmetrical logic has functioned prominently in colonialist expansion, slavery, and gender relations.[42] Because the need for orientation and welcome is so strong, a person can come to recognize herself as inferior and dependent in the eyes of another who feigns putative superiority and self-sufficiency.

To this degree, subscribing to the imposing view of another can be idolatrous, a way of locking victims of domination into further cycles of victimization. Certainly this is not to blame the victim, but rather to note the nuance of sin's hold on human life. The hatred of oneself can be a way of refusing one's vulnerability, avoiding the risk of freely entering into relationships with others. Such a posture is equally egocentric, for it allows one to be determined by the idolatry of others. But it does so as a reversal of pride.[43] Ironically, it is a will to control that hides behind the veil of what others deem one to be, attached to some finite good or convention as if it offered security. Perhaps this is the most insidious temptation for people with disabilities, in that it lets the vision of the cult of normalcy define disability. Even so, it also reflects *cupiditas*.

Sin's idolatry, then, can take the form of either overinflating pride or underinflating hiding and flight, each of them being a denial of vulnerability in its ideal mode of creativity, relationality, and availability.[44] For people with disabilities, sin is often experienced as oppression, exclusion, and isolation from others. While these have social origins, there are personal consequences in that they ignore, suppress, or harm the image of God in people, depriving them of creative, relational, and available possibilities for being. Here the tyranny of the cult of normalcy idolizes certain conventions, norms, and standards that reduce persons to their body capital and ability to purchase recognition. Insofar as this kind of reduction is internalized or adopted, it is difficult for people with disabilities to flourish as subjects of their own experiences. Hence, *cupiditas* has a dehumanizing domino effect that breaks down and distorts human relationships and the creative impulse to life.

In contrast to *cupiditas*, however, Augustine positions true love or *caritas*— genuine charity, not the condescending form of pity and charity that we described earlier in chapter 4. *Caritas* is the human desire for welcome centered properly in God.[45] It thus represents a restoration of the *imago Dei*, for this love orders all finite objects of desire according to their rightful relation to God. It is crucial to note, however, that *caritas* is not the negation of human desire, but rather its transformative fulfillment through the gratuitous and loving activity of God in Christ.[46] It is the product of God's gratuitous love acting upon human desire, breaking us out of the self-enclosed tyranny of desires trained upon their own satiation and opening us anew toward loving others and the world as a part of God's sacred realm.[47] *Caritas* is an ongoing effect of salvation, the healing of broken relatedness via the conversion and redirection of desire. The will now begins to exercise itself in righteousness (i.e., right relatedness), and desire attaches itself to God as a longing (*desiderium*) that awaits its final consummation in the beatific vision. Seen in this way, the whole Christian life is a pilgrimage traversed on the road of the affections. Augustine's idea of the two cities rests upon the distinction between desire as *cupiditas* and desire as *caritas*, the latter being the primary attribute of the community of the saved.

While this discussion of Augustine is sketchy, for lack of space, it highlights a key component in a classic view of sin and its redemptive overcoming that runs deep in Christian theology. Sin is the condition of being bound by an inordinate and self-absolutizing desire that has turned away from God by fixing itself on the immediacy of finite goods in order to find fulfillment. It is the *imago Dei* corrupted and turned in on itself. But salvific healing signifies the redirection of desire toward its ultimate end, with the dominating power of self-enclosure turned inside out so the dynamics of idolatry are broken. Instead of being "ego-logically" directed toward its own satisfaction and self-perpetuation, human desire modulates into a love desiring and delighting in other persons and the world within the horizon of God's all-encompassing love. This is a self-transcending love opened out toward and disposed to receiving the other, attuned creatively to the other's goodness in an attitude of availability. Jonathan Edwards, I think, captures something similar in suggesting that true virtue is a disposition of benevolence toward being in general, a relation of goodwill toward all things.[48] Far from being bloodless, such a posture of goodwill cannot help but attend to the value of the concrete and vulnerable other. Put differently, as the Hebrew prophets proclaimed, it is the widest form of hospitality toward the stranger.[49] The love of God entails a love of the other.

So the process of redemption reverses the tendencies of sin by transforming the affections toward God and others, making trust possible. For the Christian, desire becomes *caritas*, a love of God that overflows with an inclusive concern for the other as one's neighbor without thought of a self-serving return. This is possible because of a kind of release, a letting go of the anxiety-ridden urge to guarantee welcome, an emptying of the need to be securely in control by accepting one's vulnerability. A reality more precious than any I can guarantee to myself has bid me consent to my own vulnerable, relational, and creaturely status before its divine face. With awe and admiration I worship it as God, following its trace of grace in the gospel accounts of Jesus of Nazareth. In this acknowledgment of relation to God, a basic sense of and desire for right relatedness in creation is engendered and borne out in an attitude of vulnerability and benevolent openness to being, expressed in an ongoing posture of care for others and the world.[50] God becomes, as Carter Heyward notes, "our power in mutual relation . . . by (which) we can act, responsibly and joyfully, on behalf of the liberation of all people and creatures, including ourselves, from bondage to wrong relation."[51] There is a strong prophetic ring to desire transformed into the repentant, non-idolatrous, and compassionate relatedness—that is, availability—of *caritas*. Reoriented outwardly in love, the desire for welcome finds its center in God. And the result is a moral disposition, a *habitus*, of creative availability.

III. Reconsidering Redemption in Jesus Christ

Redemption in Christ effects a transformative reversal of the fear-based mistrust we have characterized as the basic impetus to sin. It makes possible a conversion (*metanoia*) to God that promises new life amidst the perils of tragedy, trading paradoxically on the experience of vulnerability and lack as a harbinger of divine abundance. This does not entail submissiveness and lack of power in relation to God's self-possessive omnipotence. To the contrary, Christ embodies God's self-emptying embrace of creaturely limitation and interdependence, making possible our active openness to God and others. The power of God is unseemly and strange, disclosing itself paradoxically not in autonomy but in relational vulnerability. It makes space for others, strangers, persons with disabilities—those without autonomy, power, and completeness measured in terms of the cult of normalcy. Hence, far from vindicating the conventional and normal, Christ's work actually subverts it by pointing to the palpable and life-giving presence of the divine in human vulnerability.

To exist as a finite creature is to be contingent and vulnerable. This means humans are beings that face limitations and can suffer from a range of impairments. And it is precisely such vulnerability that God embraces in Christ, entering fully into the frailty of the human condition, even unto a tragic death. Jesus is Emmanuel, God with us. Sharing the divine self in this way sends a distinct message: God is in solidarity with humanity at its most fundamental level, in weakness and brokenness. This is not to romanticize weakness. Here God reveals the divine nature as available to creation not only by undergoing or suffering with human vulnerability, but also by raising it up into God's own being. Jesus Christ is the icon of a vulnerable God. And as such, Jesus is the transforming presence of God at work in our midst, reinvigorating by recapitulating the *imago Dei*; that is, summing up what it truly means to be human in the image of God—creative, relational, and available.

Jesus as the Icon of a Vulnerable God—Redemptive Revelation

The center of the Christian witness radiates with an inclusive and vulnerable love that is christological in shape. God's enfolding love sympathetically enters into our midst and spills over with unconditional regard for all persons. That is, Jesus becomes an iconic or transparent image of God's own radical openness to what is other than God, an openness that affirms creatively the goodness of being itself in each particular creature. The term "icon" is instructive here because it connotes a finite reality that surpasses itself, conveying meanings that are divine in origin.[52] Paul speaks of Christ as the *eikon tou theou tou aoratou*, the icon or image of the invisible God (Col. 1:15). Something tangible conveys the intangible in a way that connects the two terms without reducing the latter to the former. The well-known Greek father John of Damascus famously speaks of icons as bodily images that are revelatory, giving provisional access to secrets hidden in God's transcendence.[53] Icons usher us into a prototype that remains beyond them. Reference to Christ as an icon, then, helps articulate his dual character as both human and divine. That is, Christ opens humanity up to what God is like, but does so by being fully human. He represents the passion of God for humanity and humanity's passion for God rolled into one.

For Christians, Jesus is revelatory because his openness to God is understood to be God's openness to humanity. God's power is creative and relationally available to creation, and Jesus is the icon of such a God, bringing out, focusing, and rendering that power efficacious in human life. It is through Jesus we become taken up as immigrants into the encompassing drama of God in history, shaped by the particular power he represents.[54] In this way Christianity is no abstract monotheism, but is anchored in the kerygmatic affirmation that God was in Jesus. Jesus is proclaimed as Christ not out of mere speculation but according to his redemptive significance for the new community that coalesced around him. The experience of redemption is the lens through which Jesus is understood as Christ. Jesus is revelatory, the image of divine love, designated as God's only son by the emerging Christian community to express the special iconic character of his relation to God. To ascribe divinity to Jesus means thus to portray the experience of his power to effect redemption, which implies the abiding and co-constitutive presence of God's saving power in his humanity.

Confessing Jesus as Christ is not merely giving an intellectual assent to a state of affairs, creeds, or metaphysical propositions; it is to be newly created, brought into a new state of being, a new way of relation to others (2 Cor. 5:17). It entails being made aware of the distortions of sin's self-securing idolatry and a conversion or turning (*metanoia*) toward God, being reconfigured according to the shape of divine love. In these ways it is to represent and give witness to the Christ event. As authors like Leonardo Boff and Jon Sobrino have stressed, such confession is not mere belief but a praxis, an acting with God's life-giving work in a broken world.[55] It is to be united with and have the same mind—the same love—that was in Jesus Christ (Phil. 2:1–5). Put differently, in the words of the sixteenth-century Lutheran Philip Melanchthon, "to know Christ is to know his benefits."[56] And insofar as his benefits open up trust in the unconditional love of God they mark the passion of God for humanity, a passion that denounces sin and seeks the well-being of the creature.

The passion of God for humanity is evident throughout scripture. The divine suffers with and for others. We see this in the theology of creation, in God's continual preserving love. We also see it in God's covenant with Israel, in a promise-laden engagement available to the people even when it is rejected. It is also evident in God's privileging of the disinherited and marginalized. In fact, Israel's faithfulness to the covenant is refracted through embracing vulnerable aliens in their midst. Covenant even blurs the lines between insiders and outsiders, as God calls the people to care for the stranger, the orphan, and the widow: "The alien who resides with you shall be to you as the citizen among you; you shall love the alien as yourself" (Lev. 19:34; cf. Deut. 24:19–22).[57] For the stranger is also a child of God, loved into being. Indeed, covenant is intended for Israel to bless all nations and peoples (Gen. 12:3). The chosen people intercede on behalf of humanity. God's purpose of redemption is fulfilled through their relationship with God, and such redemption frees humanity for what it was created to be. Creation, covenant, and love of the vulnerable are interwoven elements in one saving tapestry.

God's creative activity, which was inaugurated at the beginning of creation, seeks continually to bring restorative life and well-being. But as sin has ruptured relation with God, human beings, and creation, redemption is needed. Fretheim states it well: "*Redemption is in the service of creation*, a creation that God purposes for all. Because God is a God of life and blessing, God will do redemptive work, should those gifts be endangered."[58] While God is present throughout creation, God is especially present to human beings in certain circumstances—that is, when the sanctity of the *imago Dei* is threatened. Redemption thus is focused upon (1) justice and love for the vulnerable, the stranger and the marginal, and upon (2) exposing and healing the rift in relationships fostered by sin. The two are intrinsically connected; the latter opens up the possibility of the former. In redemption the image of God in human beings is restored, the sanctity of life blessed. And ultimately this points toward a new creation, a new heaven and earth (Isa. 65:17; 2 Cor. 5:17). Redemption is creative power. It is the humanizing power of God.

This is why, for Christians, the ultimate act of humanizing value can be found in Jesus Christ. The New Testament asserts that Jesus fulfills the covenantal intention of God found in the history of Israel. The Hebraic principle of covenant is borne out in Jesus as Messiah, the one who represents Israel's blessing to humanity, the one with whom God identifies so as to take the human plight up into the divine self, thus bringing about the promise of redemption for all humankind. Jesus restores right relations with God and between human beings. How so? In that he represents what human beings were intended to be. Jesus is the exemplar of the fully human life because he embodies God's loving regard for, and gratuitous solidarity with, humanity precisely in its incapacity, vulnerability, and indeed its brokenness. Rather than shunning weakness, Jesus embraces it as a means of becoming available to others. Rather than displaying power, as he was tempted to by the devil, Jesus remains open to God and identifies the redemptive work of God in him with that of the stranger, the weak, and the destitute, suggesting that by welcoming such persons one welcomes him (Matt. 25:35, 40). This identification affirms humanity to the core by embracing it at its most vulnerable points. It disrupts the human tendency to secure itself by strength, power, domination, wealth, status, and even religious association. Blessed are the meek, the needy, the vulnerable, for God is especially present to them (Matt. 5:3–5).

Jesus invites the poor, the unclean, the outcasts, and the immoral to the divine banquet, an inclusive table fellowship of unconditional regard. For example, in Luke's Gospel we find: "But when you give a feast, invite the poor, the maimed, the lame, the blind, and you will be blessed, because they cannot repay you. You will be repaid at the resurrection of the just" (14:14). As Christ welcomes, so he calls his followers to welcome others (cf. Rom. 15:7). And in turn, by receiving others Christ's followers receive God's blessing. Matthew's Jesus states it bluntly: "Truly, I say to you, as you did it to one of the least of these my brethren, you did it to me" (25:45). Here the saving presence of God, the person of Jesus, and welcoming the vulnerable are interconnected. In God's encompassing banquet no one can claim special entitlement—rich and poor, righteous and sinful, women and men, sick and healthy alike are welcomed.

Such welcome displays God's creative, relational, available power. It is thus no accident that early Christians would come to understand Christ as the "image of the invisible God, the firstborn of all creation, for in him all things in heaven and on earth were created" (Col. 1:15–16; cf. Heb. 1:3). The redemptive effect of Jesus is the welcoming presence of God in the shape of a human being who makes himself vulnerable in welcoming others. This is the stuff of divine creativity, a creativity that fashions a world to which it is vulnerable and available. Jesus embodies what we saw in the last chapter as God's capacity to be with, to suffer with, the beloved creature for its well-being. This is the iconic logic of incarnation. The prologue to the Gospel according to John articulates it in terms of the preexistent Word (*logos*) of God, which was present in the beginning and through which all things came into being (John 1:1–3). The Word was life, a light for all people that shone out in the darkness (1:4–5). And now, where the darkness of sin obscures, the life-giving light of Jesus comes to heal and redeem broken relationality. How so? As the Word become flesh and dwelling among us (1:14). "From his fullness we have all received, grace upon grace" (1:16). Jesus Christ is the one who makes known what is invisible, revealing God's heart for humanity (1:18). His fullness is a welcoming into God's embrace that is the opposite of triumphal, sovereign power. It is a vulnerable love that comes in humility and weakness.

God's redemptive presence draws near unlike what we might expect, embedded as we are in systems of relationships that thrive on efficiency, strength, ability, and independence. The self-revelation of God traffics in vulnerability. First as a baby born scandalously out of wedlock, wrapped tightly in a manger outside during the cold night, later as a wandering preacher with no home, and finally as a crucified criminal, God in Christ is a margin dweller, a stranger in our midst. Indeed, he welcomes the outcasts and sinners into his fold. This is why, as John's Gospel puts it, "the world did not know him" (1:10). For according to the sin-infected dynamics of human life, Jesus represents what has no value or worth. The redemptive work of God dives into the lowest point in order to raise human beings into divine welcome. Insofar as those in his presence received him, Jesus transformed mistrust into a trust in God's love. Jesus then becomes the human icon of a vulnerable God. He is God's creative embracing of human life, in all its fragility and suffering. In Christ nothing human is alien to God.

Jesus—The Fully Human Person

What we have been saying so far indicates a dramatic reversal of human expectations according to the cult of normalcy. It subverts the purity laws of the Leviticus tradition, a tradition that is only one example of how human societies distinguish classes of things and measure the worth of people accordingly (clean vs. unclean, normal vs. abnormal, etc.). The sacredness of vulnerability is affirmed. Purity laws are overturned to include the outsider, the oppressed, those who are thrust to the margins because of impurity and/or sin. The grace Jesus offers turns the distinction between insider and outsider inside out. For example, he challenges those who would stone the adulteress caught in the act (John 8:3–11). In this context Jesus suggests that the adulterer is us all—weak, defiled, unwholesome, sinful, and yet loved by God nonetheless.

The reversal of expectations here also eschews the temptation to the heresy of docetism that lingers among those too eager to stress Jesus's flawlessness as a spiritualized human body. Docetism was a second- and third-century form of Gnosticism that asserted Jesus only seemed or appeared to be human (from the Greek *dokeo*), being instead completely spiritual and divine. Such a view illustrates a tendency to distance spirit from body. It assumes that God's transcendence is such that it cannot embrace the physical, and that the body and its vulnerability is something to be overcome because redemption is the release of spirit from its captivity to the flesh. This understanding, however, is contrary to the vision of God and humanity we find in scripture. Jesus embraces the bodies of others, and does so as flesh and blood himself. The spiritual life is part of embodied life; indeed, it is at the center of embodied life, connected to our relationships with each other.

This leads to a further point. That Jesus embodies God's love for humanity in its vulnerability helps us move away from an individualistic hero model of Christ. Christ is no superhuman, beyond struggle, pain, or the possibility of deformation. His body was a conduit for accessibility to those who were disempowered and weak, with whom he in fact identified. His redemptive presence was interwoven with others. He did not occupy a lone space, a hero figure of autonomous individual strength. He was vulnerable, and made himself vulnerable, to others. The point is illustrated by Jesus's weeping over the death of Lazarus. Through his embodied vulnerability he forged a physical space of sharing amidst weakness. The person and work of Jesus represents a model of relational interdependency.[59] He is fully human, subject to the tragic contingencies of finite existence.

What is more, for Christians Jesus is so fully human that he marks the veritable presence of God in history. With this notion we dive directly into the recapitulation theme advanced by Irenaeus: the glory of God is the human fully alive (*gloria Dei vivens homo*).[60] The person and mission of Jesus—and the two go hand-in-hand—are transparent to the divine because Jesus is human, the second Adam (1 Cor. 15:45). Jesus is the complete human, the one who is like us in all respects except sin (Heb. 4:15). How so? He embraced his own humanity and that of others in light of the radically inclusive welcome of God, living out the image of God in himself neither by denying nor by suppressing human limitations, but by opening them up to God in a relational praxis of transformative love. His trust in God is humankind's creaturely possibility in full bloom. As one whose life consisted of being available for others, Jesus is the image of God. Because of this, others encountered the divine in him. In the words of Dietrich Bonhoeffer, Jesus's "'being there for others' is the experience of transcendence." That is, "God in human form" consists of the "man for others," who in living for others "lives out of transcendence."[61] The person and mission of Jesus (iconically) manifest God by signifying the glory and power of God that abides in the frailty of a human person. Thus, Jesus transforms what it means to be human, reversing conventional standards of human worth. The integrity of the human is neither a function of exchange value and productive ability nor a spiritualized body, but rather is based on God's unconditional regard. And this is manifest most powerfully in a vulnerability infused with creative, relational, and available power.

Jesus as God's Solidarity with Humanity—Incarnation, Cross, and Resurrection

The New Testament remembrances of Jesus corroborate such a paradoxical picture in three basic ways. First, the notion of incarnation indicates God's embodiment in the human condition. The writings of Paul speak of the preexistent Christ emptying (*kenosis*) his divine abilities to embrace humanity's inabilities by taking on the shape of a human life (2 Cor. 8:9; Phil. 2:6–8). The shape of God's saving presence comes to us not as what we might expect, as grandeur and perfection, but as humility and weakness, even unto death on the cross. And it is through entering into the human condition to the point of a humiliating death that the broken body of Jesus is then exalted in glory by God (Phil. 2:8–9). The paradox here, as Paul states elsewhere, is that the power of God appears in frailness, the wisdom of God as foolishness (1 Cor. 1:18–25). The infancy stories make the point in another way, as the divine manifests itself in a child, perhaps the most poignant metaphor of vulnerability and dependence.[62] These examples direct us to a central theological affirmation: in pouring the divine self into the world God affirms the embodied finite creature.

Such an incarnational vision radiates with sacramental power. Not only is humanity created in God's image; God also draws near to abide in, validate, and empower human vulnerability as loved by God. God's nearness is one of dramatic solidarity. God shows solidarity with human weakness and suffering by embracing the physical. We are bodies, desirous, restless, broken, and twisted. The divine is not set apart from this because Christ becomes united with it. Thus there is a revaluing of the human through Christ as God with us (Emmanuel). God desires to be with humanity, not by transforming differences into a homogeneous stock or functional normalcy but by accepting vulnerability as a route to welcome differences as good, as blessed. God is not self-sufficient, but has pathos for humanity in all its diversity. God enters sympathetically into the life of the other, emptying divinity of itself to participate in the life of the other. Such emptying is not an imposed duty administered by a third party. It is a gift freely offered to the other, for the other. It is grace. The kenotic, self-emptying love of God as disclosed in Christ is a dynamically attuned and indiscriminate love for others and the world. God, as the fullness (*pleroma*) of self-giving power (*kenosis*), desires the world, bound to it in a relationship of availability toward all that has been created.

This becomes even more pronounced in the second of three ways, the passion and death of Jesus on the cross. The paradox here, according to Paul, is that God's power is made manifest in destitution and complete inability (2 Cor. 13:4). Jesus avails himself to God to such a degree that he is deprived of all dignity, even to the point of being mocked for his inability to save himself. And yet impotence is reversed to become power. At the cross the dehumanizing powers of domination and exclusion, against which Jesus stood, overextend themselves and become exposed for what they are—evil. The paradox revealed here is that precisely at the juncture where God is most conspicuously absent, God's power is made palpably real. Jesus succumbs to death rather than mitigate the message of love. At this moment of brokenness and baseness the world becomes complete and reconciled to God (Gal. 3:13). The depth of God's kenotic love is manifest at the cross. Christ's death proves God's love for us (Rom. 5:6–8).

In his Heidelberg Disputation (1518), Martin Luther famously calls this view a theology of the cross (*theologia crucis*), and contrasts it with the theology of glory (*theologia gloriae*).[63] Whereas the theology of glory wants to assert divine wisdom and triumph in Christ, and do so according to contrived human standards of knowledge and power, the theology of the cross proclaims divine hiddenness and weakness, revealing a starkly different kind of God than what humans of their own accord expect to find in Christ. God comes not in glory but humility and foolishness, a merciful and compassionate presence that suffers with the finite creature in closeness, not distance. The cross is the supreme example of a God who draws near, not to conquer or vanquish suffering and tragedy, but to engage it and open it up anew to the promise of love built into creation.[64] Accordingly, as Jürgen Moltmann powerfully articulates, the cross becomes a vehicle of hope.[65] New possibilities are unleashed, not in achievement and power, but precisely in the depths of anguish.

Human creatureliness, then, is affirmed not from above but from below, by a vulnerable God who shares the suffering of the creature. The divine participates unconditionally in the conditions of imperilment that encumber human beings. This marks a movement of God toward the world which begins in birth and follows through in death, suffering the finite creature's condition fully.[66] However, we must be cautious to avoid claiming that suffering is the goal of such movement, for this would valorize suffering. Suffering is not a good, but a consequence of love's risk opening itself to become available for the other, flowing freely and bestowing good upon that which is imperiled by sin and distorted in its way of being. Suffering as Jesus did is not a requirement for love. God did not need a sacrifice to satisfy God's offended sense of honor in order to love. God loves us enough to die for our sake while we are yet sinners (Rom. 8:5). In this way, Luther speaks of the love of the cross (*amor cruces*), the love revealed in the death of Christ. This is not cheap or sentimental love, but love that undergoes and compassionately suffers with the other. Accordingly, along with Nancy Eiesland, it is possible to suggest that through the cross Christ becomes the disabled figure of God, the icon of a God with disabilities, a God who undergoes physical deformity and stigmatization for the sake of love.[67]

The symbol of the cross is so powerful because it is not something foreign to human experience. It not only depicts the height of our inhumanity toward one another, an instrument of torture that illustrates the extent to which human sinfulness traffics in abusive power. It also indicates the inevitable disability and death to which we are all subject. As Douglas John Hall notes, if "it is the will of God in the Christ to seek solidarity with humankind—to be Emmanuel—then we must assume that the cross, while it is certainly (for us) the cross of Jesus Christ, is a symbolic statement about the human condition generally. Jesus' cross has its high significance for faith, in fact, because faith perceives it to be the closest God comes to us, where *we* are."[68] That is, in the lowly destitution of the cross we find what we are looking for—a God who comes to us, welcoming us into the divine presence in and through direct solidarity with us, both as temporarily non-disabled persons and persons with disabilities. God's power is loving, vulnerably present in the depths of the tragic, both in terms of being victimized by instruments of domination as well as in terms of identifying with death itself. This is why Moltmann calls Christ crucified humanity's "true theology and knowledge of God."[69] The cross becomes the standard for thinking about God; otherwise, as Luther would contend, the human tendency is to fashion a triumphal God of absolute privilege and power in the theology of glory.

For Christians, in the tragedy of the cross the powers of human brokenness coalesce to reject God's vulnerable savior. His kingdom of love was not digestible to the world's kingdoms of power. Paradoxically, however, this tragedy is subverted by

God to bring the possibility of new life out of Jesus's powerlessness and rejection. In the moment when it appears that Jesus can do nothing, his ministry collapsed and his disciples scattered, Jesus's availability to God becomes identified with God's availability to humanity, such that tragedy is incorporated into the divine life. In Christ, the truly human person, God takes up the suffering of the world. The negation of life ironically becomes reversed to affirm life, yielding redemption. Not by appeasing the justice of God's vengeful anger over human sin, but by God's love for human beings, which embraces their tragic situation at its core. God's apparent absence is divine presence. Moltmann writes: "To recognize God in the cross of Christ, conversely, means to recognize the cross, inextricable suffering, death and hopeless rejection in God."[70] God does not enter into human finitude and vulnerability in the abstract, but enters into it by means of human brokenness and sin. So Jesus's cry, "My God, my God, why have you forsaken me?" becomes God's own participation in the pain and destitution of human alienation from God. The cross marks the intersection of divine love with human travail. And the result is at once scandalous and transformative. As Dietrich Bonhoeffer suggests, "Christ helps us not by virtue of his omnipotence, but by virtue of his weakness and suffering." This is what leads him to state, "Only the suffering God can help."[71]

The suffering God marks the transformative power of love, which sympathetically shares the other's condition for its sake. In this way, Christ as the crucified God unmasks the powers of human idolatry in their self-destructive bent. Idols are mechanisms of *cupiditas* that express the human will to control, obscuring the *imago Dei* and rupturing right relationships with God, other human beings, and all creation. What the scandal of the cross does is to undercut the insidious hold of idols upon humanity, reaffirming that human beings are loved by God, even as prodigals who have gone astray: "For God so loved the world that he gave his only Son . . . in order that the world might be saved through him" (John 3:16–17), not because we are able-bodied, normal, productive, and so on, but because we are first loved. Again, Moltmann's words powerfully express the point: "To know God in the cross of Christ is a crucifying form of knowledge, because it shatters everything to which a man can hold and on which he can build . . . and precisely in so doing sets him free."[72] God offers the restorative gift of forgiveness and goes the distance, so to speak, even unto death on the cross at the hands of the beloved. Hence, Jesus's death on the cross reveals God's compassionate determinedness to accept humanity, justifying it before the divine presence by bestowing unmerited goodness. God's love is a grace freely given. The cross highlights the extent of this love's openness. It shares vulnerability and suffering, going through death. Nothing human remains outside God's enfolding embrace. Thus, divine love opens up possibilities beyond the tragic, taking up all human crosses by refusing to let them be the final word of human existence.[73]

Not only does this expose idolatry for its wrongfulness, it also identifies with the victims of idolatry—the excluded and stigmatized. Through the cross God shows solidarity with the plight of those suffering from social, economic, and political oppression. This solidarity is a welcome that effectively reverses any and all human economies of exchange based upon production and ability. The cross disrupts the established order of the status quo, turning value appraisals upside down—not the strong but the weak, not the insiders but the disinherited, not ability but disability. Human beings are affirmed in their vulnerable differences and united by God's love in Christ: "There is no longer Jew or Greek, there is not longer slave or free, there is no longer male and female; for all of you are one in Christ Jesus" (Gal. 3:28). Not human power, which divides and excludes, but God's love is fundamental. The cross frees people for their own possibilities, to be subjects of their own future as vulnerable creatures loved by God. Such freedom does not suggest the immediate removal of suffering, but rather points to transformative possibilities, because God shares suffering. God becomes a companion in human suffering, thus empowering the possibility of renewal and liberation. Why empowering the possibility of renewal? Because God is the creative-redemptive source of all existence, offering not merely a freedom that releases from bondage, but also a freedom that restores for new life, for being the creatures we were created to be. As Kathryn Tanner summarizes, "The whole point of God's dealing with us as creator, covenant partner, and redeemer in Christ is to bring the good of God's very life into our own."[74] And God shares in human suffering to bestow blessing. Love shares life in sharing suffering. In an additional way, this sharing is why the resurrection becomes so important.

We thus come to the third of the ways mentioned at the outset of this section: resurrection. The cross has the power it does because of Easter Sunday. The resurrection confirms the power of love over the apparent finality of the tragic. Here tragedy is absorbed and transformed into new possibilities. Resurrection marks something unexpected and extraordinary, and it happens in the midst of destitution and despair, not in achievement and power. When all seems lost new life arrives, a life that is stronger than dissolution and death. Not that suffering and loss are triumphantly eradicated, but rather that they are transposed into the promise of a fullness yet to come. In this way, the followers of Jesus experience the risen Christ as an abundant resource of gratitude and hope precisely in their loss and confusion. Jesus's ministry of radical love is validated when he is raised from the grave. His anguish and humiliation are reversed into glory and exaltation (Phil. 2:6–11). For the disciples, resurrection ratifies Jesus's special role in God's saving plan. It means that God really is the way Jesus revealed God to be. Jesus is Christ, the Messiah. And now Jesus is experienced as the ongoing presence of the divine for those in the community. His ministry of reconciliation and welcome continue in a transformed way with God, part of God's creative, redeeming work. The risen Christ goes ahead of his followers, offering the promise of new life to come—indeed, making it possible. Jesus is not simply a past teacher or prophet but a living reality. Hope is more fundamental than despair. Jesus is alive, opening up possibilities of faith, hope, and love beyond powers that deny life's goodness.

Important consequences follow. The resurrected body of Christ is not merely a resuscitated or reanimated physical corpse. Neither is it an apparition or some spiritualized and fleshless pseudobody. It is a transcendent body, appearing and disappearing abruptly, unrecognizable in some instances until memories of his ministry are evoked (Luke 24:13–35; John 20:11–18), passing through walls (John 20:19), and even floating away into the air (Acts 1:9). But it is Jesus's body nonetheless, for the tomb is proclaimed empty. Jesus also appears bearing wounds from the cross. To be sure, the Gospel passages that refer to his scars emphasize bodily recognition: "Look at my hands and my feet; see that it is I myself. Touch me and see; for a ghost does not have flesh and bones as you see that I have" (Luke 24:39; cf. John 20: 24–29). However, there is more meaning at stake than Jesus's attempt to prove it is really his risen body. His risen body demonstrates the extent to which God affirms the created and whole person. As Jesus goes before us into transcendent life in God as a body, so too shall we follow as bodies—what Paul calls spiritual bodies, a perishable body that "puts on imperishability" beyond time and space (1 Cor. 15:44–45, 53–54). Liberation for new life confirms the goodness of creation, the goodness of the *imago Dei* in its embodied form, but it does so by transforming it into a heavenly form. Hence, redemption is not *from* bodily existence, but *for* bodily life in all its capacities—that is, creativity, relationality, and availability—the richest possibilities of which lie in communion with God.

What is more, Jesus's risen body is impaired. Eiesland eloquently draws out the profound implications for people with disabilities, so it is worth quoting her here at length.

> At the resurrection, the disciples understood the person Jesus for who he really was. . . . In the resurrected Jesus Christ, they saw not the suffering servant for whom the last and most important word was tragedy and sin, but the disabled God who embodied both impaired hands and feet and pierced side and the imago Dei. . . . Here is the resurrected Christ making good on the incarnational proclamation that God would be with us, embodied as we are, incorporating the fullness of human contingency and ordinary life into God. In presenting his impaired hands and feet to his startled friends, the resurrected Jesus is revealed as the disabled God. Jesus, the resurrected Savior, calls for his frightened companions to recognize in the marks of impairment their own connection with God, their own salvation. In so doing, this disabled God is also the revealer of a new humanity. The disabled God is not only the One from heaven but the revelation of true personhood, underscoring the reality that full personhood is fully compatible with the experience of disability.[75]

At the cross Jesus subjects himself to disability, and his resurrected body continues to bear his scars as a sign of God's solidarity with humanity. The disabled body of Jesus represents one who understands by embodying disability even in his transformed, resurrected body. Furthermore, it suggests that disability indicates not a flawed humanity but a full humanity. Our bodies participate in the *imago Dei* in and through vulnerability and its consequent impairments, not despite them.[76]

The resurrected Christ thus embodies the blessed contingencies and dependencies of human life and places these in the heart of God. The impaired body of Christ is an icon of the disabled God, a God whose vulnerability is thus palpably real.

Eiesland's notion of the disabled God helps us understand the christological implications of Paul's paradoxical proclamation in 2 Corinthians 12:9–10, namely, that the saving power of God is made manifest and perfected in weakness or the lack of ability (*astheneiai*). This is neither to valorize disability nor to glorify suffering. If Jesus is God with us, then his very person entails metaphorical reversal of human expectations insofar as they are informed by the cult of normalcy. Neither self-sufficient power and independence nor hierarchical power structures retain authority. Paradoxically, vulnerable love does. Yet the love of God does not seek suffering, but rather bears it as a consequence of its availability for human existence. Consequently, human beings do not get to God by seeking suffering to find its moral message, but rather by recognizing the graced contingency of human life, which is subject to suffering but also, as symbolized by the risen Christ, points beyond it to new life. Hope is possible through the compassion of God in Christ, who undergoes human inability to reconcile humanity with God. Instead of doing away with the capacity to suffer, redemption transforms vulnerability into a communion with God, prefiguring the final eschatological horizon to come when all things will be transformed.

Accordingly, McCloughry and Morris note how understanding "Christ as the disabled God challenges the idea that non-disabled people are the theological norm."[77] Responding to this challenge entails several factors. As Eiesland's quote above suggests, it means moving away from the suffering servant model of Christ's death, which has all too often been coopted by the privileged as a means of perpetuating the status quo and justifying oppression and exclusion. For example, that model is associated with the denigrating view that disability is the product of sin and with the trivializing view that disability is a cross to bear (recall the discussion in chapter 1). It also means moving away from the conquering lord model where Jesus's risen body overcomes his humanity and vulnerability. The wounds remain, only now they are taken into the life of the divine.[78] Keeping in mind the theology of the cross previously discussed helps in combating such an approach. Finally, responding to this challenge means moving away from the vision of redemption and promised new life in terms of homogeneity, wherein all people are normalized according to the ideal non-disabled body. Jesus's risen body marks God's identification with human vulnerability, such that differences are confirmed rather than pressed into ghost-like conformity. Bodies differ in their relational capacities, even as each participates in the image of God. There is no assimilation into normalcy in the new life to come. Certainly, as Paul notes, all will be transformed and changed (1 Cor. 15:51), the sting of suffering taken away in a way that we cannot fathom. Even so, however, we shall remain who we are, not standardized and folded into a homogenized common stock.[79]

Indeed, the redeemed life—which points toward the life to come—is marked by a new commitment to one another. It is no accident that the resurrection appearances charge the disciples with a task—to be a new community oriented lovingly toward each other and the world in God (Matt. 28:16–20; John 20:21–23). Bestowed with blessing, the community is to be a blessing to others, radiating the promise latent within the good news that God has drawn near and reconciled the world through Christ (2 Cor. 5:19). What matters most here is *whose we are*, not *what we are* measured in terms of values fostered by human economies of exchange. For the Christian community is what it is by being identified with God in Christ, participating in the divine economy of grace. Real value, then, is based in God's unconditional affirmation of human beings. It is the divine gift of grace that is fundamental. For humans are loved into being and nurtured by God, endowed with integrity and value by the sheer fact of existing. The creative-redemptive love of God in Jesus Christ opens us anew to this wondrously good news, empowering us to be the creatures we are intended to be in faith, hope, and love. Finally, it opens us anew to be in communion with others, in one body, the body of Christ (Rom. 12:5; 1 Cor. 12:12–31). With these themes we have already ventured into material that will compose the substance of our final chapter.

Conclusion: Reversing Disability's Disability

Having explored the character of human beings created in the image of God, the distortions of sin, and redemption in Christ, we return to a theme expressed in the first pages of this chapter: the moral sense of creation. If God's love spills outward toward creatures, sweeping immanently through the fabric of the universe, and if this love is imaged in the shape of human persons, then gratitude and hope entail giving recognition to the inherent worth of others, accepting the generosity that God has already given and letting it run over into the landscape of human relations. Finite gestures of compassionate regard for others are themselves sacred invocations that participate in the infinite, life-giving generosity of the divine. That is, loving others is a form of loving God, and vice versa. The "yes" to another reflects the divine "yes" that is embodied in the gift of existence itself, and more, in the redemptive and reconciling love of God in Christ. Indeed, Jesus is experienced by those surrounding him as representing the strange power of God's compassion for and solidarity with human beings. His death on the cross is the radical extension of a life lived consistently in radical openness to others in God's love. Further, his resurrection signifies the overcoming of the world's death-giving economies of domination, exclusion, and violence. In Christ, God's recreative power of love brings the vulnerable but distorted and sinful life of human beings into a relational wholeness with others as graced and loved by God, such that trust in God is restored and humans are freed to love others. There is something deeper than tragedy at work in the world, and this is affirmed in responses of faith, gestures of hope, and acts of love.

Within this kind of framework, human disability becomes central to the affirmation of God's work of transformative love. Indeed, disability is tragically but redemptively fundamental. On the one hand, it is tragic in that it concerns involuntary impairments and real suffering, much of which is the consequence of disabling social alienation and exile. This implicates human sin more than it does a flawed humanity evoking condescending acts of pity. In fact, the very idea that disability reflects a deficiency implicates sinful mechanisms of interchange, including the cult of normalcy, which denies vulnerability in favor of the illusion of control. Disability is redemptive, on the other hand, because God affirms by embodying it in Christ, contesting exclusion and ratifying vulnerability and relational interdependence as normative. God's power is made complete and perfected in weakness. The upshot of this is that there is, strangely enough, strength in weakness, usefulness in being of no use. As God embraces human weakness and inability in Christ, we are empowered to welcome weakness in others as God's beloved. And conversely, it is by encountering weakness in another that we come to discover it in ourselves as God's beloved.

We are all at the core vulnerable, receiving our existence from one another and ultimately from God. This is why Moltmann can claim, "a person with disabilities gives others the precious insight into the woundedness and weakness of human life. But a person with disabilities also gives insight into the humanity of his own world. Through persons with disabilities, other people can come to know the real, suffering, living God, who also loves them infinitely."[80] Jean Vanier corroborates the point in noting how persons with disabilities call us into acknowledging our own human weaknesses and thus open us up more radically to God's grace.[81] Disability is a profound symbol of human vulnerability, of our need for each other and God. It is not merely a symbol, for this would trivialize persons with disabilities. So we must hasten to add, using Johann Baptist Metz's term, that disability is a "dangerous memory" holding our societies, theologies, and church communities accountable.[82] Disability is not an issue invoked merely when people with disabilities factor in the equation. Rather, it is a ubiquitous element in all economies of interchange that presume normalcy as their touchstone and rule out of play the non-normal by raising access barriers. Disability is the site of not only overt but also covert and hidden gestures of exclusion, and intentional and unintentional acts of oppression. Furthermore, by fostering such exclusion and oppression non-disabled people ironically suppress or deny their own vulnerability, and in so doing avert what is perhaps most human about us all—the need for welcome, to be recognized as valuable. As a result, we shun the ultimate act of humanizing value found in Jesus Christ.

In the end, because Jesus is the icon of a vulnerable God, the veritable crux of the Christian witness is an inclusive love of difference that is christological in shape. In the Christ event God's enfolding love sympathetically enters into the

midst of human vulnerability and suffering and resonates outward with unconditional regard for all persons. This means more than merely a confirmation of the
basic human right to respect. The nature of this creative-redemptive love fosters a
recognition and acceptance of human vulnerability and disability as bearing the
image of God. And it does so in a gesture of trusting welcome. The moral thrust
of Christian community has its origin here.

Notes

1. Miroslav Volf expresses this powerfully in *Free of Charge: Giving and Forgiving in a Culture Stripped of Grace* (Grand Rapids: Zondervan, 2005), chap 1.

2. H. Richard Niebuhr, *Radical Monotheism and Western Culture* (Louisville: Westminster John Knox Press, 1943), 32.

3. Paul Ricoeur, "Love and Justice," *Figuring the Sacred: Religion, Narrative, and Imagination*, trans. David Pellauer, ed. Mark I. Wallace (Minneapolis: Fortress Press, 1995), 325. See also Volf, *Free of Charge*, 45–47.

4. Roy McCloughry and Wayne Morris, *Making a World of Difference: Christian Reflections on Disability* (London: Society for Promoting Christian Knowledge, 2002), 34.

5. Terence E. Fretheim, *God and World in the Old Testament: A Relational Theology of Creation* (Nashville: Abingdon Press, 2005), 48–49.

6. Ibid., 49.

7. See William P. Brown, *The Ethos of the Cosmos: The Genesis of Moral Imagination in the Bible* (Grand Rapids: Eerdmans, 1999), 42–52.

8. Fretheim, *God and World in the Old Testament*, 49.

9. Ibid., 49–52.

10. Jürgen Moltmann, *God in Creation: A New Theology of Creation and the Spirit of God*, trans. Margaret Kohl (San Francisco: Harper and Row, 1985), 190.

11. Brown, *The Ethos of the Cosmos*, 44–46.

12. See Fretheim, *God and World in the Old Testament*, 55.

13. Daniel L. Migliore, *Faith Seeking Understanding* (Grand Rapids: Eerdmans, 1991), 124.

14. Dietrich Bonhoeffer, *Creation and Fall, Temptation: Two Biblical Studies*, trans. John C. Fletcher and Kathleen Downham (New York: Macmillan, 1959), 46.

15. An excellent argument for this point can be found in Alasdair MacIntyre's *Dependent Rational Animals: Why Human Beings Need the Virtues* (Peru, IL: Carus Publishing Company, 1999), see chaps. 1–5.

16. For a scientifically savvy statement of this theme, see Ian G. Barbour, *Nature, Human Nature, and God* (Minneapolis: Fortress Press, 2002).

17. Moltmann, *God in Creation*, 185.

18. Fretheim, *God and World in the Old Testament*, 58.

19. See Migliore, *Faith Seeking Understanding*, 125–28.

20. Jonathan Sacks, *The Dignity of Difference: How to Avoid the Clash of Civilizations* (New York: Continuum, 2002), 59.

21. John Macquarrie, *Principles of Christian Theology*, 2nd ed. (New York: Charles Scribner's Sons, 1977), 231.

22. Some scientist theologians call this the "anthropic principle," which names human beings as beings through which the universe is designed to become aware of itself. See the classic study by John D. Barrow and Frank J. Tipler, *The Anthropic Cosmological Principle* (Oxford: Oxford University Press, 1986).

23. For further discussion of meaning and vitality as coordinated terms, see chap. 4 in my *The Broken Whole: Philosophical Steps toward a Theology of Global Solidarity* (Albany: State University of New York Press, 2005).

24. Eugene TeSelle, *Augustine* (Nashville: Abingdon Press, 2006), 43.

25. For examples, see "The Trinity," in *Augustine: Later Works*, ed. and trans. John Burnaby (Philadelphia: Westminster Press, 1955), 8, 6ff., 43ff. and 15, 38ff., 166ff.; *The Confessions*, trans. Maria Boulding, OSB (New York: Vintage Books, 1998), 13, 10, 310; and "The Soliloquies," in *Augustine: Earlier Writings*, ed. and trans. J. H. S. Burleigh (Philadelphia: Westminster Press, 1953), 6, 12ff., 31–32.

26. Augustine *The Confessions* 1, 1, 3.

27. Migliore, *Faith Seeking Understanding*, 128.

28. Ibid., 101 (emphasis in original).

29. Bonhoeffer, *Creation and Fall*, 37.

30. Macquarrie, *Principles of Christian Theology*, 230.

31. McCloughry and Morris, *Making a World of Difference*, 25–26.

32. Ibid., 29.

33. Ibid., 31.

34. Fretheim, *God and World in the Old Testament*, 74.

35. Ibid.

36. Ibid., 73.

37. Ibid., 77.

38. Ibid., 78. See also note 19, 323.

39. For a classic twentieth-century depiction of sin along these lines, see Reinhold Niebuhr, *The Nature and Destiny of Man: A Christian Interpretation*, vol. 1 (London: Nisbet and Co., 1941). In another vein, Emmanuel Levinas suggests something similar when he speaks of totality as the reduction of the other to the same. See *Totality and Infinity: An Essay on Exteriority*, trans. Alphonso Lingis (Pittsburgh: Duquesne University Press, 1969).

40. See *The Confessions* 6, 10, 15ff., 64ff. and 10, 6, 8–9, 201–3.

41. I am influenced here by Valerie Saiving's important essay "The Human Situation: A Feminine View," in *Womanspirit Rising: A Feminist Reader in Religion*, ed. Carol Christ and Judith Plaskow (San Francisco: HarperSanFrancisco, 1979), 25–42.

42. See Frantz Fanon, *The Wretched of the Earth* [1963], 3rd ed., trans. Constance Farrington (Harmondsworth: Penguin Books, 1990); Robert C. Young, *Colonial Desire: Hybridity in Theory, Culture and Race*; and Edward Said, *Orientalism: Western Conceptions of the Orient* (New York: Vintage, 1979). On gender relations, see Luce Irigaray, *This Sex Which Is Not One* (Ithaca, NY: Cornell University Press, 1977); and the essays in *A Mind of One's Own: Feminist Essays on Reason and Objectivity*, eds. Louise M. Antony and Charlotte Witt (Boulder, CO: Westview, 1993).

43. Migliore, *Faith Seeking Understanding*, 131–34.

44. I discuss this in terms of a dialogical form of reason in *The Broken Whole*, 127–30.

45. See *On Christian Doctrine*, trans. D. W. Robertson, Jr. (Indianapolis: Bobbs-Merrill Educational Publishing, 1958), 3, 16; and *The City of God*, trans. Henry Bettenson (New York: Penguin Books, 1984), 14, for a discussion of *cupiditas* vs. *caritas*. For excellent commentary, consult John Burnaby's classic study *Amor Dei* (London: Hodder and Stoughton, 1938), and also William S. Babcock's essay "*Cupiditas* and *Caritas*: The Early Augustine on Love and Fulfillment," in *Augustine Today* (Grand Rapids: Eerdmans, 1993), 1–34.

46. For example, see *The Confessions* 7, 20, 26ff, 141ff.

47. See "The Trinity" 8, 10ff., 51ff., and *The Confessions* 7, 18.24f., 139f.

48. Jonathan Edwards, *The Nature of True Virtue* (Ann Arbor: University of Michigan Press, 1960), 3–4.

49. On this ideal and its Christian implications, see the excellent study by Thomas W. Ogletree, *Hospitality toward the Stranger: Dimensions of Moral Understanding* (Philadelphia: Fortress Press, 1985).

50. For a well-written and powerful contemporary revisionism of the Christian themes of self and God, see Lucinda A. Stark Huffaker, *Creative Dwelling: Empathy and Clarity in God and Self* (Atlanta: Scholars Press, 1998).

51. Carter Heyward, *Touching Our Strength* (San Francisco: HarperSanFrancisco, 1989), 188–89. 52. For a more in-depth and philosophical discussion of the icon versus the idol, see my *The Broken Whole*, 179–86.

53. A good discussion of John of Damascus and images as icons can be found in Jaroslav Pelikan's *The Spirit of Eastern Christendom* (Chicago: University of Chicago Press, 1974), 117–33.

54. See H. Richard Niebuhr, *The Meaning of Revelation* (New York: Macmillan, 1941), 115–16.

55. See Leonardo Boff, *Jesus Christ Liberator: A Critical Christology for Our Times* (Maryknoll, NY: Orbis Books, 1978); and Jon Sobrino, *Jesus the Liberator: An Historical-Theological Reading of Jesus of Nazareth* (Maryknoll, NY: Orbis Books, 1994).

56. Philip Melanchthon, *Loci Communes Theologici*, trans. Lowell J. Satre; in *Melanchthon and Bucer*, ed. Wilhelm Pauck (Philadelphia: Westminster Press, 1969), 21.

57. David H. Jensen, *Graced Vulnerability: A Theology of Childhood* (Cleveland: Pilgrim Press, 2005), 17.

58. Fretheim, *God and World in the Old Testament*, 125 (emphasis in original).

59. Nancy L. Eiesland, *The Disabled God: Toward a Liberatory Theology of Disability* (Nashville: Abingdon Press, 1994), 103.

60. Irenaeus, *Against Heresies* 4, 19, 7 in *Ante-Nicene Fathers* (Peabody, MA: Hendrickson Publishers, 1994), 1: 490. See also 3, 21, 10, 1:454.

61. Dietrich Bonhoeffer, *Letters and Papers from Prison*, ed. Eberhard Bethge, trans. Reginald Fuller, et al. (New York: Macmillan, 1971), 381–82.

62. Jensen, *Graced Vulnerability*, 19–22.

63. See Timothy F. Lull, ed., *Martin Luther's Basic Theological Writings* (Minneapolis: Fortress Press, 1989), 30ff.

64. Douglas John Hall, *The Cross in Our Context: Jesus and the Suffering World* (Minneapolis: Fortress Press, 2003), 30–31.

65. Jürgen Moltmann, *Theology of Hope: On the Grounds and Implications of a Christian Eschatology* (New York: Harper and Row, 1968).

66. Hall, *The Cross in Our Context*, 38–42.

67. Eiesland, *The Disabled God*, 98–105.

68. Hall, *The Cross in Our Context*, 70 (emphasis in original).

69. Jürgen Moltmann, *The Crucified God: The Cross of Christ as the Foundation and Criticism of Christian Theology*, trans. R. A. Wilson and John Bowden (Philadelphia: Fortress Press, 1974), 212.

70. Ibid., 277.

71. Bonhoeffer, *Letters and Papers from Prison*, 360–61.

72. Moltmann, *The Crucified God*, 212.

73. Jensen, *Graced Vulnerability*, 27.

74. Kathryn Tanner, *Economy of Grace* (Minneapolis: Fortress Press, 2005), 85.

75. Eiesland, *The Disabled God*, 99–100.

76. Ibid., 101.

77. McCloughry and Morris, *Making a World of Difference*, 68.

78. Eiesland, *The Disabled God*, 102–3.

79. McCloughry and Morris, *Making a World of Difference*, 73.

80. Moltmann, "Liberate Yourselves by Accepting One Another," 121.

81. Jean Vanier, *Becoming Human* (Mahwah, NJ: Paulist Press, 1998), 39–41.

82. Johann Baptist Metz, *Faith in History and Society: Toward a Practical Fundamental Theology*, trans. David Smith (New York: Seabury Press, 1980).

7

Being Together

Love, Church, and Hospitality

For Christ plays in ten thousand places,
Lovely in limbs, and lovely in eyes not his
To the Father through the features of men's faces.

Gerard Manley Hopkins,
from "As Kingfishers Catch Fire"

It was a beautiful moment. Chris had just returned home from a brief stay at a psychiatric hospital, and immediately upon getting out of the car he reached out and eagerly hugged his brother, Evan. It was clear that greeting his brother was the most important thing on his mind at that instant. Evan reciprocated, a bit shyly turning his head in the process, slightly embarrassed that his parents were watching, and perhaps taken aback by his brother's abounding joy. But Evan's joy at reuniting was equally obvious. Despite the fact that he and Chris, like most siblings, seem to endlessly bicker and argue, and despite the fact that he has had to adjust in countless ways to accommodate to his brother's disabilities, Evan was genuinely glad to see Chris. This kind of welcome was a tremendous joy to witness.

I have not spoken much of Evan in this book, but it would be dishonest to overlook him and avoid detailing, even if briefly, the unique power of his presence in our household. Evan, now fourteen, is an amazingly perceptive and caring young man. Often overshadowed by the largeness of Chris's needs, he remains a luminous testimony to availability, to how its moral fabric is developed and stitched into ordinary life. True, Evan gets frustrated and even angry with Chris. Beneath this, however, runs a current of deep respect, fidelity, and compassion. His openness to Chris refreshes itself with each day. Mary and I saw this at work early on in his childhood. Evan's boundless trust in Chris, whom he affectionately called "D" (for reasons unknown to us), seemed incapable of being let down. He was quick to reconcile, forgiving time and again after Chris had hurt him, even in cases where Chris was deliberately manipulative or verbally abusive. Evan seemed to understand his brother on an intuitive level, a level beyond our ability to comprehend but obviously powerful and real, for it cemented a relational connection that grew stronger with time. To this day Evan is remarkably patient and forgiving. Mary and I marvel at his love for Chris. Such love humbles us. Evan seems able to "go with the flow" and attend to Chris's unique tempo and character much easier than I do, despite my best efforts to be accommodating and open.

This helps me understand why Jesus often refers to children as examples of the vulnerable and trusting openness characteristic of the kingdom of God. For example, at one point, after realizing that the disciples were shunning children from Jesus's presence, Jesus exclaims, "Let the little children come to me; do not stop them; for it is to such as these that the kingdom of God belongs. Truly I tell you, whoever does not receive the kingdom of God as a little child will never enter it" (Mark 10:14–15). Here the childlike disposition of discipleship is privileged over the adult-like obsession with attending to "important" matters, which are often dictated by economies of exchange that obscure the divine economy of grace. The adult world is often competitive and caught up in proving value and ability. Children, on the contrary, are often simply ready to accept persons without presumptive expectations. Indeed, they must be taught to mistrust in order to protect themselves from harm.

This is spelled out in a passage from Matthew's Gospel where the disciples, upon getting competitive with one another, ask Jesus, "Who is the greatest in the kingdom of heaven?" Jesus's response illustrates the child-focused nature of God's kingdom as compared to the competitive kingdoms and economies of the adult world, marked as they are by mistrust and greed. He calls a child among them and states, "Truly I tell you, unless you change and become like children, you will never enter the kingdom of heaven. Whoever becomes humble like this child is the greatest in the kingdom of heaven. Whoever welcomes one such child in my name welcomes me" (Matt. 18:3–5). Mark's version of the story qualifies this further in Jesus's declaration, "Whoever wants to be first must be last of all and servant of all" (Mark 9:35, cf. 9:36–37). Jesus is emphatic about pointing us to the humble and trusting nature of children and, consequently, to their particular vulnerability.[1] Indeed both are connected, for children are as eager to welcome as they are in need of welcome. Such interdependence is the fulcrum from which both trust and vulnerability emerge as testimonies to the kingdom of God. Hence, discipleship is about trusting enough to welcome without reserve, caring for the vulnerable in the process.

The example of children has radical implications. First, it indicates that human vulnerability—along with the weakness and inability that it entails—marks a need for welcome found through loving relationships. Second, it means that vulnerability is privileged and loved by God, as are children, and that mutual dependence upon one another and God is a sacred blessing. Third, it means that the inability and weakness of vulnerable persons can be a vehicle for healing liberation, the strange power of God revealed in and through weakness. These are lessons that reach into the heart of Christian faith. They have dramatic consequence for thinking about disability.

With this in mind, the task of this final chapter is to explore the strange power of God at work in the humble and open love of neighbor, particularly persons with disabilities. The communal context for this love is found most pointedly in the idea of church (*ecclesia*), the household of God composed of those called out to be the living body of Christ. Living with others in such a household communion is no ordinary act of dwelling together; it is an icon of God's redemptive work in the world. The question for us is, how? We have already seen that becoming like children is necessary for becoming genuine followers of Christ. Let us now push further, exploring such a vision in full bloom.

I. To Love as Christ Loves: Loving Chris as Christ Loves and Loving Christ as Chris Loves

In Dostoevsky's classic novel *The Brothers Karamazov*, the most morose and cynical of the three Karamazov brothers, Ivan, makes a confession to his brother Alyosha that is at once amazingly perceptive and disturbing. He avers, "I never could understand how it's possible to love one's neighbors. In my opinion, it is precisely one's neighbors that one cannot possibly love. . . . It's still possible to love one's neighbor abstractly, and even occasionally from a distance, but hardly ever up close." While Ivan admits that selfless acts up close do occur, he claims they are for the most part disingenuous, stemming more from what he calls "the strain of a lie, out of love enforced by duty, out of self-imposed penance," than from genuine kindness or care. He goes on, "If we're to come to love a man, the man himself should stay hidden, because as soon as he shows his face—love vanishes."[2] Yes, people may seem altruistic, but they are either living in a dream world, loving humanity in some vague and general sense, or else repudiating themselves in an act of prescribed self-hatred. And for Ivan, neither option has integrity.

I must admit that when I first read *The Brothers Karamazov*, my initial reaction to the conversation between the two brothers favored the viewpoint of the tender and good-hearted Alyosha, who believes in the redemptive possibility of Christ-like love for one's neighbor in everyday life. Ivan's appraisal of humanity seemed hopelessly pessimistic. But now, upon further reflection, I have reconsidered my initial inclination. There is a hard truth to Ivan's perspective. Indeed, the social barriers and exclusionary practices that persons with disabilities often encounter seem to support it. Compassionate regard and self-giving care do seem easier and more alluring as general ideals than as particular realities. Once we encounter other human beings and acknowledge their genuine difference from us, recognizing the peculiar ways they call us to respond to and affirm their uniqueness apart from our own agendas or expectations, it is difficult to love. At close range, the little details get in the way. But the truth is: it is only at close range that love becomes active and real.

Love is compassionate regard that draws near and attends to the beloved for her own sake and with her good in mind. It means adjusting or even giving up our hold on reality as we see it and opening ourselves to the unfamiliar, strange, perhaps even threatening presence of another. And it means doing so without imposing conditions that restrict or exclude their own particular capacities and ways of being human. Genuine love indicates that we have been summoned into a relational space of giving and receiving that happens outside preset calculations and expectations, beyond the ordered boundaries of economies of exchange. This is why Ivan is right to note how difficult love is. Love is, in fact, traumatic. Its gesture of giving hinges around letting go of those things by which we domesticate and manage reality so as to feel ourselves secure and in control. But love is also life-giving generosity that plugs into the radiant pulse of God's presence throughout creation, sharing it with others. Love is the inner purpose of all relationships, an inbuilt possibility for human life based upon the creatively relational and available *imago Dei*.

Love up close is the path to human wholeness. And wholeness is a way of living vulnerably and interdependently with others before God in creation. It is a relational term, the product of a love for God manifested concretely in relation with others, and vice versa, a love for others manifested concretely in relation to God. For Christians, this is made possible by being transformed and made new via the redeeming power of Jesus Christ, whose life, death, and resurrection reorient human beings toward God, each other, and creation. Remembering the story of Jesus opens up new possibilities for being in covenantal relation to God and neighbor over and against human efforts at self-security and satiation. Accordingly, redemption is a freedom from being under the distorting influence of sin as a will-to-control, which in fear seeks to guarantee its own existence by controlling all else around it. As conformity to the shape of God's image in Jesus Christ, redemption is also a freedom for relation to God and neighbor in the mode of openness and hospitality. On the one hand, this means radical openness to a transcendent God who is yet near, who is close like a parent, who has compassion for and is in nurturing relationship with the world. Paul often speaks in the language of obedience to convey such openness to God, expressing it negatively as a self-emptying. Put in a positive light, we can say redemption means being ready for and available to God. On the other hand, openness to God means also to be with and for others, for the whole of humanity. It is to be ready for and available to the stranger, one who is different. Love of God and love of neighbor are twin moments of the same redemptive momentum.

Perhaps this is why, in *The Brothers Karamazov*, Dostoevsky offers another vision of love in the beautifully narrated story of a holy man, Father Zossima, and his encounter with a woman who doubts her faith. The woman asks him how we can prove the existence of God and the reality of life after death. Father Zossima replies that there is no proof available, though we can be convinced by "the experience of active love." He proposes that she strive to love her neighbor, suggesting that to the degree she perfects this task she will grow surer of the presence of God and her immortal soul.[3] But Father Zossima recognizes that this is no easy task. He goes on to say that active love is hard labor and requires fortitude, a "harsh and fearful thing compared with love in dreams"—that is, with abstract or overly romanticized love from a distance.[4] Up close, love is difficult, and thus Father Zossima exhorts the woman to be patient and forgiving of herself. In this, Father Zossima preaches that love is not only possible, it is a window into the divine. Its "yes" reflects the divine "yes" that is embodied in the gift of existence itself, and in the person and work of Jesus Christ.

So while there is truth to Ivan's view of human love, there is a much richer tapestry woven into human relations than Ivan recognizes. Along with Father Zossima, I affirm the possibility of genuine love at close range, the possibility that love is more than an imposed duty or superficial feeling of benevolence for humanity in general, more than stoic self-sacrifice or a state of emotional elation that is a mile wide but an inch deep and all too easily manipulated to cloak self-serving agendas. Love is something already at work at the deepest level of existence, a creative and expansive relational power into which we enter as the ultimate source and consummation of our lives together. This is what the life, death, and resurrection of Jesus Christ reveal.

I make such an assertion not simply because of its theological heft, but also because of how my life has been opened up to new possibilities through being present with Chris. Learning to attend to Chris with compassionate regard has been a life-transforming process that might best be expressed in religious terms as a kind of redemptive healing. Abstract love from a distance is not an option here. It would be absurd to speak of loving my son in some disinterested or general sense. Indeed, it is hard to think of a more concrete example of love up close than such familial love. Learning from him what it means to let go and genuinely attend to a life at once inseparably joined with yet distinct from my own, I have been persuaded that concrete love—up close—opens to a surplus of grace that can only be called divine. Present in the concrete, relational experience of love's welcome is a universal dynamism at work. It is touched by the power of God that is disclosed in Christ. Love is at the heart of the universe. Let us now attend to how this is borne out concretely in the ministry of Jesus and those who followed him.

II. The Strange Kingdom of God: Restoring the *Imago Dei* in Right Relationships

Jesus's ministry embodies divine love through what we have been calling a metaphorical reversal. The center is not the strong but the weak, not those who have it all but those who are without, not the privileged but the disinherited, not the insider but the outsider. This reversal is unseemly and foolish if we operate within the sway of the cult of normalcy, for the integrity of personhood here is measured according to productive ability and bounded space. That is, health and wholeness are appraised in terms of physical, cognitive, and emotional abilities which correspond to the capacity to control one's body and authorize actions that stay within proscribed boundaries. These boundaries outline what counts for purity and moral integrity; they mark body capital in an economy of exchange. As we discussed in chapter 2, standing outside these boundaries means to be perceived as running against the fabric of a community's sense of good. The "out-of-control" body is thus stigmatized because its behaviors reflect what is taboo. Jesus's ministry upsets this order. Through Jesus the creator God comes to us not as what we might expect—a possessing, domineering, displacing, or controlling presence—but rather in the form of self-giving love, inviting or luring us into relational creativity and wholeness.

The power of Jesus's presence in this way is received as a liberating gift as well as a provocative demand.[5] It is the promise of a reconciling and emancipatory love upon which those who follow set their hopes in the expectation of an ultimate fulfillment. And it is this promise that in turn elicits a *metanoia*, a transformative allegiance and repentance which obligates persons to accept and themselves embody that love. Jesus's followers are called to become as little children, selling all they have, becoming last, becoming vulnerable caregivers in the service of others. Indeed, Jesus himself embodies this by constantly crossing boundaries and turning around conventional expectations. For him the kingdom of God (*basileia tou theou*) resides in a boundary-transgressive openness to God and others. His is a love without borders, trafficking in an economy of grace incapable of being measured by economies of exchange, based as they are in the ability to produce and purchase welcome. In the kingdom of God all persons are gifts to be welcomed, not simply because of neediness but because each human being is loved into being by God in the image of God—authorized by God and given unique abilities by God. It is not scarcity that governs the kingdom of God but abundance. God's love knows none of the conventional distinctions between "pure" and "impure" or "good" and "bad." The kingdom of God is radically inclusive.

The Creative Power of Inclusion—Welcoming (in) the Kingdom

Stated succinctly, the kingdom of God is a relational realm shaped by the creatively self-giving and available love manifested in and proclaimed by Jesus Christ. It comes both as the anticipated nearness of a new fellowship of radical other-centeredness and as a prophetic critical principle exposing the structures of relational distortion and violence for what they are, calling people to accountability. It is an openness to the infinite that is at the same time an openness to others, to the stranger, to genuine difference. And this confounds the principalities and powers of life ordered by the will-to-control: not the power of economic success but the power of poverty; not the power of lordship, dominance, and sovereignty but the power of self-giving and servanthood; not the first but the last; not blood relationships but universal ethical relationships; not the logic of reward and punishment, of master and slave, but the logic of grace, forgiveness, liberation, and inclusive love.[6] Accordingly, the kingdom of God acts as an empowering leaven (Matt. 13:33) that manifests itself in a creative and reconciling love which transforms and draws together those touched by its power into an open and inclusive community.

In Luke's rendering, the beginning of Jesus's ministry is punctuated by a lesson drawn from Isaiah 61 to announce that the kingdom of God is at hand: "The Spirit of the Lord is upon me, because he has anointed me to bring good news to the poor. He has sent me to proclaim release to the captives and recovery of sight to the blind, to let the oppressed go free, to proclaim the year of the Lord's favor" (4:18–19). It is fitting that Jesus would employ such imagery to outline his vocation, for Jesus is Jewish and thus shares the history and hopes of his people. "The kingdom of God," as Donald Senior notes, "was not an invention of Jesus or the gospels. The theme had deep roots in Israel's religious history." God's promise had been proclaimed before, grounded in the themes of covenant and creation, which point toward "an ultimate act of redemption that would bring about a new act of life-giving mercy."[7] Israel's hope was in a faithful God who would eventually rescue the people from sin and oppression and bestow blessing. Indeed, the "year of the Lord's favor" indicated in the passage Jesus reads from Isaiah refers to the ancient Jubilee practice of Israel wherein debts would be canceled and slaves set free. Jesus draws from such rich imagery to suggest that God is now in the process of doing the new thing promised long ago. God is drawing near to restore Israel and remake the world, a world where justice and mercy would prevail and mistrust and hostility cease (Isa. 11:6–9).[8] Jesus thus calls people to participate actively in God's present work of reconfiguring the world.

Hence, "kingdom" is not a static term, but a communal and social metaphor for a realm shaped in all its activities by God's empowering rule. The great paradox, however, is that this rule is constituted not by power but by vulnerable self-giving. It does not take shape through coercion, domination, exclusion, and violence, but through compassionate, gratuitous, and unconditional regard. Neither does it call people into a club of the privileged, of "the blessed" versus "those others," but rather it is marked by a love that is not restricted by conventional barriers, where there is mixing because there is no inside versus outside, where one's neighbor even includes one's enemy (Matt. 5:43–45). The kingdom portrays a reversal that destabilizes the economies of exchange that prop up the cult of normalcy. This is pointedly manifest in Jesus's table fellowship, which intentionally undermines exclusive conventions by inviting outcasts—the despised, the destitute, the poor, the unclean, the sick—to share in God's banquet (Mark 2:15; Luke 15:1–2). This also comes out with frankness in many of Jesus's parabolic sayings, which jolt the reader's attention to the inclusion of the stranger by reversing expectations: not the first, but the last; not the strong, but the weak; not the privileged, but the underprivileged. God works in, through, and for the vulnerable and broken, fashioning a community of beloved people, people loved for who they are as creatures made in God's image.

Jesus proclaims that this kind of community is in the process of becoming. It is being created. It is at hand but has yet to arrive in the fullest sense, though it soon will. Thus, Jesus's gestures of inclusion present the kingdom of God as both a present reality and future hope. The decisive factor, however, is how one responds now and participates in God's creative work. Responding means repenting and becoming open to God. But it also means loving one another. In this new kind of community, love of God and love of neighbor are connected at the root. Jesus sums up the prescription for the kingdom in Mark's Gospel, and he does so by answering a question about which commandment is the greatest: "The first is, 'Hear, O Israel: the Lord our God, the Lord is one; you shall love the Lord your God with all your heart, and with all your soul, and with all your mind, and with all your strength.' The second is this, 'You shall love your neighbor as yourself.' There is no other commandment greater than these" (Mark 12:29–31; cf. Matt. 22:34–40 and Luke 10:25–28). "On these two commandments hang all the law and the prophets" (Matt. 22:40). Devotion to God implies welcoming and sharing with others, a total dedication to the well-being of the human family. This involves no less than feeding the hungry, aiding the poor, tending to the orphan and widow, forgiving those who injure us, washing one another's feet, claiming a humble instead of prestigious place, denying ourselves and taking up the cross, and bearing one another's burdens. Paul echoes this theme in Jesus's teaching by claiming that loving each other fulfills the whole law, striking the fundamental chord of his announcement that the kingdom of God is at hand (Rom. 13:8; Gal. 6:2). Conversion to God is a conversion to the other, for the other, with the other.

Hence, living in openness to God is inherently connected with the question, "Who is my neighbor?" In Luke 10:29–37, Jesus tells a parable of the Good Samaritan to drive home the point. The message comes across with disorienting clarity. Here, a pious priest and privileged Levite each pass by the vulnerable victim of injustice. In fact, they go out of their way to avoid him. Who else helps? Contrary to what we might expect, it is the half-breed heretic, the Samaritan, who offers himself and shows mercy. Mercy here means giving one more than is due them by right, according to conventional standards of exchange. By right, the Samaritan should have been the one who passed by. He is a busy merchant and an ostracized foreigner of mixed blood and questionable religious descent. But he does not pass; he gives. The unexpected happens. Who is the neighbor? In this parable it is the Samaritan. Jesus has turned the question around. It is not who our neighbor is that matters—that is, who has prestige, who believes the right things, who has body capital, and thus deserves care and love. It is who we are as neighbors that matters, that is, how we act toward others set before us in their vulnerability as human beings.[9] The Samaritan offers a gift of inclusive grace. He is an unexpected symbol of God's self-abandoning love. He is the one who welcomes. And who is the recipient? The one who ostensibly has nothing to offer in return, from whom nothing can be expected. This story artfully displays the radical reversal we have seen endemic to the kingdom of God. The vulnerable outcast welcomes the vulnerable victim. Neighborly love joins the two as kindred souls.

Such love marks an economy of grace within which there is no outcast. Jesus's family is all humanity. Boundaries are leveled. No one can claim special entitlement; no one is exempt from God's love, left on the outside. The meaning is made prophetically palpable by Jesus's constant privileging of vulnerable outcasts. Blessed *are* the poor, the marginalized, and the weak. Not blessed *will be* the poor and weak once they get it all together and become acceptable or normal. Grace already abounds, right now. Abundance is not something to be achieved; it is at hand. And what is more, as one shows grace by welcoming the vulnerable, one rides the wave of divine abundance, and indeed welcomes the divine (Matt. 25:35, 40; Heb. 13:2). Jesus proclaims God's solidarity with humanity at its weakest points and invites all human beings to participate in it.

The kingdom is the self-giving shape of God's nearness. In such nearness, three kinds of human vulnerability are involved. First, there are those who are most vulnerable, needing protection and care in a direct and concrete manner—for example, children, the elderly, sick, destitute, or homeless, as well as people with certain kinds of disabilities. God especially privileges and cares for these people so the image of God may be recognized and affirmed in them, in whom the *imago Dei* faces the potential of being socially and personally obscured, of going unnoticed or rejected and thus disempowered. This privileging, second, calls all people to recognize their human vulnerability and dependence upon God and one another. All human beings are loved into being by God and receive their existence from each other. No one is autonomous and invulnerable. Accepting this brings an attitude of openness and acceptance toward others, who share a common humanity before God. In fact, acknowledged vulnerability can be life-giving. Hence, third, vulnerability facilitates love. This involves an explicit solidarity with those who are more vulnerable, not as pity but creative availability. It elicits resistance to exclusion and nurtures advocacy that aims to create an empowering space for and on behalf of vulnerable persons. This is not merely something necessary for "them"—those weaker others—but is something important for all human beings, for a wider and more inclusive "us." Exclusion anywhere is a threat to inclusion everywhere. In the end, rich and poor, righteous and sinful, women and men, healthy and sick, able-bodied and disabled, are joined together in a relational wholeness constituted by grace.

Seen in this way, the ideal of God's kingdom, along with its correlative elements of human vulnerability, is not just announced by but embodied in Jesus's way of being in relation to others. Jesus is the emblem of inclusion in its most genuine sense, widening space for others to be what they are created to be in the image of God: creative, relational, and available. And it precisely because of this that the theological meaning of incarnation and the cross gain significance, for they exemplify God's welcome, a welcome that is central to Jesus's mission. The kingdom is manifest in the relational praxis of Jesus, who becomes a visible image—an icon—of the way God acts in the world, transforming and healing historical existence. Jesus acts as though only God reigns, and thus incarnates the shape of right relatedness to God and to others. By identifying with the vulnerable and existing with them on the margins, Jesus presents the power of God's impartial welcome. Accordingly, he effects a subversive reversal of prevailing social patterns and structures of power, revealing a non-domineering and radically egalitarian way of dwelling together through God's redemptive presence. He embodies what it means to be vulnerable and open to God and each other. For those surrounding him, Jesus reveals the abundance of God's gracious welcome.

Healing Power—Welcome, Transformation, and Wholeness

The healing narratives confirm this point. Through Jesus the blind see, the lame walk, the deaf hear. But we must be circumspect about understanding the meaning of Jesus's healings, for there is more at stake than might be apparent. It is not simply the physical healing that is important, as if Jesus intends only to cure by making normal what was previously abnormal and faulted, lacking humanity. In fact, it is crucial to distinguish between the words "cure" and "heal." The latter signifies something much deeper than the former. Cure tends to be understood medically as a restoration of function, a making right of what was broken, seen in terms of the cult of normalcy. Jesus does not condescend to take pity on persons with disability that their defects might be eliminated. True, he seeks to alleviate suffering, and does not make an explicit distinction between physical restoration and healing. Nevertheless, it is clear that healing means something more fundamental than curing. It means promoting wholeness as well-being.[10] And, as shall become evident, one does not have to be cured to experience this kind of healing. Jesus offers life abundant (John 10:10). He restores the image of God, touching with healing power the creative, relational, and available depths of human existence.

First of all, it is clear that Jesus does not stigmatize persons with illnesses, diseases, and impairments. Rather, he invites people considered defiled or unclean into his presence, deliberately unconcerned with the purity codes governing temple practices. Wherever Jesus goes the destitute, sick, impaired, and vulnerable in society come to the fore and gather around him. Why? Not simply because they seek Jesus. Rather, because Jesus seeks them. He esteems vulnerability and weakness, not power and ability, as the criteria for genuine personhood in relation to God. So Jesus intentionally ignores social barriers, going against the norm by actively gathering in those whose lack of body capital placed them on the margins of society. He embraces what is taboo to include it in the kingdom of God. In fact, this practice is part of his overall intent to pull the margins to the center: the first shall be last, and the last first.

Second, we must remember that in the ancient world, as in today's, health is not just a matter of the individual, a state of body functioning. It is also tied to the community and the economies of exchange that govern social life. Understood in these terms, sickness causes relational isolation and alienation, interfering with a person's sense of being in community. It is perceived as a limitation, deviation, or devaluation that has dramatic social consequences. The result is exclusion. What Jesus does to remedy this, as Kathy Black notes, is cross boundaries "in order to reconcile the one excluded with the community."[11] In Jesus's ministry, then, welcome seems to be the primary event. And this highlights a love that redeems by including, consequently radiating with healing power. Why? Because the gift of wholeness is a relational dynamic and not simply a factor of the individual, measured by means of one's body capital. It is matter of affirming the image of God in persons and facilitating new opportunities for creativity, relationality, and availability.

Contrary to societal mechanisms of exclusion that pit normal against abnormal, lack of ability is not the truly defining characteristic of the people Jesus heals. Social exclusion is. Thus, God's redemptive and reconciling grace takes precedence over the cure. It is not merely that healing becomes liberating because those who are sick and impaired now gain access to the social life of the community as able-bodied people, made strong and "fully human." Rather, Jesus's community includes the broken and destitute from the start, thereby bringing wholeness to what was alienated. Life abundant is not a matter of eliminating bodily deficiencies so that persons can now participate in God's kingdom by being restored to "normal" functioning. Sick and disabled persons are welcomed as persons by Jesus into God's kingdom such that healing takes place. Healing is the effect of inclusion. To be sure, curing an illness or impairment entails healing. But healing should not be reduced to curing.[12] For the illness or disability is not the primary focus of Jesus's attention. The person is—who is made whole by being accepted first as they are, loved by God. A focus on the cure suggests the opposite, namely, that the person is not acceptable until he or she first becomes restored and made complete—normal like everyone else.[13] Jesus goes the other direction, seeing and affirming the humanity of the dehumanized and bringing it symbolically to wholeness by welcoming them to the divine banquet. Healing is a correlate of being welcomed.[14] And being welcomed opens up anew the image of God in human beings, such that the goodness and preciousness of human life resonates with restored clarity.

Third, that the healing narratives in many cases are not primarily about curing people is evidenced in several ways. One way is by their christological focus. That is, as Colleen C. Grant suggests, they emphasize not the people healed but instead the healer, describing who Jesus is as Christ. Only limited detail is given of people's afflictions. Instead, attention is directed to Jesus as a healer and miracle worker (Mark 1:31–34; 3:7–12; Luke 4:40–41), one who has compassion for those in need (Mark 1:40–45; 20:30–34; Matt. 14:14; Luke 7:13), and who has been given divine authority, especially over the Sabbath (Mark 3:1–6; Matt. 12:9–14; Luke 13:10–17).[15] These healing narratives give testimony to his messianic status, the fact that in his ministry the kingdom of God is at hand, and the power of God is at work (John 9:1–41). They also are used to demonstrate how Jesus fulfills messianic prophesies from the Hebrew Bible (Matt. 8:16–17; cf. Isa. 29:18–19 and 35:5–6). Jesus heals people in order to confirm that he is from God. To be sure, Jesus does not cure all those around him who are ill and disabled. He leaves towns without curing everyone (Mark 1:38; Luke 4:42–43). But some are cured to demonstrate his divinely authorized healing power, a power that indeed affects all. Healing miracles are a visible sign of God's power over evil, a mark of a kingdom that while yet incomplete is beginning to unfold, the ultimate victory of which is assured.[16] The point is not merely the curing, but Jesus's redemptive presence as Christ. And this presence testifies to how God privileges the vulnerable outcast in order to build a new community for all based upon mercy and love.

However, as Grant points out, there is another type of healing narrative beside the christologically shaped narrative, which shifts the emphasis from Jesus to those being healed.[17] This kind of account shows how it is neither by extraordinary ability nor even by magical curative powers that one is given access to God's love, but rather by the heartfelt acknowledgment of one's need for grace in faithful discipleship. Again, the predominant theme is not so much the physical elimination of impairments and illnesses as it is the personal transformation that takes place vis-à-vis Jesus's presence. The story of Bartimaeus being healed is noteworthy in this regard (Mark 10:46–52; Luke 18:35–43). Bartimaeus is a blind beggar on the roadside who, upon hearing Jesus is near, cries out for mercy. While he is rebuked by many and told to be quiet, he persists, thus drawing Jesus's attention and invitation, "What do you want me to do for you?" Bartimaeus voices the desire of his heart by responding, "My teacher, let me see again" (Mark 10:51). Jesus replies, "Go; your faith has made you well." Bartimaeus is not just healed, but more importantly follows Jesus along the way (10:52). Healing here accompanies persistent faith and committed discipleship, embodying a trust in what God is doing through Jesus. Similar connections between healing and faithful discipleship are found in the story of the two blind men whose faith empowers healing (Matt. 9:28–29), and that of the woman suffering from bleeding whose faith saves her (Mark 5:34).[18]

On the basis of these kinds of narratives, the reader might easily come to the conclusion that faith and discipleship yield healing, such that failure to be healed indicates a lack of faith or personal flaw.[19] But again, we must remember that physical restoration is not the sine qua non for entry into the community that Christ inaugurates. Membership in the kingdom of God is indiscriminate and lavish, beginning with God's gracious welcome and not human strength, ability, and health. Indeed, God's reign privileges the vulnerable and weak, the marginalized and outcast, drawing near principally through and among them. Recall that his table fellowship symbolizes a divine banquet in which the last are first and the weak have a special place, not because they are cured and made strong along the lines of normalcy, but because they are more ready to accept being welcomed by God for who they are. Wholeness and healing run deeper than the restoration of bodily function, for becoming able-bodied is not the criterion for membership in the kingdom. When healing occurs, it is the result of being redeemed, stemming from a faithful response to God's welcome, a yes proclaimed in gratitude to God's prior yes. Faith involves experiencing oneself within the arc of God's love. It may or may not entail physical restoration.

This means, as McCloughry and Morris claim, that physical "healings were not an end in themselves. They were not the ultimate in what the Kingdom offered to all. The gospel was the presence of Jesus himself. . . . His salvation was more than physical healing." The main event consists of "accepting Christ and becoming spiritually whole."[20] God reaches out to people before they are healed, not because they are healed. Jesus does not say to Bartimaeus, "Your faith *will* make you well"; rather, "Your faith *has* made you well." And while in some cases faith does yield physical healing, faith does not guarantee physical health. Becoming able-bodied is not a necessary correlation of faithful discipleship. So the healing narratives should not be seen according to the medical model, as a remedial cure. Rather, as a testimony to God's loving power, an example of how God privileges the vulnerable, sick, and impaired—not to fix but to welcome. Such welcome is transformative because it ennobles the human capacity to accept God's gratuitous and loving regard. God's love restores the image of God, reconciling human beings with one another and God.

The healing narratives give witness to this in other cases by highlighting the power of Jesus to forgive sins. As we noted in chapter 1, these stories are especially ambiguous and potentially dangerous for people with disabilities, for they can be read as indicating a connection between impairments and sin, ability and righteousness. Indeed, this connection was common in the ancient world, and has biblical precedent. Psalm 32 gives evidence of believing healing from affliction is a sign of God's forgiveness (1–2, 10). Proverbs 11 does as well (8, 19, 21). John 5:2–9 also suggests the connection. Here Jesus heals a man by the pool of Bethesda and later encounters him, stating, "See, you have been made well! Do not sin any more, so that nothing worse happens to you" (5:14; cf., Luke 5:18–26).[21] Jesus calls the man to live a transformed life, the life of faithful discipleship. Another example is Matthew 9:1–8, which portrays Jesus as healing a paralyzed man via forgiving his sin. Interestingly, it is not the man's faith here that has made him well, but God's forgiveness, which precedes the subjective act of faith (cf. Mark 2:1–12). But does this link sin and impairments inextricably, as a general principle? Certainly not, for elsewhere Jesus subverts the common assumption of a causal linkage between previous sin and present suffering.

A powerful example is found in John 9:1–41, the story of the healing of the man born blind. Upon encountering this man, Jesus's disciples ask who sinned so that he was born blind, he or his parents. Breaking the link between sin and impairment as divine punishment, Jesus answers, "Neither this man nor his parents sinned; he was born blind so that God's works might be revealed in him" (9:3). The real focus is neither sin nor disability, but the purposes of God. In the end, he affirms Jesus by stating, "Lord, I believe" (9:38). Hence, as Grant notes, the man becomes "the quintessential model of a disciple," his eyes opened to the identity of Jesus as Christ.[22] In entering into communion with Christ, the man evidences the work of God. The focus is not merely on his impairment. Neither is it on the physical restoration. He is rather an example of faith for all human beings insofar as he witnesses to Jesus and becomes a partner in the kingdom of God.

By forgiving sins, Jesus acts as a surrogate for the temple rites by which one could obtain forgiveness. This is important because sick people and people with disabilities are excluded from the temple by virtue of their blemish. But Jesus welcomes all into his presence, forgiving sins by his own authority, outside the purity codes governing temple practices. In this he subverts the cult of normalcy, effectively claiming to do what God does, acting as an agent of the grace-giving activity of God. Hence, as McCloughry and Morris suggest, Jesus is showing "that he has authority to forgive sins by demonstrating his power to heal and restore. The two go hand in hand not because they are cause and effect as was popularly thought, but because they are both evidence that the Kingdom has come in Jesus, the Christ."[23] In the kingdom, bodily reparation is not an end in itself, as if the only thing to do with a paralyzed or blind person is to cure them. Inclusion is the more fundamental reality, which is fostered by a forgiveness that reconciles people to God and the community. While in some cases sickness and impairment may be the result of human sin—for example, in the form of carelessness or irresponsibility—this correlation is not generally in accordance with Jesus's own understanding. Furthermore, it is first the act of God that forgives and saves, that restores wholeness to the *imago Dei*, which subsequently cultivates the response of faith and, in some cases, leads to physical healing. But again, we must fervently stress that, even in these cases, healing is a broader reality that has more to do with salvation than simply being cured.

We must also stress that Jesus himself criticizes the public for their demand for healing wonders, as if only these could count as symptoms of salvation and forgiveness. As mentioned above, the christological miracles serve to draw attention to Jesus's messianic role in God's saving plan. But Jesus at times denounces the need for supernatural miracles in order to believe. For example, in John's Gospel, after having been approached by an officer who pleaded for Jesus to heal his dying son, Jesus replies sardonically, "Unless you see signs and wonders you will not believe" (John 4:48). He then heals the officer's son, though the context here suggests that faith/belief was not the condition for the healing, but rather the outcome. For upon hearing that his son recovered, the officer believed, along with his whole household (4:53b). Healing happens in this case for lack of faith, not because of it, and Jesus states his dismay over how the public expresses such lack of faith in craving for miraculous signs as a display of his power. In the end, genuine healing is exhibited not through power and might, through supernatural strength, but in a vulnerability and weakness that follows the way of the cross.

So as overall strategies, it is problematic to link harm with sin, and physical cures with righteousness. Such connections wrongly emphasize the individual and overlook the social powers of exclusion that Jesus is addressing. Faith is a matter of becoming whole in terms of creative, relational, and available possibilities, a recreation of self in connection with God and other human beings that does not operate according to norms fashioned in economies of exchange, but according to God's economy of grace. Moreover, as we saw in chapter 1, linking sinfulness with illness or impairments too closely associates the kingdom of God with faulted theodicy questions, which go against the grain of Jesus's way of being in relation to those who are marginalized and oppressed. Jesus does not set out to explain why someone is the way he or she is, looking for mysterious purposes at work or something to blame; rather, he is present to them in a way that brings wholeness and abundant life. He welcomes as God welcomes. Yet this is not to romanticize sickness and impairments as somehow special in God's view. Jesus focuses on the person, not the ailment as something that defines them. He sees vulnerable people as more than examples of weakness and brokenness; they are privileged as contributing partners in the kingdom—which leads us to a further theme.

Cross as Inclusive Solidarity—The Power of Inability

It is clear then that Jesus does more in physically restoring people than cure them. He heals, offering a redemptive wholeness that connects with God's presence, not only by means of welcoming the outcast, sinful, weak, impaired, and sick to the divine banquet, but also by taking on and experiencing their vulnerability directly, such that he compassionately suffers with them. Jesus draws near and aligns himself in solidarity with otherwise destitute or unwelcome persons, bearing their burdens and sharing their plight. Understood in this way, Jesus's healing power is not simply magical, wonder-working power. It is the power of his availability for others, which becomes manifest in his capacity to love vulnerably. This is the power that reflects the radiant love of God. Jesus's practice of inclusion and healing serves an iconic end by revealing God's love.

The point was detailed in the last chapter, so it will suffice here to summarize that Jesus is sympathetically attuned to human vulnerability in three ways. First, he is fully and vulnerably human. Second, he specifically directs his ministry toward human vulnerability, embracing it completely in the life-giving shape of welcoming persons who are in a variety of ways especially vulnerable and without welcome. The marginalized and oppressed thus find liberation through Jesus's presence. Third, they find liberation not by sheer power and might, which Jesus intentionally avoids, but by love's vulnerable solidarity. As Matthew's Gospel proclaims, healing the sick fulfills what had been spoken prophetically by Isaiah: "He took our infirmities and bore our diseases" (53:4; Matt. 8:17). Jürgen Moltmann notes the importance of this: "He heals, not by casting aside and getting rid of the sicknesses, but by taking them on himself. People are not healed by Jesus' supernatural powers, but rather by his wounds."[24] Thus, the radical character of Jesus's availability is exemplified dramatically at the cross. His brokenness and weakness on the cross manifests the hidden power of God's healing presence. The cross then graphically portrays the extent of God's sharing of human vulnerability and suffering, going through death. Precisely at this point human inability and impoverishment become harbingers of divine grace. Hence, nothing human remains outside God's enfolding embrace.

Through the cross, divine love opens up possibilities beyond the tragic. At this low point of utter destitution, God takes up all human tragedies and in so doing refuses to let them be the final word on existence. Jesus is no mere scapegoat sacrificed to appease God's wrath. Rather, he goes the distance required by the nature of his availability for others. And this act of giving for humanity becomes the veritable love of God at work in the world, bringing healing and reconciliation—in a word, atonement—by making tragedy part of the divine life. The cross is a site of divine welcome, such that tragedy's suffering, impoverishment, and alienation are taken up into the abundant and life-giving core of God's being. The paradoxical reversal gets to the very heart of the kingdom of God, where the weak are blessed, the last are first, and the poor are rich. God's power identifies with human vulnerability, even unto death, so that human vulnerability may be made to participate in the liveliness of God. Healing, then, is the result of sharing in divine gratuity, of being welcomed by God. Moltmann declares: "God heals us in that he participates so much in our pains that they become part of his eternal love."[25] This does not necessarily mean physical restoration. What it does mean, however, is that tragedy can be transformed into creative, relational, and available possibilities, nurturing gratitude and hope in the midst of imperilments. God is with us. And this "with" yields healing wholeness.

A poignant example of how the cross paradoxically couples Jesus's impoverishment with God's love is found in Matthias Grünewald's famous painting on the Isenheim Altar. Created between 1513 and 1515 for the chapel at a hospital for dying plague victims in Isenheim, France, the front panel displays a disfigured Jesus on the cross, covered with lacerations similar to the ulcers afflicting the patients. In this painting, as Moltmann notes, the sick "recognized themselves in the man of pain, because he had become one of them. And in looking at this picture they experienced the eternal, unbreakable fellowship with the crucified God."[26] Even as death approached, this fellowship brought healing. For the viewers saw divine solidarity, compassion, and forgiveness in this suffering figure. They were not alone.[27] Jesus's passion was understood to be God's compassion for all humanity precisely in its vulnerability to tragedy.

However, the viewers also saw another adjacent panel by Grünewald, this one depicting the resurrected Christ, which glowed with splendor. The good news for people dying of the plague was that new life was possible. Just as Jesus died and rose again, so too could they. From tragedy rose new beginnings, new life. Death and dissolution had become the way to liberation, to a sense of being included in God's banquet of grace. Despair was thereby robbed of its power. Not because the people were merely encouraged, but because they were empowered to share in new life, a life stronger than tragedy, the currents of which flowed from the divine itself. Weakness and brokenness yielded way to a deeper grace—that is, a sense of being loved by God.

To human beings in the midst of tragic circumstances, the gospel message does not say "hang in there," or "it is not really so bad." With characteristic pastoral sensitivity, Henri Nouwen points out that the gospel promise is entirely new: "The most tragic, the most painful, the most hopeless circumstances can become the way to the liberation you long for most of all."[28] It is this kind of affirmation that allowed plague victims to see their existence as full of promise, to see that vulnerable life is stronger than its disintegration in sickness and death. By implication, for all people the cross—a sign of death—becomes a sign of hope through the resurrection, marking the vitalizing prospect of renewal over and against despair. Indeed, resurrection is what happens when tragedy is taken into the compassionate and life-giving core of God.

Grünewald helps us access a key message in the gospel: namely, that suffering and death do not bar the way to new life, but through Jesus become the way to it. God liberates humanity not from tragedy, but rather amidst and through it.[29] Suffering is not necessarily removed, but suffering can yield new life. By sharing tragedy with us, God empowers its transformation, making genuine healing possible. God is with us. In the depths, God's creative-redemptive presence is at work. The sympathetic love revealed at the cross highlights God's relational vulnerability, God's capacity to undergo the finite creature's tragic situation. Because of this, the cross is not the end. It points toward resurrection. And resurrection is a vivid symbol for the irrepressible character of the kingdom of God, embodying the resilient promise of a realm of renewed life and reconciled relationships shaped by divine abundance and love. But the wounds of the cross remain even on Christ's risen and transformed body. Thus as disciples, Christians are called to imitate Christ by taking up the cross in anticipation of the arrival of the kingdom. We await resurrection in gratitude and hope, amidst finite imperilments.

Disability and the Imitation of Christ

This is precisely why the apostle Paul employs the model of Christ crucified as basic to his ministry. Paul acknowledges that his weakness (*astheneiai*), his impairment, a "thorn in the flesh," is a vessel for God's saving power to become complete in him (2 Cor. 12:5–10). Indeed, it is through his lack of ability that Paul finds his gift as a disciple of Christ, compelled to depend on God's grace rather than his own strength. For it is in inability that God's saving presence is made real. Paul recalls God speaking to him, saying, "My grace is sufficient for you, for my power is made perfect in weakness" (12:9). Not only is this weakness displayed in Christ's death on the cross, the power of God appearing in frailty, the wisdom of God in foolishness (1 Cor.1:18–25), it also becomes palpable and real in Paul's own experience of impairment. If God's glory is made manifest at the point where the Messiah, the anointed one, is dispossessed of ability and made weak, so too, in conformity with Christ the faithful disciple experiences the glory of God in weakness. The sympathetic activity of God is revealed through human inability. Christ crucified is axiomatic for the Christian life (1 Cor. 1:23; 2:2; Gal. 6:14). "For he was crucified in weakness, but lives by the power of God. For we are weak in him, but . . . live with him by the power of God" (2 Cor. 13:4). The theological thrust is this: God not only acts in solidarity with weakness, God acts through weakness. The way to God is in taking up the cross. The marks of Jesus's wounds are branded on our bodies (Gal. 6:17).

By no means does this romanticize suffering or trivialize disability by somehow making it redemptive. Rather, it directs us to the unexpected character of God's healing presence in human life. The cross reveals the worth of what is considered worthless, welcoming it into the divine life. God is sympathetically attuned to human beings at their weakest point. And surprising things happen. Simon Horne comments upon this paradox, noting how "within inability is striking capability."[30] Human limitations in one area can open up unexpected possibilities in other areas that might otherwise go unnoticed or remain dormant. In a unique, vulnerable, and dependent way, each person has something to offer to the human family and to the kingdom of God. What is more, we discover this through interdependent relationships with each other. It is here that we accept someone not because of what they can offer—according to established conventions and economies of exchange—but rather because of who they are, precious and loved into being by God in the image of God. Only in this sense do we come to experience the creative gifts that a person can truly offer, which often surprise with unexpected and enriching possibilities. So, as we have noted time and again, suffering and limitations carry the power to open up human beings to each other in mutual vulnerability, and open us to the presence of God. For example, God chooses Moses for a special leadership role neither despite his speech impairment—as something God regrets but will put up with—nor without it—as something God eliminates or cures—but along with it, providing him with provisions that nurture an ongoing trust in God's faithfulness (Exod. 4:10–17). And because of some physical inability, Paul is first empowered to preach to the people of Galatia (Gal. 4:13). Elsewhere, Paul claims that the source of his ability does not reside in his own strength or wisdom, "but in the power of God" (1 Cor. 2:1–5; cf. 2 Cor. 4:7). Inability is not itself a redemptive gift, but a site of divine giftedness, a place where God's vulnerable power comes to abide.[31]

The message, then, is more than learning to accept one's weakness and dependence, as if impairments are negative anomalies simply to be endured or put up with. The biblical witness points to acknowledged weakness and dependence as positive sources of unexpected ability and grace. Redemption does not happen because of disability, but amidst it. Light can shine out amidst the darkness; failures can become virtues. Why? Because darkness and failure are not the utter evils we attribute to them. From the perspective of God's love they are possibilities, as chaos is the potential for creative-redemptive vitality and wholeness. Even tragedy can give way to wholeness, not necessarily—as if through some fait accompli—but through its possibility for transformation. As the cross is real in the depths of every human life, so is the possibility of resurrection.

Hence, in God's economy of grace there is no shame in weakness, no need to hide from vulnerability and pretend to be strong, striving to become somebody. The "out-of-control" body is normative and has creative, relational, and available potential. Christ crucified dethrones the powers and principalities of the cult of normalcy and enfolds humanity in a loving embrace that brings the margins to the center. Far from something to be cured and gotten rid of, then, disability is a locus of divine relational power. Furthermore, far from being a cross to bear so redemptive healing takes place, disability is welcomed as part of who a person is. There is no moral meaning to disability per se. Even as a privileged site of divine welcome, God does not teach lessons through disabilities. Disability can indeed help bring home the moral meaning of vulnerability and weakness as the fulcrum of what it means to be human and created in the image of God. But it should not therefore be understood as a generic symbol of human weakness, for there are many kinds of disabilities. A person with autism and a person who is blind cannot be reduced to some generic condition of disability as if they experience the same thing. If preference is to be given to the persons with disabling conditions, variety must be taken into account. In fact, all people experience limitations and inabilities—along with abilities—that are of different degrees and qualities. So having disabilities does not measure an individual. What it does measure, paradoxically, is the lavishly abundant character of God's love, given neither because of nor despite lack of body capital, but rather because all people are loved into being by God and thus intrinsically precious, vulnerable creatures in need of God and one another.

In sum, the radical healing power of Jesus's ministry, death, and resurrection consists in the revelation of every human being's infinite worth in God, even as some may be considered worthless non-contributors in human economies of exchange. Redemption is the experience of being welcomed into the kingdom of God. This is the new creation that Christ inaugurates. It is the fulfillment of what creation intends, the restoration of the image of God in human beings, for we are created that God's love might be revealed through us.

III. The Strange Household of God: Church as the Ongoing Presence of Christ

Jesus's proclamation of the kingdom of God consists of welcoming outcasts, the poor, and people with disabilities to the banquet of divine grace. His ministry of healing uproots social barriers and creates communal inclusion, challenging the notion that disability is a flaw or punishment for sin. Indeed, as we have seen, the physical healings themselves are not the main event, a counter to the problematic urge by non-disabled people to cure disability. In the bigger picture, Jesus's healings both confirm his identity as Emmanuel—God with us—and embody the features of the kingdom. Jesus is no stranger to disability; he seeks to be with people with disabilities and identifies himself with them, for them. At the cross Jesus subjects himself to disability, his resurrected body continuing to bear his scars as a sign of God's solidarity with humanity.

Let us now explore how Christians come to participate in this solidarity in the ongoing life of the church, being the collective and Spirit-filled body of Christ. How does this take shape? As a household of God managed according to an economy of grace. This vision has dramatic implications for reconsidering the church as a community of faith founded upon the memory that God was in Christ reconciling the world (2 Cor. 5:19). The implications spill over into praxis-oriented considerations that affect people with and without disabilities alike.

Church as the Household of God—A New Covenant

It is no accident that the biblical narratives portray a kind of salvation that, far from vindicating the conventional and normal, actually undercuts it by pointing to the palpable presence of God in human vulnerability as a locus of relational interdependence. Jesus proclaims the nearness of God's kingdom, inviting people to participate in God's present work of reconfiguring the world. For those who find themselves caught up in this redemptive momentum, he offers a new covenant, a new way of being in relation to God and each other based upon grace and shaped by God's empowering love. This new covenant anticipates the arrival of God's kingdom, and accordingly challenges the world's economies of dominance, exclusion, and violence, not by brute force, but by the creative life-giving power of compassion and unconditional regard—in a word, availability.

The character of the new covenant is made concrete in Christ's death (Luke 22:20; Heb. 9:15), which demonstrates a love that goes the distance and knows no barriers, where walls between people are broken down to create one new humanity

(Eph. 2:14–15). Indeed, death on the cross is the seal of Jesus's ministry, the emblem of the way he iconically embodies the way God acts in the world. Why? Because even in death, Jesus acts as though only God reigns; in this radical openness God's love is revealed and becomes efficacious. Jesus represents the new covenant because he incarnates the shape of right relatedness to God and to others, then makes this possible for those who follow him. Hence, Jesus offers reconciling and liberating possibilities for the community that remembers him. That is, re-membering the story of Jesus opens up new possibilities for being in covenantal relation to God and neighbor over and against the cult of normalcy and its way of perverting and feeding upon the need for welcome as a will to control. It is this positive potential that coalesces into a household of God.

Paul acknowledges that one who is in Christ has become a new creation (2 Cor. 5:17), made fully alive and restored to what she or he is meant to be as a creature created in the image of God. However, being remade in Christ is not simply a private, individualistic affair. Insofar as the image of God is relational in character, being in Christ has an unavoidably communal quality. This is why Paul uses cor-porate metaphors to describe it. Speaking to Gentile Christians, he claims, "You are no longer strangers and aliens, but you are citizens with the saints and also members of the household of God" (Eph. 2:19). Through Christ, all are joined together into a holy temple, a dwelling place for God (2:21–22). The metaphor of a house/temple is instructive not merely because of its spatial connotations, but because of the solidarity implied between people as a sign of solidarity between humanity and God.

A house is a dwelling place for those related to a shared heritage or purpose, a common reference point harboring them and providing refuge—a home. Through dwelling within its frame, persons gain resources for considering themselves a community, tied together in daily activities by patterns of mutual care, concern, and memory. A domestic economy is created that nurtures a sense of belonging. Hence, the *ecclesia*, those "called out" to be a new community, functions like a household in that it signifies a people tied together and nourished by reference to the saving work of God in Christ. This is what makes the house a temple. It is a place founded by the new covenant. Within it we are members of a family of faith (Gal. 6:10).

The household of God is a dwelling place structured according to a divine economy of grace. The Christian cannot be faithful alone or in isolation. Oth-ers are implied who, in different ways, also find themselves taken up into God's transformative work. There are thus many rooms, each joined together by a shared field of resonance that makes them something larger than they are alone. This field of resonance is grace, and such grace is experienced insofar as genuine solidarity and communion in Christ is made real. The church (*ecclesia*) is not a bureaucratic system of administration governed by yet another human economy of exchange. To be sure, it involves institutional processes and offices, the structures of which provide for necessary continuity and preservation. But these are not fundamental.

Grace is fundamental, grace which creates a fellowship (*koinonia*) based upon mutual vulnerability in faith, hope, and love. This means that the new community is not privileged, restricted, or provincial; it is not based upon blood, sex, ethnicity or race, inheritance or property. It is intrinsically non-provincial and radically universal: "There is no longer Jew or Greek, there is no longer slave or free, there is no longer male and female; for all of you are one in Christ Jesus" (Gal. 3:28).

As a temple, the household of God is an open household, where each room has a self-surpassing character connecting it to others. There is one communion. This fellowship of Christ is thus open to differences, built up by a compassion wherein others are welcomed and served as part of the household. There is no absolute stranger. Difference is not merely tolerated; it is constitutive of the new community, which is a *koinonia* through and not in spite of diversity. As redemption in Christ legitimates no divisions or restrictions on the grounds of race, ethnicity, gender, or ability, the household of God is indiscriminate and nonexclusive. It is an inclusive stretch of unconditional regard for others where grace abounds. The church is a people joined together by God's gracious welcome. We are no longer separate; we are one in God through Christ's love. There is one household of God (1 Tim. 3:15; Heb. 3:6; 1 Pet. 2:5; 3:17).

Church as the Body of Christ

The stress on mutuality and inclusion in God's household is why Paul employs the metaphor of "body" to illustrate what it means to be church. How are Christians drawn together? By an economy of grace that unites all persons into a shared identity representing the ongoing presence of Christ. Paul speaks of Christ as the "head" of the church—the post-resurrection incarnation of his body (Eph. 1:22–23; 5:23; Col. 1:18–20). All members are reconciled and brought together by being "baptized into one body" (1 Cor. 12:13). Furthermore, all participate in Christ and are linked inextricably through the Lord's Supper: "The cup of blessing that we bless, is it not a sharing in the blood of Christ? The bread that we break, is it not a sharing in the body of Christ? Because there is one bread, we who are many are one body, for we all partake of the one bread" (1 Cor. 10:16–17). The whole community—not simply several of its stronger or more spiritual members—is the body of Christ, the continuation of his saving presence in the world. As God's gracious availability to humanity became manifest in Christ, so the church is called to manifest God's availability as Christ's body. The household of God is a redemptive body animated by an economy of grace. And the body of Christ is a "solidarity of others."[32]

The organic nature of the body as a metaphor for God's presence in the shape of a new community is charged with multiple meanings. First, it suggests that the nature of this community is defined by the loving service it offers to others. As Jesus "came not to be served but to serve, and to give his life as a ransom for many" (Mark 10:45), likewise members of his body are called to be servants—"slaves for Jesus' sake" (2 Cor. 4:5).[33] Daniel Migliore notes that such service reflects Jesus's twofold commandment to love God and neighbor. This command indicates that the church's reason for existence lies not in itself—in its own preservation as a kind of club—but instead in its task, which prays, praises, and worships God as well as witnesses to God's gracious welcome and prophetically works for justice by privileging the vulnerable.[34] In fact, the new community itself becomes vulnerable by identifying with Christ, such that loving God and loving others are twin aspects of the same redemptive pulse. Its availability to God makes vulnerable the service it renders to others; and its service to others consecrates its openness to God. Far from being a community of the privileged and powerful, the church ideally is comprised of people who take up the cross and suffer with and for others. Jesus outlines what this involves, asserting that "whoever wishes to be great among you must be your servant, and whoever wishes to be first among you must be your slave" (Matt. 20:26–27). Not the rich but the poor; not the strong but the weak. As the body of Christ, the church is called to embody this paradoxical reversal in its ministry, existing in compassionate solidarity with the human family just as God does in Christ. This makes it a community of vulnerable caregivers.

Given this, a second meaning comes to the fore. For Paul, existence in Christ—as the body of Christ—makes each member of the new community vulnerable "members of one another" (Rom. 12:5). The church is a household of welcome, in which every member belongs to and receives sustenance from others in the economy of the whole. Bound together in interdependence, each is "given grace according to the measure of Christ's gift" (Eph. 4:7), and each is given specific gifts "for building up the body of Christ" (4:12), fostering growth into the fullness of Christ, "from whom the whole body, joined and knit together by every ligament with which it is equipped, as each part is working properly, promotes the body's growth in building itself up in love" (4:16). No part of the body is left out; all are related in love—with and for each other. In Christ's love, Christians are part of one another, caught up in a web of mutual belonging such that when one member suffers, all suffer together, and when one member rejoices, all rejoice together (1 Cor. 12:26). Love is the hallmark of the body of Christ, a love that imitates God and embodies the love revealed in Christ (Eph. 5:1; cf. 1 Cor. 13:1–7).

Furthermore, within the throes of such love all members are welcomed as having unique gifts to contribute to the community. Paul is emphatic in encouraging the Christian communities in Rome, Ephesus, and Corinth to live in harmony and peace, noting that not all members of the body have the same function, but have different gifts according the grace given (Rom. 12:4–8; 1 Cor. 12:12; Eph. 4:2–3, 7–8). Aware of the lure of the world's economies of exchange, which measure value according to status, performance, or strength, he warns against the temptation to think more highly of a person's gifts (perhaps one's own) than is fitting, pleading for humility and graciousness among community members; for in the body of Christ all members are indispensable. "Indeed, the body does not consist of only one member, but many" (1 Cor. 12:14). Consequently, one part should not exclude another as unimportant, nor should one part exclude itself as unimportant. God arranges the members of the body in different ways, each according to their own unique gifts (12:18).[35] The differences are good, precisely amidst their various abilities and disabilities.

Simon Horne takes this point even further by noting Paul's vigorous claim that God's power is manifest in the communal body of Christ not merely through a mutual concern that champions all members as indispensable, but through a privileging of those members who lack ability and respect.[36] Again, Paul underscores that it is through inability that God's saving presence is made real. Only now the focus is communal in nature. It is worth quoting him at length:

> As it is, there are many members, yet one body. The eye cannot say to the hand, "I have no need of you," nor again the head to the feet, "I have no need of you." On the contrary, the members of the body that seem to be weaker are indispensable, and those members of the body that we think less honorable we clothe with greater honor, and our less respectable members are treated with greater respect; whereas our more respectable members do not need this. But God has so arranged the body, giving the greater honor to the inferior member, that there may be no dissension within the body, but the members may have the same care for one another. If one member suffers, all suffer together with it; if one member is honored, all rejoice together with it. (1 Cor. 12:20–26)

The identity and mission of the church is rooted in welcoming and caring for those at the margins. Understood in terms we have employed in this book, Paul directs our attention to those whose body capital might seem unworthy of welcome according to normal conventions and expectations. This kind of vision squares with that of Jesus: not the first, but the last; not the strong, but the weak; not the privileged, but the underprivileged. God works in, through, and for the vulnerable and broken, drawing together a community of the beloved based upon radical inclusion. Here, all have the same care for one another so that no one should be excluded and everyone treated as equal; for all members are gifts, loved into being and redeemed by God. Diversity and equality are two sides of the same coin in God's economy of grace.[37]

Thus, excluding one member of the body of Christ mars its image. This is of crucial importance, for the image of God is restored only in relationships of vulnerable interdependence that connect us with one another in the new community. Christians are less than whole without one another, without the contributions that all make to the household of God. This is why it is necessary to recognize the unique gifts that each person brings to the divine banquet. Moreover, it is why, as Paul states, bearing one another's burdens is the path to fulfilling the law of Christ (Gal. 6:2). Such love yields communion. It also highlights vulnerability. And, in the words of Jean Vanier, "communion is mutual vulnerability and openness one to the other."[38] We find life through inclusion, through belonging to each other; we give life through inclusion, through belonging to each other. This seems to be at the heart of what it means to be the body of Christ. By remembering excluded differences, then, we "re-member" and so constitute the body of Christ. Accordingly, in Frances Young's words, "the image of God is restored in the Body of Christ, in which every individual is affirmed for the bit they have to contribute to the total image, but none can claim to be the image of God on their own."[39] The image of God is the creative, relational, and available community of faith.

Theologically speaking, then, the body of Christ is fractured when people with disabilities are excluded from full participation in the church. Genuine love is prevented from coming to fruition when physical and social barriers prevent access. Yet access is not something to be provided out of charity or pity, which often merely contributes to the problem. Access is not an extra option, an afterthought derived from feeling bad for persons who lack body capital. It is mandated by the very character of what it means to be church, a people joined together by God's gracious gift of welcome. By refusing to welcome some, the church refuses to embody the love incarnate in Christ, the love to which it is called. And insofar as love of others is linked to love of God, this means that the church refuses to love God. For the body of Christ is shaped by the bodies of people with disabilities, not as people who are lacking in humanity, but as people who are different and equally loved into being by God. And if we follow Paul's logic, especially because disability is accorded less respect in the church, it should be privileged and accorded special respect and honor. In God's economy of grace the margins are the center. Christians should receive each other's difference as life-giving sources of communion. Welcoming and being present with people with disabilities makes the church more able to be the body of Christ. As Stanley Hauerwas aptly concludes, "only when we learn how to be with those different from us can we learn to accept the love that each of us needs to sustain a community capable of worshiping God."[40]

Church as Anticipation—The Not Yet Kingdom of God

Sadly, however, the conventions of the cult of normalcy survive in the new community. This underscores the fact that the church (*ecclesia*) is a human communion, a corporate body or household that anticipates the arrival of the fullness of God's kingdom (*basileia*), but in finite and piecemeal ways. The church is not the kingdom, only a prefiguring of it. Indeed, the new community cannot strictly be identified with the kingdom of God without becoming itself idolatrous and self-serving. Its mission focuses not on preserving itself, but on serving God and neighbor. The church is thus more an ongoing task than an essence to be guarded. It is ever on the way, waiting with active faith, hope, and love, seeking to serve God and neighbor with an ever wider inclusive stretch. As such, however, it is fallible, all too easily coopted by human mechanisms of closure. This is why the church is an *ecclesia semper reformanda*, an assembly of the people of God that is always being reformed. Because the kingdom is "not yet," remaining in the process of coming, the church must be vigilant against becoming static and self-satisfied. The kingdom of God remains an ideal, a transcendent and heavenly reality not yet entirely present on earth. Yet it is also present, a paradigm of right relation to God and others—an economy of grace—that summons the corporate body of Christ to be transformed into the image of Christ, the relational wholeness of which constitutes the collective restoration of the image of God.[41]

As a productive paradigm, the kingdom operates as a prophetic call for justice and equality, a call that seeks to liberate persons with disabilities from forces that nullify the gift of being created in the image of God. Freedom for being the body of Christ means freedom from alienating and dehumanizing powers that debilitate it by excluding persons. Without this, the church cannot be church. Thus, as Brett Webb-Mitchell puts it, the prophetic message for the church today is: "If the Church is to be like the Kingdom of God, then it too must invite, welcome, and accept the presence of those who are considered poor, 'the crippled, the blind, and the lame,' in our world today."[42] Precisely this message is why, as we shall now explore, hospitality is at the core of the new community as the Spirit's fundamental work.

IV. Hospitality: Welcoming (in) the Spirit

Up to this point we have employed the images of household of God and body of Christ to illustrate the nature of *ecclesia*. This could be misleading, however, for Paul also uses language of the Holy Spirit to describe the church. In 1 Corinthians, he makes the basic claim that "no one can say 'Jesus is Lord' except by the Holy Spirit" (12:3), going on to suggest that the work of the Spirit creates unity in diversity: "To each is given the manifestation of the Spirit for the common good" (12:7). Indeed, "in the one Spirit" Christians are "baptized into one body," different gifts being given "as the Spirit chooses" (12:11–13). The church is a "communion of the Holy Spirit" (2 Cor. 13:13), a community of the spirit, a "sharing in the Spirit" (Phil. 2:1). It is the spirit of God that creates and nurtures the *koinonia* fellowship that embodies the love of Christ, building together a corporate dwelling place for God (Eph. 2:22). If Christ is the foundation, the Holy Spirit is the cement that holds together the household of God, which is a "spiritual house" (*oikos pneumatikos*, 1 Pet. 2:5). And in this household a single new humanity is created, breaking down barriers that once existed between differences. There are no longer strangers and aliens, but fellow citizens of one community (Eph. 2:19). The creative work of God as spirit quickens the body of Christ.[43] The Spirit functions to gather together what was separate and unrelated, and enlivens the communion that results through its indwelling power.

In the Hebrew Bible, the Spirit takes on the meaning of wind or breath (*ruach*) which indwells creation as the nearness of God (*Shekinah*). The spirit of God hovers over the face of the deep in the creation story as the shaping and vivifying element of God's creative presence (Gen. 1:2). God breathes the divine spirit into Adam, and he becomes a living and whole being (2:7). The connection between creation and *ruach* is evident elsewhere, a metaphor for the life-giving energy of

God (cf. Job 26:12–13; 33:4; Ps. 104:27–31).[44] All creation participates in the spirit of God, which stretches everywhere. There is no place where God is absent: "Where can I go from your spirit? Or where can I flee from your presence?" (Ps. 139:7). The spirit also becomes manifest concretely in special moments, endowing people with charisms or gifts that otherwise would not be possible, such as wisdom (Gen. 41:38–39; Exod. 28:3; 35:31; Deut. 34:9), leadership (Judg. 14:6, 19; 15:14–15), and prophecy (Isa. 61:1; Ezek. 2:1–2; Zech. 7:12). Regarding prophecy, the Spirit validates the message as "the word (*dabhar*) of the Lord."[45] In all these functions, it has an empowering and enlivening role to play.[46]

The New Testament picks up on and augments the role of the spirit (*pneuma*) as a way of speaking about God's anointing and ingathering power. Here, as Bradley C. Hanson notes, the Spirit has a twofold relation to Jesus. Jesus is both "bearer of the Spirit," in the sense that he is given a full measure of its consecrating authority as a special representative of God (Mark 1:10–11; Luke 4:18ff.; John 3:34), and "giver of the Spirit," as he bestows it upon his followers (John 20:22). These meanings allow Paul to employ "in Christ" and "in the Spirit" interchangeably: to participate in Christ is to participate in the Spirit.[47] And through that Spirit, Christ's presence continues after his resurrection, consecrating the new community at Pentecost by endowing people with special gifts (Acts 2:4; 8:16; 10:44–46). The Spirit builds up the household of God, animating its economy of grace and directing its life-giving ministry. It grants new life and bears fruits, the first of which is love (Gal. 5:22–23). In this way, the Spirit is the source of communion, which is the fruit of love. So it is a manifestation of God's loving presence. Paul sees the coming of the Spirit in the church as the firstfruits of God's coming reign (Rom. 8:23). We might then say that as the Spirit both indwells Jesus and animates his ministry, it also indwells and animates the post-resurrection church as Christ's body. As Paul states: "God's love has been poured into our hearts through the Holy Spirit that has been given to us" (Rom. 5:5). This makes Christ present in an ongoing way, creating new life in freedom for and with others—that is, in a *koinonia* fellowship of grace.[48] The Spirit energizes and opens up the image of God in human beings, nurturing creative relations of availability to God and others.

Hospitality—Inspirited Openness to the Other

The household of God is charged with the power of the Spirit. As such, it is a life-giving freedom from the cult of normalcy, along with its modes of communal closure and freedom for one another and God. In Paul's writing, the letter of the law functions in a way strikingly parallel to the cult of normalcy, confirming value and worth in people according to their ability to fulfill certain prescribed roles and duties. But as no one can be righteous in these terms, all fall short of the glory of God (Rom. 3:23). Similarly, as was discussed in chapter 2, all fall short of the conventions demanded by idealized notions of normalcy. In the widest sense, then, right relation to God and neighbor is precluded within the cult of normalcy, for its mechanisms exemplify sin as a will to control, a desire to manage and guarantee welcome. The reversal exemplified by the new covenant, in contrast, breaks the hold of this obsession with securing welcome in human terms, working instead according to the Spirit: "for the letter kills, but the Spirit gives life" (2 Cor. 3:6), and "where the Spirit of the Lord is, there is freedom" (3:17). In Paul's understanding, such freedom from the letter is freedom for love. Christ's welcome is made manifest in the Spirit, making possible a love without boundaries—that is, a love that does not predetermine or measure in advance the conditions for serving one another. God's grace is not meted out according to the acquisition of body capital but is gratuitously given. Accordingly, serving one another gratuitously is the hallmark of the kingdom of God, summing up the positive aim of the law: "You shall love your neighbor as yourself" (Gal. 5:14). This means bearing one another's burdens and so fulfilling the law of Christ, the law of love (6:2).

The moral sense of such a law might best be described as hospitality, a welcoming of one's neighbor that bears and invites him or her into a shared space of mutuality, a household. If the body of Christ is a solidarity of others, the Spirit is the empowering hospitality that builds up this solidarity as a communion of differences. Hospitality is the means to solidarity. This goes beyond the common usage of the term as a way of talking about etiquette and throwing parties. As Christine Pohl observes, hospitality connotes extending to the unfamiliar alien a "quality of kindness usually reserved for friends and family," those within the boundaries of a common social network.[49] The root context is the dwelling space of the home, the shared environment of those closest and most familiar to us. In the biblical traditions, the household is considered primary. It has centering and cohesive power, serving as the basis for identity and orientation toward the public life of a community, its culture, politics, and religion.[50] Hospitality, then, is an opening up of the household to provide and care for another whose place of origin is elsewhere. It is the practice of making room to include the stranger, an act of sharing with and for another as oneself.

Hospitality embodies divine love. It neither condescends out of pity nor forces the other to conform or assimilate to the household rule, but rather lets the other be, yielding space for the other's freedom and difference. In this it recognizes the preciousness of the other as a person loved by God. Hospitality opens copiously to host the other.[51] It is both liberating and reconciling, welcoming in a way that at once empowers the other to be who he or she is while building a link with the other in solidarity. This kind of freedom and cohesion is present through the power of the Spirit, which empowers and gives life at the same time that it draws together. And precisely this is why the church is a unity in diversity, a gathering of differences that share a mutual communion.[52] As Moltmann puts it, "The fellowship of the Spirit is the free space in which the manifold and many-faceted gifts of the Spirit can be awakened and grow."[53] Hospitality names the character of this fellowship, testifying to the Spirit's work of bringing diverse parties into solidarity.

The Spirit turns xenophobia into *philoxenia*, the fear of the stranger into a love of the stranger.[54] And the love of the stranger, the alien, the foreign, and the different has an important place in the biblical traditions. In the Near Eastern context, hospitality emerged as a practice of tending to sojourners, travelers requiring shelter, nourishment, and protection. Such persons were conspicuous in their strangeness and difference, indicating that they hailed from outside established social and kinship frameworks—from beyond the tribe. Made vulnerable by this lack of place, the stranger was regarded as a person in need, on a par with the marginalized in the community (e.g., orphans and widows). He or she, therefore, possessed no evident exchange value, no resources, no ability to purchase response. Accordingly, the moral obligation of gracious hosting became paramount. Especially in a nomadic context, anyone could find her or himself a stranger in one circumstance or another. This ethic of exchange suggests that human beings share a baseline nature that is vulnerable and can be imperiled when exposed, fostering a dependence upon the generosity of others. Justice requires an economy of compassionate reciprocity that welcomes the vulnerable stranger.

In the Hebrew Bible this notion is given religious justification. Indeed, the Israelites are exhorted by God not to oppress or harm the stranger, and reminded that they too endured similar circumstances in the land of Egypt (Exod. 22:21). Furthermore, God commands the Israelites to provide for and attend to the stranger as a native among them, loving him or her equally as one of their own (Lev. 19:33–34). The resounding message is this: as the covenanted people of God were themselves aliens, and remain vulnerable sojourners with God, provided for and loved by God (Lev. 25:23), so too should they love others. The memory of being an outsider and subsequently being welcomed thus provides impetus to empathize with other outsiders. In fact, God promises to dwell with the people insofar as they act justly and offer hospitality, caring for the alien, the widow, the orphan, and so on (Jer. 7:5–7).

At stake is far more than superficial civility or niceness. First, hospitality is a radical form of reciprocity that creates space for identifying with and receiving the stranger as oneself. It is what humanity shares—vulnerability—that grants the capacity to recognize and become available to the alien or foreign as someone not entirely different. All human beings are vulnerable strangers in one sense or another, and at one time or another. The stranger has inherent value as a human being precisely in his or her dependence, in lacking the ability to reciprocate in kind. This leads to a second point. Hospitality trades on a prior sense of abundance and gratitude that of its own accord spills outward in a welcoming gesture neither calculating merit in advance nor expecting it in return. Its generosity evolves from the humble acknowledgment of being graced, of having been given something to offer. Hospitality is built upon the premise that a host can and should give because she or he has first received—that is, since it has already been given to you, you should give to others. Out of this sense of being gifted grows an obligation that is much more than the logic of giving in order to receive (*du et des*) that animates normal economies of exchange.[55] The two points stated here join creatively into a single thread: gratitude is possible only in light of the recognition that one is vulnerable, a stranger who has now been given the gift of being the host. This is the stuff of human availability, and compassionate generosity spills over as the aftereffect.

Hospitality itself involves vulnerability, a mixing between guest and host that undoes the distinction between outsider and insider. Doors swing open and strangers are welcomed as part of the household. Here boundaries shade into one another, for the generosity of hospitality consents to a kind of role reversal that now also leaves the host vulnerable and dependent. Once the stranger is invited in, the host yields stability and control, adjusting the household to accommodate and attend to the guest's unique needs as they became apparent. Offering hospitality in this way invites disruption in household order and routine. The status quo is challenged, for the home is made different, even strange, vis-à-vis the presence of the stranger. The familiar is defamiliarized. Things do not remain as they were. The center of gravity shifts. A liminal zone of mutual sharing is created, a kind of covenantal exchange that both receives and gives. And in this exchange something counterintuitive happens. As the host gives to the guest, the host paradoxically gains a gift, unexpectedly becoming more than he or she was before. The host becomes honored and enhanced. A larger mutual indebtedness emerges in which both host and guest remain distinct yet fundamentally connected.[56]

With this we come to the theological root of hospitality. In a phrase, God blesses through the stranger. How so? In hospitality the center of gravity lies neither in the home nor in the stranger, neither in host nor guest, but in the God of both who is discovered redemptively in the meeting—indeed, in the role reversal. As boundaries become fluid, the vulnerable stranger, the one who ostensibly has nothing to offer, becomes a source of enrichment to the reconfigured household. This marks the upbuilding and bonding work of the Spirit, through whom the center of the household—animated by God's economy of grace—is not on the inside of a closed circle, protected by fortified walls, but rather on the margins of an open circle. Perhaps, then, in hospitality the Christian community ideally becomes what it is by extending outside of its own identity, by building border crossings that serve as connecting points for reconciliation and partnership between differences instead of separation. This kind of paradox is displayed poignantly in stories of hospitality that depict hosts "entertaining angels unaware" (Heb. 13:2). The guest who receives honor ironically turns out to be a divine visitor who bestows honor.[57] An example is Genesis 18, where Abraham and Sarah welcome three mysterious guests. Through such generosity and risk God blesses the hosts by granting Sarah a child. Unexpectedly, the strangers become a harbinger of divine abundance. As rabbi Jonathan Sacks writes, "God creates difference; therefore it is in one-who-is-different that we meet God."[58] Hospitality, then, is a window into blessing, a veritable trace of God's presence in the Spirit.

The New Testament corroborates such a picture. Indeed, Jesus himself is a sojourner in need of hospitality. More than this, however, Jesus embodies hospitality toward others, welcoming all to share in the divine banquet. His is a love without boundaries, a love that does not ask by what right the beloved deserved welcome. A gift is given, the value of which cannot be measured according to conventional mechanisms of exchange based in self-interest or calculated outcomes. Here the stranger is welcomed as a neighbor, recognized as kin with subversive effect. This disorients and overturns standards of value founded upon status, race, gender, religion, and so on, forcing a reevaluation of what it means to have a household, an identity. The home is for giving, indeed, for giving way to others. The model of hospitality dramatized by Jesus, therefore, undercuts self-righteousness or self-protection, postures that treat with condescension, suspicion, or outright hostility those others—those outsiders—whose difference threatens the status quo. Strangers—people who are despised, poor, unclean, sick, or have disabilities—are invited into the household of God.

Radical implications follow. Christine Pohl puts it succinctly, "Jesus welcomes and needs welcome; Jesus requires that followers depend on and provide hospitality."[59] The second part of this statement builds upon the first. And the point is this: Jesus identifies the redemptive work of God in himself with that of the stranger, the weak and destitute, suggesting that by welcoming such persons one welcomes him. This identification affirms humanity to the core by embracing it at its most vulnerable points. It disrupts the human tendency to secure itself by strength, power, domination, wealth, status, and even religious association. Blessed are the meek, the needy, the vulnerable, for God is especially present to them. Matthew's Jesus states it bluntly: "Truly, I say to you, as you did it to one of the least of these my brethren, you did it to me" (25:45). Christians meet Jesus in showing hospitality to the stranger: "I was a stranger and you welcomed me" (25:35). The saving presence of God, Jesus, and the stranger are interconnecting threads in one tapestry.

As we have seen, the redemptive logic of this is spelled out metaphorically in terms of a banquet.[60] For example, in Luke's Gospel we read, "But when you give a feast, invite the poor, the maimed, the lame, the blind, and you will be blessed, because they cannot repay you. You will be repaid at the resurrection of the just" (14:14). As Christ welcomes, so he calls his followers to welcome others (John 15:12; Rom. 15:7). And in turn, by receiving others Christ's followers receive God's blessing. Welcome leads to welcome, leading to further welcome. Being a follower of Christ then means to be taken up into the circle of God's hospitality, which spills outward in the Spirit toward others in the shape of a radically welcoming and inclusive community symbolized by an open table fellowship. The sharing of food and drink is perhaps the most vivid example of the redemptive circle of hospitality. Out of the experience of abundance, abundance is given. Boundaries are transgressed. Hospitality is a gift that arises neither out of an expectation for something in return, nor merely because of a command. It does not give in order to get, or in order to fulfill an imposed duty. It gives because a gift had first been given: "We love because he first loved us" (1 John 4:19). The love of God becomes a love of neighbor; and conversely, the love of neighbor becomes a way of loving God. Within an economy of grace, we love others with the love of God, which gives life, revealing to people their value and beauty, and their capacity also to love and give life.[61]

Hospitality and Disability

In hospitality, the Spirit is at work creating relations of reciprocity between God's children. This includes persons with disabilities, not as an afterthought but as essential to the well-being of the household. For the moral measure of a community lies in the way it treats its most vulnerable members, those strangers who exist on the margins. Paradoxically, however, in the community managed by God's economy of grace, the vulnerable stranger is at the center as one in whom the presence of the divine becomes real. The face of Christ is the face of the stranger. This is certainly not because he or she is special in God's eyes as a stranger, because of having disabilities; nor because he or she represents an opportunity for non-disabled people to show hospitality out of guilt, duty, pity, or the desire to gain stature, thanks and recognition by others as noble and loving. Nor is it because of the personal benefits of showing hospitality, such as satisfaction and self-esteem, for these are only secondary blessings that emerge as a consequence and not as the condition for serving others. If hospitality is shown in order that something is gained, it becomes reduced to helping another out a position of superiority and strength. But hospitality is not a matter of "us" serving "them," those weaker others who need us to achieve something they do not have. Rather, it is a matter of becoming a more inclusive and interdependent "us" fostered within relations of mutual giving and receiving. The stranger is the center of a household of vulnerable members equally loved into being by God. Accordingly, the stranger allows a broader "us" to be constituted within the presence of each other, in and through a Spirit-infused relationship.

Welcoming another makes room for a relation that transforms both the one who welcomes and the one who is welcomed. The encounter transforms both parties and hallows a sacred place, consecrating the remade household. By empowering people with disabilities to find a place in the church, to creatively contribute to the life of the community, the church becomes itself—that is, a place of redemption for all. What is church but the mutual exchange of gifts given by the power of the Spirit? And such gifts reside in all people, precisely amidst various disabilities and alleged limitations. God is present in the mutual relation of receiving and giving, present in a way that yields wholeness and makes possible further acts of hospitality. Christians find divine welcome in welcoming others. This is why exclusion is devastating for the church. It prevents it from fulfilling its mission: to embody God's hospitality toward humanity, which is shown in Christ.

How might hospitality be demonstrated specifically regarding people with disabilities? First, by recognizing the presence of persons with disabilities. This involves more than a superficial acknowledgment of people's needs. Rather, it entails being sympathetically attuned and available to the presence of others with unique gifts as well as particular concerns and needs. Becoming sensitized to the range and diversity of persons in general might be one way that such availability can be nurtured with regard to people with disabilities. Also important is becoming aware of how the community might be excluding some people unknowingly by participating in disabling practices and attitudes. The prophetic element is essential here, for the church's vision is narrowed when programmed according to the cult of normalcy. Letting go of the need to control and learning to accept people for who they are without calculating in advance what they can do or achieve for the group is fundamental to letting differences be. Hospitality is the opposite of conformity; it allows persons with disabilities to be heard and seen without pressure to accommodate to a version of normalcy.

Second, then, hospitality means accommodating to others as uniquely precious persons, acting for their benefit. It makes space for people with disabilities so as to empower their flourishing as subjects of their own experience and as persons capable of contributing to the community. This involves decentering norms and curbing prejudgments that might curtail another's freedom to be who they are precisely amidst disabilities. Recall that disability is not a deficit, and does not define a person. Acknowledging this requires churches to welcome without over-focusing on specific disabilities as the main thrust of a person's life. There is more to being a person than the disabilities someone may happen to have.

Nonetheless, churches must also be circumspect in the way that language is employed. For instance, metaphors of blindness, deafness, impairments, and so on, can work in subtle ways to build linguistic barriers to exclude people with disabilities and contribute to disabling attitudes among non-disabled people.[62] Inclusive language is crucial to accommodation. Yet because people with disabilities have unique bodily needs, accommodation also involves adapting the physical environment to make it accessible. The extent to which the community should modify its environment to make it accessible of course depends on the specific situations of persons that comprise the community. This will naturally require negotiating awkward situations that force reenvisioning the character of the community to make possible the full participation of all. It will also require the redistribution of church resources to prioritize accessibility; not out of charity, but rather, in the words of Webb-Mitchell, "from a desire to receive one another as a source of life and communion."[63]

Accordingly, and third, hospitality means advocacy. Advocacy in this sense indicates a reaching out with and not only for people with disabilities. In advocacy, hospitality stands with the stranger on the margins. It understands the world as another understands it and works with that understanding to promote his or her well-being. This is the stuff of genuine solidarity. Through it we all become strangers, vulnerable creatures animated together by grace. It is no accident that the Holy Spirit (the Paraclete) is seen as an advocate, one who exhorts, supports, comforts, and dwells in the new community as an active agent of God's presence (cf. John 14:16, 23–26).[64] For advocacy is the work of God's spirit, joining together and breathing a new corporate life into being. Given this, people with disabilities are not an anomaly but an instance of the creative capacity each human being has to share in the lives of others, mediated by vulnerability and empowered by that spirit.

Real community is made by sharing one another's burdens and weaknesses, such that each becomes empowered to be who they are—loved into being by God and in the image of God. And the Spirit comforts and gives strength along the way. In Jean Vanier's words, "community is made of the gentle concerns that people show each other every day. It is made of small gestures, of services and sacrifices which say 'I love you' and 'I'm happy to be with you.'"[65] This is what hospitality in the mode of advocacy is. And it means, as Vanier continues, "letting down the barriers which protect our vulnerability and recognizing and welcoming our weakness," such that "people who are separated from the community" experience genuine welcome.[66]

Hospitality as recognition of, accommodation for, and advocacy with people with disabilities is necessary for the church to be church. We are prone to hide from vulnerability, subsequently shunning it in others. Yet, as Frances Young puts it, "before God, we are all equally vulnerable—it is no good pretending to him; and vulnerability shared in his name is the way to real human fellowship."[67] In a position of feigned strength and putative ability this truth falls flat. But as hospitality opens to receive another, the host comes to recognize her or his own vulnerability and need. And because of this, Young goes on to claim, "we can receive the gospel, we can receive the ministry of others. To receive from someone is to accord them a deeper respect, and to do them far more good than to give them our charity."[68] This is the paradox of hospitality: through receiving another the host in turn receives. In acts of receiving and sharing with one another, God's economy of grace becomes manifest and the church fulfills itself, pointing in fallible ways to the kingdom that is yet to come in all its fullness.

Vulnerability, then, is the fulcrum of God's creative-redemptive work in the Holy Spirit. It is the means to the wholeness that comes from welcoming and being welcomed. Hospitality to people with disabilities is both a way to God and a way that God reaches to us.[69] Loving others amounts to knowing God (1 John 4:7). Or, in the words of Dietrich Bonhoeffer, "'being there for others' is the experience of transcendence."[70] Indeed, the presence of Christ lies in the presence of the stranger. Insofar as people with disabilities are welcomed, Christ is welcomed. This is one particularly powerful way to interpret the lines of Gerard Manley Hopkins that opened this chapter.

Conclusion: Kindling Hope for the Church as a Communion of Strangers

To be Christian is to strive for the actualization of God's kingdom of loving reconciliation. It is an openness to the infinite that is at the same time an openness to others, to the stranger, to difference, to people with disabilities. To be a church means such openness in community with and for others. Monica Hellwig sums it up nicely:

> To be a follower of Jesus means in the first place to enter by compassion into his experience, with all that it expresses of the divine and of the human. And it means in the second place to enter with him into the suffering and the hope of all human persons, making common cause with them as he does, and seeking out as he does the places of his predilection among the poor and despised and oppressed.[71]

Given our focus in this book, we might add to Hellwig's statement in the following way: if it is true, as H. Richard Niebuhr contends, that Jesus is the human through whom the whole of human history becomes our history as Christians,[72] then the church—precisely as the body of Christ—must fully include the experiences and contributions of people with disabilities. This is no imperialistic act of assimilation, but rather, a decentering act of hospitality that opens outward toward others.

In Jesus we are all vulnerable marginal dwellers in God's encompassing drama of salvation history. Difference here is not merely tolerated; it is celebrated as the key to the story, for the power of God is unseemly and strange. It discloses itself paradoxically not in uniformity and sameness but through differences, not in autonomy but through dependency and lack of ability. The stranger is at the center, but not merely as moral lesson. He or she is a person full of dignity, full of humanity, whose call is for us to be present and listen and to open up and share our lives. And by welcoming such a person in love, we love God, becoming whole ourselves with them. Hospitality emerges from a thankful heart, a heart that has received God's welcome and overflows with gratitude and hope. Ultimately, the stranger is us all (universal), but only insofar as (particular) strangers—people with disabilities—are first recognized and welcomed.

I can think of no better way to illustrate this than to speak of my relationship with Chris.

It has been my deepest wish to make room for Chris, to make time for him, to share life with him on his terms, not mine. But this has not been easy, for the daily challenges have tempted me to close the doors of my heart and shut down. Indeed, during the process of writing this book our family has passed through its darkest days. At one point Chris was hospitalized briefly, as all other resources grew ineffective in helping him traverse his days. The Green Bay Crisis Center has gotten to know us well. Yet new possibilities always emerge. And Chris's unyielding spirit of goodness continues to shine forth, constantly disturbing my pretenses by knocking at the doors of my heart, as if to say, "I am here, welcome me." His presence is beautiful, vulnerably precious in its own right. What can I do but recognize this and accommodate, advocating with him on his behalf? Chris is a bearer of Christ—his name indeed embodies the point. He opens me up time and again to love.

It is on this more personal level that this book began, and so shall it conclude. Disability is no abstract field of study to which I find myself attracted. It has reshaped my life, reorienting my way of thinking theologically and acting Christianly. For example, recently I was invited to read some of my writing at a conference on autism and advocacy as part of a group of five parents with children on the autism spectrum. What struck me about every reading at this session—including mine—was the powerful desire for gratitude and hope at work. Each sought to find connecting points of vulnerability with their child, to find humanizing means of relating more lovingly with their child in situations that at times appeared dehumanizing and tragic. The emotion of the event was overwhelming; I held back the tears and, at one point, even had to get up to walk around for a moment. More concretely and certainly more substantively than any of the words I have written in this book, I witnessed the vulnerable and strange power of love. It was a humbling privilege. I felt the presence of God amidst us, in the flesh through the testimony of lives lived hospitably for others.

The experience confirmed my own desire for Christian communities to welcome with wider embraces. There are many lives in our midst that call us to hospitality. I could not agree more with Jean Vanier when he states: "This is my vision for our churches: that they become places of belonging, places of sharing . . . [among] broken, wounded men and women, like you and like me."[73] Accordingly, as Vanier goes on, "our belonging, our commitment, is a response to a call from God."[74] Precisely this call comes from those in our midst whose vulnerability calls us to open our hearts, our communities, our lives. Life is a gift to be given with and for others, together in a life-giving circle of hospitality. This is what I have learned by experience from Chris. Furthermore, it is what lies at the core of the biblical witness.

For Christians, Jesus decenters the established principalities and powers and re-centers human lives toward a new order, an order of love. An economy of grace displaces economies of exchange based in the cult of normalcy. In this new economy, this household of God, we are transformed, remade interdependently with each other as vulnerable beings loved into being by God. How so? As we welcome Jesus the stranger into our home. This is why disability is redemptively fundamental: by welcoming people with disabilities into our church communities, our churches become communions bearing witness to God's creative-redemptive power, a strange power that works not through strength but weakness and vulnerability to give life. And when our church communities traffic in such power, they cannot help but spill outward to transform the world in a God-ward direction. It is perhaps fitting to conclude with wisdom from Vanier, whose lifework incarnates the vision of this book:

> In the midst of our broken world our communities and our families are called to become like small oases, humble places of love where we try to live covenant between us and in solidarity with the weak and the suffering throughout the world.

Our communities are not cut off from the world. They are open to others in the local community and neighbourhood, as well as to those who are far away. We are all part of one and the same body, each one of us, in his/her own way, breathing the same breath of the Spirit of God.[75]

Notes

1. David H. Jensen, *Graced Vulnerability: A Theology of Childhood* (Cleveland: Pilgrim Press, 2005), 126.

2. Fyodor Dostoevsky, *The Brothers Karamazov* (New York: Vintage, 1991), 236–37.

3. Ibid., 56. See also Mary Jo Leddy, *Radical Gratitude* (Maryknoll, NY: Orbis, 2002), 66–67.

4. Ibid.

5. See Schubert Ogden, *The Reality of God* (Dallas: Southern Methodist University Press, 1992), 188–205.

6. Peter C. Hodgson, *Revisioning the Church: Ecclesial Freedom in the New Paradigm* (Minneapolis: Fortress Press, 1988), 36.

7. Donald Senior, *Jesus: A Gospel Portrait*, rev. ed. (Mahwah, NJ: Paulist Press, 1992), 48.

8. Ibid., 50.

9. Ibid., 89–90.

10. Roy McCloughry and Wayne Morris, *Making a World of Difference: Christian Reflections on Disability* (London: Society for Promoting Christian Knowledge, 2002), 102. See also Kathy Black, *A Healing Homiletic: Preaching and Disability* (Nashville: Abingdon Press, 1996), 53.

11. Black, *A Healing Homiletic,* 50.

12. Ibid., 181.

13. Ibid., 52.

14. McCloughry and Morris, *Making a World of Difference*, 107–8.

15. Colleen C. Grant, "Reinterpreting the Healing Narratives," in *Human Disability and the Service of God: Reassessing Religious Practice* (Nashville: Abingdon Press, 1998), 73.

16. Senior, *Jesus: A Gospel Portrait*, 105.

17. Grant, "Reinterpreting the Healing Narratives," 74.

18. Ibid.

19. Ibid., 77–78. See also Nancy L. Eiesland, *The Disabled God: Toward a Liberatory Theology of Disability* (Nashville: Abingdon Press, 1994), 117; and McCloughry and Morris, *Making a World of Difference*, 98.

20. McCloughry and Morris, *Making a World of Difference*, 56.

21. Ibid., 54; see also Grant, "Reinterpreting the Healing Narratives," 76.

22. Grant, "Reinterpreting the Healing Narratives," 84.

23. McCloughry and Morris, *Making a World of Difference*, 55–56.

24. Jürgen Moltmann, "Liberate Yourselves by Accepting One Another," in *Human Disability and the Service of God*, 115.

25. Ibid., 117.

26. Ibid. See also Henri J. Nouwen, *Letters to Marc about Jesus*, trans. Hubert Hoskins (New York: Harper-Collins, 1998), 23–25.

27. Nouwen, *Letters to Marc about Jesus*, 25.

28. Ibid., 15.

29. Ibid., 30–31.

30. Simon Horne, "'Those Who Are Blind See': Some New Testament Uses of Impairment, Inability, and Paradox," in *Human Disability and the Service of God*, 89.

31. Ibid., 94–95.

32. See Anselm Kyongsuk Min, *The Solidarity of Others in a Divided World: A Postmodern Theology after Postmodernism* (New York: T. & T. Clark, 2004), chap. 7.

33. Daniel L. Migliore, *Faith Seeking Understanding* (Grand Rapids: Eerdmans, 1991), 191.

34. Ibid.

35. McCloughry and Morris, *Making a World of Difference*, 75.

36. Horne, "'Those Who Are Blind See," 96.

37. McCloughry and Morris, *Making a World of Difference*, 75.

38. Jean Vanier, *Becoming Human* (Mahwah, NJ: Paulist Press, 1998), 28.

39. Frances Young, *Face to Face: A Narrative Essay in the Theology of Suffering* (Edinburgh: T. & T. Clark, 1990), 192.

40. Stanley Hauerwas, "The Church and the Mentally Handicapped: A Continuing Challenge to the Imagination," in *Critical Reflections on Stanley Hauerwas' Theology of Disability: Disabling Society, Enabling Theology*, ed. John Swinton (Binghampton, NY: Haworth Press, 2004), 62.

41. See Hodgson, *Revisioning the Church*, 60.

42. Brett Webb-Mitchell, *Unexpected Guests at God's Banquet: Welcoming People with Disabilities into the Church* (New York: Crossroad, 1994), 20.

43. Hodgson, *Revisioning the Church*, 33–34.

44. See Jürgen Moltmann, *The Spirit of Life: A Universal Affirmation*, trans. Margaret Kohl (Minneapolis: Fortress Press, 2001), 40–43.

45. Alister E. McGrath, *Christian Theology: An Introduction* (Oxford: Blackwell, 2001), 309. See also Moltmann, *The Spirit of Life*, 43–47.

46. Min, *The Solidarity of Others*, 95.

47. Bradley C. Hanson, *Introduction to Christian Theology* (Minneapolis: Fortress Press, 1997), 226–27. See also Moltmann, *The Spirit of Life*, 60–65.

48. Min, *The Solidarity of Others*, 95–100.

49. Christine D. Pohl, *Making Room: Recovering Hospitality as a Christian Tradition* (Grand Rapids: Eerdmans, 1999), 19.

50. Ibid., 40–41.

51. This idea reflects the substance of Jennie Weiss Block's excellent book *Copious Hosting: A Theology of Access for People with Disabilities* (New York: Continuum, 2002).

52. Lucien Richard, OMI, *Living the Hospitality of God* (Mahwah, NJ: Paulist Press, 2000), 70–71.

53. Moltmann, *The Spirit of Life*, 194.

54. Min, *The Solidarity of Others*, 110.

55. On the notions of abundance and gratitude, see Mary Jo Leddy, *Radical Gratitude* (Maryknoll, NY: Orbis Books, 2002).

56. See John B. Bennet, *Academic Life: Hospitality, Ethics, and Spirituality* (Bolton, MA: Anker Publishing, 2003), 46–49, 54.

57. This divine visitor theme is found in many Near Eastern and Mediterranean religious traditions. See Thomas M Bolin, "The Role of Exchange in Ancient Mediterranean Religion and Its Implications for Reading Genesis 18–19," *JSOT* 29.1 (2004): 37–56; and Amy G. Oden, ed., *And You Welcomed Me: A Sourcebook on Hospitality in Early Christianity* (Nashville: Abingdon Press, 2003).

58. Jonathan Sacks, *The Dignity of Difference: How to Avoid the Clash of Civilizations* (New York: Continuum, 2002), 59.

59. Pohl, *Making Room*, 17.

60. Webb-Mitchell spells this out at length in *Unexpected Guests at God's Banquet*.

61. Vanier, *Befriending the Stranger* (Grand Rapids: Eerdmanns, 2005), 59.

62. See Black, *A Healing Homiletic*, for an in-depth treatment of such perils.

63. Webb-Mitchell, *Unexpected Guests at God's Banquet*, 19.

64. Block, *Copious Hosting*, 140.

65. Jean Vanier, *Community and Growth: Our Pilgrimage Together* (New York: Paulist Press, 1979), 19. This quote is cited in Hauerwas, "Timeful Friends: Living with the Handicapped," in *Critical Reflections on Stanley Hauerwas' Theology of Disability*, 23.

66. Ibid.

67. Young, *Face to Face*, 99.

68. Ibid., 100.

69. See Richard, *Living the Hospitality of God*, 52.

70. Dietrich Bonhoeffer, *Letters and Papers from Prison*, ed. Eberhard Bethge, trans. Reginald Fuller et al. (New York: Macmillan, 1971), 381–82.

71. Monika K. Hellwig, *Jesus: The Compassion of God* (Wilmington, DE: Michael Glazier, Inc., 1983), 108.

72. H. Richard Niebuhr, *The Meaning of Revelation* (New York: Macmillan, 1941), 115–16.

73. Vanier, *Befriending the Stranger*, 12.

74. Ibid., 17.

75. Ibid., 128.

Index